The Spirit of Atonement

T&T Clark Systematic Pentecostal and Charismatic Theology

Series editors
Daniela C. Augustine
Wolfgang Vondey

The Spirit of Atonement

*Pentecostal Contributions and Challenges
to the Christian Traditions*

Steven M. Studebaker

LONDON • NEW YORK • OXFORD • NEW DELHI • SYDNEY

T&T CLARK
Bloomsbury Publishing Plc
50 Bedford Square, London, WC1B 3DP, UK
1385 Broadway, New York, NY 10018, USA
29 Earlsfort Terrace, Dublin 2, Ireland

BLOOMSBURY, T&T CLARK and the T&T Clark logo are trademarks of
Bloomsbury Publishing Plc

First published in Great Britain 2021
Paperback edition published 2022

Copyright © Steven M. Studebaker, 2021

Steven M. Studebaker has asserted his right under the Copyright, Designs and Patents Act, 1988, to be identified as Author of this work.

For legal purposes the Acknowledgments on p. x–xi constitute an extension of this copyright page.

Cover design by Anna Berzovan
Cover image © naqiewei / GettyImages

All rights reserved. No part of this publication may be reproduced or transmitted in any form or by any means, electronic or mechanical, including photocopying, recording, or any information storage or retrieval system, without prior permission in writing from the publishers.

Bloomsbury Publishing Plc does not have any control over, or responsibility for, any third-party websites referred to or in this book. All internet addresses given in this book were correct at the time of going to press. The author and publisher regret any inconvenience caused if addresses have changed or sites have ceased to exist, but can accept no responsibility for any such changes.

A catalogue record for this book is available from the British Library.

Library of Congress Cataloging-in-Publication Data
Names: Studebaker, Steven M., 1968- author.
Title: The spirit of atonement: Pentecostal contributions and challenges to the Christian traditions / Steven M. Studebaker.
Description: London; New York, NY, USA : Bloomsbury Academic, 2021. | Series: T&T Clark systematic Pentecostal and charismatic theology |
Identifiers: LCCN 2020045380 (print) | LCCN 2020045381 (ebook) | ISBN 9780567682369 (hb) | ISBN 9780567699251 (paperback) | ISBN 9780567682406 (ebook) | ISBN 9780567682376 (epdf)
Subjects: LCSH: Atonement–Pentecostal churches. | Pentecostal churches–Doctrines.
Classification: LCC BT265.3 .S778 2021 (print) | LCC BT265.3 (ebook) | DDC 234/.5–dc23
LC record available at https://lccn.loc.gov/2020045380
LC ebook record available at https://lccn.loc.gov/2020045381

ISBN: HB: 978-0-5676-8236-9
PB: 978-0-5676-9925-1
ePDF: 978-0-5676-8237-6
Book: 978-0-5676-8240-6

Series: T&T Clark Systematic Pentecostal and Charismatic Theology

Typeset by Deanta Global Publishing Services, Chennai, India

To find out more about our authors and books visit www.bloomsbury.com and sign up for our newsletters.

*For "Doc" (Daniel) Pecota (1997†) and Darrell Hobson, professors at Northwest University. My journey in theology began in your classrooms.
And . . .
for Bruce L. Fields (2020†), your teaching at Trinity Evangelical Divinity School exemplified theological curiosity and charity.*

Contents

Preface	viii
Acknowledgments	x
1 Introduction	1
Part One Theology of Atonement	15
2 Pentecost	17
3 Incarnation	40
4 Crucifixion	56
5 Resurrection	77
6 Eschatology	93
Part Two Practicing Atonement	107
7 Empowering All People	109
8 Renewing Embodied Life	128
9 Living in the Way of the Cross	150
10 Waking to New Creation	164
11 Going Home	179
12 Epilogue	200
Subject Index	203
Modern Name Index	205

Preface

A pentecostal theology of the atonement, really? Is there such a thing? While writing this book, students and colleagues often asked about my current research project. Sharing that I was working on a pentecostal theology of the atonement that highlights the role of the Holy Spirit, provoked looks of incredulity, followed by something like, "Isn't atonement about Christ and the cross?!" Well, yes, it is. But it is also about the Holy Spirit and Pentecost.

This book, consequently, is critical and constructive. It critiques and ultimately rejects the fundamental paradigm of redemption that was the gateway to my conversion. I became a Christian in the living room of two friends. We were co-workers at a small furniture manufacturer. They hosted a Bible study sponsored by Forest Grove Assemblies of God. On a Monday in early September, I accepted their invitation to attend. I was nineteen. And, like many of the Pentecostals described in this book, my life was in desperate straits. I am grateful for their concern for me because accepting their invitation and going to the Bible study that night transformed my life and set it on a trajectory I could never have imagined. As the Apostle Paul indicates, "No eye has seen, no ear has heard, no mind has conceived what God has prepared for those who love him" (1 Cor. 2:9). At some point during the evening, a burly looking biker guy shook his meaty finger at me and said, "God brought you here tonight to save you, if you don't accept Christ tonight, you are lost." Convinced he was right, I took his advice. The Bible study group then circled around me and led me through the sinner's prayer. According to which I prayed that God would forgive my sin because Christ died on the cross. Because they were Pentecostals, a few minutes later they told me I could receive the baptism in the Holy Spirit. I needed everything I could get from God, so they circled me again, laid hands on, and prayed over me. Within a few minutes I received what Pentecostals call Spirit baptism—an ecstatic, emotionally charged experience attended with speaking in tongues. My personal conversion is cookie-cutter evangelical and classical pentecostal. This book calls into question the theology that framed my conversion. My goal, however, is not to repudiate that conversion experience and the subsequent life of transformation that led me to Northwest University in Kirkland, Washington, and the friends I met there, to my wife Sheila, to ministry in Seattle and in Northern Minnesota, to graduate school in Chicago and Milwaukee, to two marvelous kids, to teaching for Emmanuel College in Franklin Springs Georgia, and now to McMaster Divinity College in Hamilton, Ontario. All of these experiences and many more are ways that the Holy Spirit empowered my life to participate in the narrative of redemption. The problem is not the experience of life transformation that my friends from work introduced to me at the Bible study. The problem is the theology behind it. A theology that is overly Christocentric and judicial. A theology that subordinates receiving the Holy Spirit and the ongoing renewal of life to the forgiveness of sins based on Christ's penal death on a Roman cross.

The constructive goal of this book is to articulate a theology that reflects the pneumatological, holistic, and life-renewing and empowering character of pentecostal experience. I do not believe the inherited categories Pentecostals used to articulate their theology are adequate to the task. Indeed, they ultimately do an injustice not only to pentecostal experience but to the Spirit's place in the wider biblical narrative of redemption. This book argues that atonement is the fundamental work of redemption. But, atonement is not primarily a judicial story about a heavenly court room where an avenging God assuages his wrath for sin by punishing his Son on a cross. That penal narrative reduces the biblical vision of redemption to receiving forgiveness of sin and freedom from God's punishment of eternal torment in hell. Forgiveness of sins and reconciliation with God are important and part of atonement, but a richer vision of redemption is found in the Bible. It is a story that begins with creation and carries on to the eschatological new creation. And, the Spirit of Pentecost plays a leading role in this narrative of atonement. This project tells that story.

I completed this book while the world was coming apart. During the spring and early summer of 2020, the COVID-19 pandemic put the world under lockdown. American cities and some around the world erupted with protests and riots because of the police killing of an unarmed and incapacitated George Floyd. Strife, polarization, hostility, and vitriol characterize public life today. We live in a world rent by hatreds and grievances. We live in a world of vengeance. We live in a world of enmity. We live in a world where Cain kills Abel. "Peace" too often means getting retribution. We want the pound of flesh. Much of classical atonement theology, unfortunately, reflects this pattern. It calls the killing of the innocent Christ on the cross an act of divine justice. This story of redemption is a worldly one. It operates according to the punitive and vindictive logic of retribution and redemptive violence. Christ's suffering and death on the cross appease God's anger over sin and secure salvation from eternal punishment in hell. In other words, someone was wronged, in this case God, and someone must pay for it, in this case Christ's humanity vicariously for human beings. That makes sense to us. And, that is why we should be suspicious of it. Jesus warned us that his "new wine" would "burst . . . the old wineskins" (Lk. 5:37). The Christian doctrine of atonement addresses the fundamental rift that separates human beings from their God, each other, and the life for which their God created them. But, atonement does not play on our terms. It subverts them. Atonement reconciles us to each other and to God so that we can live without racism, without fear of brutality, and without the inequities of condescending conceit. Atonement takes us to the place where we do not need to hide from God and each other. It takes us to a place beyond fig leaves and animal skins, beyond the thistle and thorn and into a "good and spacious land" where the many tongues of all people are brought together in the fellowship of the Father, the Son, and the Holy Spirit (Gen. 3:18, Exod. 3:8, and Acts 2:17). This is the work of atonement, the work of the Spirit of Pentecost.

Acknowledgments

The genesis of this book project was Wolfgang Vondey's invitation to give the Annual Walter J. Hollenweger Lecture in conjunction with the Centre for Pentecostal and Charismatic Studies and the Cadbury Centre for the Public Understanding of Religion at the University of Birmingham in June 2017. Giving that lecture was a rich experience. The audience was warm, receptive, and invigorating. My respondents Mikael Stenhammar and Simo Frestadius were critical and constructive. I enjoyed two excellent dinners with my hosts Wolfgang Vondey and Allan Anderson (the Balti Curry was delicious!). I developed the material presented at the Hollenweger Lecture into a proposal for the Systematic Pentecostal and Charismatic Theology Series edited by Daniela C. Augustine and Wolfgang Vondey. I am grateful for everyone involved in the academic experience at Birmingham. Special thanks and heartfelt gratitude to Daniela Augustine and Wolfgang Vondey, editors of the SPCT series, and to Anna Turton and Veerle Van Steenhuyse, editors at Bloomsbury, all of whom facilitated the completion of this project.

Looking back, this project is also the result of a longer journey of thinking about the nature of a pentecostal theology of the Holy Spirit. It began in the first semester of my doctoral studies at Marquette University. Professors such as Michel René Barnes, Patrick Carey, David Coffey, D. Lyle Dabney, and Ralph Del Colle catalyzed my thinking. They were foundational for introducing me to the pneumatology and trinitarian theology of the wider Christian traditions that became resources for this theological project. Also important for nurturing these budding ideas were conversations with friends such as Jeff Barbeau, Skip Jenkins, Cheryl Peterson, Jason Nicholls, Wolfgang Vondey, Richard Weber, and Jeffrey Wilcox in the Marquette classrooms, halls, and theology department parties. Days long gone, but not forgotten.

I completed the substantive writing of this book while on a research leave in the fall semester of 2019. I want to thank the leadership of McMaster Divinity College, President Stanley E. Porter, Vice President Academic Phil Zylla, and Board members for supporting faculty research with regular research leaves. You deserve recognition for creating an academic environment that supports and encourages research and writing. I also appreciate my colleagues at McMaster Divinity College. They are a source of encouragement while researching and writing as well as critical foils for discussing theological ideas. Your friendships make work a blessing.

Thanks also to my ever-growing kids, Gabby and Max. Our summer afternoon movies and trips to Buffalo for exploring new eating establishments in summer 2019 were the substance of life and a welcome diversion from the research and writing bunker. Although the COVID-19 summer of 2020 prevented cross-border excursions to Buffalo, we made up for it with living room YouTube exercise videos, bike rides, and Netflix. They were golden moments in the twilight of your teen years. Finally, my wife, Sheila, remains a perennial source of encouragement and inspiration. You are an amazing woman, full of fortitude, energy, and wit.

Fonthill, Ontario
July 13, 2020

All Scripture quotations, unless otherwise indicated, are taken from the Holy Bible, New International Version®, NIV®. Copyright ©1973, 1978, 1984, 2011 by Biblica, Inc.™ Used by permission of Zondervan. All rights reserved worldwide. www.zondervan.com. The "NIV" and "New International Version" are trademarks registered in the United States Patent and Trademark Office by Biblica, Inc.™

1

Introduction

The atonement is about Christ and his crucifixion on the cross. That is true. But it is a constricted narrative. Why? Because atonement is also about the Holy Spirit and Pentecost. This book highlights the Holy Spirit's role in the atonement and in doing so also proposes a pentecostal theology of the atonement. Hermeneutically that means developing a theology of the atonement from the perspective of the Spirit of Pentecost. Theologically that means atonement is receiving and participating in the Spirit of Pentecost. Pentecostal atonement is to participate in the Spirit-breathed life fulfilled in Jesus Christ, in the coming of the eschatological new creation, and the offering of that Spirit-breathed life to the "all people" of Pentecost (Acts 2:17). Pentecost is the nexus in the narrative of redemption from the particularity of the Spirit-breathed life fulfilled in Jesus Christ to the horizon of the new creation. Considering atonement from the perspective of the Spirit of Pentecost should be prima facie for pentecostal theology, but it is not. Why? To answer that question, I want to address first the context of this project and then turn to the problem of pentecostal praxis and rhetoric and finally address matters of method and content.

Context

The confessional context of this project is Classical Pentecostalism and Western objective theories of the atonement. First, why focus on this tradition of pentecostal theology given that contemporary Pentecostalism is a global and diverse movement? Classical Pentecostalism emerged during the formation of pentecostal denominations in North America and remains popular in North America and in many global pentecostal movements. Pew Research Center's survey and report, *Spirit and Power: A 10-Country Survey of Pentecostals*, shows that Classical Pentecostals remain in the majority among Protestant Renewalist Christians ("'Renewalist' is an umbrella term that refers to both pentecostals and charismatics as a group").[1] Given the representative nature of Pentecostals in North America and around the world, Classical Pentecostalism is the background for what I call traditional pentecostal theology. Contemporary pentecostal theologians such as Daniel Castelo, Frank Macchia, David Perry, A. J.

---

[1] See *Spirit and Power: A 10-Country Survey of Pentecostals*, The Pew Forum on Religion and Public Life (October 2006), 3. https://www.pewresearch.org/wp-content/uploads/sites/7/2006/10/pentecostals-08.pdf.

Swoboda, Wolfgang Vondey, and Amos Yong have expanded and in important ways moved beyond these traditional theological categories with respect to a pentecostal theology of grace.[2] This project is in concert with and contributes to this constructive trajectory of pentecostal theology. It does so by proposing a systematic theology of the atonement on the basis of the Spirit of Pentecost. The primary backdrop for its intra-ecclesial dialogue, however, is Classical Pentecostalism.

Second, why take Western, and especially Protestant evangelical, atonement theology as the backdrop for this project? Because they shaped the fundamental assumptions about Christ and the Holy Spirit in classical pentecostal theology. Thus, critical analysis of Christocentric and crucicentric objective atonement theology and its influence on Classical Pentecostalism is necessary to create the space to propose a constructive and systematic pentecostal theology of the atonement.[3] In evangelical theology, atonement customarily deals with the life and ministry of Jesus Christ, especially his death on the cross, with little reference to the Holy Spirit.[4] Indeed, as Clark H. Pinnock put it, "has not the cross (or more properly, a theory of the atonement) usurped center stage in theology?"[5] This project takes another approach. It presents Pentecost as a culminating point in the biblical narrative of redemption and considers Christ from the perspective of Pentecost.[6] But, what can be said more specifically about the relationship between traditional evangelical penal atonement theology and classical pentecostal theology?

Classical Pentecostalism is a product of late-nineteenth-century evangelical theology.[7] As such, its theology bears the Christocentric and crucicentric characteristics of this tradition of theology. The popularity of penal-substitutionary atonement in classical pentecostal theology is a key indicator of this influence. For traditional Protestant, evangelical, and classical pentecostal theology, atonement is Christological, not pneumatological. Atonement is the work of Christ. It takes place on the cross, not at Pentecost. Jesus Christ provides salvation through his death on the cross. This

---

[2] See Amos Yong, *Spirit of Love: A Trinitarian Theology of Grace* (Waco: Baylor University Press, 2012); Frank D. Macchia, *Baptized in the Spirit: A Global Pentecostal Theology* (Grand Rapids: Zondervan, 2006) and *Justified in the Spirit: Creation, Redemption, and the Triune God* (Grand Rapids: Eerdmans, 2010); A. J. Swoboda, *Tongues and Trees: Toward a Pentecostal Ecological Theology* (Blandford Forum: Deo, 2013); and Wolfgang Vondey, *Pentecostal Theology: Living the Full Gospel* (London: Bloomsbury, 2017).

[3] For my earlier work on this subject, see "Pentecostal Soteriology and Pneumatology," *Journal of Pentecostal Theology* 11, no. 2 (2003): 248–70; *The Trinitarian Vision of Jonathan Edwards and David Coffey* (Amherst: Cambria, 2011), 167–205; and "Pentecostal Soteriology: Overcoming the Ecumenical Impasses of Classical Pentecostalism and Charismatic Experience," in *Pentecostal Theology and Ecumenical Theology*, ed. Peter Hocken, Tony Richie, and Christopher Stephenson, Global Pentecostal and Charismatic Studies Series (Leiden: Brill, 2019), 283–307.

[4] For example, Fleming Rutledge, *The Crucifixion: Understanding the Death of Jesus Christ* (Grand Rapids: Eerdmans, 2015) and Eleonore Stump in her philosophical theology approach to atonement in *Atonement*, Oxford Studies in Analytic Theology (New York: Oxford University Press, 2018), 7–8.

[5] Clark H. Pinnock, "Salvation by Resurrection," *Ex Auditu: An International Journal of Theological Interpretation of Scripture* 9 (1993): 1.

[6] Craig S. Keener develops the case for reading Scripture in light of Pentecost as well. He emphasizes that pentecostal emphasis on empowered mission, charismatic experience, and eschatological realization should provide lenses for reading Scripture. See Keener, *Spirit Hermeneutics: Reading Scripture in Light of Pentecost* (Grand Rapids: Eerdmans, 2016), esp. chapter 2.

[7] For this background, see Donald W. Dayton, *Theological Roots of Pentecostalism* (Grand Rapids: Francis Asbury/Zondervan, 1987).

tradition of atonement theology and its influence on pentecostal theology are the primary background for the critical aspects of this project. But is penal-substitutionary atonement widely held among Pentecostals outside of North America? Although Pew does not provide data specific to atonement beliefs, they do record that Pentecostals and Charismatics (Renewalists) hold a high "obligation to evangelize."[8] This commitment to evangelism is "consistent with the widespread belief among Pentecostals that faith in Jesus Christ represents the exclusive path to eternal salvation" and "is the only way to be saved from eternal damnation."[9] Although admittedly conjecture, this view of salvation is consistent with the classical pentecostal (and evangelical) view of salvation framed in terms of penal-substitutionary atonement—that is, faith in Christ's sacrifice on the cross provides forgiveness of sins and redemption from God's wrath and judgment. I recognize that it does not represent the view of atonement held by all Pentecostals. This view of atonement, however, likely represents many and probably a majority of what Pew describes as Protestant Pentecostals and Charismatics.

Given the emergence of Classical Pentecostalism from the evangelical revival movements of the late-nineteenth and early-twentieth centuries, the important question is: Is pentecostal theology more than or something different than its evangelical predecessors? In other words, does Pentecostalism have a distinct theological voice and tradition to contribute to the global Christian traditions or is it evangelical theology plus charismatic gifts? Terry Cross effectively states the question, can Pentecostals bring the "main course" or only the "relish tray" to the ecumenical table?[10] The answer depends on the starting point. Beginning with classical pentecostal theology means being content with bringing the relish of speaking in tongues and charismatic experience. Although Pentecostalism has robust charismatic experience and over a century of exponential global growth, its traditional theology of baptism in the Holy Spirit demonstrates theological capture by traditional Protestant evangelical theology. The early Pentecostals articulated their experience of the Holy Spirit in theological categories they inherited from their evangelical predecessors. The doctrine of Spirit baptism, regarded by many Pentecostals as their "distinctive" doctrine, showcases this influence. Theologically, classical pentecostal theology is evangelical. It inherited its primary structure and content from its evangelical predecessors. This project critically examines the way this historical influence shaped pentecostal atonement theology and constructively proposes a *pentecostal* theology of the atonement based on the Spirit of Pentecost. But why is the evangelical influence on classical pentecostal theology a problem?

Problem

A profound irony characterizes traditional pentecostal theology. What is the nature of that irony? On the one hand, pentecostal religious experience (praxis) and the place

---

[8] *Spirit and Power: A 10-Country Survey of Pentecostals*, 29.
[9] *Spirit and Power: A 10-Country Survey of Pentecostals*, 29.
[10] Terry L. Cross, "The Rich Feast of Theology: Can Pentecostals Bring the Main Course or Only the Relish Tray?," *Journal of Pentecostal Theology* 8, no. 16 (2000): 32–6.

of Pentecost in the narrative of redemption emphasize the Holy Spirit. On the other hand, classical pentecostal theology (rhetoric) reflects neither the pneumatological praxis of Pentecostals nor the place of the Spirit of Pentecost in the narrative of redemption. The problem is not the pneumatological nature of pentecostal praxis, but the Christocentric and crucicentric character of classical pentecostal theology. In short, the theological rhetorical categories of Classical Pentecostalism—indeed, even its sine qua non of Spirit baptism—represent the colonization of pentecostal praxis by Western, Protestant, and evangelical atonement theology.[11] Douglas Jacobsen and L. William Oliverio document the development of classical pentecostal theology and describe it in terms of pentecostal scholasticism and the Bible Doctrines approach to pentecostal theology.[12] This formative pentecostal theology reflected the influence of the conservative evangelical approach to theology. Cheryl Bridges Johns characterizes the consequence of this influence. Pentecostals were "like David in Saul's armor, second- and third-generation Pentecostals have tried to fit into Evangelical approaches to hermeneutics, education and worship. The result has at times been disastrous and humorous."[13] The theological structure and content of what became Classical Pentecostalism was widespread in North American Protestant Evangelicalism of the late-nineteenth and early-twentieth centuries.[14] Understanding that structure and content and its influence on pentecostal theology is vital for understanding the atonement theology popular in Classical Pentecostalism. The following outlines the structure and content of that theology and highlights its influence on the classical pentecostal theology of atonement.

The structure and content of evangelical theology is Christocentric and crucicentric. These characteristics coalesce around penal-substitutionary atonement. Christocentrism, crucicentrism, and penal-substitutionary atonement predominate evangelical theology because its fundamental way of framing redemption is judicial. The structure has two echelons—Christological-judicial-objective and pneumatological-transformational-subjective. The work of Christ on the cross is the objective work of atonement. The cross pays the penal payment of sin and is the foundation of forensic justification. The Holy Spirit plays no role in the atonement. The Holy Spirit's work falls under the subjective and transformational work of sanctification. Consequently, this theology not only distinguishes the saving work of Christ on the cross from the Holy Spirit's inner sanctifying work but also subordinates the Holy

---

[11] A case in point is the long-standing influence of Myer Pearlman's *Knowing the Doctrines of the Bible*, rev. ed. (1937; Springfield: GPH, 1981).

[12] Douglas Jacobsen, "Knowing the Doctrines of Pentecostals: The Scholastic Theology of the Assemblies of God, 1935–1955," in *Pentecostal Currents in American Protestantism*, ed. Edith L. Blumhofer, Russell P. Spittler, and Grant A. Wacker (Urbana: University of Illinois Press, 1999), 90–107 and L. William Oliverio, Jr., *Theological Hermeneutics in the Classical Pentecostal Tradition: A Typological Account* (Boston: Brill, 2012), 116–31.

[13] Cheryl Bridges Johns, *Pentecostal Formation: A Pedagogy among the Oppressed*, Journal of Pentecostal Theology Supplement Series, 2 (Sheffield: Sheffield Academic Press, 1993), 7. D. Lyle Dabney later used the same metaphor of David in Saul's armor to highlight the problematic of trying to articulate pentecostal theology in the register of evangelical theology in "Saul's Armor: The Problem and the Promise of Pentecostal Theology Today," *Pneuma: The Journal of the Society for Pentecostal Studies* 23, no. 1 (2001): 115–46.

[14] See Dayton, *Theological Roots of Pentecostalism*.

Spirit's sanctifying work to Christ's atoning work. Sanctification is not denied or intentionally minimized. But since the crux of salvation is Christ's atonement that provides forensic justification, sanctification necessarily plays a secondary role. Since the Spirit's primary work is sanctification, the Spirit's work, by default, is subordinate to the work of Christ.[15] In this theology of grace, atonement is exclusively Christological, crucicentric, and an extrinsic or objective work of redemption. This theology was the framework for the development of classical pentecostal theology. The influence of this tradition of theology prevented Pentecostals from developing a theology in general and an atonement theology in particular that matches its pneumatological praxis and the role of the Spirit of Pentecost in the narrative of redemption.

Adopting these traditional categories of Christology and pneumatology, Pentecostals articulated their theology of Spirit baptism in terms of a gateway experience to empowered ministry and to exercising spiritual gifts. In other words, the chief feature of pentecostal praxis, Spirit baptism, was articulated as a subset of the subjective work of grace. Assemblies of God theologians William W. Menzies and Robert P. Menzies, for example, argue that the "Pentecostal gift . . . provides for witness not justification before God or personal cleansing."[16] The Assemblies of God doctrinal statement states that Spirit baptism gives power for Christian life and ministry and imparts spiritual gifts for the work of ministry.[17] Classical Pentecostalism includes pentecostal groups that regard Spirit baptism as a post-conversion experience. Speaking in tongues is often the initial sign of this experience, but not all Classical Pentecostals insist on tongues as evidence for the experience of Spirit baptism.[18] The defining feature is that Spirit baptism is distinct from and subsequent to salvation (subsequent, at least, experientially) and is for the purpose of empowering ministry and higher levels of Christian spirituality and spiritual gifting. The problem, as Lisa P. Stephenson argues, is that Classical Pentecostalism reduces Spirit baptism, and hence

---

[15] Gary D. Badcock suggests that the Reformation doctrine of justification "results in a certain displacement of the Spirit from the center of the scheme of salvation" in *Light of Truth and Fire of Love: A Theology of the Holy Spirit* (Grand Rapids: Eerdmans, 1997), 97. William G. Rusch also remarks that Protestant Orthodoxy tends to objectify soteriology and subordinate pneumatology; see Rusch, "The Theology of the Holy Spirit and the Pentecostal Churches in the Ecumenical Movement," *Pneuma: The Journal of the Society for Pentecostal Studies* 9, no. 1 (1987): 17–30.

[16] William W. Menzies and Robert P. Menzies, *Spirit and Power: Foundations of Pentecostal Experience* (Grand Rapids: Zondervan, 2000), 115.

[17] See "Our 16 Fundamental Truths," number 7. https://ag.org/Beliefs/Statement-of-Fundamental-Truths#7. The Pentecostal Assemblies of Canada also stipulates that Spirit baptism is a post-conversion experience that gives "power to witness and grow spiritually." https://paoc.org/docs/default-source/fellowship-services-documents/statement-of-fundamental-and-essential-truths.pdf?sfvrsn=153a1d6a_0.

[18] For example, the Assemblies of God of Great Britain affirms that speaking in tongues is "the essential, biblical evidence," but not the "initial physical sign" of Spirit baptism as does their American counterpart (see Assemblies of God Great Britain, "What We Believe, Baptism in the Holy Spirit," https://www.aog.org.uk/what-we-believe). The Elim Pentecostal Church in the United Kingdom and Ireland affirms a distinct experience of Spirit baptism but makes no mention of an initial sign (see Elim Pentecostal, "What We Believe, The Holy Spirit," https://www.elim.org.uk/Articles/417857/Our_Beliefs.aspx). The issue of tongues, moreover, has not played the sine qua non role of identifying authentic Pentecostalism among South African Pentecostals as it has among Western Pentecostals; see Matthew S. Clark, "Initial Evidence: A Southern African Perspective," *Asian Journal of Pentecostal Studies* 1, no. 2 (1998): 207–8.

pentecostal pneumatology, to the functional role of charismatic gifting.[19] Rather than the Holy Spirit playing a soteriological role, the Spirit is a *donum superadditum* to a salvation and atonement already achieved and received based on the work of Christ.

Classical Pentecostalism theologically marginalizes the place of the Holy Spirit in pentecostal praxis. It does so because the theological framework of Classical Pentecostalism is not indigenous to pentecostal praxis. Indeed, Classical Pentecostalism assumes Christological and crucicentric categories that prevent the theological articulation of the Spirit's place in pentecostal praxis and, for that matter, in the biblical narrative of redemption. Where classical pentecostal rhetoric reflects evangelical theology, pentecostal praxis reflects the narrative of the Spirit of Pentecost—the embodied life and material redemption described in the Hebrew Bible stories of the Spirit and carried on in the life of Jesus Christ. Rather than assimilating pentecostal praxis to an evangelical theological paradigm, pentecostal theology needs to develop an atonement theology that reflects the prominence of the Holy Spirit in pentecostal praxis as well as in the biblical narrative of redemption. Toward that goal, this book offers a pentecostal theology of the atonement that integrates pneumatology and Christology by recognizing that pentecostal praxis is indicative of the place of the Holy Spirit in the biblical narrative of redemption. In doing so, this book speaks to the wider traditions of Christian theology by proposing a holistic, transformational, and pneumatological atonement theology. This project also provides a corrective to Evangelicalism's and Classical Pentecostalism's tendency to reduce atonement to Christological, crucicentric, and forensic categories.

Method

The Holy Spirit is central to pentecostal praxis.[20] The place of the Holy Spirit in pentecostal praxis indicates a pentecostal hermeneutic for systematic theology in general and atonement theology in particular. Why? Because the place of the Holy Spirit in pentecostal praxis corresponds with the role of the Spirit of Pentecost in the narrative of redemption. The correlation between pentecostal praxis and the Spirit's role in the narrative of redemption means that the pentecostal experience of the Holy Spirit is theologically significant, indeed, it is fecund for theology. Before proceeding to detail this theological principle and its implications for method, note that "pentecostal praxis" and "pentecostal experience" are functionally equivalent. Praxis is a broad term. It includes explicit charismatic experiences among Pentecostals, such as speaking

---

[19] Lisa P. Stephenson, *Dismantling the Dualisms for American Pentecostal Women in Ministry: A Feminist-Pneumatological Approach*, Global and Charismatic Studies, 9 (Boston: Brill, 2012), 91–9 and 107–14.

[20] See my extended argument for this theological method in *From Pentecost to the Triune God: A Pentecostal Trinitarian Theology* (Grand Rapids: Eerdmans, 2012). For similar approaches, also see Kenneth J. Archer, *A Pentecostal Hermeneutic: Spirit, Scripture, and Community* (Cleveland: CPT, 2009) and Amos Yong, *Spirit-Word-Community: Theological Hermeneutics in Trinitarian Perspective* (Eugene: Wipf & Stock, 2002). The progenitor for taking pentecostal praxis as informative for pentecostal theology is Steve J. Land, *Pentecostal Spirituality: A Passion for the Kingdom* (1993; Sheffield: Sheffield Academic Press, 1997).

in tongues and emotionally fervent worship. It also includes healing, deliverance, and liberation, which may not have an explicit charismatic character. My focus on pentecostal praxis usually indicates the personal and life-transforming dimensions rather than church-based charismatic experience. I am not discounting charismatic experience. Indeed, it is often the place where the Holy Spirit's renewal of life emerges. But this book is on the holistic, transformative, and pneumatological nature of atonement and not on the practice of charismatic and spiritual gifts per se. Central and common to the range of personal and communal experiences of pentecostal praxis is the Holy Spirit. What does this premise about the centrality of the Holy Spirit in pentecostal praxis and its correspondence with the Spirit of Pentecost mean for the theological approach of this book?

First, pentecostal praxis orientates a theological method that takes the Spirit of Pentecost as the systematic principle of a pentecostal atonement theology. Pentecostal experience (praxis) of the atonement is holistic, transformational, and pneumatological. Historical and global accounts of Pentecostalism illustrate the holistic nature of the pentecostal experience of grace.[21] I recognize that I am using atonement as a broader category of grace than is common in traditional theology. I provide the rationale for this use later. Returning to the point on Pentecost as the systematic principle of this theology, the Holy Spirit is central to the pentecostal praxis of atonement. Spirit baptism is the biblical and liturgical term used to denote that praxis. The Holy Spirit, the Spirit of Pentecost, also plays a decisive role in the narrative of redemption. The prominence of Pentecost in the biblical story of redemption corroborates the priority of the Spirit in pentecostal praxis. The prominence of the Holy Spirit in pentecostal praxis, moreover, sensitizes a reading of Scripture that recognizes the Holy Spirit's role rather than subordinating it to a Christological narrative. Methodologically, taking Pentecost as a culminating moment in the narrative of the atonement is not a matter of reading off theology from pentecostal experience. Pentecostal praxis/experience of the Spirit of Pentecost is theologically indicative of a hermeneutical approach to reading Scripture and developing a theology of the atonement, but only because that praxis reflects the role of the Holy Spirit in the biblical narrative of redemption. Without biblical corroboration, pentecostal praxis would not indicate a hermeneutic. The problem is that Christological and crucicentric narratives have so

---

[21] For historical, see Allan Anderson, *Spreading Fires: The Missionary Nature of Early Pentecostalism* (Maryknoll: Orbis, 2007); Douglas Jacobsen, *Thinking in the Spirit: Theologies of the Early Pentecostal Movement* (Bloomington: Indiana University Press, 2003); and Grant Wacker, *Heaven Below: Early Pentecostals and American Culture* (Cambridge, MA: Harvard University Press, 2001). For more contemporary and global, see Sammy Alfaro, *Divine Compañero: Toward a Hispanic Pentecostal Christology* (Eugene: Pickwick, 2010); Clifton Clarke, ed., *Pentecostal Theology in Africa* (Eugene: Pickwick, 2014); Harvey Cox, *Fire from Heaven: The Rise of Pentecostal Spirituality and the Reshaping of Religion in the Twenty-first Century* (Reading: Addison-Wesley, 1995); Walter J. Hollenweger, *Pentecostalism: Origins and Developments Worldwide* (Peabody, MA: Hendrickson, 1997); Ogbu Kalu, *African Pentecostalism: An Introduction* (New York: Oxford University Press, 2008); Martin Lindhardt, *Practicing the Faith: The Ritual Life of Pentecostal-Charismatic Christians* (New York: Berghahn, 2011); Amos Yong and Estrelda Y. Alexander, *Afro-Pentecostalism: Black Pentecostal and Charismatic Christianity in History and Culture* (New York: New York University Press, 2011); and the four volume *Global Renewal Christianity*, gen. ed. Vinson Synan, Amos Yong, and Miguel Álvarez (Lake Mary: Charisma, 2015–).

dominated atonement theology that the role of the Holy Spirit has been sidelined. The pneumatological nature of pentecostal praxis helps to recover a reading of Scripture that recognizes the place of Pentecost and the role of the Holy Spirit in the wider narrative of redemption. Doing so does not displace Christology but reinforces the synergy between pneumatology and Christology. Thus, a pentecostal theology of the atonement does not supplant Christology. It does not replace Christocentrism with pneumacentrism. On the contrary, it integrates the works of the Holy Spirit and of Christ in a more comprehensive and unified vision of redemption.

But does starting with the Spirit of Pentecost arbitrarily privilege pentecostal preferences? Theology must start somewhere. Protestant (indeed much of Western) atonement theology starts and, for the most part, ends with Christ on the cross. Christocentrism and crucicentrism characterize most Western atonement theologies from Anselmian satisfaction, penal substitutionary, and moral exemplar to nonviolent and solidarity-in-suffering views. Jesus' suffering and death on the cross are certainly vital to the atonement. But they do not tell the whole story of atonement. Indeed, focusing almost exclusively on them obscures the fundamental nature of the atonement, which is receiving and participating in the Spirit of Pentecost. All theology starts at a particular place. No theology is initially or eventually totally all-inclusive. Being Christocentric is not being more biblical and more authentically Christian, if it means marginalizing the role of the Holy Spirit in the work of redemption.

Second, framing atonement in terms of the Spirit of Pentecost and the Spirit's role in the wider narrative of redemption means embracing a broader vision of atonement than is common in traditional Western theology. Atonement theology customarily engages Hebrew Bible sacrificial practices and New Testament accounts and theologies of the cross (e.g., Paul and Romans). But what is the fundamental meaning of atonement? Reconciliation. Atonement means "the reconciliation between God and the world which is the heart of Christian teaching."[22] The common assumption is that atonement means to "undergo some kind of pain or sacrifice for wrongful acts . . . a demand for punishment . . . by the gift of a bloody sacrifice." But "the resumption of friendly relations" is its basic meaning.[23] In other words, as a reconciling activity, atonement takes in the primary redemptive activity of God. The fundamental problem in the narrative of redemption for human beings is alienation from God, each other, and the world in which God created them. For example, Genesis 3 narrates alienation in terms of the shame of nakedness that Adam and Eve experience first between each other and then with God. Their expulsion from the Garden of Eden completes their estrangement from the life for which God created them. Jesus completes his teaching ministry with his disciples in Jn 17:20-26 with a prayer for atonement/reconciliation with God and each other. Reconciliation to the life for which God created human

---

[22] Colin E. Gunton, *The Actuality of Atonement: A Study of Metaphor, Rationality and the Christian Tradition* (Grand Rapids: Eerdmans, 1989), 2. Atonement as reconciliation is the common meaning of the term. See Paul S. Fiddes, *Past Event and Present Salvation: The Christian Idea of Atonement* (London: Darton, Longman, and Todd, 1989), 3–4 and Paul R. Eddy and James Beilby, "The Atonement: An Introduction," in *The Nature of the Atonement: Four Views* (Downers Grove: InterVarsity Academic, 2006), 9.

[23] Stump, *Atonement*, 7.

beings—atonement—is made complete in the new heaven, the new earth, and the new Jerusalem (Rev. 21–22). The point is that atonement deals with the fundamental nature of redemption.

The popular view of penal-substitutionary atonement, for example, also regards atonement as the fundamental redemptive work. But it truncates that redemptive work. Indeed, the traditional theology of atonement is almost exclusively a discussion of the meaning of Christ and the cross. Paul S. Fiddes, for example, claims that the cross is the "cross-roads" of human experience. "Atonement happens because of the death of Jesus in a Roman execution one Friday afternoon."[24] Atonement is a judicial story of Jesus Christ paying the penal price of sin on the cross. The essence of salvation, according to this view, is receiving the imputed righteousness of Christ and the forgiveness of sins before God's heavenly tribunal. The result is that atonement is all important, but, because of its juridical Christocentrism and crucicentrism, denotes only a very narrow aspect of the comprehensive work of redemption. All the dimensions of grace beyond Christ's penal death of atonement are superfluous. Now, the objection is that God sanctifies the justified. OK. But theologically, sanctification is not part of atonement. It is not ultimately what saves a person before the holy wrath of God. Only the death of Christ does that. So, in the end, only the death of Christ on the cross really matters. Everything else, everything that the Spirit of Pentecost brings to the table of redemption is a "relish tray."[25]

The argument here is that the history of redemption is a narrative of atonement. But it is also a narrative of the Holy Spirit, the Spirit of Pentecost. It is the history of the Spirit of atonement. Atonement takes in the comprehensive history of God's redemptive work and the Holy Spirit plays a leading role in that narrative. The outpouring of the Holy Spirit on the Day of Pentecost is a key event not only in the New Testament but in the entire history of redemption. Joel 2 identifies the outpouring of God's Spirit as the eschatological work of redemption. The life and ministry of Jesus Christ reflect this anticipation. Jesus' saving work does not reach its climax on the cross or even in the resurrection, but on the Day of Pentecost with the outpouring of the Holy Spirit. The Day of Pentecost is a decisive scene in the drama of redemption. Pentecost paradoxically culminates and carries on the great movement of redemption that began with the Spirit hovering over the waters, breathing life into the dirt, and bringing about the incarnate life of Jesus Christ. Pentecost is penultimate. Not because Pentecost is deficient and needs something else to complete it. The outpouring of the Spirit of Pentecost is the perennial condition of the ongoing narrative of redemption. Pentecost is the abiding threshold to and the animating power of the kingdom of God. Thus, Peter's Pentecost sermon identifies the outpouring of God's Spirit as the eschatological work of redemption (see Acts 2:14-21). This project, therefore, considers atonement, and the meaning of Christ for redemption, from the perspective of the Spirit of Pentecost. Atonement is participating in the life the Holy Spirit realized in

---

[24] Fiddes, *Past Event and Present Salvation*, 4. Although Christocentric, Fiddes' theology of atonement recognizes and integrates pneumatological and transformational elements; as such, it is not subject to critical issues I raise later in the book in respect to substitutionary atonement. See Fiddes, *Past Event and Present Salvation*, 53, 99, 153–5, and 166–8.

[25] Cross, "The Rich Feast of Theology," 27–47.

Jesus Christ—fellowship through the Spirit with Christ and the Father, the fellowship with all those who participate in the community of Pentecost, the community created by the Spirit of Christ, and the renewal of life in this world, ultimately achieved in the new creation, but foreshadowed in Christ's healing ministry and resurrection and the incipient eschaton of that new creation in the experience of grace. Thus, a pneumatological and pentecostal theology of the atonement shows that the Spirit of Pentecost's renewal of life, not Christ's penal punishment and death, is the primary plotline and nature of the atonement.

Third, the formative context of this project shapes its scope. A fair question is, why focus on Classical Pentecostalism and Western atonement theology rather than putting forth a unified atonement theology that speaks for global Pentecostalism? Developing a comprehensive atonement theology for the diverse manifestations of global Pentecostalism seems beyond the capacity of any one book. Indeed, such an effort may in fact be contrary to the diverse tongues of the Spirit of Pentecost. The Spirit of Pentecost is inimical to totalizing theologies. The limits of theology are intrinsic to the pneumatological subject matter of theology and the diverse particularities in which God's Spirit engages human life (indeed, this is one reason why the early Pentecostals were often non-creedal). Consequently, I work from the tradition of Pentecostalism in which my faith formation and ministry practice took place. Although contextual, this jumping-off point is not parochial because this tradition of Pentecostalism remains a popular form of theological self-understanding for Pentecostals in North America and around the world. In this respect, the book speaks to classical pentecostal communities and Pentecostals seeking a theology that better articulates their praxis of the Spirit of Pentecost. Although primarily engaging in critical conversation with classical pentecostal theology and Western atonement theology, this project is not insular. It draws on historical and contemporary resources that do not fit within and may even challenge Classical Pentecostalism. It also dialogues with alternatives to the objective theories of the atonement, such as the moral exemplar, nonviolent suffering, and solidarity-in-suffering views of atonement. In terms of correspondence with historical atonement theologies, this project shares closest affinity with Eastern Orthodox theologies of grace. Its transformative vision of grace and accented role of the Holy Spirit is closer to pentecostal praxis than Western views that tend toward juridical Christocentrism and crucicentrism.

Fourth, taking Pentecost as a grounding event and a primary theological category has precedent among pentecostal theologians. For Daniela Augustine, the outpouring of the Spirit of Pentecost establishes the church and empowers its Christ-like way of life, making it the earthly icon of the fellowship of the triune God.[26] The outpouring of the Spirit of Pentecost plays a systematic role in Wolfgang Vondey's *Pentecostal Theology*. For Vondey, "Pentecost is the core theological symbol" of pentecostal theology and the narrative for detailing that symbol is the Full Gospel.[27] Like Vondey,

---

[26] Daniela C. Augustine, *Pentecost, Hospitality, and Transfiguration: Toward a Spirit-inspired Vision of Social Transformation* (Cleveland: CPT, 2012). She further developed this pentecostal principle of theology in *The Spirit and the Common Good: Shared Flourishing in the Image of God* (Grand Rapids: Eerdmans, 2019).

[27] Vondey, *Pentecostal Theology*, 1.

Pentecost is a fundamental plotline of this project, but I also turn to the narrative of biblical redemption to situate and frame the narrative of the Spirit of Pentecost. My case for taking the Spirit of Pentecost as foundational for pentecostal atonement also stands in continuity with Frank D. Macchia's pentecostal theology of justification and his emphasis on Spirit baptism as a primary category for pentecostal theology.[28] But it also differs. The main point of departure is that my argument situates Christ within and as the outcome of the narrative of the Spirit, a narrative that culminates with the Holy Spirit offering to all people the Spirit-breathed life fulfilled in Christ. Macchia also focuses on the doctrine of justification, where I consider the keystone doctrine of atonement—justification usually regarded as the primary soteriological result of the atonement. At the same time, my case for pentecostal atonement is a continuation and development of the important work in this trajectory initiated by Macchia. Like Macchia, I am addressing a traditional doctrinal category—atonement—from a pneumatological and pentecostal perspective and endeavoring to "expand the boundaries of Spirit baptism and justification [in my case atonement] so as to discover the vastness of their eschatological scope."[29] Amos Yong's *Spirit of Love: A Trinitarian Theology of Grace* (Baylor, 2012) also points in the direction of my project. Yong's goal is to articulate a theology of the Holy Spirit that extends beyond traditional pentecostal theology, which locates the work of the Holy Spirit in spiritual gifts and empowered ministry. For Yong, the experience of the Holy Spirit as divine love is at the root of pentecostal experience and ministry. The Holy Spirit is the loving presence of God, as grace. Spiritual gifts and signs of Spirit are the tangible manifestations of God's loving presence in the Spirit. I share this goal to envision a more fundamental pneumatology for pentecostal theology. Where Yong focuses on divine love as the grace of the Spirit and engages the issue of divine love vis-à-vis contemporary scientific accounts of altruism, my project considers the place of the Spirit in the doctrine of the atonement. Yong also develops the inclusive nature of the outpouring of the Spirit of Pentecost that speaks in the tongues of the nations and that transcends ethnic, gender, religious, cultural, and class distinctions.[30] These themes dovetail with the global resources and social transcending and empowering nature of the Spirit of Pentecost developed throughout this book.

Content

The pentecostal method outlined earlier shapes the content matter of this project. The book has two parts—"Theology of Atonement" and "Practicing Atonement." The

---

[28] For his theology of justification, see Macchia, *Justified in the Spirit* and for the priority of Spirit baptism, see Macchia, *Baptized in the Spirit*.

[29] Macchia, *Justified in the Spirit*, 99.

[30] Amos Yong, *In the Days of Caesar: Pentecostalism and Political Theology—The Cadbury Lectures 2009*, Sacra Doctrina: Christian Theology for a Postmodern Age series (Grand Rapids: Eerdmans, 2010); *Hospitality and the Other: Pentecost, Christian Practices, and the Neighbor*, Faith Meets Faith series (Maryknoll: Orbis, 2008); and *The Spirit Poured Out on All Flesh: Pentecostalism and the Possibility of Global Theology* (Grand Rapids: Baker Academic, 2005).

structure of Parts One and Two assumes synergy between pentecostal atonement *theology* and *practice*. I argue at several places in this book that classical pentecostal theology disrupts the resonance between pentecostal theology and practice/praxis. But that is a problematic this book endeavors to overcome. The goal is to strike harmony between the theology and praxis. The first part of this book develops a pentecostal theology of atonement based on the biblical narrative of the Spirit of Pentecost. Indicating the method, it begins with the outpouring of the Holy Spirit on the Day of Pentecost as the telos of the history of redemption. It systematically considers the atonement from the perspective of the Spirit of Pentecost. In place of the Christocentric and crucicentric hermeneutic of traditional Protestant and evangelical atonement theology that also shapes classical pentecostal theology, it presents a pneumatological and holistic pentecostal theology of the atonement. The chapters in Part One do not trade Christocentrism for pneumacentrism but achieve a more comprehensive and unified understanding of the atonement. Part One has five chapters that start with Pentecost and then move to Incarnation, cross, resurrection, and eschaton. Although Pentecost comes "late" in the biblical narrative of redemption, it anchors the systematic approach of this book. Why? Because the Spirit of Pentecost is the telos of the narrative of redemption from creation to eschaton. Pentecost is not an isolated but an integrative atonement metaphor. It is an eschatological event in the history of redemption. The point here is that Pentecost, as an eschatological event, on the one hand, culminates the narrative of the Spirit that began in Genesis and, on the other hand, expands, extends, and opens a new chapter. It is the prism for understanding Incarnation, cross, resurrection, and eschaton (note that Pentecost is eschatological and that Pentecost informs the nature of the eschatological promise). Pentecost needs to be understood in the context of and as a culminating event in the wider story of God's redemptive work. Pentecost, therefore, serves as the systematic theological category for this theology of atonement. Constructively, these chapters set forth a pentecostal rhetoric or theology of atonement based on the Holy Spirit's role, as Spirit of Pentecost, in the biblical narrative of redemption. Critically, they offer an alternative to traditional pentecostal rhetoric/theology that gives voice neither to the fundamental nature of the Holy Spirit's work in the history of redemption nor to holistic and transformative pentecostal experience of the Holy Spirit.

Part Two also consists of five chapters that mirror and correspond to the chapters in Part One. The purpose of these chapters is to carry on a conversation between the atonement theology developed in Part One and pentecostal praxis today and yesterday. They show ways the narrative of the Spirit connects with and can shape pentecostal practice. Pentecostal atonement encompasses the narrative of the Spirit of Pentecost and pentecostal praxis. Indeed, pentecostal atonement entails pentecostal praxis because atonement is participation in the narrative of the Spirit of Pentecost. Pentecostal praxis does not constitute atonement. The Spirit of Pentecost, the Spirit of atonement, nevertheless produces the holistic life transformation that characterizes pentecostal praxis. In other words, pentecostal atonement theology is incomplete without considering its meaning for and expression in pentecostal experience—that is, the pentecostal praxis of atonement. The goal of these chapters is to explore past and current pentecostal experience from the perspective of the pentecostal theology set forth in Part One. Each chapter has critical and constructive elements. Critically, they identify and interact with ways that pentecostal praxis diverges from the Spirit Pentecost. Constructively, they show that pentecostal praxis (historical and contemporary) reflects the pentecostal atonement theology developed in Part One, but they also suggest ways that theology points the way toward a more expansive praxis of the Spirit of Pentecost for contemporary Pentecostals. Thus, the result is a holistic account of pentecostal praxis that integrates pneumatology and Christology as well as the transformational and material nature of the pentecostal experience of redemption. These chapters ground their interaction between the pentecostal theology of atonement and pentecostal praxis, for the most part, in historical and empirical studies of global Pentecostalism. Part Two, moreover, is not only historical—asking questions about how to account for pentecostal praxis of the Spirit in the past—but also forward looking. It proposes what the Spirit of Pentecost, the Spirit of atonement, means for pentecostal communities of faith today. The five chapters in Part Two follow the same order as Part One—Pentecost, Incarnation, cross, resurrection, and eschatology.

The two phases in this theological project are not simple linear movements from theory or theology to application and practice. This method assumes a feedback loop between pentecostal praxis and theology. Pentecostal praxis provides the indicator for a pentecostal hermeneutic that recognizes the central place of the Spirit of Pentecost in the biblical narrative of redemption and, thus also, in a pentecostal atonement theology. The constructive theology that emerges from this pentecostal hermeneutic (Part One) informs a wider vision of pentecostal praxis of atonement (Part Two).

Part One

Theology of Atonement

2

Pentecost

The Spirit of Pentecost is central to the narrative of redemption and pentecostal experience. But Pentecost does not feature prominently in either traditional Protestant evangelical or pentecostal atonement theology.[1] Recognizing that the outpouring of the Spirit of Pentecost is fundamental to the narrative of redemption and to the atonement resolves this dissonance. Pentecost is not an adjunct to Christ or a subsidiary experience (e.g., Spirit baptism) to the salvation provided by Christ on the cross. The outpouring of the Holy Spirit on the Day of Pentecost is the critical nexus not only in the New Testament but also in the entire history of redemption. Pentecost is where the narrative of redemption comes together. Pentecost structures the history of redemption. It provides theological coherence to the narrative parts. From Genesis to Pentecost and the new creation that emerges from it, the history of redemption is a story of the Holy Spirit.[2] Pentecost *reveals* the perennial and universal work of the Holy Spirit that began with creation and comes to full historical manifestation in the particular history of Jesus Christ and *gives* the Spirit-anointed life of Christ a universal horizon. To understand Pentecost is to understand the history of redemption and atonement.

The argument that Pentecost is central to atonement invites critical and constructive dialogue with traditional Christocentric and crucicentric approaches to the atonement as well as the tendency in traditional pentecostal theology to bracket Spirit baptism in a post-conversion experience of grace. Subsequent chapters engage these issues at length. This chapter, however, builds the case for taking the Spirit of Pentecost as the systematic principle for a pentecostal theology of the atonement.[3] The narrative of redemption stretches from creation to eschaton and the Holy Spirit plays a central role in it. Pentecost is a critical revelatory telos and participatory nexus in that broader story of redemption. The primary content of this chapter charts scenes and themes

---

[1] See my discussion of Frank D. Macchia's and Amos Yong's work in Chapter 1 as important examples of pentecostal theologians moving beyond traditional theologies of grace.

[2] The narrative continuity in the biblical story of the Spirit follows from the correlation between the immanent identities and economic activities of the divine persons. See my *From Pentecost to the Triune God: A Pentecostal Trinitarian Theology*, Pentecostal Manifestos (Grand Rapids: Eerdmans, 2012).

[3] Wolfgang Vondey also takes Pentecost as a principle for pentecostal systematic theology and develops it in the structure of the Full Gospel in his volume in this series. See Wolfgang Vondey, *Pentecostal Theology: Living the Full Gospel*, Systematic Pentecostal and Charismatic Theology, ser. ed. Wolfgang Vondey and Daniela C. Augustine (London: Bloomsbury, 2017), 1–10.

in the history of redemption to show their pneumatological nature and proleptic relation to Pentecost. It begins, however, with a brief description of the programmatic pneumatological principle that the outpouring of the Spirit of Pentecost is the telos of the narrative of redemption (Chapter 6 extends the discussion of the telos of Pentecost/ Spirit telocity in terms of the Holy Spirit's eschatological agency in the narrative of redemption).

Pentecost: The Telos of Redemption

Pentecost, not the cross, is the *telos* of redemption. Frank D. Macchia also recognizes the eschatological nature of the Holy Spirit's work. For Macchia, Spirit baptism is the "goal of creation and the fulfillment of justice for creation."[4] I want to extend this eschatological character of the Spirit's work with the notion of Spirit telocity.[5] In my earlier work on the Trinity, I proposed "trinitarian teloi" for each divine person, according to which each divine person has a proper telos in the immanent and the economic Trinity.[6] The theology of Spirit telocity presented here is a development on that theology in respect of the Spirit and atonement.

The Holy Spirit is the telic agent of the history of redemption. The narrative of redemption has Spirit telocity.[7] "Ocity" means the quality of something. In this case, the quality of being telic or activity toward a goal. Spirit telocity has two aspects: (1) The Spirit guides the narrative of redemption and (2) the full realization of Spirit-breathed life in and for the world is the end of that narrative. Although the history of redemption, from creation to the new heaven and the new earth, bears fundamental

---

[4] Frank D. Macchia, *Justified in the Spirit: Creation, Redemption, and the Triune God* (Grand Rapids: Eerdmans, 2010), 143. Macchia's view on the eschatological nature of Spirit baptism has expanded. For example, in *Baptized in the Spirit: A Global Pentecostal Theology* (Grand Rapids: Eerdmans, 2006), he argues that Spirit baptism is eschatological because it indicates and enacts the inauguration of the kingdom of God "before it is applied to the church"; in other words, Pentecost is primarily eschatological, not ecclesiological (see pp. 85 and 102-3). A distinguishing point between the view that Macchia presents in *Justified in the Spirit* and my proposal is that I locate the Spirit's fundamental work in the Incarnation of Christ (hence, Spirit Christology), whereas Macchia places it at the baptism of Jesus (see *Justified in the Spirit*, 94). Note, however, that Macchia emphasizes the fundamental role of the Spirit in the Incarnation and coordinates it with Jesus as the Spirit baptizer in his later work, *Jesus the Spirit Baptizer: Christology in Light of Pentecost* (Grand Rapids: Eerdmans, 2018), 124-31 and 158-61. For my earlier work on the relationship between Incarnation and Pentecost, see *From Pentecost to the Triune God*, 78-94 and *A Pentecostal Political Theology for American Renewal: Spirit of the Kingdoms, Citizens of the Cities* (New York: Palgrave Macmillan, 2016), 184-8.

[5] I developed Pentecost as the telos of the work of redemption and its implications for pneumatology and trinitarian theology in *From Pentecost to the Triune God*, 165-6. After writing this chapter, I also discovered that Frank Macchia uses telos in a similar way to describe the relation between the Incarnation and Pentecost. See Macchia, *Jesus the Spirit Baptizer*, 129.

[6] See my *From Pentecost to the Triune God*, 165-6.

[7] Amos Yong seems to have a similar point in mind with the statement that the "outpouring of the Spirit indicates that eschatological salvation is . . . both historical and directed toward the future transformation of all creation in the new heavens and new earth." See Amos Yong affirms the same in *The Spirit Poured Out on All Flesh: Pentecostalism and the Possibility of Global Theology* (Grand Rapids: BakerAcademic, 2005), 96.

continuity, it is not monotonous; Pentecost takes the story to a new scene. Pentecost is a hinge of history. Pentecost is the threshold between the world of Genesis 3 and the coming of God's kingdom that culminates in the new creation.

Stated briefly, what does it mean to call Pentecost the telos of redemption? Jesus saw Pentecost as the telos of his ministry. Just before his Ascension, Christ charged his disciples, "do not leave Jerusalem, but wait for the gift my Father promised, which you have heard me speak about. For John baptized with water, but . . . you will be baptized with the Holy Spirit" (Acts 1:4-5). In other words, Jesus did not see the cross or even his resurrection as the final work of redemption. He recognized that his life, as the Spirit-anointed messiah, was the threshold to the outpouring of the Holy Spirit, an outpouring that would share his Spirit-anointed life with all people and that would culminate in the new heaven and the new earth. Jesus, therefore, affirmed the pneumatelic nature and the Spirit telocity of his life. Although Pentecost stands in continuity with the prior story of redemption, most clearly and directly in connection with Christ, it also opens a new chapter. It is the gateway through which Christ's definitive and sublime fulfillment of Spirit-breathed life becomes available to all people and ends with the new heaven and the new earth.[8] Pentecost is not the end of the narrative of redemption. But perhaps Pentecost signals the "end of the beginning."[9] Without Pentecost, Christology is not redemptive. It remains a story of the past. With the outpouring of the Spirit of Pentecost, the history of redemption crosses a threshold from the historical particularity of Christ's Spirit-breathed life to the universality of the Spirit of Pentecost.[10]

What I just outlined about the Spirit of Pentecost jars with much of traditional atonement theology. Why? Because traditional atonement theology takes Christ and the cross as the primary events in the history of redemption. Traditional atonement theology is a Christological and crucicentric narrative. Considered from the standpoint of Pentecost, however, the life and ministry of Jesus Christ take part in a wider story of the Holy Spirit. The Gospels frame Jesus' identity, ministry, and the redemption that flows from him in terms of pneumatology. This chapter describes the fundamental place of Pentecost in the wider narrative of redemption. Pentecost is an ongoing and a culminating point in the narrative of the Spirit of God that begins in Genesis 1 and culminates in Revelation 21 and 22. The common Christological emphasis in atonement theology and pentecostal approaches to the Holy Spirit divide the story of the Spirit into two narratives, one that deals with creation and one with redemption.

---

[8] Although focusing on the theology of Spirit baptism, Macchia also maintains the eschatological nature of the Spirit of Pentecost as bringing "the final dominion of life over death as all of creation becomes the dwelling place of God's Holy Spirit" (see Macchia, *Baptized in the Spirit*, 103). Later he calls Pentecost a "unique event" and "a turning point." See *Jesus the Spirit Baptizer*, 315.

[9] Winston Churchill used these words to characterize the significance of the British victory over the German Afrika Korps and its Italian allies at the Battle of El Alamein, delivered to the House of Commons, November 10, 1942.

[10] Although the language and terms differ, what I am suggesting here as the Spirit-telic nature of atonement seems to bear correspondence with the Eastern Orthodox theology of deification. As Vladimir Lossky concludes that "in breaking the tyranny of sin, our Saviour opens to us anew the way of deification, which is the final end of man. The work of Christ calls out to the work of the Holy Spirit." See Lossky, *The Mystical Theology of the Eastern Church* (Crestwood: St. Vladimir's Seminary Press, 1976), 134.

The consequence is that the Holy Spirit is either submerged in a Christological narrative or subordinated in a discrete element of the order of redemption (*ordo salutis*). My goal here is to set forth Pentecost as a systematic category for understanding the biblical narrative and the nature of the atonement and its related doctrines—that is, Incarnation, cross, resurrection, and eschaton. The following sections set the biblical narrative foundation of the Spirit of Pentecost.

Creation: Proto-Pentecost

Where does the narrative of Pentecost begin? "In the beginning, God created the heavens and the earth . . . and the Spirit of God was hovering over the waters" opens the narrative of the Spirit of Pentecost (Gen. 1:1-2). The Spirit of God stirring over the dark waters is the first outpouring of the Holy Spirit. Saying that means the Genesis 1 (as well as the Genesis 2) creation story is in fact a redemption story.[11] The pneumatological and redemptive nature of Genesis 1 and 2 are often overlooked. Why? Because common approaches to them privilege the categories of modern science and Christology. Traditional pentecostal and evangelical readings of Genesis endeavor to demonstrate that the creation stories detail scientific and historical accounts of cosmic origins. The Genesis creation stories, however, are not modern scientific reports.[12] They do not answer questions of scientific cosmology, but theological ones.[13] They portray the way that God tamed the primordial chaos and darkness and established a world of life, light, and harmony and in which human beings are meant to flourish. The Spirit of God, moreover, was the initiating agent of that redemptive process of creation. The Genesis creation stories are not rivals to Big-Bang cosmology and biological evolution. They address different concerns. Although modern cosmology explains the transition from the primordial darkness before the initial singularity to a universe filled with billions of stars and evolution accounts for the development of the chemical building blocks that led to the emergence of life, they do not explain why this took place. Genesis 1 and 2 do that. They describe God's dreams for this world and the place of human beings within it. In place of darkness, disorder, and death, the "hovering" Spirit

---

[11] Karl Löning and Erich Zenger point out that the Bible begins with the creation of heaven and earth and ends with the creation of a new heaven and a new earth. They maintain that creation theology is central to redemption theology. Although not addressing pneumatology, their view applies to this project: "it is not christology that is the hermeneutic key to understanding the theology of creation, but just the opposite: the New Testament kerygma about God's saving activity in the crucified and risen Jesus is a unique explanation of the living power of the Creator-God." See Karl Löning and Erich Zenger, *To Begin with, God Created . . . Biblical Theologies of Creation*, trans. Omar Kaste (Collegeville: Liturgical, 2000), 1–2.

[12] Robert Karl Gnuse, *Misunderstood Stories: Theological Commentary on Genesis 1–11* (Eugene: Cascade, 2014), 19.

[13] Mark S. Smith argues that ancient Near Eastern creation myths are "narratives of revelation. They allow their human audience an opportunity to step into a deeper reality, one underlying its more mundane existence. . . . Myths narrate across these realities of deities, humanity, and the world, but without explaining them, in any modern sense." See Smith, "Is Genesis 1 a Creation Myth? Yes and No," in *Myth and Scripture: Contemporary Perspectives on Religion, Language, and Imagination*, ed. Dexter E. Callender Jr. (Atlanta: SBL Press, 2014), 87–8.

of God creates the sun, moon, and stars—the latter promising that even during the night the world is not lost to the darkness of Leviathan—and brings structure to the world that enables life to flourish.[14] Genesis 2 focuses on the Spirit of God's designs for human beings. The breath of God brings forth a creature that bears the divine image. The important point for using Pentecost as the grounding metaphor for a pentecostal theology of the atonement is that Pentecost continues and develops the Spirit's place in the biblical narrative of redemption. The pneumatic imagery of the wind that tamed the abyss in Genesis 1 is the wind that accompanied the outpouring of the Spirit of Pentecost. The remainder of this section details the foundational pneumatology of the creation stories.

First, creation is the work of God's Spirit. Conditioned by Christocentrism, the common practice is to begin the creation story with the Word, "and God said" in Gen. 1:3.[15] The next step from the Word of Gen. 1:3 is the Logos of Jn 1:1, who "was with God in the beginning. [And t]hrough him all things were made" (Jn 1:2-3). The point here is not to deny the agency of the eternal Son of God in creation, but to correct Logo-centric stories. The problem with the Logo-centric readings of Scripture and the theologies they fund is not emphasizing the Son and his Incarnation in Jesus Christ. The problem is marginalizing the Holy Spirit. God's Spirit hovering over the "formless and empty" earth and the "darkness . . . over the . . . deep" is the beginning of creation (Gen. 1:2).[16] The Spirit of God is the catalyst for creation. Connecting creation to the agency of not only divine *logos*, but also God's *pneuma* in Genesis 1 is consistent with Ps. 33:6-7: "By the word of the LORD were the heavens made, their starry host by the breath of his mouth." The Spirit of God hovering over the primal elements in Gen. 1:2 is the pneumatological threshold from cosmic chaos to God's good creation. At the initiative of God's Spirit, the days of creation emerge from the primal pandemonium. The stirring Spirit of God separates the heavens and the earth, the light and the darkness, the waters above from the waters below, and the water and the land. Indeed, the hovering Spirit of God "continuously . . . [fills] the space between the heaven and the earth with his life-giving breath."[17] The Genesis 1 creation story, consequently, portrays the Spirit of God as the divine agent that redeems the elements from that dark abyss and ushers in a world ordered for the flourishing of life.[18]

---

[14] Also see Ps. 33:6 for the pneumatological agency of God's creative activity. The psalm uses the same images of God's breath and word as Genesis 1, although it reverses their order.

[15] Reflecting Christocentrism, Karl Barth maintains that the Spirit hovering over the primal elements is impotent and the power of creation lies in the Word of God. Karl Barth, *Church Dogmatics*, III/I.2, *The Doctrine of Creation*, ed. G. W. Bromiley and T. F. Torrance (Edinburgh: T & T Clark, 1958), 108. Biblical scholars are sometimes no less prone than theologians to downplay pneumatology in the creation story—for example, Bruce Waltke, *Genesis: A Commentary* (Grand Rapids: Zondervan, 2001), 69.

[16] Thomas L. Brodie, *Genesis as Dialogue: A Literary, Historical, and Theological Commentary* (New York: Oxford University Press, 2001), 133.

[17] Ellen van Wolde, "Separation and Creation in Genesis 1 and Psalm 104, A Continuation of the Discussion of the Verb ברא," *Vetus Testamentum* 67, no. 4 (2017): 632–3 and 637.

[18] Rebecca S. Watson maintains that chaos is not an appropriate concept for understanding creation in the Hebrew Bible. The elements of creation are never in real competition with the God of Israel, according to Watson. God is always in control and the stability of creation with God overseeing it is never in question. I agree with her in respect to the God-creation relationship. Although demythologized of divine warfare, the Genesis 1 creation story retains the negative connotations

Second, creation is a redemptive activity of God's Spirit. Genesis does not begin with neutral material elements. The ancient Israelite would not consider the "formless" earth and the "empty, darkness . . . over the surface of the deep" (Gen. 1:2) with the clinical detachment that a modern cosmologist might ponder the base elements the moment prior to the Big-Bang. Indeed, the latter is likely to marvel at the state of the universe just before the primal release of energy that propelled the formation of the universe. The ancient Israelite would regard them as malevolent and foreboding. The description of creation in Psalm 74 opens a window into the worldview of the ancient Near East (ANE). It declares unambiguously that creation is an act of salvation: "You, O God . . . bring salvation upon the earth. It was you who split open the sea by your power and broke the heads of the monster in the waters . . . you established the sun and moon . . . set all the boundaries of the earth" (Ps. 74:12-17; also see Pss. 18:7-15, 89:8-11, 93:1-4, 24:1-10). Job also conveys this type of creation story: "By his power he churned up the sea; by his wisdom he cut Rahab to pieces. By his breath the skies became fair; his hand pierced the gliding serpent" (Job 26:12-13; also see Job 38–41, which is an extended chaos to creation story). These creation accounts retain elements of the *Chaoskampf* characteristic of comparable ANE cosmic origin stories.[19] Creation is a battle between dragon-like chaos gods (Rahab and the multi-headed Leviathan) out of which the victor brings order and flourishing to the world.[20] Relative to Psalm 74 and Job 26 and 40–41, Genesis 1 demythologizes ANE cosmology. Yahweh does not engage in a cosmic cage match with rival deities.[21] It nevertheless retains its fundamental worldview. God tames the menacing primal sea and darkness. This raises the question, but were the primal elements created by God or did they coexist with God? Menahem Kister is correct: "The author of Genesis . . . does not give us a clue about the way in which he coped with this subtle theological question, if he recognized it at all."[22] That answer poses philosophical and theological problems for the Jewish and Christian doctrines that God alone is eternal.[23] But Genesis is not addressing the concerns of later Jewish and Christian theology. It tells the reader that from darkness

of the primal elements—for example, the darkness over the surface of the deep stands in contrast to the ordered and light-filled world that emerges in the days of creation in Genesis 1. For Watson, see *Chaos Uncreated: A Reassessment of the Theme of "Chaos" in the Hebrew Bible*, Beihefte zur Zeitschrift für die alttestamentliche Wissenschaft, vol. 341 (New York: Walter de Gruyter, 2005).

[19] For excellent comparisons of the Hebrew *Chaoskampf* creation and redemption narratives, see Hyun Chul Paul Kim, "City, Earth, and Empire in Isaiah 24–27," in *Formation and Intertextuality in Isaiah 24–27*, ed. J. Todd Hibbard and Hyun Chul Paul Kim, Ancient Israel and Its Literature 17, ser. ed. Thomas C. Römer (Atlanta: Society of Biblical Literature, 2013), 25–34; Jakob H. Grønbaek, "Baal's Battle with Yam–A Canaanite Creation Fight," *Journal for the Study of the Old Testament* 10, no. 33 (1985): 27–44; and Henry Rowald, "Mī hū' - lī hū': Leviathan and Job in Job 41:2-3," *Journal of Biblical Literature* 105, no. 1 (1986): 104–9.

[20] Eric Ortlund, "Identity of Leviathan and the Meaning of the Book of Job," *Trinity Journal* 34, no. 1 (2013): 17–30.

[21] Gnuse, *Misunderstood Stories*, 22. Rebecca Watson argues that mythic divine combat themes are not presented in the passages that portray Yahweh's interactions with the sea and dragon type monster (e.g., Leviathan and Rahab). See Watson, *Chaos Uncreated*, see esp. 369–76.

[22] Menahem Kister, "Tohu wa-Bohu, Primordial Elements and Creatio ex-Nihilo," *Jewish Studies Quarterly* 14, no. 3 (2007): 241.

[23] Indeed, the problem for monotheism posed by the apparent "uncreated primordial elements" is a possible motivation for Isa. 45:7 that makes it clear that God created the light *and* the darkness. See Kister, "Tohu wa-Bohu, Primordial Elements and Creatio ex-Nihilo," 241–2.

and desolation, God created a world of abundance and delight for human beings to enjoy, thrive in, and care for as God's image bearers.[24] The Spirit of God, moreover, is the catalyzing agent that redeems the elements from the dark abyss and ushers in a world fashioned for the flourishing of life.

The story of Noah and the flood is creation 2.0.[25] "The springs of the great deep burst forth, and the floodgates of the heavens were opened" (Gen. 7:12). The floodwaters kept rising until even the mountains were covered and "every living thing that moved on the earth perished . . . everything on the face of the earth was wiped out" (Gen. 7:17-23). When the floodwaters abate, the earth again lies in the darkness of the deep. Only the creatures stowed away in Noah's ark and the sea creatures do not perish. Like creation, the flood story is a redemption story. Freeing the earth from the floodwaters redeems the earth from the abyss. The flood story is also a story of God's Spirit. The agent of God's redemptive activity is pneumatological—a *ruach* (wind, spirit) from God blows and frees the earth from the floodwaters (Gen. 8:1-5). Just as the hovering Spirit of God freed the earth from the antediluvian flood and was the divine presence that brought forth the living creatures, the Spirit of God again makes the waters recede, land appear, and life emerge on the earth.[26] God describes human beings, moreover, as bearers of the divine image, and then blessed and called Noah and his family to "Be fruitful and increase in number and fill the earth" (Gen. 9:1 and 6-7; cf. Gen. 1:27-28 and Gen. 2:3).

Third, the creation stories present a pneumatological anthropology.[27] Although differing in important ways, Genesis 1 and 2 share points of continuity on the role of the Spirit of God in creation and especially the pneumatic nature of human life. In Genesis 1, the Spirit of God begins the days of creation that bring order and life from the abyss and darkness. The creation process that begins with the hovering Spirit of God culminates in the creation of human beings in the image and likeness of God. God speaking is also creative in Genesis 1. But breath is the foundation of speaking. The hovering Spirit of God is not an oddity that momentarily appears in Gen. 1:2 and that can be discarded once the Word arrives in Gen. 1:3. The hovering Spirit remains the ongoing and active presence of God that is the foundation and agency of the days of creation that bring forth the living creatures, which culminates in the creation of human beings.[28] The Spirit of God is the immanence of transcendence. The Spirit is the presence of God that is above and beyond the world, but also present and active in the

---

[24] Fred Gottlieb, "The Creation Theme in Genesis 1, Psalm 104, and Job 38–42," *Jewish Bible Quarterly* 44, no. 1 (2016): 31.

[25] Löning and Zenger, *To Begin with, God Created*, 20. Bradley Embry points out that the Flood and Tower of Babel narratives develop themes presented in the Garden/Fall narrative. See Embry, "The 'naked narrative' from Noah to Leviticus: Reassessing Voyeurism in the account of Noah's Nakedness in Genesis 9:22-24," *Journal for the Study of the Old Testament* 35, no. 4 (2011): 425.

[26] Van Wolde, "Separation and Creation in Genesis 1 and Psalm 104, A Continuation of the Discussion of the Verb ארב," 632–3. Van Wolde argues that the continuing presence and activity of God's Spirit is the ongoing divine agent of creation in Genesis 1. I am extending that point to God's Spirit in restoring the earth after the flood.

[27] As do Job 33:4 and 34:14 and Ps. 104:29-30.

[28] Van Wolde, "Separation and Creation in Genesis 1 and Psalm 104, A Continuation of the Discussion of the Verb ארב," 632–3.

world (also cf. Ps. 139:7).[29] Thus, the final act of the Spirit of God's redemption of the darkness of the deep is the creation of human beings in the divine image.

In Genesis 2, the breath of God initiates the emergence of human life. Both stories emphasize the place of human beings in God's creation: Genesis 1 by culminating and Genesis 2 by starting the creation of life with human beings. The work of God's Spirit brings life to the world in both Genesis 1 and 2. The barrenness of the earth before the divine breath gives life to human beings (Genesis 2) correlates with the inhospitable condition of the primal abyss (Genesis 1). Divine action by God's Spirit marks the transition from darkness to light and from dirt to life. Like Genesis 1, the creation process in Genesis 2 moves from disorder and lifelessness to structure and life. The creation of human beings begins with dirt. The Genesis 2 story emphasizes that before the creation of human beings, the earth was without life—"no shrub of the field had yet appeared on the earth and no plant of the field had yet sprung up" (Gen. 2:5). The structure of the heavens and the earth are present and the separation of the waters and the land detailed in Genesis 1 are assumed complete. But living creatures are absent. God crafts the human from the dust and then frees the human dirt statue from its inertia by breathing "into his nostrils the breath of life" (Gen. 2:7). The breath of God makes the human a living being. God redeems dirt by breathing life into it. Divine breath is theologically synonymous with the Spirit (*ruach*, wind) of God that initiated and carried out creation in Genesis 1.[30] The gift of divine breath, the Spirit of God, transforms the dirt into the human divine image bearer.[31] The creation of human life in Genesis 2 continues the portrayal of creation as an act of redemption and of God's Spirit. Human life emerges when God's Spirit breathes life into lifeless dust. The dirt is dead until the Spirit of God vivifies it.[32] The breath of God makes the dust a human being that can live in fellowship with its Creator, other human beings, and the rest of creation.[33] Genesis 2:7, therefore, presents a pneumatological anthropology. Human beings can bear the divine image and likeness because their life emerges from the very breath of God's Spirit. The pneumatic foundation of human life in Genesis points toward the Spirit of Pentecost.

---

[29] Andreas Schuele puts it this way: "The Spirit is not just a manifestation of divine presence on earth but establishes an overlap between the divine and created spheres." See Andreas Schuele, "The Spirit of YHWH and the Aura of Divine Presence," *Interpretation: A Journal of Bible and Theology* 66, no. 1 (2012): 26.

[30] For parallel use of *ruach* (spirit, wind) and *nishmat* (breath), see Job 33:44, Job 34:14, and Ps. 104:29-30.

[31] For a detailed comparative study of Adam and Eve as the divine image in the ancient Near East, see Catherine L. McDowell, *The Image of God in the Garden of Eden: The Creation of Humankind in Genesis 2:5–3:24 in Light of the mis pî and wpt-r Rituals of Mesopotamia and Ancient Egypt*, Siphrut: Literature and Theology of the Hebrew Scriptures, 15 (Winona Lake: Eisenbrauns, 2015).

[32] John R. Levison, *Filled with the Spirit* (Grand Rapids: Eerdmans, 2009), 14–15; George T. Montague, *The Holy Spirit: Growth of a Biblical Tradition* (New York: Paulist, 1976), 5; and John H. Walton, *Genesis*, The NIV Application Commentary Series (Grand Rapids: Zondervan, 2001), 166.

[33] After developing this tri-relational nature of human beings as divine image bearers, I came across Marsha M. Wilfong's use of them in "Human Creation in Canonical Context: Genesis 1:26-31 and Beyond," in *God Who Creates: Essays in Honor of W. Sibley Towner*, ed. William P. Brown and S. Dean McBride, Jr. (Grand Rapids: Eerdmans, 2000), 42–6.

Eden: Proto-Charismatic Community

The outpouring of the Holy Spirit on the Day of Pentecost creates a charismatic community. The charismatic community of Pentecost corresponds to the three relationships that define the fabric of Spirit-breathed life in Genesis—relationship with God, other human beings, and the earth. "Charismatic" is a widely used term and usually refers to spiritual gifts attributed to the Holy Spirit and the emotionally charged experiences that often attend pentecostal worship and spirituality. While not questioning that use of the term, I want to apply it to the fundamental nature of the life the Spirit of God brought forth for human beings. Thus, charismatic takes in the relationships human beings have with God and with each other as well as with their life in this world. The starting place for understanding these relationships and the type of life the Spirit of God intends for human beings is the Genesis creation stories, especially Genesis 2 that presents the creation of Adam and Eve and their life in, and expulsion from, the Garden of Eden.

First, God's Spirit-created human beings for edenic life.[34] Eden is a picture of abundant life in this world. Genesis 2 uses the evocative metaphor of nakedness to describe that abundant life. Prior to being expelled from Eden, Adam and Eve are naked. Nakedness, more than a statement on their lack of clothing, portrays the condition of their lives. Nakedness and its loss capture the three relationships that define the nature of Spirit-breathed life. The Spirit of God creates human beings for relationship with God, with each other, and with the land.[35] First, they are God's companions. The most intimate relationship human beings have is with their creator God. The breath of God animates their very life and remains the foundation and horizon of their life. Expressing the theology of Gen. 2:7, the Psalmist puts it this way: "when you take away their breath, they die and return to the dust. When you send your Spirit, they are created, and you renew the face of the earth" (Ps. 104:29-30; also see Gen. 6:3 and Job 34:14-15). The Spirit of God is the perennial foundation of human life. When the Spirit of God leaves human beings, they return to the dust; they are no more. Second, they feel safe in each other's presence. Although existentially and teleologically defined by the indwelling presence of God's Spirit to bear the divine image, relationships with other human beings are intrinsic to bearing the divine image. God declares, "It is not good for the man to be alone" (Gen. 2:18). Although Adam enjoyed relationship with God, he was without human companionship. Genesis 2 indicates that God did not create human beings for a mono-dimensional divine relationship. Life in community with other people is intrinsic for the fullness of human life. Third, human beings were made from and for this world. Genesis 1 describes human beings as created in the "image" and "likeness" of God (Gen. 1:26-27). God charges the human beings to "rule" and to "be fruitful and increase in number; fill the earth and subdue it" (Gen. 1:27-28). Their stewardship and productivity roles correlate with God's creative activity in the

---

[34] Löning and Zenger argue that creation "is constituted by the goal toward which the relationship that links the creator and 'his' creation is aimed" (*To Begin with, God Created*, 10).

[35] Sibley W. Towner, "Clones of God: Genesis 1:26-28 and the Image of God in the Hebrew Bible," *Interpretation* 59, no. 4 (2005): 350.

days of creation. As God tamed the primordial elements, human beings image God by carrying on the work of creation through their culture building activities. Genesis 2:7, moreover, shows that the human ability to image God derives from the presence of God's Spirit that gives human beings the ongoing capacity for life in the likeness of God. After animating Adam with the divine breath and placing him in the Garden of Eden, God calls him "to work it and take care of it" (Gen. 2:15). Relationship with God and with each other as well as a meaningful activity in this world is the multifaceted telos of Spirit-breathed life.

Second, the Spirit of God brings forth human beings for embodied life on earth, not spiritual life in heaven.[36] Genesis 2:7 does not portray a body getting a soul or a spirit, but God's Spirit animating dirt. The entirety of human life is a gift of God's Spirit and not only its inner spiritual element. Adam does not possess a "natural" life that later receives a "spiritual" life. Relationship with God is not a *donum superadditum* of grace layered over human beings otherwise living natural, secular, and nonspiritual lives. The biblical creation story does not support a "supernatural anthropology."[37] Giving Adam the breath of life created his life and created it for no other reason than for Adam to live in this world in loving relationship with God and eventually with Eve and the rest of creation. Adam never had a "natural" existence. He was, from the beginning, created for nothing other than relationship and life with God in and for this world. What Gen. 2:7 means for pneumatology and theological anthropology is that the totality of human life arises from the breath of God's Spirit. The Spirit of God's redeeming activity does not paste a spiritual life onto a lesser natural life. The life given by the Spirit, moreover, is not for heaven, but for this world.

Third, after eating the forbidden fruit, Adam and Eve lost their nakedness and, in its place, lived in shame. Rather than going to greet, they hide from their God in the Garden. They also hide from each other. Why? Because they no longer feel safe in each other's presence.[38] Rather than a companion, their counterpart is now a threat. But the Fall effects their relationship with the earth as well. No longer an edenic paradise, the earth becomes a place of futility, frustration, and failure. In place of the largess of the verdant garden, Adam gets "thorns and thistles," the "sweat of the brow," and "painful toil" until he returns to dust (Gen. 3:17-19). Eve gets birth pangs and misogyny (Gen. 3:16). The question of whether or not childrearing was painful before the Fall misses the point of the story. Genesis 3 is not about obstetrics. Genesis 2 and 3 narrate the tragic irony of the human condition. Reading Genesis 2, our hearts resonate with Eden and nakedness, we say, "yes, that's what I was made for, that's what life should be like." It also invokes nostalgia. It evokes memories of furtive experiences of Eden—perhaps an embrace in a father's arms that conveyed

---

[36] For the embodied nature of the divine image, see J. Richard Middleton, *The Liberating Image: The Imago Dei in Genesis 1* (Grand Rapids: Brazos, 2005), 54–5. For further discussion on this topic, see Studebaker, *A Pentecostal Political Theology for American Renewal*, 178–9.

[37] For this term, see Craig Martin, *Capitalizing Religion: Ideology and the Opiate of the Bourgeoisie* (New York: Bloomsbury, 2014), 56. Martin argues that the separation of the spiritual and physical derives not so much from lingering vestiges of Platonism but from late Medieval and early Reformation currents in theology (Martin, *Capitalizing Religion*, 54–6).

[38] Rebecca Thomas and Stephen Parker, "Toward a Theological Understanding of Shame," *Journal of Psychology and Christianity* 23, no. 2 (2004): 179.

unmitigated love. The utterly selfless concern showed by a teacher who noticed your downcast spirit alone in a crowd of students in a high school hall. But with bitterness and despair, we recognize that Genesis 3 characterizes the more common experience of life in this world. The business office, for example, should be a place of mutual collaboration where colleagues foster each other's creative capacities for a common purpose (Genesis 2), but is more often the place of petty power-mongering, turf wars, incompetence, and backstabbing (Genesis 3). Human beings were made for more than the dysfunction, austerity, grind, and abuse that too often characterize life. Giving birth to a child should be attended with celebration and anticipation for the future. But the pain of childbirth too often in the ancient world meant the death of mother and/or child and in the world today the poverty and despair of single parenthood. Genesis 2 and 3 indicate that human life finds its richness in nurturing human relationships and meaningful activity in this world. And yet, the travails pictured in Genesis 3 are the more frequent companions of life, which finally ends with returning to the dust. All of these, from estrangement from God and from each other to the activities that should invest life with significance are the loss of nakedness and the experience of shame. Shame severs people, whether perpetrator or victim, from the fundamental relationships that make life meaningful.

But how does the nakedness and shame of Genesis 2 and 3 relate to the Spirit of Pentecost? God's Spirit-created Adam and Eve "naked, and they felt no shame" (Gen. 2:25). Jesus' exposed body on the cross is the nadir of the human experience of nakedness and shame. Stripped, tortured, humiliated, the object of derision, insult, and finally execution, Jesus bears the collective nakedness and shame of the human race. But his life does not end in a meaningless denouement in the dust. The Spirit of God raises him from the dead. The Spirit of Pentecost then becomes the way for all to participate in the resurrected life of Christ.

Fourth, the coming of the Spirit of Pentecost brings, at its most fundamental level, the renewal of the three relationships that defined human life in the Garden. Receiving the Spirit of Pentecost brings the risen Christ and restores human relationship with God the Father. The Christ seated at the right hand of God the Father is not far off, but present in the Spirit of Pentecost. In the Gospel of John, Jesus promises that he will send the Holy Spirit and that through the presence of the Spirit he and the Father will make their home with his disciples (Jn 14:15-23; also see Lk. 11:13 and 24:49). In the Spirit of Pentecost, God comes to fellowship with his human divine image bearers living east of Eden. Indeed, in the new heaven and new earth the edenic vision is finally consummated (Rev. 22:1-5).

The Spirit of Pentecost's outpouring on all people—"sons and daughters . . . even my servants, both men and women"—and their common sharing of life begins to restore the charismatic community (Acts 2:17-18) and overcome the shame of the human condition. The Holy Spirit spoke in the tongues of the nations to renew their relationships with each other. Language and ethnic and class identities unfortunately serve as the basis to exploit, degrade, and dehumanize people outside the privileged group. Pentecost promises an end to degrading hierarchy whereby some "rule" over others. The early pentecostal community unseated demeaning power structures and want. The Spirit of Pentecost begins to remove the animal skins and restore people to their nakedness and life without shame. Acts, therefore, describes the new Spirit-baptized pentecostal community's life together in the following terms,

> They devoted themselves to the apostles' teaching and to the fellowship, to the breaking of bread and prayer.... All the believers were together and had everything in common. Selling their possessions and goods, they gave to anyone as he had need.... They broke bread in their homes and ate together with glad and sincere hearts. (Acts 2:42-47)

The Spirit of Pentecost, in other words, started removing the "fig leaves" and animal skins (Gen. 3:7 and 21) that alienate people from each other and restoring them to each other in a community of love and care.

The renewal of embodied life is also a principal feature of the Spirit of Pentecost. Addressing the crowd on the Day of Pentecost, Peter declares God neither "abandoned [Christ] to the grave, nor did his body see decay. God has raised this Jesus to life.... Exalted to the right hand of God, he has received from the Father the promised Holy Spirit and has poured out what you now see and hear" (Acts 2:31-33). The Spirit of God raising Adam from the dust in Gen. 2:7 finds its dramatic climax in the resurrected life of Christ. The resurrected life of Christ is not a one-off, but the promise for all who receive the Spirit of Pentecost (Acts 2:38). Illustrating the renewed life brought by the Holy Spirit, shortly after the Day of Pentecost Peter touches a physically disabled man with the result that "instantly the man's feet and ankles became strong. He jumped to his feet and began to walk . . . [and] went with them to the temple courts, walking and jumping, and praising God" (Acts 3:7-9). Peter's healing of the disabled man, due not to his innate power but to the Spirit of Pentecost, correlates with Christ's Spirit-empowered healing. Physical healing was a prominent feature of Christ's ministry. It was not, however, a parlor trick to dazzle people. His healing ministry was a foretaste of his resurrection by the Spirit of God and the renewal of life that the Spirit of Pentecost would offer to "all people" (Acts 2:17). Christ, moreover, attributed his ability to heal to the Spirit of God. In Matthew 12, Jesus heals a man with a shriveled hand and frees a "demon-possessed man who was blind and mute" by the Spirit of God (Mt. 12:13, 22, and 28). In other words, Christ's power to heal the body is derived from the presence of the Spirit of God upon him: the same Spirit of God that infused human beings with life in Genesis 2.

Exile and Exodus: Anticipating Pentecost

Exile-exodus is a primary theme of the narrative of redemption.[39] The exodus of the people of Israel from Egypt is the most well-known version of this theme. The

---

[39] The influence of N. T. Wright for highlighting the importance of these themes in biblical theology is vital. For an introduction to Wright's theology and scholarly support and criticism of his work on the theme of exile, see James M. Scott, ed., *Exile: A Conversation* (Downers Grove: IVP Academic, 2017).

redemptive arc of exile-exodus, however, characterizes the basic structure of the Spirit's work in the history of redemption. In other words, creation, exodus, and restoration from exile are correspondents. The pattern of exile and exodus resonates throughout the history of redemption from the deep to creation, from dust to divine image bearers, from bondage in Egypt to deliverance in the Promised Land, from exile in Babylon to new exodus and restoration to homeland, from Christ's crucifixion to his resurrection, and from life under the pall of death in the world of Genesis 3 to the emergence of the new creation with the outpouring of the Spirit of Pentecost in Acts 2. The Spirit's work in the creation of the world (Genesis 1) and the divine image bearers (Genesis 2) is paradigmatic for the exile-exodus redemptive narrative that characterizes the work of God's Spirit throughout the history of redemption. This section highlights the common motifs of the Spirit's work in creation, exodus, and restoration.[40] Each one adds texture to the Hebrew Bible's narrative of God's Spirit that points the way toward Pentecost.

First, exodus is a Spirit-empowered journey toward Eden. The book of Exodus has two back-to-back accounts of the deliverance of the people of Israel from Egypt. Both use pneumatological imagery to describe the divine agency of their salvation. In the prose account, "the LORD drove the sea back with a strong east wind and turned it into dry land" (Exod. 14:21). The poem or the Song of Moses intensifies the personal connection of the wind that drives back the water of the sea. Exodus 15:8 and 10 declare "by the blast of your nostrils the waters piled up . . . you blew with your breath and the sea covered them." The song attributes both restraining the waters for the Israelites (deliverance) and swamping Pharaoh's army (judgment) to the *ruach*/Spirit of God.[41] Both texts interpret the physical phenomenon that caused the sea to recede for the Israelites and cascade over the Egyptians as the direct intervention of Israel's God and describe that activity in pneumatological terms.[42] The exodus from Egypt and return to the land of Canaan is the paradigmatic salvation saga in the Hebrew Bible. The exodus redeems the people of Israel from servitude in Egypt and eventually establishes them in the land of promise in order to create a people who embody the divine purpose of human life in their relationship with God and with each other (Lev. 20:22-24). The exodus, in other words, was a Spirit-empowered journey to restore the people to the edenic condition of life. Redemption is a return to creation.

Second, the exile-restoration motifs in the Hebrew prophets recapitulate the creation and exodus sagas. In other words, exile to Assyria and Babylon and

---

[40] Lisa P. Stephenson also uses the themes of exodus, exile, and new exile to develop a pentecostal feminist theology. She shows that Jesus Christ and the Spirit's work in Christ stand in continuity with the prophetic tradition that anticipated a new exodus and messiah. See Stephenson, *Dismantling the Dualisms for American Pentecostal Women in Ministry: A Feminist-Pneumatological Approach*, Global and Charismatic Studies, 9 (Boston: Brill, 2012), 99–114.

[41] Al Wolters argues that Exod. 15:8 does not refer to the deliverance of the Israelites, but that Exod. 15:8 and 15:10 both refer to the flood of water that destroyed the Egyptian forces. Although I agree with Wolters that the Song of Moses primarily showcases the destruction of Pharaoh and his army, Exod. 15:8 and 10 appear to integrate the two aspects—deliverance and judgment—of the one event. See Wolters, "Not Rescue but Destruction: Rereading Exodus 15:8," *Catholic Biblical Quarterly* 52, no. 2 (1990): 223–40.

[42] For the connection between wind and the Spirit of God, see Studebaker, *From Pentecost to the Triune God*, 54–60.

restoration to the land of Israel are a second experience of exodus in the life of the people of Israel (cf. Isa. 48:20-21). But they are also new creation events. The Spirit of God's cultivation of the earth for life, breathing life into human beings, leading the people out of Egypt, and restoring them to their homeland are iterations of a common redemption story. Making a distinction between creation and redemption, however, is common. According to this view, what God did in creation and exodus are distinct providential programs. The logic is, God created the world and then, when it fell into sin, saved it. But that misunderstands the theology of creation, pneumatology, and especially the connection between creation and pneumatology for the "redemptive" works of exodus and restoration. The primary redemptive motifs and events in the Hebrew Bible—exodus, exile, and restoration—reiterate the creation stories. Put another way, creation is an exile-exodus story and the exodus is a creation story. The primal abyss is the earth in "exile." The Spirit of God stirring over the waters frees the earth from its exile in darkness and disorder and delivers it by bringing it to a place of order and life. Creation is the exodus of the earth from its "exile" in primal oblivion. The exodus from Egypt created Israel. Thus, the Song of Moses in Deuteronomy says "Is he [Yahweh] not your Father, your Creator, who made you and formed you? . . . who fathered you; you forgot the God who gave you birth" (Deut. 32:6 and 18).

Isaiah reinforces the connection between creation and exodus and God's Spirit as their agent. Isaiah 63 directly attributes the divine agency in the exodus to the Spirit of God. Isaiah 63:10-14 declares,

> Yet they rebelled and grieved his Holy Spirit. . . . Then his people recalled the days of Moses and his people—where is he who brought them through the sea, with the shepherd of his flock? Where is he who set his Holy Spirit among them, who sent his glorious arm of power to be at Moses' right hand, who divided the waters before them . . . who led them through the depth? . . . [T]hey were given rest by the Spirit of the LORD.

Here the Spirit of God's role in the narrative of the exodus mirrors creation in Genesis 1. In creation, the Spirit of God is present hovering over the darkness of the deep. The deliverance of the exodus begins when God "set his Holy Spirit among them" (Isa. 63:11). As the Spirit of God separated the primal waters and made dry land appear, so the Spirit of God divided the waters and made a dry passageway for the people of Israel. The Spirit that brought forth an abundant earth from the primal chaos leads the people into the land of promise. Creation and exodus, moreover, end with "rest" (Gen. 2:2-3 and Isa. 63:14).

Isaiah also links creation, exodus, and restoration. In the late-sixth century, the people of Judah were exiled to Babylon (taking place over three phases in the years 597, 586, and 582 BCE). The destruction of Jerusalem and her temple was a national and religious tragedy. Was Yahweh, the God of Israel, powerless before the might of Babylon's divine protectors and martial forces? It sure looked that way. The prophets, however, declared that exile was not the end of the story of Yahweh and the people of Israel. They promised a future restoration to the land of promise. In this vein of prophetic promise, Isaiah connects creation, exodus, and restoration from exile. Anticipating return from exile, Isa. 51:9-11 declares:

> Was it not you who cut Rahab to pieces, who pierced that monster through. Was it not you who dried up the sea, the waters of the great deep, who made a road in the depths of the sea so that the redeemed might cross over? The ransomed of the LORD will return. They will enter Zion with singing; everlasting joy will crown their heads.

The correlation between creation, exodus, and restoration is clear. The God who redeemed the earth from the chaos monster, divided the sea, led the people of Israel to freedom from Pharaoh and eventually to inhabit the land of Canaan, now will return them from exile in Babylon to their homeland.[43]

Creation, exodus, and restoration from exile are not exactly the same, but creation is like the exodus and exodus and restoration are like creation.[44] The abyss of Genesis 1 and the Leviathan in Job, Psalms, and Isaiah are distinct motifs that illustrate redemption and that are applied variously to creation, the exodus, and restoration. They portray God taming the primordial chaos, although Genesis 1 is without the dragon monster found in Job, Psalms, and Isaiah. In creation, the God of Israel defeated Leviathan, in the exodus the same God vanquishes Pharaoh.[45] Leviathan is not just a mythic creation symbol for Pharaoh or the king of Babylon. Leviathan is a fungible symbol. Leviathan was the primal chaos monster (e.g., Tiamat in the *Enuma Elish*). Pharaoh and the Babylonian king were no less chaos figures that threatened the life of Israel than the primal abyss that threatened life on earth. Just as Yahweh "crushed Rahab" and "founded the world and all that is in it" (Ps. 89:10-11), so Yahweh "will slay the monster of the sea," restore the exiles from Assyria and Egypt, and cause "Israel [to] bud and blossom" (Isa. 27:1, 6, and 13).[46] The *Chaoskampf* can refer to the cosmic battle of creation (sometimes conceived as an annual re-creation in the ANE) or a symbol for political polemics. Hyun Chul Paul Kim clarifies that "a double meaning seems to be intended." They can refer to Yahweh's victory over "the most formidable chaotic forces

---

[43] Philip B. Harner makes this point in respect to Exodus "providing a model for the imminent restoration of Israel." See Harner, "Creation Faith in Deutero-Isaiah," *Vetus Testamentum* 17, no. 3 (1967): 300.

[44] Ortlund, "The Identity of Leviathan and the Meaning of Job," 21.

[45] John N. Day, "God and Leviathan in Isaiah 27:1," *Bibliotheca Sacra* 155, no. 620 (1998): 432-3.

[46] Note that as a continuation of the means of renewal promised in Isaiah 26, the scope may extend eschatologically to all of the earth and not only to the restoration of Israel. See Stephen L. Cook, "Deliverance as Fertility and Resurrection: Echoes of Second Isaiah in Isaiah 26," in *Formation and Intertextuality in Isaiah 24-27*, ed. J. Todd Hibbard and Hyun Chul Paul Kim, Ancient Israel and Its Literature 17, ser. ed. Thomas C. Römer (Atlanta: Society of Biblical Literature, 2013), 165-82 and Kim, "City, Earth, and Empire in Isaiah 24-27," 25-48. Also, pinning down the exact reference of the Leviathan in Isa. 27:1 is difficult. It could refer to Egypt, Tyre, or Babylon, depending on the period of its composition and redaction. Kim argues that its meaning is "open-ended" so that it can be applied with increasing scope to forces at odds with Yahweh and his people. See Day, "God and Leviathan in Isaiah 27:1," 434; John T. Willis, "Yahweh Regenerates His Vineyard: Isaiah 27," in *Formation and Intertextuality in Isaiah 24-27*, ed. J. Todd Hibbard and Hyun Chul Paul Kim, Ancient Israel and Its Literature 17, ser. ed. Thomas C. Römer (Atlanta: Society of Biblical Literature, 2013), 203; and Kim, "City, Earth, and Empire in Isaiah 24-27," 46-8.

in the celestial realm" and "these mythological figures can symbolically represent the menacing empires on the political realm, which are denounced and denied of their power by the righteous God."[47]

Third, the role of creation and the exodus for imagining restoration from exile, however, should not give the impression that the anticipated work of God is only backward looking. The exodus from Egypt is a model for God's work, but it does not exhaust it. God's redemption is expansive and progressive. Isaiah, therefore, while using the exodus as a pattern for restoration from Babylonian exile, also sees restoration on a larger, even cosmic, eschatological scale.[48] Isaiah 43:18-19 declares "Forget the former things; do not dwell in the past. See, I am doing a new thing! Now it springs up; do you not perceive it? I am making a way in the desert and streams in the wasteland." Yet, even here, where the prophet calls the people of Israel to anticipate "a new thing," the creation and the exodus remain informative for God's redemptive work—"I am making a way in the desert and streams in the wasteland." Isaiah 65 indicates the scope of the eschatological work: "Behold, I will create new heavens and a new earth. The former things will not be remembered . . . I will create Jerusalem to be a delight and its people a joy. . . . [T]he sound of weeping and of crying will be heard no more" (Isa. 65:17-19). The passage goes on to describe the new heavens and new earth in edenic imagery of abundance, peace, and prosperity (Isa. 65:20-25).[49] The Spirit's work in the exile-exodus pattern is not a redundant cycle but a progressive narrative with eschatological expansiveness.

Fourth, the outpouring of the Holy Spirit on the Day of Pentecost carries on the Spirit of God's role in the exile-exodus narratives. The connection to Pentecost is the divine agency that overcomes the chaos monsters is pneumatological. This is the case whether Yahweh's redemptive activity is conceived in the creation stories or the ongoing religious and political circumstances of Israel vis-à-vis nations such as Egypt, Assyria, and Babylon (e.g., Isa. 27:8, "By warfare and exile you contend with her [cf. "Leviathan the gliding serpent . . . the monster of the sea" in Isa. 27:1]—with his fierce blast he drives her out, as on a day the east wind blows"). Isaiah 42:5-7 succinctly nits together creation, exile, and restoration, and bases them on a messiah anointed by the Spirit of God. Isaiah portrays Yahweh declaring,

> he who created the heavens and stretched them out, who spread out the earth and all that comes out of it, who gives breath to its people, and life to those who walk on it. "I, the LORD, have called you in righteousness; I will take hold of your hand. . . . [T]o free captives from prison and to release from the dungeon those who sit in darkness."

Because Yahweh created the heavens and the earth (Genesis 1) and gave the breath of life to its people (Genesis 2), Yahweh can free the people of Israel from exile (Isa.

---

[47] Kim, "City, Earth, and Empire in Isaiah 24–27," 32–3.
[48] Harner, "Creation Faith in Deutero-Isaiah," 303–4.
[49] Richard L. Schultz, "Intertextuality, Canon, and 'Undecidability:' Understanding Isaiah's 'New Heavens and New Earth' (Isaiah 65:17-25)," *Bulletin for Biblical Research* 20, no. 1 (2010): 33.

41:6-9). On the Day of Pentecost, the Holy Spirit appears in the "blowing of a violent wind" and the "tongues of fire that separated and came to rest on each of them" (Acts 2:1-3). The outpouring of the Spirit of Pentecost stands in continuity with the history of redemption's earlier exile-exodus events. Pentecost also advances the narrative of redemption by initiating the eschatological exodus from exile in the world of Genesis 3 to the world of the new heaven and the new earth of Revelation 21 and 22.

People, Place, Messiah: The Promise of Pentecost

Exodus from exile is a primary redemptive theme in the story of the Spirit set forth in the Hebrew Scriptures. But what is the content of the promise of restoration? It is twofold. First, the central features of Spirit-breathed life remain the subject of the Spirit's redemptive work. Three fundamental relationships define human beings as Spirit-breathed divine image bearers—relationship with God, with each other, and with creation. The biblical Fall was the loss of relationship with God, people, and place. Life east of Eden is one of exile from God, people, and place. Redemption is exodus from this exile. Redemption, therefore, is the Spirit of God restoring people to God, to each other, and to a place in creation. The Hebrew prophets Isaiah, Ezekiel, and Joel highlight that the outpouring of God's Spirit renews these primary relationships. The promise of restoration to the land of Israel inextricably involves reconciliation with God, renewal of the community of God's people, and restoration to abundant life in the world. Second, the narrative of the Spirit expands to include a Spirit-anointed messianic figure. Using pneumatological imagery the Hebrew prophets envision the coming of a Spirit-anointed messiah who will lead the people out of exile and renew the earth and their life with God and the people of God.

People

First, Ezek. 37:1-14 draws on Gen. 2:7 to imagine the restoration of the people of Israel from exile. Ezekiel 37, moreover, shows the theological range of the creation story. Ezekiel 37 is not only about the creation of one person, Adam, but the Spirit's creative and restorative work to renew a community of human life. God created human beings for relationship with God and with each other. It also shows that the creation of Adam story was a redemption story. Thus, Ezekiel uses the imagery of God's Spirit breathing life into Adam to inform the valley of dry bones vision in which the same Spirit of God infuses new life into the people of Israel. Ezekiel also shows that God's Spirit comes to renew a certain quality of life. The Spirit will transform the heart of stone into a heart of flesh. The people will be rekindled in their relationship with God. The Spirit renews them in righteousness, cleansing them of their moral and religious impurities. The purpose is to restore the fellowship with God for which human beings were created— "you will be my people and, I will be your God" (Ezek. 36:28). God renews the people in righteousness not because God is a cosmic judge that is fastidious about moral and religious purity for its own sake. Holiness—moral and religious—is the context in which flourishing human life takes place. The Spirit of God renews the hearts of the people so that they can thrive with each other and their God.[50] Ezekiel 36 and 37 do not specifically name Adam and Eve. Ezekiel, however, uses the Gen. 2:7 Spirit infusion of Adam's life to portray the renewal of Israel (Ezek. 37:1-14) and refers to Eden (Ezek. 36:35) as a model for the renewal of the land. These allusions suggest that the life Adam and Eve enjoyed with each other and with God in Eden is the basal vision for the Spirit of God's work of restoration.[51] As in Adam, the Spirit of God, moreover, works not as an extrinsic, but as an intrinsic agent. Thus, the renewal of the people derives from the indwelling presence of God's Spirit. God will renew the people by putting his Spirit in them (Ezek. 36:26-27).

Second, Isaiah extends the communal scope of the gift of God's Spirit. Isaiah 42:5 begins with the investiture of God's Spirit on a messianic figure (Isa. 42:1-4), but then shifts to the Spirit's presence on a collective "people" (Isa. 42:5-6). The group intended in the original context was likely the Judean exiles in Babylon.[52] Yet, the universal and inclusive purpose is present in Isaiah 42. Even if the people receiving the Spirit have a Jewish scope, they receive the Spirit to be a "light for the Gentiles" (Isa. 42:6). This wider scope, moreover, parallels the Holy Spirit's presence in Christ and the universal outpouring of the Spirit of Pentecost.[53] Elsewhere Isaiah's vision of redemption also entails a renewal that includes the nations. Not only Israel, but the nations, even former enemies (e.g., Egypt and Assyria), will be included among God's people (Isa. 19:19-25). Isaiah begins and ends with a cosmopolitan vision of inclusivity and peace among the nations (Isa. 2:3-4 and Isa. 66:18-22). Isaiah's vision of people gathered from the nations correlates with Joel's vision of the Spirit being poured out on "all people" (Joel 2:28).

Third, the prophet Joel particularizes and universalizes the presence of the Spirit among the people. Not only the collective, but Joel 2:28 announces that "I will pour out my Spirit on all people."[54] Clarifying "all people," Joel promises that "sons," "daughters," "old men," "young men," and "even my servants, both men and women" will receive

---

[50] Disagreement among OT scholars exists over whether the "new spirit" refers to moral renovation or to the Spirit of God (i.e., an "anthropological" or a "theological" meaning). I agree with Verena Schafroth's argument that Ezekiel 36 entails the moral and religious cleansing of the human heart by God's Spirit. See Schafroth, "An Exegetical Exploration of 'Spirit' References in Ezekiel 36 and 37," *Journal of the European Pentecostal Theological Association* 29, no. 2 (2009): 67–8.

[51] Levison, *Filled with the Spirit*, 101.

[52] See Schuele, "The Spirit of YHWH and the Aura of Divine Presence," 23–4. For the significance of Isaiah in the book of Acts, see Jon Ruthven, "'This is My Covenant with Them': Isaiah 59:19-21 as the Programmatic Prophecy of the New Covenant in the Acts of the Apostles (Part 1)," *Journal of Pentecostal Theology* 17, no. 1 (2008): 32–47.

[53] Andreas Schuele highlights the shift from an individual Spirit bearer to a group of people, as taking place most likely in the context of Judean exiles in Babylon. See Schuele, "The Spirit of YHWH and the Aura of Divine Presence," 23–4.

[54] Note also that Joel connects the outpouring of the Spirit with an allusion to the Exodus—"I will show wonders in the heavens . . . the sun will be turned to darkness" (Joel 2:30-31). Cf. with the three days of darkness that fell over Egypt (Exod. 10:21-23). At this point, "all people" probably meant all Israel, Peter's Pentecost sermon includes a wider scope; although as the books of Acts demonstrates even Peter struggled to grasp that "all people" really meant *all* people and not only Jews. Peter Nagel, "The *Schechina* Concept(s) in Acts: The Formation Potential of Old Testament Citations," *Neotestamentica* 51, no. 1 (2017): 117.

God's Spirit and display charismatic gifting (Joel 2:28-29). The outpouring of God's Spirit is inclusive. It is not reserved for political and priestly elites. Indeed, the absence of reference to kings and priests signals a progressive eschatological expectation. The Spirit's anointing of the leaders of Israel was not unusual. Moses and the elders of Israel received the Spirit of God to equip them for their leadership roles. After entering the land of Canaan, Israelite figures such as Othniel, Gideon, and Samson received the Spirit of Yahweh, usually to empower them for successful military campaigns against their oppressors (e.g., Judg. 3:10, 6:34, and 14:6). Joel, however, emphasizes that the Spirit of God is for all people, even people considered menial and marginal by the culturally privileged. But this inclusive gift of the Spirit was not entirely unanticipated. Moses declared to Joshua, "I wish that all the LORD's people were prophets and that the LORD would put his Spirit on them!" (Num. 11:29). Moses also attributes technical craft skills to the Spirit of God—"he has filled [Bezalel] with the Spirit of God, with skill, ability and knowledge in all kinds crafts . . . to carry out all the work of constructing the sanctuary" (Exod. 35:30-35). In other words, precedent is here for an inclusive vision of the Spirit of God's presence among the people of God. The offer of the Spirit of Pentecost to reconcile "all people" fulfills this vision for divine presence among the people of God.

Place

Ezekiel's promise of the outpouring of God's Spirit and restoration to the land bears strong parallels with the creation and Fall stories in Genesis 2 and 3. First, the Fall narrative is fundamentally a story of exile from the place the Spirit of God created for human life. Adam and Eve's death was the incremental and terminal experience of exile from the life the Spirit of God created for them. After breathing life into Adam, the "LORD God took the man and put him in the Garden to work it and take care of it" (Gen. 2:15). The breath of God gives life to Adam, and he as well as Eve enjoy fellowship with their God and abundant life in the Garden of Eden; they live without shame before God and before each other. Adam was, however, warned not to "eat from the tree of the knowledge of good and evil" (Gen. 2:17). Why? Because in doing so, he would know evil. The consequence of which was death—"for when you eat of it you will surely die" (Gen. 2:17). Now, Adam, did not suddenly fall dead when he ate the forbidden fruit. But the relationships that defined his God breathed life were shattered. He was estranged from God and Eve and banished from the Garden. His ultimate return to the dust was but the nadir of that initial taste of death—the experience of fear and shame that made him hide from Eve and then from God. Death, from the first drop of the sweat of the brow to the return of the body to dust, is alienation from the place the Spirit of God created for human life.

Second, the parallels between Spirit-breathed life, relationship with God and other people, and abundant life in Genesis and Ezekiel's vision of their renewal in the Promised Land are clear. The breath of God gives life to Adam and Eve to enjoy fellowship with their God and abundant life in the Garden of Eden (Gen. 2:7 and 15). Choosing the path of fear and shame, however, Adam and Eve are exiled to the east of Eden where life is by the sweat of the brow. In Ezekiel, the outpouring of God's Spirit correlates with the restoration of their relationship with God and "each other" (i.e., the renewal of the people of Israel). Like Adam and Eve, Israel was placed in a land of promise and, after eating the forbidden fruit of idolatry and debauchery, experienced shame—the people are separated from God and their land and humiliated before the nations. Because of disobedience to their God, Israel is cast out of Eden—in Joel the locust plague desiccates the land, and later, Jerusalem and its temple are razed, and the people exiled east to Babylon. The shame and separation from God in exile (Yahweh hides his face, Ezek. 39:29) parallels the experience of Adam in the Garden of Eden. In other words, Israel lost their Spirit-breathed life and died. But, Ezekiel promises the return of God's Spirit that will "cleanse [them] from all [their] impurities and from all [their] idols . . . [and they] will be my people, and I will be [their] God. . . . I will no longer hide my face from them, for I will pour out my Spirit on the house of Israel" (Ezek. 36:25-28 and 39:26-29). Ezekiel continues with the promise that Yahweh

> will make breath enter you, and you will come to life. . . . "O my people, I am going to open your graves and bring you up from them; I will bring you back to the land of Israel. . . . I will put my Spirit in you and you will live, and I will settle you in your own land." (Ezek. 37:4 and 14)

Restoration from exile removes their shame. In Ezekiel 37, the breath of God will raise Israel's dry bones to new life and "settle" them in their land "that has become like the garden of Eden," which removes their fear and shame (Ezek. 37:5-14, 36:35, and 39:26).

I am not suggesting that Adam and Eve are simply a parable of Israel's exile and restoration. Something to the effect that Adam's sweat of the brow is a symbol for exile and the desolation of the land of Israel and striking the head of the serpent a symbol for Yahweh setting them free from Babylon and returning them to the land of promise. But God's creation of Adam and placing him in Eden and then exiling him from the Garden, the exodus from Egypt to the land of promise, and exile to Babylon and return to the land of promise are similar to one another and programmatic for the Spirit of God's work in the history of redemption. As Adam and Eve were exiled from the Garden, so was Israel. Outside the garden, Adam and Eve's Spirit-breathed life dissipated and they died. In exile, Israel is without the Spirit of Yahweh. They are dead. As God promised to strike the serpent that beguiled Adam and Eve, through Ezekiel Yahweh promises to raise the people to new life by putting the Spirit of God in them and restoring them to their land so that "it will become like the garden of Eden" (Ezek. 37:1-14 and 36:35).

Third, Isaiah's visions of redemption share common themes with the anticipations for renewal in Ezekiel, but they also give the vision universal scope. First, creational imagery is a consistent feature of Isaiah's vision of redemption. Isaiah promises a renewal of the land and life within it. The rebirth of the land, moreover, has intertextual parallels with the Genesis 1 and 2 creation stories. Isaiah 65:17-18 reflects the language of Genesis 1 when it declares, "Behold, I will create new heavens and a new earth. The former things will not be remembered . . . for I will create Jerusalem to be a delight and its people a joy." Earlier, Isaiah compares rejuvenation of the land to Eden: "The LORD will surely comfort Zion . . . he will make her deserts like Eden, her wastelands like the garden of the LORD" (Isa. 51:3; cf. 35:1-10). Earlier I called the flood in Genesis 8 creation 2.0. Without discounting the differences, the exodus from Egypt and the return of the people of Israel from Babylonian exile are creation 3.0 and 4.0 (the new heaven and new earth in Revelation 21 and 22 is creation 5.0). But that is not quite correct. The vision of renewal in these Isaiah passages is not only a return to a primeval pristine state of the first heaven and earth of Genesis 1 and 2.[55] They project an eschatological enrichment (see Chapters 6 and 11 for development of this expansive eschatology). Note, for example, the striking similarity between the cosmopolitan and eschatological visions of nations coming to the glory of the renewed Jerusalem in Isaiah 60 and 65–66 and Revelation 21 and 22.[56] The reference to the city of Jerusalem and the cultural activity that flourishes is a key development. Although Eden has cultural activity—for example, God charges Adam to work and to take care of the garden (Gen. 2:15)—it does not reach the level of sophistication portrayed in the reconstruction of Jerusalem. The fundamental conditions of life in the new heaven and the new earth, nevertheless, bear fundamental continuity with the environment described in Genesis 1 and 2.[57] The land teems with fecundity and plenty. People no longer live in fear, shame, and want. Children no longer die in infancy. Tears are dried. Weeping turns to joy. Longevity increases. People build homes and enjoy the fruit of their labor. Parents see their children prosper (Isa. 65:19-23). Second, the Spirit of God is vital to this use of creation imagery to describe the renewal of the land and the people. Isaiah 32:15-18 identifies God's Spirit as the agent for the transformation of the desert into a place of fertility: "till the Spirit is poured upon us from on high, and the desert becomes a fertile field, and the fertile field seems like a forest. Justice will dwell in the desert and righteousness live in the fertile field.... My people will live in peaceful dwelling places in secure homes, in undisturbed places of rest." The renewal brought by the outpouring of God's Spirit resonates with the blessing, the rest (Gen. 1:28 and 31 and 2:2), and the abundance of life (i.e., Eden) described in the Genesis creation stories and the exodus (Deut. 8:7-10 and Isa. 63:14).

Spirit-Anointed Messiah

Isaiah introduces a Spirit-anointed figure that will be instrumental for realizing the restoration of the people (Isa. 11:1-2, 42:1, and 62:1). Pneumatology defines the identity and ministry of the messiah. The redemption brought by the Spirit-anointed messiah, moreover, is consistent with the work of the Spirit from creation to exodus and restoration. The presence of the Spirit of the LORD identifies the messianic figure.[58]

---

[55] Schultz, "Intertextuality, Canon, and 'Undecidability,'" 33.
[56] Ulrich W. Mauser, "Isaiah 65:17-25," *Interpretation* 36, no. 2 (1982): 182.
[57] Although continuity is not a mainstream pentecostal way of thinking of the relationship between the current and the eschatological world, it has precedence in early Pentecostalism. See Jeffrey S. Lamp, "New Heavens and New Earth: Early Pentecostal Soteriology as a Foundation for Creation Care in the Present," *Pneuma: The Journal of the Society for Pentecostal Studies* 36, no. 1 (2014): 68–73.
[58] Isaiah's emphasis on a Spirit-anointed messianic leader is anticipated in the Hebrew Bible. Previous figures such as Moses and the seventy elders, the judges, and David received their capacity for leadership from the Spirit of the Lord (Num. 11:17 and 25; Judg. 3:10 and 14:6; and 1 Sam.

Isaiah describes Yahweh giving his Spirit to (Isa. 42:1) and the Spirit of the LORD resting on the figure (Isa. 11:2 and 61:1). The presence of the Spirit also defines the ministry of the messianic leader—"I will put my Spirit on him and he will bring justice to the nations" (Isa. 42:1). The Spirit-anointed leader brings redemption in the form of justice. But what kind of justice? Not primarily retributive justice, rather God's justice aligns with contemporary notions of social or restorative justice. Not the hammer blow of penal judgment, the prophetic vision focuses on the justice that heals the bruised reed and kindles the ember into a flame (Isa. 42:3). The Spirit-anointed redeemer acts on behalf of the "poor" and "needy" (Isa. 11:4), frees the captives, comforts the brokenhearted, and brings joy and abundance to those trapped in misery and austerity. Isaiah's vision is not heavenly, but earthy. The freedom, comfort, and prosperity are not "spiritual," but earth bound. The people will rebuild their cities, restore their commerce, and live in righteousness with each other and their God (Isa. 61:1-9).[59] The justice of retribution is not absent. Isaiah 11:4 warns, "He will strike the earth with the rod of his mouth; with the breath of his lips he will slay the wicked." The focus remains, however, on social justice. The judgment visited upon the "wicked" comes because they have oppressed and exploited the poor. Rather than saving the bruised reed, they trampled it. Although judgment remains, the vision of justice is not penal, but social and restorative.

The ministry of the Spirit-anointed messiah deals directly with the shame of the human condition introduced in Genesis 3—alienation from God and abundant life. Adam turned away from bearing Spirit-breathed life and began his descent to the dust. He lived in shame. Shame, however, is not simply an emotional state of embarrassment, but the material deprivation of embodied life. As Adam was cast out of Eden to fend for himself by the sweat of the brow and ultimately to return to the dirt, the Spirit-anointed messiah will give the people a "double portion," which is a return to abundant life in the land of promise—for example, "freedom for captives ... to comfort all who mourn ... a garment of praise instead of a spirit of despair ... rebuild the ancient ruins ... renew the ruined cities" (Isa. 61:1-4). Isaiah promises that the Spirit-anointed messiah will remove Israel's shame and disgrace: "[i]nstead of their shame my people will receive a double portion, and instead of disgrace they will rejoice in their inheritance; and so they will inherit a double portion in their land, and everlasting joy will be theirs" (Isa. 61:7). The Spirit of Yahweh that anoints the messianic figure is, moreover, the same Spirit of creation—"the Creator of the heavens, who stretches them out, who spreads

---

16:13-15). Jacqueline Grey makes the case, using Speech-Act theory, that Yahweh accomplishes renewal through the Spirit of God and the words of the prophet Ezekiel. The Spirit of God is the foundation and source of renewal but works through human agency to renew the exilic community and, eschatologically, the world. See Jacqueline Grey, "Acts of the Spirit: Ezekiel 37 in Light of Contemporary Speech-Act Theory," *Journal of Biblical and Pneumatological Research* 1 (2009): 79–80.

[59] As Ulrich Mauser points out, "New heavens and new earth are not at all the products of a tired turn to 'spiritual values' but the fervent affirmation of the goodness of life and land. . . . It must not, indeed it cannot, be said that this displays a sub-Christian attitude. Peace on earth in its most comprehensive meaning is the hope of Isaiah 65:17-25. Peace on earth is announced when the Christ is born (Luke 2:14)." See Mauser, "Isaiah 65:17-25," 185–6.

out the earth with all that springs from it, who gives breath to its people, and life to those who walk on it" (Isa. 42:5).[60]

At this point one may wonder, what does this trek through the Hebrew Bible pneumatology and theologies of creation, exodus, and restoration have to do with the atonement and Pentecost? It is fundamental. The purpose of the Spirit of Pentecost, the Spirit of atonement, cannot be understood outside of this wider narrative of the Spirit of God. Atonement begins, from the perspective of pneumatology, with the Spirit hovering over the primal waters. The Spirit of God redeemed the earth from darkness and lifelessness by crafting it into a world of abundant life that culminates in human beings as the divine image bearers. The wind of the Holy Spirit that came on the Day of Pentecost continues that work, one that will not be completed until the Holy Spirit liberates creation from its bondage to decay and raises the children of God for life in the new heaven and the new earth and the New Jerusalem (Rom. 8:18-21 and Rev. 21 and 22). The biblical stories of the creation of the heavens and the earth and of human life are proto-pentecostal and prescriptive for the narrative of God's Spirit. They display God's dream for Spirit-breathed life. The presence and activity of God's Spirit give structure and life to the world. To be human is to be a creature vitalized by God's Spirit for a unique relationship with God, other human beings, and creation. Joel 2 identifies the outpouring of God's Spirit as the eschatological work of redemption. The life and ministry of Jesus Christ reflect this anticipation. Jesus' saving work does not reach its climax on the cross or even in the resurrection, but on the Day of Pentecost with the outpouring of the Holy Spirit. The Day of Pentecost is a decisive scene in the drama of redemption. It culminates the great movement of redemption that began with the Spirit hovering over the waters, breathing life into the dirt, that continues on in the exodus, restoration from exile, and most dramatically in bringing about the incarnate life of Jesus Christ.

Conclusion

Pentecost is the centerpiece of the history of redemption. This chapter sets forth the narrative scenes and themes of the history of redemption. These include creation, exile-exodus, and the restoration of people to their God, each other, and a place in this world for abundant life. It argues that the outpouring of the Spirit of Pentecost is the telos that gives theological coherence to this narrative. Pentecost is the culminating threshold in the emergence of the new creation. Pentecost structures the narrative of redemption. As the Spirit of God first redeemed the primal elements from the darkness and animated human beings for life with God, each other, and in creation, so the outpouring of the Spirit of Pentecost is the eschatological commencement of restoring this life for all people and all creation. The Spirit of Pentecost, therefore, is foundational for atonement theology.

---

[60] For an elaboration of the connection between God's Spirit, the messianic figure, and creation in Isaiah 42 and 61, see Schuele, "The Spirit of YHWH and the Aura of Divine Presence," 24–6.

3

Incarnation

Interpreting the Incarnation from the perspective of Pentecost shows that Spirit Christology provides foundational content for a pentecostal theology of atonement.[1] What is that content? An organic, participatory, and trinitarian paradigm of grace. The Spirit of Pentecost shares with the world the Spirit-anointed life brought forth in the life of Jesus Christ.[2] The Incarnation is fundamental to the atonement. But it is an Incarnation based on Spirit Christology, rather than the traditional near-exclusive reliance on Logos Christology, which makes little place for the Holy Spirit in either the Incarnation or Christ's work of atonement. The Incarnation points to the fundamental nature of God's redemptive work. The Spirit's Incarnation of the Son of God in Jesus Christ reveals that creation and embodied life are the subject matter of atonement. The Spirit's agency in the Incarnation, moreover, continues the story of redemption that began with the creation of the world and of human beings as Spirit-breathed divine image bearers. Jesus displays what it means to fulfill the human calling to bear the divine image. Christ brings God's dream for human life to its most sublime historical manifestation. Jesus fulfilled the human vocation because he was the Spirit-anointed Christ. The Holy Spirit was the foundation of his identity as the incarnate Son of God.[3] The same Spirit that was the source of Christ's incarnate life comes to renew all human beings in the image of Christ. Everything achieved in the life of Jesus Christ arises from the Holy Spirit's union of the Son of God with the human nature of Jesus. What the Holy Spirit did in the particular life of Jesus Christ is the pinnacle of the work began with hovering over the darkness of the deep and becomes available to all people through the Spirit of Pentecost. Thus, the narrative trajectory of Jesus Christ's life is

---

[1] I made this connection between pneumatology and Christology in terms of Spirit Christology and the Trinity in *From Pentecost to the Triune God: A Pentecostal Trinitarian Theology* (Grand Rapids: Eerdmans, 2012), 88–100 and 165. Later Frank D. Macchia also drew out the synergy between the Incarnation and Pentecost in *Jesus the Spirit Baptizer: Christology in Light of Pentecost* (Grand Rapids: Eerdmans, 2018), 124–34.

[2] Although arguing from a Christological orientation, Thomas H. McCall argues for the importance of grounding the atonement in the Incarnation and the trinitarian relations in *Forsaken: The Trinity and the Cross, and Why It Matters* (Downers Grove: IVP Academic, 2012), 119–20.

[3] Vladimir Lossky also emphasizes redemption as renewing the divine image in Christ and affirms the Holy Spirit's activity in the Incarnation. The Spirit's role remains, however, an affirmation. Here I develop that role at length and coordinate the work of the Spirit in Christ with a pneumatological theology of atonement. Spirit Christology gives the linkage for the correspondence that Lossky affirms between "incarnation . . . and deification." For Lossky, see *The Mystical Theology of the Eastern Church* (New York: St. Vladimir's Seminary Press, 1976), 136 and 158.

Pentecost, not the cross. Chapter 2 argued that Pentecost is the telos of the history of redemption and, therefore, central to atonement. This chapter locates the Incarnation in that longer narrative of the Spirit of God and shows that the Holy Spirit's work in the Incarnation is the paradigm for Pentecost. But before detailing that, the first section highlights the incarnational deficiency of traditional Western atonement theology.

Pneumatological and Incarnational Deficit

The first step in this chapter is critical assessment of the incarnational deficit of traditional Western atonement theologies from the perspective of the Spirit of Pentecost. The problem is twofold. On the one hand, traditional Western atonement theology has almost no role for the Holy Spirit; it is almost entirely a Christological narrative. On the other hand, the Incarnation of Christ plays no fundamental role in the atonement; it is a crucicentric narrative. This section treats these problems in turn.

First, traditional Western Christology restricts the role of the Holy Spirit, for the most part, to empowering the human nature of Jesus. As Donald Macleod maintains in the context of rejecting any correlation between the union of the Son in the Incarnation and the Christian experience of grace, "[t]here is, of course, continuity between Christ and the Christian disciple and this continuity includes the fact that he was the recipient of grace to the extent that his human obedience depended on the ministry of the Holy Spirit."[4] Linking the Holy Spirit to the moral empowerment of Jesus' human nature makes the Spirit extrinsic to the Incarnation. Incarnation is something the Son does. While incarnate, the Son foregoes divine prerogatives and relies on the Holy Spirit, not because he needs to, but to provide a moral analog for the Christian experience of sanctification—that is, as the Holy Spirit-empowered Jesus' human nature, so the Spirit sanctifies the Christian. The Spirit comes upon Jesus Christ to provide a moral assist because the Son set aside his divine powers while incarnate in Jesus Christ. But had he so desired, the incarnate Son could have lived a sanctified life without the help of the Holy Spirit. The role of the Holy Spirit in Jesus' life becomes a pantomime for grace and offers nothing essential to the Incarnation itself or erstwhile that the Son needed. Spirit Christology seeks a more integrated and trinitarian understanding of the Incarnation. The goal here is to showcase that the Holy Spirit's role in the Incarnation is more than the moral empowerment of Jesus' human nature on his way to penal sacrifice on the cross. The Holy Spirit was intrinsic to the Incarnation. The Holy Spirit catalyzed the Incarnation of the Son of God in Jesus Christ. More technically, the Holy Spirit was the principle of the hypostatic union of Jesus' human nature with the Son of God. As such, the Holy Spirit was the foundation of Christ's life and ministry and, therefore, of the atonement.

Second, the Incarnation plays little role in popular evangelical and pentecostal atonement theology. Despite their theological differences, Evangelicals and Pentecostals often hold a penal view of the atonement. It goes like this: human beings

---

[4] Donald Macleod, *The Person of Christ*, Contours of Christian Theology, gen. ed. Gerald Bray (Downers Grove: InterVarsity Press, 1998), 191.

are sinners, God demands obedience, and in order to retain the integrity of divine justice, God requires a penalty for sin and perfect obedience to make up for human sin; therefore, Christ dies on the cross to satisfy the demands of divine justice. The atonement, moreover, is God-centric. Placating God's wrath and demonstrating God's glory through judicial penalty is the plot of the atonement. The pardon from punishment human beings receive is secondary to God demonstrating his glory by exacting a penalty for human sin in Christ's death on the cross.[5] The work of Christ is objective, which means it is a judicial transaction between God the Father and God the Son and utterly external to human beings.[6]

In this atonement theology, the Incarnation plays no central role. Thomas R. Schreiner, for example, develops an account of the atonement with no discussion of the Incarnation.[7] One could object that the Incarnation is assumed in the penal view of the atonement. Granted. But the Incarnation as such offers nothing to penal atonement theology. The Son of God takes on humanity in Christ in order to live a sinless life and then die on the cross to satisfy the judicial demands and to assuage the wrath of God.[8] In other words, the union of God with humanity in the Incarnation does not illuminate anything about the fundamental nature of redemption, which is penal redemption and pardon for sin. The Incarnation is simply the prerequisite for Christ obeying the law and offering his life as a penal sacrifice or, as Wayne Grudem calls it, as a "judicial execution."[9] The union of the Son of God with the humanity of Jesus Christ illuminates nothing about the nature of redemption in this traditional Western atonement theology. Donald Macleod, for example, argues that "it is not helpful to compare the personal union involved in the incarnation to the union established by grace between Christ and his people."[10] Rejecting a correlation between the union of God in Christ and in grace, however, is not uniform among evangelical theologians. Incredibly, in the same series as Macleod's volume, Robert Letham, arguing the opposite, maintains that "Our union with Christ is grounded in his union with us."[11] Letham's direction is

---

[5] Wayne Grudem affirms this view of the atonement in his popular *Systematic Theology: An Introduction to Biblical Doctrine* (Grand Rapids: Zondervan, 1994), 570, 575, and 577. Grudem's work is valuable for its articulation of the popular evangelical theology of the atonement.

[6] Joel R. Beeke makes this point in presenting the atonement theology of the Reformed theologian Herman Bavinck in "The Atonement in Herman Bavinck's Theology," in *The Glory of the Atonement: Biblical, Historical, and Practical Perspectives*, ed. Charles E. Hill and Frank A. James, III (Downers Grove: IVP Academic, 2004), 341. Indeed, the Incarnation receives no substantial treatment in this entire volume. It is possible for evangelical theologians to outline "*Biblical, Historical, and Practical Perspectives*" on the atonement and give no serious and sustained attention to the most fundamental event in the history of redemption—the Incarnation. Thomas F. Torrance also draws this assessment in respect of the marginalization of the Incarnation as such in traditional Western atonement theology. See Torrance, *The Mediation of Christ*, rev. ed. (Colorado Springs: Helmers & Howard, 1992), 40–1.

[7] Thomas R. Schreiner, "Penal Substitution View," in *The Nature of the Atonement: Four Views*, ed. James Beilby and Paul R. Eddy (Downers Grove: IVP Academic, 2006), 67–98.

[8] Grudem, *Systematic Theology*, 578.

[9] Grudem, *Systematic Theology*, 579.

[10] Macleod, *The Person of Christ*, 190. Macleod addresses the Holy Spirit's role in the creation of the human nature of Jesus more than most scholars, but he does not do so for the Spirit's role in the Incarnation itself (see Macleod, *Person of Christ*, 25–43).

[11] Robert Letham, *The Work of Christ*, Contours of Christian Theology, gen. ed. Gerald Bray (Downers Grove: InterVarsity, 1993), 77.

the correct one. As James R. Payton Jr. notes in his introduction to Eastern Orthodox soteriology, "the incarnation was not merely getting the Savior on the ground, as it were, so that he could eventually save . . . but the incarnation was itself salvific."[12] Daniel J. Treier, in an excellent overview of the current state of atonement theology, suggests that treating Incarnation and atonement as distinct elements of atonement are "popular aberrations" in evangelical theology.[13]

One source of this problem is the assumption that the narrative roles of Christ and the Holy Spirit map directly to the categories of the *ordo salutis*—justification and sanctification.[14] Treier thinks "classic Protestant" atonement theology is not subject to this problem.[15] I disagree. The distinction between justification and sanctification is the hinge that divides classical Protestant and Roman Catholic theology. Although Luther recognized the curative dimensions of grace, the seeds of popular evangelical atonement theology are present in his forensic and extrinsic notions of justifying grace. The same can be said for Calvin.[16] The solution is to understand Jesus Christ's life and ministry in terms of the wider narrative of God's Spirit rather than the systematic theology categories of justification and sanctification. Doing so shows that the Spirit's Incarnation of the Son of God in Jesus Christ is fundamental to the atonement. T. F. Torrance moves in this direction. He makes the Incarnation the foundation of the atonement. Why? Because the life and ministry of Christ derive from the hypostatic union of the Son of God in Jesus Christ. The union of the Son in Christ, moreover, brings the trinitarian life of God into union with human nature and reciprocally brings human nature into communion with the trinitarian life.[17] Torrance's theology brilliantly integrates Incarnation and atonement on the basis of a fundamental trinitarian theology. It falls short, however, of articulating the Holy Spirit's role in the Incarnation, and thereby also in the atonement. Although recognizing the Holy Spirit's role in the conception of Jesus Christ, the Spirit remains, for the most part, the source of the subjective application of grace.[18] As Torrance points out, people "are incorporated into Christ by the power of his Holy Spirit. . . . Thus it may be said that the 'objective' union which we have with Christ through his incarnational assumption of our humanity into himself is 'subjectively' actualized in us through his indwelling Spirit."[19] This chapter argues that a fully trinitarian theology of the Incarnation and thus also of the atonement requires a fuller account of the Holy Spirit's role in Jesus

---

[12] James R. Payton, Jr., *The Victory of the Cross: Salvation in Eastern Orthodoxy* (Downers Grove: IVP Academic, 2019), 78.
[13] Daniel J. Treier, "The New Covenant and New Creation: Western Soteriologies and the Fullness of the Gospel," in *So Great a Salvation: Soteriology in the Majority World*, ed. Gene L. Greene, Stephen T. Pardue, and K. K. Yeo (Grand Rapids: Eerdmans, 2017), 28–9.
[14] Treier, "The New Covenant and New Creation," 14 and 33.
[15] Treier, "The New Covenant and New Creation," 29.
[16] For demonstration of the extrinsic and forensic theology of grace in the Protestant tradition, see my *The Trinitarian Theology of Jonathan Edwards and David Coffey* (Amherst: Cambria, 2011), 170–80.
[17] Torrance, *The Mediation of Christ*, 61–5.
[18] Torrance, *The Mediation of Christ*, 62.
[19] Torrance, *The Mediation of Christ*, 66–7. For an excellent presentation and analysis of Torrance's Christology and atonement, see Martin M. Davis, "T. F. Torrance: Union with Christ through the Communion of the Spirit," *In Die Skriflig* 51, no. 1 (2017): 1–9.

Christ's Incarnation and atoning work. In short, it develops a pentecostal theology of atonement grounded in a Spirit Christology of the Incarnation.

From Spirit of God to Spirit of Christ

Locating Christ in the wider narrative of the Spirit of Pentecost is the necessary first step for developing a pentecostal theology of the atonement that integrates pneumatology and Christology. The work of God in Christ is unique and definitive in certain respects, but it also stands in continuity with the preceding history of redemption. Indeed, the Incarnation of the Son of God in Jesus Christ carries on a story of God's Spirit that began with creation. That work consisted in creating human beings for relationship with God and with each other and for abundant life in this world. In Christ, the Spirit of God brings that previous work to its zenith in the particular life of Jesus Christ. In other words, the Incarnation reveals the Spirit of God as the Spirit of Christ and points toward the Spirit of Pentecost. The Spirit's work in the Incarnation, thus, gives this wider work of the Spirit Christological clarification. As Lisa P. Stephenson points out, Spirit Christology highlights "Christ's mission as an aspect of the Spirit's mission, rather than vice versa."[20] Yet, while recognizing growth in revelation—from the Spirit of God to the Spirit of Christ, the fundamental continuity in the Spirit's work must be kept in mind. What the Spirit did in Christ carries on the story of the Spirit that began with the Spirit's first stirring over the primal darkness of the deep and giving the breath of life to dirt. This section shows first that the New Testament interprets Jesus in continuity with and as carrying on the longer history of God's redemptive work and second that the Holy Spirit is the source of the incarnate Christ's life and ministry. In making the case for continuity between the Incarnation of the Son of God in Christ and the longer history of the Spirit of God, I am diverging from the common emphasis that the Holy Spirit's work in Jesus Christ "was a totally unique and unparalleled action of the Holy Spirit," but moving in concert with scholars who maintain that Jesus must be interpreted in light of the history of Israel.[21]

First, the work of the Holy Spirit in Christ stands in continuity with the work of the Spirit of God that began with creation. The Gospel of John connects Christ with creation: "In the beginning was the Word, and the Word was with God, and the Word was God. He was with God in the beginning. Through him all things were made. . . . In him was life, and that life was the light of mankind. The light shines in the darkness, and darkness has not overcome it" (Jn 1:1-5). The Word, the Son of God, was there in

---

[20] Lisa P. Stephenson, *Dismantling the Dualisms for American Pentecostal Women in Ministry: A Feminist Pneumatological Approach*, Global and Charismatic Studies, 9 (Boston: Brill, 2012), 125.

[21] Millard J. Erickson, *The Word Became Flesh* (Grand Rapids: Baker, 1991), 23. Also see Macleod, who emphasizes the discontinuity of Jesus' human nature with the rest of human beings and of the miraculous nature of the Holy Spirit's creation of Jesus' human nature, in *The Person of Christ*, 25–43 and 191. For continuity, see H. Ray Dunning, *Grace, Faith, and Holiness: A Wesleyan Systematic Theology* (Kansas City: Beacon Hill, 1988), 309; Peter J. Leithart, *Delivered from the Elements of the World: Atonement, Justification, Mission* (Downers Grove: IVP Academic, 2016), 288 and 294; and N. T. Wright, *The Day the Revolution Began: Reconsidering the Meaning of Jesus' Crucifixion* (New York: HarperOne, 2016).

Genesis 1 and was the light that shined in the primordial darkness and brought life to the world, especially God's divine image bearers. John continues that this Word "became flesh and made his dwelling among us" (Jn 1:14). What John attributes to the Son of God, the Hebrew Bible passages discussed in the previous chapter associated with the Spirit of God, namely creation and God coming to dwell with his people (e.g., Ezek. 36:26-28). This correspondence between the presence and agency of God's Spirit and the Son of God in creation suggests continuity with their work in the Incarnation. John's emphasis on the Word becoming flesh, however, is the basis of traditional Logos Christology. Logos Christology emphasizes a descending Christology. God the Son was in eternity with the Father and then came down and became incarnate in Jesus Christ. Logos Christology is not problematic as such, but, by itself, it is incomplete. The important question is, how did the divine Son take on humanity? To answer that question requires a turn to pneumatology and Spirit Christology.[22]

The Synoptic Gospels locate Jesus' identity in the narrative of God's Spirit. The Gospels of Matthew and Luke testify to the pneumatological foundation of Jesus Christ. Consider the conception narratives. Struck with fear and bewilderment at an unplanned pregnancy from someone other than her fiancé, the Angel Gabriel comforts Mary, "Do not be afraid . . . the Holy Spirit will come upon you . . . [s]o the holy one to be born will be called the Son of God" (Lk. 1:35). The Holy Spirit descending on Mary echoes the Spirit of God hovering over the primal abyss. It also connects with God's glory that fills the tabernacle in the first exodus (Exod. 40:35) and the promised outpouring of the Spirit that transforms the desert into a fertile field in the second exodus (Isa. 32:15).[23] The result is the production of life—Israel, the renewal of Israel, and the incarnate Christ as the messiah. Distraught at the news of Mary's condition, an angel assures Joseph that "what is conceived in her is from the Holy Spirit" (Mt. 1:20). The pneumatic conception of Jesus should not be entirely surprising. As the angel reminded Joseph with the words of Isaiah, "The virgin will conceive and give birth to a son, and they will call him Immanuel" (Mt. 1:23, Isa. 7:14). Isaiah, moreover, foretold that this messianic figure will be the "shoot . . . from the stump of Jesse" that "the Spirit of the LORD will rest on" (Isa. 11:1-2). Matthew's genealogy identifies Jesus as this Davidic descendant. Jesus Christ is the Spirit-anointed messiah foretold in Isaiah. Jesus Christ is the unfolding of the redemptive work of God's Spirit. Whatever uniqueness theology attributes to Christ—for example, he is the Incarnation of the Son of God—it must also situate Christ in the wider narrative of the Spirit of God. As a new chapter in this wider narrative of redemption, the Incarnation reveals the Spirit of God as the Spirit of Christ. The Spirit of God brings about the union of the Son of God in the humanity of Jesus Christ. Spirit Christology supplies the missing link in Logos Christology. Namely, what transpired between Jn 1:1 and Jn 1:14 was the work of the Holy Spirit.

---

[22] For a full development of Spirit Christology, see Myk Habets, *The Anointed Son: A Trinitarian Spirit Christology*, Princeton Theological Monograph Series (Eugene: Pickwick, 2010). For a briefer account, see my *From Pentecost to the Triune God*, 78–87.

[23] My thanks to Lisa P. Stephenson for highlighting these connections in Exodus, Isaiah, and Luke. See Stephenson, *Dismantling the Dualisms for American Pentecostal Women in Ministry*, 103.

But the Spirit's work in Christ goes even deeper into God's redemptive history than Isaiah's Spirit-anointed messiah of Davidic descent. John says that in Christ God "made his dwelling among us" and Matthew calls Christ "Immanuel" or "God with us" (Mt. 1:23). The Hebrew Bible associates divine presence with the Spirit of God. In Genesis 1, the Spirit of God initiates creation. The Spirit of God renews the face of the earth from the floodwaters. The Spirit of God makes the passage through the sea for the Israelites' flight from Egypt. The Spirit of God restores the people to their homeland after exile. But the breath of God that animates and sustains human life is the most intimate manifestation of divine presence in creation. The Holy Spirit's activity in the Incarnation not only parallels the breath of God that brought forth human life in Gen. 2:7 but brings that life to its most radical expression. The Incarnation of the Son of God by the Holy Spirit is the definitive dwelling of God "with us" (Mt. 1:23). For this reason, Paul says that "He is the image of the invisible God. . . . For God was pleased to have all his fullness dwell in him" and "in Christ all the fullness of the Deity lives in bodily form" (Col. 1:15 and 2:9, also see 2 Cor. 4:4). Hebrews describes the Son of God in Christ as "the radiance of God's glory and the exact representation of his being" (Heb. 1:3). The Apostle Paul also contrasts Jesus Christ as the "last Adam" with the "first . . . Adam" (1 Cor. 15:45). Where the first Adam "became a living being" and "was of the dust" (1 Cor. 15:45 and 47), the last Adam was a "life-giving spirit" (1 Cor. 15:45). Paul's point is that the descendants of Adam die; they return to the dust, but those who bear the "likeness of the man from heaven" shall put on immortality (1 Cor. 15:49 and 53). Why did Adam return to the dust after becoming a "living being"? Because he forsook his Spirit-breathed life. Jesus Christ became a life-giving spirit because he embraced his Spirit-breathed life as the incarnate Son of God. Although Paul juxtaposes Adam and Christ in 1 Corinthians with respect to their destinies—for example, dust versus imperishable life, in Romans 1 he identifies Jesus' continuity with Adams' earthly life. Paul affirms that the Son of God in Jesus Christ "was a descendant of David" according to his "human nature" (Rom. 1:3). But he was also the Son of God through his resurrection by the Spirit of God—that is, "the Spirit of holiness" (Rom. 1:4). Jesus Christ became a "life-giving spirit" because his Spirit-anointed life was raised from the dead (1 Cor. 15:20-23 and 15:45). The promise of redemption is that all who share the "likeness" of the first Adam can share the "likeness" of Christ, the second Adam. As the first Adam represents the failure of humankind to fulfill its destiny as Spirit-breathed divine image bearers, Jesus Christ embodied its success. The Spirit that was the foundation and source of Christ's life, exemplified in resurrection, promises to give that life to all people as the Spirit of Pentecost. The Spirit of God's gift of life to human beings in Gen. 2:7 finds its most radical particular and historical expression in the Incarnation of the Son of God in Jesus Christ and its eschatological fulfillment when the Spirit of Pentecost offers to all people that Spirit-breathed life actualized in Christ.

So far, I have emphasized the continuity between the Holy Spirit's work in the incarnate Christ and the previous work of the Spirit in the Hebrew Bible, but the Incarnation was also sui generis. Jesus Christ was the Incarnation of the Son of God. The Incarnation has an incomparable quality. Traditional Western atonement theology correctly wants to preserve the uniqueness of Christ. Part of the motivation in denying correlation between the union of God in Christ and in grace is to preserve the divinity of Christ and to avoid drifting into works righteousness. What the Spirit of God brought about in Jesus Christ was unique. It was the Incarnation of the Son of God in the particular humanity of Jesus Christ. But the exclusive emphasis on the exceptional nature of the Incarnation obscures its place in the wider narrative of the Spirit and diminishes its relevance for redemption, aside from being a prerequisite for judicial fulfillment (perfect obedience and penal payment on the cross). The goal here is to affirm the uniqueness of the Spirit's work in the incarnate Christ, but also its continuity with the Spirit's work in the wider history of redemption. So, when Frank J. Matera says Christ "has a unique relationship to God, different from any other human being," that is true, but requires qualification.[24] The Incarnation is part of the ongoing work of the Spirit of God that began with creation and finds fulfillment in new creation.[25] The Incarnation is not an aberration in the long history of redemption. The Incarnation is a continuation of the work of creation. Making creation the place for the dwelling of God and the manifestation of the divine life is the perennial and fundamental work of the Holy Spirit. Considered from the vantage of Pentecost, the Incarnation is neither an anomalous nor an alien act of God, but the particular fulfillment of the Spirit's sharing of divine life with and in creation.

Second, the Spirit is the abiding source of Jesus Christ's life and ministry. Considering Christology from a pneumatological perspective (i.e., Spirit Christology) means that Jesus, throughout his life and not only in his conception, was the Messiah in and through the agency of the Holy Spirit.[26] The Holy Spirit, in other words, is the ongoing foundation of Jesus Christ's incarnate life and ministry. The Spirit's role in the life of Jesus again parallels the Spirit's role as the animating source of human life. In the Hebrew Scriptures, the Spirit of God was neither a momentary catalyst nor a transient agent of human life. The Spirit is the enduring source of human life. Death, the return to the dust, occurs when the Spirit departs. The loss of "his spirit" also marks Jesus' death (Jn 19:30; also Mt. 27:50, Mk 15:37, and Lk. 23:46).[27] The Spirit's investiture of the breath of life in human beings (Gen. 2:7) corresponds to the Spirit's catalyzing of

---

[24] Frank J. Matera, *New Testament Christology* (Louisville: Westminster John Knox, 1999), 29.
[25] Although not addressing the Spirit's role in the process, Marsha M. Wilfong makes the point that the "purpose of the new creation in Christ is the same as the original intention of human creation. It consists in and makes possible faithful relationships with God within human community and with the rest of creation." See Wilfong, "Human Creation in Canonical Context: Genesis 1:26-31 and Beyond," in *God Who Creates: Essays in Honor of W. Sibley Towner*, ed. William P. Brown and S. Dean McBride, Jr. (Grand Rapids: Eerdmans, 2000), 51.
[26] Although not developed at length, Matera affirms the ongoing role of the Holy Spirit in Jesus as the Spirit-anointed messiah. See Matera, *New Testament Christology*, 56.
[27] Scholars represent several views of "my spirit." It can refer to his physical death, the effusion of the Holy Spirit on the disciples at the cross, or a synthesis of the first two. David Crump advances a trinitarian interpretation that has Jesus returning to the Father the Holy Spirit he received at his baptism. For my part, Jesus' committing "his spirit" and breathing "his last" parallels the pneumatological anthropology of the Hebrew Scriptures—for example, people become living beings by the breath of God and return to the dust when the Spirit of God departs (Gen. 2:7, 3:19, and 6:3; Ps. 104:29-30; and Job 34:14-15). In death, Jesus shares the fate of all people who receive the breath of life, but live "by painful toil," amid "thorns and thistles," and "by the sweat of [their] brow" (Gen. 3:19). For Crump, see "Who Gets What? God or the Disciples, Human Spirit or Holy Spirit in John 19:30," *Novum Testamentum* 51, no. 1 (2009): 78–89.

the Incarnation of the Son of God in Jesus Christ (Mt. 1:18 and Lk. 1:35).[28] The Spirit's role in the Incarnation of Jesus Christ is an ongoing phenomenon, just as the Spirit of God is the abiding source of human life, and especially human life that bears the divine image. The Gospels of Matthew and Luke present Jesus Christ as the Spirit-anointed messiah. In doing so they express the messianic expectation of Isaiah, which based the messiah's ministry on pneumatology: Because the "Spirit of the LORD rests on him" he will govern with "wisdom" and "justice" (Isa. 11:1-9).[29] "Returning to Galilee in the power of the Spirit," Jesus enters the synagogue in Nazareth on the Sabbath. There he reads from the scroll of Isaiah: "The Spirit of the LORD is on me, because he has anointed me to preach good news to the poor. He has sent me to proclaim freedom for the prisoners and recovery of sight for the blind, to release the oppressed, to proclaim the year of the LORD's favor" (Lk. 4:14-19). Thus, Jesus recognized that the presence and power of the Holy Spirit constitutes him the Christ and empowers his ministry.[30] The Holy Spirit not only initiated the union of the Son of God with Jesus' humanity but was the abiding foundation of his incarnate life and ministry.

From Spirit-Anointed Christ to Spirit-Baptized World

To this point, I have argued that Jesus carries on a narrative of the Spirit of God that began with creation, continues through the history of Israel, and is foretold by the Hebrew prophets. Placing Jesus in this pneumatological narrative yields a Spirit Christology. The Holy Spirit is the abiding foundation of Jesus Christ's incarnate life and ministry. But how does placing Christ in this wider story of the Spirit of God contribute to the work of redemption—atonement—brought about through Christ's life and ministry? The following outlines general features of that redemptive work, Chapters 4 and 5 deal directly with the implications of a pentecostal understanding of the cross and resurrection. Recognizing the Spirit's work in the Incarnation of Jesus Christ has several results.

First, the Holy Spirit's incarnation of the Son of God in Jesus Christ is the fundamental work of atonement.[31] Although not emphasizing the Holy Spirit, Thomas F. Torrance is correct when he remarks that "the atoning reconciliation began to

---

[28] Although the Spirit Christology developed here and its connection to the Spirit's work in grace differ, they share correspondence with Incarnation and grace (i.e., deification) in Eastern Orthodox theology. See Lossky, *The Mystical Theology of the Eastern Church*, 136.

[29] Andreas Schuele, "The Spirit of YHWH and the Aura of Divine Presence," *Interpretation: A Journal of Bible and Theology*, 66, no. 1 (2012): 22-6.

[30] James D. G. Dunn surmises that the "Spirit of Christ . . . [is] that power which determined Christ in his ministry and in so doing provided a pattern of life in the Spirit." See Dunn, *Romans 1-8*, Word Biblical Commentary (Waco: Word, 1988), 446. For other New Testament scholars making similar points, see Robert Jewett, *Romans: A Commentary*, Hermeneia: A Critical and Historical Commentary on the Bible (Minneapolis: Fortress, 2007), 106-7 and 492; Grant R. Osborne, *Romans*, IVP NTCS (Downers Grove: InterVarsity Press, 2004), 32 and 201; and Peter Stuhlmacher, *Paul's Letter to the Romans: A Commentary*, trans. Scott J. Hafemann (Louisville: Westminster/John Knox, 1994), 19 and 122.

[31] Note that when I use "incarnation" as a verb to indicate the Holy Spirit's role in the Incarnation, I lower case the word.

be actualized with the conception and birth of Jesus of the Virgin Mary when he identified himself with our fallen and estranged humanity."[32] The most fundamental gift that Christ comes to share with the world is what he most fundamentally was. The dwelling of God with humanity through the Holy Spirit. What the Holy Spirit did in Christ is what the Spirit does in grace. Although not highlighting the Holy Spirit's role in the matter, Vernon White emphasizes that Christ in the Incarnation enters into the human condition and lived in faithfulness to God ("he died to self and lived to God") and through participation in his life of love to God and neighbor, human beings are made righteous.[33] People are predestined in Christ "before the creation of the world," not because God foreordained the fall into sin and a select group for salvation, but because the Spirit-anointed life realized in Jesus Christ was always God's dream for human beings that bear the Spirit-breathed divine image (Eph. 1:3-14). Genesis 2:7 and Acts 2:1-4 are one story of the Spirit. The Spirit of Pentecost, as Spirit of Christ, gives the story of the Spirit Christological clarification. The Incarnation puts on full display the life that God imagined for human beings the first moment the Spirit-breathed life into dust. The Spirit of Pentecost comes to fulfill the Spirit-breathed divine image and makes available to all people what the Spirit brought about in the life of Jesus Christ. Through the Spirit of Pentecost all people can be scripted into the narrative of redemption—a narrative that is pneumatological and Christological. The particular fulfillment of human life in Jesus is the archetype for the Spirit's inclusion of "all people" in the narrative of redemption (Acts 2:17). The Spirit endeavors to realize in all human beings what the Spirit accomplished in the life of Jesus Christ.

Second, Spirit baptism is the symbol for the Spirit of atonement. If we ask, "what does the Spirit-anointed Christ come to do?" The answer is "baptize in the Holy Spirit." The Spirit baptizes Jesus, then comes upon "all people" as the Spirit of Pentecost. Jesus Christ shares what he was and received through the Holy Spirit—Spirit-baptized life. For this reason, the Gospels frame Jesus' redemption in terms of Spirit baptism. The baptismal narratives in the Gospels define the nature of Christ's redemptive work in terms of pneumatology—Spirit baptism.[34] Heralding the coming of the Messiah, John the Baptist also declares the nature of his salvation—"I baptize you with water . . . [h]e will baptize you with the Holy Spirit" (see Mt. 3:11, Mk 1:8, Lk. 3:16, and Jn 1:33). In the Gospel of Luke, Jesus indicates that the goal of his work is sharing the gift of the Holy Spirit. In Lk. 11:13, he promises that the "Father in heaven [will] give the Holy Spirit to those who ask him." Not just one among other gifts, the promise of the Holy Spirit is the gift par excellence. The Gospel of Luke closes with Jesus assuring the disciples that they will receive the promise of the Father and be "clothed with power from on high" (Lk. 24:49). Jesus saw his life and ministry culminating in the gift of

---

[32] Torrance, *The Mediation of Christ*, 41.
[33] Vernon White, *Atonement and Incarnation: An Essay in Universalism and Particularity* (New York: Cambridge University Press, 1991), 54–5.
[34] For pentecostal views on the gift of the Spirit, see Frank D. Macchia, *Baptized in the Spirit: A Global Pentecostal Theology* (Grand Rapids: Zondervan, 2006); Wolfgang Vondey, *Pentecostal Theology: Living the Full Gospel*, Systematic Pentecostal and Charismatic Theology, ser. ed. Wolfgang Vondey and Daniela Augustine (London: Bloomsbury, 2017); and Amos Yong, *Spirit of Love: A Trinitarian Theology of Grace* (Waco: Baylor University Press, 2012).

the Holy Spirit. Why? Because the Spirit of Pentecost shares Christ's fulfillment of the human vocation to embody the Spirit-breathed image of God with all people. Spirit baptism is, therefore, the fundamental nature of the atonement.

An obvious objection to this point is that Christ's baptism by the Holy Spirit is distinct from his Incarnation. True in respect of Jesus' historical experience. He was conceived at one point and baptized in the Holy Spirit some three decades later. It is not distinct, however, from the theological perspective of his identity as the Spirit-anointed messiah. How does Christ's pneumatic conception relate to the Spirit's descent upon him at the river Jordan? The latter is the confirmation of the former. It also marked the public announcement of his identity as "my servant whom I have chosen, the one I love, in whom I delight; I will put my Spirit on him, and he will proclaim justice to the nations" (Mt. 12:18). Thus, "As soon as Jesus was baptized, he went up out of the water. At that moment heaven was opened, and he saw the Spirit of God descending like a dove and lighting on him. And a voice from heaven said, 'This is my Son, whom I love; with him I am well pleased'" (Mt. 3:16-17). The manifestation of the Holy Spirit at Jesus' baptism declares to the world what the angels said to Mary and Joseph: "the Holy Spirit will come upon you . . . [s]o the holy one to be born will be called the Son of God" (Lk. 1:35) and "what is conceived in her is from the Holy Spirit" (Mt. 1:20). The outpouring of the Holy Spirit on Jesus at his baptism was a public confirmation of his perennial pneumatological identity as the Spirit-anointed messiah. The descent of the Holy Spirit during his baptism did not involve an ontological change in the Holy Spirit's presence in Jesus' life. It was a public manifestation of the Spirit's abiding presence.

From Incarnation to Trinitarian Fellowship

The Incarnation is a trinitarian and participatory nexus of atonement. It is the place of the economic manifestation of the triune fellowship of God that is offered to all people through the outpouring of the Spirit of Pentecost. This final section presents the relational, participatory, and trinitarian nature of atonement in conversation with the traditional subjective view of the atonement and the Eastern Orthodox theology of grace.

First, the trinitarian nature of the Incarnation and atonement invites interaction with the moral-subjective approaches to atonement. They are called "subjective" atonement theories for three reasons. (1) They make human beings the subject of the atonement rather than positing a transaction between the Father and the Son (e.g., usually either a satisfaction rendered, or penalty paid by Christ on the cross to the Father for human sin). (2) They emphasize that Jesus Christ's life and death demonstrate God's love for human beings and provide a model for human morality. (3) They see Christ's entire life as part of his atoning work, rather than focusing primarily on the cross.[35] In these respects, the subjective views are correct. God's love is the motivating

---

[35] Richard Rohr presents a fine case for this atonement theology in "The Franciscan Option," in *Stricken by God? Nonviolent Identification and the Victory of Christ*, ed. Brad Jersak and Michael

factor of atonement and the transformation of human life is its goal. Nevertheless, atonement theology of this kind can make the grace that comes through the life of Christ extrinsic. Although called "subjective" because the love and example given in Christ focus on changing human beings in their relationship with God and other people, the life of Christ itself remains objective. Christ demonstrates God's love, which leads people to love God. Subjective change takes place, but it is not necessarily organic or participatory with Christ. Christ's life is the historical and moral exemplar, not an indwelling and transformative divine presence. Extrinsicism misses the trinitarian and participatory nature of the Incarnation and the atonement. Christ undeniably demonstrates God's love for human beings and gives them an example of what it looks like to love God and neighbor. But Christ and the atonement are much more than that. Jesus Christ is the economic manifestation of God's triune life in humanity. He embodies, moreover, the fullness of life for which human beings were created. Not only as a historical example to follow, but as a vector in which all people can participate through the Spirit of Pentecost. Paul S. Fiddes is correct that integrating the traditional objective and subjective or past event and current experience of atonement is the vital task of theology.[36] God desires to share the triune life with every person. The Spirit of God brought forth human life to bear the divine image. God created human beings to manifest in their embodied life, the life, love, and creative fecundity of the triune God. The Incarnation provides the particular fulfillment of that life in Jesus Christ as the Spirit-anointed messiah. Then, through the Spirit of Pentecost, the triune God makes that life available to all people, thus providing atonement. Admittedly, I am interacting with Gustav Allen's ideal type of the subjective theory of the atonement popular in Protestant Liberalism.[37] Participation can be part of a subjective view of atonement.[38] Nevertheless and with some irony, the traditional subjective theory's emphasis on God's love and atonement as moral transformation, even if not based in Chalcedonian Christology and divine participation, resonates more with my proposal for a pentecostal theology of the atonement than the penal-substitutionary view that has historically been popular among Pentecostals.

Second, the grace of atonement is relational, participatory, and trinitarian. God desires to renew and dwell in the hearts and the lives of people. Faith opens the

---

Hardin (Grand Rapids: Eerdmans, 2007), 206–12. Also see, Peter Schmiechen, *Saving Power: Theories of Atonement and Forms of the Church* (Grand Rapids: Eerdmans, 2005), 288–97 and 305–9. Although not a systematic theology of subjective atonement per se, an excellent presentation of its biblical basis is Donald Senior's *Why the Cross?* Reframing New Testament Theology, ed. Joel B. Green (Nashville: Abingdon, 2014), see esp. 29–92.

[36] Paul S. Fiddes, *Past Event and Present Salvation: The Christian Idea of Atonement* (London: Darton, Longman, and Todd, 1989), 26.

[37] Gustav Aulén, *Christus Victor: An Historical Study of the Three Main Types of the Idea of Atonement*, trans. A. G. Herbert (1969; reprint, New York: Macmillan, 1979), 3, 133–42, and 145–54.

[38] Paul Fiddes, for example, presents a subjective approach to atonement that emphasizes the "the cross of Jesus as an event which has a unique degree of power to evoke and create human response to the forgiving love of God . . . that goes far beyond an 'example' or 'window into God's love.'" See Fiddes, *Past Event and Present Salvation*, 29. Although emphasizing that Christ demonstrates God's love and provides a moral and spiritual pattern, Rohr and Senior also affirm participation, thus suggesting compatibility between this and a pentecostal approach to the atonement. See Rohr, "The Franciscan Option," 210 and Senior, *Why the Cross?* 92–3.

human heart to know and to love God. Knowing and following in the love of God demonstrated in Christ means relational participation in that love and life. God first loved human beings by giving them the breath of life and communing with them in the Garden of Eden. In the Incarnation, God goes beyond walking with human beings in the Garden and takes on their humanity and walks with them in the world. John describes the Incarnation as an act of God's love—"For God so loved the world that he gave his one and only Son" (Jn 3:16). Evangelical and pentecostal Christians can become inured to these words in John's Gospel. They need to be heard again. They describe the fundamental meaning and way that God loves human beings. God dwells with them and in doing so gives and renews their life. Life-giving and redemptive presence is the way God loves human beings. God relates to human beings by participating in their embodied life. The Holy Spirit actuates the Incarnation—God's participation in humanity—in order to renew relationship with people. Jesus Christ, the incarnate Son of God, is an act of God's love because in Christ, God is Immanuel—"God with us" (Mt. 1:23). Consequently, the story of redemption continues in the outpouring of the Spirit of Pentecost according to which "God has poured out his love into our hearts by the Holy Spirit, whom he has given to us" (Rom. 5:5; cf. 1 Jn 3:7-16).

Jesus' Farewell Address highlights the trinitarian, participatory, and relational nature of the atonement. These chapters in John's Gospel are Jesus' last teachings to his disciples before his arrest and crucifixion. The Farewell Address comprises four of twenty-one chapters, which is roughly 20 percent of the Gospel of John. The Holy Spirit and trinitarian communion are central to these chapters. John 14 opens with Jesus assuring his disciples that although he will be leaving, they should not fret because he will return to his Father and make a home for them so that they may be "where I am" (Jn 14:3). At this point, Jesus sounds like he will leave and come back at a later date and take them with him. But later in the same chapter, Jesus comforts them by promising that he will send the Holy Spirit to be with them. The Spirit, however, is not a surrogate for the departed Christ. The Holy Spirit will bring the Son and the Father to make their home with the disciples (Jn 14:17 and 23). Jesus uses the language of his relationship with the Father to describe the relationship they will have with him and the Father. In his last prayer, he looks forward to all who will come to him and says, "that all of them may be one, Father, just as you are in me and I am in you. May they also be in us so that world may believe that you have sent me . . . [and] that the love you have for me may be in them and that I myself may be in them" (Jn 17:21 and 26). Christ also prays that his disciples will be sanctified as he is sanctified (Jn 17:18-19). At the close of his time with his disciples, Jesus defines his ministry in terms of sharing the triune relationships and sanctified life he experienced with his disciples. How does he share it with them? Through the Holy Spirit. This promise of renewal of life and of relationship with God through the Spirit corresponds to the promise of Ezekiel 36—a renewal of the human heart and life by the indwelling Spirit of God (see Chapter 2 for discussion of Ezekiel 36 as a precursor for the Spirit of Pentecost).

The Farewell Address also describes, what trinitarian theology calls, Jesus' economic relationship with the Father. But, the economic relationships and activities of Jesus derive from immanent relationships.[39] In other words, theology takes the relationship that Jesus experienced as the incarnate Son of God as indicative of the Son's eternal relationship with the Father (i.e., their immanent relationships). Jesus experiences filial love with the Father because the Son and Father existed that way from eternity. The Holy Spirit, moreover, brings the Son into union with the humanity of Jesus and constitutes the Incarnation of the Son's relationship with the Father because the Spirit does so in the immanent Godhead. Jesus Christ is the result of the Holy Spirit incarnating the Son of God in his particular humanity and life, and his personal experiences arise from that trinitarian dynamic.[40] But the Farewell Address is not only about Jesus' relationship with the Father and the Holy Spirit. Jesus indicates that the triune life of God he enjoys is available to all who will believe in him. His last words to his disciples are the promise that they too can share in that trinitarian source of life and love (Jn 17:26). The Incarnation and atonement, therefore, have trinitarian symmetry. What the triune God most fundamentally is, a fellowship of love, comes to manifestation in the Spirit's Incarnation of the Son of God in Jesus Christ. The life of Christ provides atonement because, through the Holy Spirit, the Spirit of Pentecost, the triune fellowship Christ experienced becomes available to all people.

Third, this pentecostal approach to the Incarnation and atonement invites ecumenical and critical dialogue with Eastern Orthodox theology. This pentecostal proposal connects with the theology of Eastern Orthodoxy, but also differs. Sergius Bulgakov, for example, recognizes the work of the Holy Spirit in the Incarnation, but also sees the Incarnation as opening up a new kind of the Spirit's work. He suggests that the "church of the Old Testament had for its purpose . . . the preparation of holy humanity worthy to receive the Holy Spirit."[41] Bulgakov correctly critiques the extrinsicism of Western objective atonement theology, which regards the Incarnation as a stepping stone to penal payment, rather than as the substantive character of redemption. He, nevertheless, retains an extrinsicism of the Spirit. The pre- and post-Incarnation work of the Spirit—that is, the outpouring of the Spirit of Pentecost—is distinct. The Incarnation and, afterward, the outpouring of the Spirit of Pentecost may fulfill the human vocation, but they mark a new kind of work in the history of redemption for Bulgakov.[42] Vladimir Lossky maintains that the Holy Spirit is present and at work in the world prior to Christ's outpouring of the Spirit. But "the operation of the Holy Spirit in the world before the Church and outside the Church is not, therefore, the same as His presence in the Church after Pentecost."[43] Thus, Lossky distinguishes

---

[39] The correspondence between the immanent and economic Trinity is fundamental to trinitarian theology. For example, see Karl Barth, *Church Dogmatics*, vol. 1, The Doctrine of the Word of God, § 8–12 The Revelation of God: The Triune God, ed. G. W. Bromiley and T. F. Torrance (New York: T & T Clark, 2009), I.1.8.9.3 (pp. 78–9) and Karl Rahner, *The Trinity*, trans. Joseph Donceel, intro. Catherine Mowry LaCugna (1970; reprint, New York: Crossroad, 1988), 22. At the same time, the economic Trinity does not fully reveal the immanent Godhead, as God remains transcendent to creation and human comprehension—see Barth, *Church Dogmatics*, I.1.9.3 (p. 79).

[40] For my fuller development of a pentecostal trinitarian theology and its implications for Spirit Christology, see *From Pentecost to the Triune God*, 78–87 and 94–100.

[41] Sergius Bulgakov, "The Virgin and the Saints in Orthodoxy," in *Eastern Orthodox Theology: A Contemporary Reader*, ed. Daniel B. Clendenin (1995; Grand Rapids: Baker Academic, 2003), 66.

[42] Bulgakov, "The Virgin and the Saints in Orthodoxy," 66.

[43] Lossky, *The Mystical Theology of the Eastern Church*, 157.

between the Spirit's work in creation and the post-Pentecost and ecclesiastical work of the Spirit. Moreover, although Lossky affirms the Spirit's role in the Incarnation, he emphasizes the distinction of the Holy Spirit's mission in the economy of redemption. This emphasis seems to arise from trying to retain the distinct procession of the Holy Spirit relative to the Son's, which distinguishes Eastern Orthodox theology from its Western counterpart.[44] In other words, maintaining the distinction of the Spirit's mission relative to the Son's derives from the Spirit's non-Son dependent immanent procession (non-*filioque*).[45] The result is an argument that recognizes the integrity of the Holy Spirit's mission, on the one hand, and, on the other hand, retains a Christocentric structure in which Christ essentially achieves redemption (fulfills the divine likeness in human nature) and the Holy Spirit applies it (enables individual persons to participate in Christ's fulfillment of the likeness). This approach is personal, participatory, and transformational in contrast to the forensic and extrinsic nature of much of Western atonement theology.[46] Overplaying the differences between my proposal and Eastern Orthodoxy serves no useful purpose.[47] But it is not a distinction without a difference. The Holy Spirit's work in the Incarnation of Christ stands in continuity with the Spirit's work from creation to eschaton. The Incarnation emerges from the narrative and mission of the Spirit of God. The mission of the Spirit is not the consequence of the Son's mission. Subordinating the Spirit's mission to Christ's arises from the logic of the eternal processions of the divine persons. Even though Eastern Orthodox trinitarian theology avoids the subordinationist implications of the Western *filioque*, it nevertheless takes the order of processions as indicative of a relational and missional order between the Son and the Holy Spirit.[48]

No distinction pertains between the pre- and post-incarnational work of the Holy Spirit. Making this distinction introduces discontinuity into the economic work of not

---

[44] Lossky, *The Mystical Theology of the Eastern Church*, 156–60.
[45] Referencing Lossky, John Meyendorff makes a similar argument. See John Meyendorff, *Byzantine Theology: Historical Trends and Doctrinal Themes*, 2nd ed. (New York: Fordham University Press, 1979), 172 and 159.
[46] Christoforos Stavropoulos explains that "the work of our theosis, which . . . Christ accomplished objectively, is completed by the Holy Spirit, adapting it to the life of every faithful Christian." He also says that "Christ realizes in time . . . the Holy Spirit completes and perfects and adapts this work to people." This language reflects the paradigm that Christ accomplishes the objective work of redemption and the Spirit subjectively applies the benefits of redemption. It connotes extrinsicism to the Spirit because Christ, not the Spirit, is the primary agent of "accomplishing" redemption; the Spirit subsequently applies Christ's redemption to individuals. See Christoforos Stavropoulos, "Partakers of the Divine Nature," in *Eastern Orthodoxy: A Contemporary* Reader, ed. Daniel B. Clendenin (1995; Grand Rapids: Baker Academic, 2003), 188–9. For a critical evaluation of the objective-subjective paradigm, see my "Pentecostal Soteriology: Overcoming the Ecumenical Impasses of Classical Pentecostalism and Charismatic Experience," in *Pentecostal Theology and Ecumenical Theology: Interpretations, Intersections, Inspirations*, ed. Peter Hocken, Tony L. Richie, and Christopher A. Stephenson, Global Pentecostal and Charismatic Studies, 34 (Leiden: Brill, 2019), 283–307.
[47] For example, Stavropolous' essay "Partakers of the Divine Nature," notwithstanding my critical comments earlier, puts participation and transformation at the heart of redemption, which dovetails with the pentecostal theology of atonement developed in this project. See Stavropolous, "Partakers of the Divine Nature," 184 and 187–8.
[48] For a more extended analysis of Eastern Orthodox and Western trinitarian theologies, see my *From Pentecost to the Triune God*, 101–46.

only the Holy Spirit but the Trinity as well. In other words, it suggests a discrepancy between the immanent identity and economic activity of the Holy Spirit. The Spirit of Pentecost fosters life filled with love, compassion, and joy. Does the work of the Spirit prior to Pentecost engender something else? No. The work of the Holy Spirit throughout the biblical narrative of redemption bears the same character. The reason is trinitarian. The Holy Spirit's economic activities derive from the Spirits immanent identity. The Holy Spirit is the divine person who completes the fellowship of the triune God and, consequently, provides the narrative structure to the history of redemption. Thus, the biblical narrative of the Spirit of Pentecost and principles of trinitarian theology suggest that creation and redemption are not two stories but one. Genesis 2:7 and Acts 2:1–4 are one story of the Spirit. The Spirit of God creating the world, giving the breath of life, catalyzing the Incarnation of the Son of God, coming as Spirit of Pentecost, and finally bringing the new creation are one story of the Spirit. The nature of the Spirit's work in each part of the story is the same. Pentecost is a threshold in the work of redemption, but not to a new kind of work by the Spirit. The Spirit that gave the breath of life gave that life to enable human beings to bear the divine image. This mission of the Spirit finds particular fulfillment in Christ and is revealed as a universal opportunity in the outpouring of the Spirit of Pentecost. The Spirit of Pentecost, as Spirit of Christ, gives the story of the Spirit Christological clarification. Again, the differences should not be exaggerated because Eastern Orthodoxy's more pneumatological and organic understanding of the Incarnation shares more in common with this pentecostal theology of the atonement than do its Western counterparts.

Conclusion

The Holy Spirit narrates the comprehensive history of redemption in the life of the incarnate Christ. The Incarnation displays in vivid clarity God's vision for human life. What Christ was is what Adam and Eve were meant to be. God's Spirit brought forth embodied human life, life to be lived in and for this world and in loving fellowship with the triune God and other human beings. The Holy Spirit brought that life to its fullest manifestation in the Incarnation of the Son of God in Jesus Christ. The Spirit's role in the Incarnation of Christ establishes the fundamental nature of atonement—the Spirit of Pentecost shares the life realized in Christ with all people. This chapter began by evaluating the place of the Incarnation in traditional atonement theology. It then framed the Holy Spirit's work in Christ in the wider narrative of redemption, detailed the Holy Spirit's role in Christ in terms of Spirit Christology, and showed that this Spirit Christology informs a pentecostal theology of atonement. It concluded with the trinitarian and participatory nature of atonement.

4

Crucifixion

Christ and the cross are central to Christianity. The cross is the center piece of most atonement theologies.[1] Indeed, many atonement theologies are almost exclusively narratives of the cross and Christ's death. This chapter articulates the place of the cross in a pentecostal theology of the atonement. It considers the cross from the perspective of the Spirit of Pentecost. For a pentecostal theology of the atonement, the justice of the cross resides in Christ's fulfillment of the human vocation to bear the Spirit-breathed image of God and the promise that through the Spirit of Pentecost all people can participate in his fulfillment. In other words, this pentecostal theology of the atonement is not exclusively or even primarily a penal view of the cross. But as Darrin Belousek points out, rejecting penal substitution is not rejecting the justice of the cross.[2] Dispensing with a retributive theory of justice, it affirms a vision of justice that integrates Christ and the Holy Spirit in a restorative and transformational theology of atonement. This chapter develops the first facet of a pentecostal theology of the cross and its meaning for atonement. It focuses on the Spirit Christological categories of atonement and the cross. Chapter 9 sets forth additional considerations of the cross as a pneumatological and participatory paradigm of atonement. Developing this pentecostal theology of the cross includes several steps. Reframing atonement in terms of the mission of the Spirit of Pentecost instead of Western atonement theology's judicial lens is the first one. The second shows that the cross is the climax of Jesus fulfillment of Spirit-breathed life (righteousness). The third develops a theology of Christ's substitutionary life and death that provides a foundation for a pneumatological and participatory theology of atonement. The fourth presents an account of Jesus' death as the sacrifice for sin.

Christ, the Cross, and the Mission of the Spirit of Pentecost

The basic point of a pentecostal theology of the atonement is that the cross finds its meaning in the broader narrative of the Spirit's redemptive mission and work.[3] That

---

[1] Crucicentrism can also characterize intentional efforts to develop atonement theologies distinct from the common penal-substitutionary view. See, for example, Kate Eisenbise, *Cooperative Salvation: A Brethren View of the Atonement* (Eugene: Wipf & Stock, 2014), 4.
[2] Darrin W. Snyder Belousek, *Atonement, Justice, and Peace: The Message of the Cross and the Mission of the Church* (Grand Rapids: Eerdmans, 2012), 171–2.
[3] Other scholars also call for understanding Christ and the cross in terms of the history of Israel and its Scripture. E.g., see H. Ray Dunning, *Grace, Faith, and Holiness: A Wesleyan Systematic Theology*

is not the case for traditional Western atonement theology, which usually has little to no role for the Holy Spirit and interprets atonement almost everything in terms of the cross.[4] Atonement is a crucicentric narrative.[5] The concern here is not to chronicle a detailed history of the genesis and development of Western atonement theology, but to identify its primary way of understanding Christ and the cross. Anselm's satisfaction theory of atonement, if not started, solidified a tendency toward crucicentrism in Western atonement theology.[6] The sixteenth-century Protestant reformation theologies of justification by faith intensified this trajectory around penal and judicial themes.[7] Traditional pentecostal theology (at least in Western contexts) for the most part borrowed the evangelical version of this atonement theology.[8] Marginalizing the cross is the purpose here. The cross is vital to Christian theology. But recognizing the importance of the cross and embracing the penal view of the cross are not one and the same. This section treats two narratives of the cross. The first is the cross in Western atonement theology and the second is the cross in the narrative of the Spirit of Pentecost.

First, although the cross is central to the penal view of atonement, judicial presuppositions predominate its understanding of the cross.[9] The setting of atonement

---

(Kansas City: Beacon Hill, 1988), 309 and Peter J. Leithart, *Delivered from the Elements of the World: Atonement, Justification, Mission* (Downers Grove: IVP Academic, 2016), 18.

[4] Crucicentrism is not only a feature of penal-substitutionary atonement but other approaches as well. Paul S. Fiddes, articulating a contemporary approach starting with the traditional subjective aspect of atonement, maintains that "the cross of Jesus ... [occupies] the centre of all life. The many strands of human experience run through the cross-roads of the cross ... [and] atonement *depends* upon that moment." Fiddes, *Past Event and Present Salvation: The Christian Idea of Atonement* (London: Darton, Longman, and Todd, 1989), 3–4. Although critiquing penal-substitutionary atonement and recommending diverse images based on biblical theology, Joel B. Green and Mark D. Baker assume a crucicentric approach to atonement in *Recovering the Scandal of the Cross: Atonement in New Testament and Contemporary Contexts* (Downers Grove: InterVarsity Press, 2000). More recently, see Fleming Rutledge, *The Crucifixion: Understanding the Death of Jesus Christ* (Grand Rapids: Eerdmans, 2015) and Marit Trelstad, ed., *Cross Examinations: Readings of the Meaning of the Cross Today* (Minneapolis: Augsburg, 2006).

[5] Note that Eastern Orthodox theology is also crucicentric. It does not, however, valorize penal justice, but the cross as Christ's victory over death, the principal consequence of sin. See Georges Florovsky, *Creation and Redemption*, Collected Works, vol. 3 (Belmont: Nordland, 1976), 96–104.

[6] Although affirming "penal representation" within a larger theology of the cross as God's hospitality, Hans Boersma links the problems with Western satisfaction and penal atonement (i.e., its "juridicizing, individualizing, and de-historicizing" tendencies) to a particular stream of Augustinian theology. See Boersma, *Violence, Hospitality, and the Cross: Reappropriating the Atonement Tradition* (Grand Rapids: BakerAcademic, 2005), 153–70.

[7] Excluding Luther from this trajectory, Gustav Aulén also argues this point for the subsequent Protestant tradition in *Christus Victor: An Historical Study of the Three Main types of the Idea of Atonement*, trans. A. G. Herbert (New York: Macmillan, 1969), 2–3, 123–4, and 128–9.

[8] See American Assemblies of God theological textbook by William W. Menzies and Stanley M. Horton, *Bible Doctrines: A Pentecostal Perspective* (1993; 7th printing, Springfield: Logion, 2000), 99–100. Charismatic theologian, Larry D. Hart, although affirming a holistic approach to redemption, affirms a penal and forensic view of atonement and justification in *Truth Aflame: Theology for the Church in Renewal* (1999; reprint, Grand Rapids: Zondervan, 2005), 354. Church of God, Pentecostal-Holiness theologian, R. Hollis Gause also emphasizes holistic salvation, but retains the traditional penal and forensic view of atonement and justification in *Living in the Spirit: The Way of Salvation*, Revised and Expanded Edition (Cleveland: CPT, 2009), 43–8.

[9] I am not the first to make this characterization. See Fiddes, *Past Event and Present Salvation*, 88–9 and 96–104. Affirming this viewpoint, I. Howard Marshall argues that justification in the New

is the heavenly courtroom.[10] God the Father presides as judge. Human sinners stand guilty before the seat of judgment. Unable to satisfy the demands of divine justice, they face "God's wrath," "hatred," and "hostility" and are doomed to everlasting torment in hell.[11] The solution to this courtroom drama is the cross. Christ interposes his blood shed on the cross. God the Father accepts Christ's life of obedience to the law and penal death on the cross as fulfilling the requirements of justice.[12] All those who place their faith in Christ have his righteousness imputed to them.[13] Imputed righteousness does not change anything in believers in Christ. God simply chooses to treat them as if they were as righteous as Christ. The cross is the centerpiece of this redemption narrative. Although Christ's entire life of obedience contributes to the redemptive work, the cross is preeminent. John Calvin clarifies, "to define the way of salvation more exactly, Scripture ascribes this as peculiar and proper to Christ's death."[14] Calvin, although discussing the "synecdoche" of cross and resurrection, maintains that "we have in his death the complete fulfillment of salvation, for through it we are reconciled to God, his righteous judgment is satisfied, the curse is removed, and the penalty is paid in full."[15] More recently, Bruce Demarest gives Christ's "active obedience" only passing mention, while focusing on the penal death of Christ on the cross as the foundation of atonement.[16] Demarest sharpens the focus on the cross with "Christianity is Christ, and the crucial fact about Christ is his passion on the cross."[17] Penal-substitutionary atonement, therefore, is not only Christocentric but also crucicentric.[18]

Someone might object that Martin Luther and John Calvin affirmed that grace is transformational.[19] Yes, they did, as do most all Christian theologians in one way or

---

Testament is "best understood against a legal background" and is "an act of acquittal." See Marshall, *Aspects of the Atonement: Cross and Resurrection in the Reconciling of God and Humanity* (London: Paternoster, 2007), 121.

[10] For the courtroom imagery in John Calvin, see *Calvin: Institutes of the Christian Religion*, 2 vols., ed. John T. McNeil, trans. Ford Lewis Battles (Philadelphia: Westminster, 1960), 2.15.6 (pp. 501–2) and 2.16.5 (pp. 508–9) and more recently Robert Letham, *The Work of Christ*, Contours of Christian Theology, gen. ed. Gerald Bray (Downers Grove: InterVarsity Press, 1993), 178–81.

[11] Calvin, *Institutes of the Christian Religion*, 2.16.1–3 (pp. 504–5).

[12] Calvin, *Institutes of the Christian Religion*, 2.16.6 (pp. 510–11).

[13] Calvin, *Institutes of the Christian Religion*, 2.17.5 (p. 533).

[14] Calvin, *Institutes of the Christian Religion*, 2.16.5 (p. 507).

[15] Calvin, *Institutes of the Christian Religion*, 2.16.13 (pp. 520–1).

[16] Bruce Demarest, *The Cross and Salvation*, Foundations of Evangelical Theology, 1 (Wheaton: Crossway, 1997), 158 and 173.

[17] Demarest, *The Cross and Salvation*, 167.

[18] Charles Hodge clarifies that the distinction between active and passive obedience is misleading because the entirety of Christ's life was one of obedience to the law, which culminated in his death on the cross. Charles Hodge, *Systematic Theology*, 3 vols. (Peabody: Hendrickson, 2003), 3:142–3 and 161. Letham also affirms the entirety of Christ's life as part of his obedience that secures atonement, but also sees his "atoning death" as the primary act of obedience (Letham, *The Work of Christ*, 132).

[19] For example, some scholars argue that forensic categories were later corruptions of Luther's theology—for example, Aulén, *Christus Victor*, 124–5. Alister E. McGrath, however, argues that although Melanchthon accentuated the forensic character of justification, it is present in Luther's theology of the alien righteousness of Christ. See McGrath, *Iustitia Dei: A History of the Christian Doctrine of Justification*, 2nd ed. (New York: Cambridge University Press, 1998), 182 and 210–11. Hans C. Boersma argues that "the violence of an economy of exchange [that] came to dominate the understanding of the cross" in Reformed Scholasticism was present, if not as dominant, in Calvin. See Boersma, *Violence, Hospitality, and the Cross*, 170, 59–60, and 163–70.

another. The point is that their way of understanding Christ, the cross, atonement, and justification make the relational and transformational elements of redemption, such as union with Christ and sanctification, marginal. Union with Christ and sanctification ultimately have nothing to do with atonement and justification and, therefore, nothing to do with the fundamental experience of salvation, which is judicial acquittal before God.[20] Union with Christ, although necessary as the conduit for receiving penal atonement, is not itself salvific. Penal atonement, moreover, makes sanctification theologically superfluous. For example, Robert Letham, although grounding redemption in union with Christ, affirms that justification is imputed righteousness and deals with legal standing before God and that sanctification is imparted righteousness "but is never perfect or complete ... since we will never be free from sin in this life." Letham nevertheless insists that sanctification is necessary. But saying it is so over and over does not make it so.[21] Consider, what is the most fundamental reality of salvation and how does a person experience it? Is it the inner renewal of sanctification? Is it to be "'born anew to a living hope' ... 'through [Christ's] resurrection'"?[22] Will a person stand before God and point to their level of spiritual renewal and moral sanctity? No. The only recourse is the imputed and extrinsic righteousness of Christ that comes from the cross. The transforming work of the Spirit in a person can never be part of atonement and justification because it is not perfect. God the Father demands perfect obedience to assuage his wrath. Only Christ's obedience that led to penal death confers the perfect righteousness that fits a person to stand before the glaring judgment of God the Father.[23] So, in the end, no level of sanctification and the Spirit's work adds anything to the fundamental nature of redemption.[24] Salvation, from beginning to end, is to receive pardon from sin and the declaration of righteousness before the heavenly tribunal of God the Father based on the imputed righteousness of Christ.[25]

This theology makes the righteousness of the cross extrinsic. The cross is a legal penalty the Son pays on behalf of sinners. The cross confers imputed righteousness, which remains *extra nos* in order to preserve salvation by grace through faith and to

---

[20] Charles Hodge, for example, affirms that union with Christ is the foundation of the benefits of Christ, but that the imputed righteousness of justification that comes through Christ's atoning death is extrinsic; it makes no inner and subjective change in the believer. See Hodge, *Systematic Theology*, 3:127 and 144–5.

[21] Letham, *The Work of Christ*, 184–5.

[22] Calvin, *Institutes of the Christian Religion*, 2.16.13 (p. 520).

[23] In his case for penal-substitutionary atonement, William Lane Craig argues that "atonement is a forensic transaction, which would be powerless to transform our lives without the work of the Holy Spirit in regeneration and sanctification. Our legal pardon by God no more transforms our character and makes us virtuous people than does a human pardon a convicted criminal." See Craig, *The Atonement*, Cambridge Elements (New York: Cambridge University Press, 2018), 95.

[24] For Luther's use of extrinsic righteousness to discuss justification and the transformational power of grace, see *Lectures on Romans: Glosses and Scholia*, ed. Hilton C. Oswald, trans. Walter G. Tillmanns and Jacob A. O. Preus, vol. 25 of *Luther's Works* (St. Louis: Concordia, 1998), 64, 79, 245, 330–42, and 370 and *Lectures on Galatians 1535, Chapters 5–6; Lectures on Galatians 1519, Chapters 1–6*, ed. Jaroslav Pelikan, trans. Jaroslav Pelikan and Richard Jungkuntz, vol. 27 of *Luther's Works* (St. Louis: Concordia, 1964), 64–5 and 75.

[25] For the imputed versus transformational elements of grace in Calvin, see *Institutes of the Christian Religion*, 2.16.5 (p. 507), 2.16.13 (p. 521), 3.11.2 (pp. 726–7), 3.11.10 (pp. 736–7), 3.11.11 (pp. 740–1), 3.14.6 (p. 774), 3.14.21 (p. 788), and 3.11.23 (p. 753).

avoid works righteousness. Penal-substitutionary atonement dislodges the fundamental meaning of the cross from the experience and transformation of redemption. According to this theology, the cross is primarily a judicial transaction between the Father and the Son. Jesus Christ offers his life to the Father as the punitive payment to pacify the demands of divine justice. Jesus Christ's perfect obedience to God's law and penal death on the cross for human sin preserves the holiness of the divine nature.[26] With God's holy wrath and anger mollified by Jesus' bloodletting, sinful human beings can appear before God the Father absolved of their guilt.[27] Yet, atonement leaves believers unchanged. Calvin insists that the righteousness of atonement and justification is extrinsic. The Christian is made "righteous, not intrinsically but by imputation."[28] Reinforcing the point, he continues that because sanctification remains imperfect, Christians remain "liable to the judgment of death before his tribunal."[29] The righteousness of atonement and justification, however, is perfect for God "does not justify in part but liberally, so that they may appear in heaven *as if* endowed with the purity of Christ."[30] The traditional formula for expressing this theology is *simul iustus et peccator* (simultaneously justified and sinful). Justified because they have received the imputed righteousness of Christ. But in themselves and even though undergoing the process of sanctification they are sinful. Thus, the righteousness of Christ conferred by virtue of Christ's atoning work on the cross is extrinsic. Yes, Calvin affirms that the "grace of justification is not separated from regeneration."[31] But then he immediately states they are "distinct."[32] What he means is that justification and regeneration are concurrent. Regeneration and its development in sanctification, however, are not part of the fundamental nature of redemption, which is legal acquittal before God's tribunal.[33]

The penal view also affirms that Jesus' blood sacrifice provides forgiveness for human sin. But it does not. God does not forgive sin. Jesus Christ pays its price. God the Father accepts Christ's death on the cross as the payment for sin. Human beings can stand before the holiness of God the Father because Christ vicariously obeyed divine law and paid the penalty for their sin, thereby fulfilling the demands of divine justice on their behalf. It makes no sense to talk of forgiveness in a theological system that requires judicial penalty. R. B. Jamieson, for example, argues that death is key to atonement— "ritual slaughter [is] prerequisite to forgiveness because, in order for forgiveness to

---

[26] Demarest, *The Cross and Salvation*, 179–80.
[27] I. Howard Marshall argues that since the Father and the Son have the same will and desire to redeem human sinners, it is wrong headed to portray the Father as the punitive judge demanding the Son's death on the cross. Marshall is correct that the divine will is one, but as he indicates the Father sends the Son and only the Son dies on the cross. Yes, the Father's sending, just as the Son's coming into to the world, arises from the loving nature of the divine will, but also from a divine nature that demands penal payment for sin. See Marshall, *Aspects of the Atonement*, 55–67.
[28] Calvin, *Institutes of the Christian Religion*, 3.11.11 (1:739).
[29] Calvin, *Institutes of the Christian Religion*, 3.11.11 (1:739).
[30] Calvin, *Institutes of the Christian Religion*, 3.11.11 (1:739); emphasis added. This theological paradigm is also present in Luther. See Luther, *Lectures on Romans*, 59, 64, 79, 245, 257–8, 268, 330–1 333–4, 336, 340, 342, and 370.
[31] Calvin, *Institutes of the Christian Religion*, 3.11.11 (1:739).
[32] Calvin, *Institutes of the Christian Religion*, 3.11.11 (1:739).
[33] E.g., also see Calvin, *Institutes of the Christian Religion*, 3.11.2 (pp. 726–7).

obtain, a life must be given for the life that is forfeit."[34] Penal substitution, in other words, obviates forgiveness because it is a system of *lex talionis*—as Jamieson argues "life for life."[35] God demands and gets the pound of flesh when Christ is hoisted on the cross. Atonement, and the justification it provides, is a legal transaction. Forgiveness is irrelevant within a court room. The key issue is being declared guilty or not guilty. The penal view of justice requires perfect obedience of the law and punishment for infraction of the law. Of course, the Gospel includes the forgiveness of sins. That is not in question, but whether or not the penal-substitutionary view of the atonement provides it within its understanding of the cross. The answer is "no." Forgiveness cannot derive from the cross in the penal view. The cross is penal payment for sin. Once payment is made, one is clear before the court. Sure, the sinner may feel bad for their sin, and seek release from their sense of guilt from the offended party. In this case, God may assure the person that wrath has been abated, but strictly speaking this assurance is not forgiveness because it has nothing to do with the penalty exacted for sin and judicial acquittal. From the perspective of the cross, there is neither guilt nor need for forgiveness because the judicial demands have been met. If the demands of justice have been met, no need for forgiveness exists. If a debt has been paid, then it does not need to be forgiven. This traditional view of the atonement posits a dialectical deity caught between divine justice and love.[36] God cannot simply forgive human sin because divine justice requires perfect law keeping and, in lieu of that, penal punishment. Although God's love is central too and motivates the Son to offer himself in Christ to pay the judicial price, a retributive theory of justice dominates this theology of atonement.[37] Because, moreover, it is a judicial system in which divine law is upheld and penalty paid, it has no forgiveness.

Second, what is the alternative to the penal theology of the cross and atonement? Placing the cross in the wider mission and work of the Spirit of Pentecost.[38] The

---

[34] R. B. Jamieson, *Jesus' Death and Heavenly Offerings in Hebrews*, Society for New Testament Studies Monograph Series, gen. ed. Edwards Adams, 172 (Cambridge: Cambridge University Press, 2019), 159. Jamieson, however, agrees with Moffit that the offering of his death as atonement for human sin takes place in heaven (19–20).

[35] Jamieson, *Jesus' Death and Heavenly Offerings in Hebrews*, 159.

[36] Adonis Vidu argues that a recognition of the doctrine of divine simplicity absolves this alleged conflict in the divine attributes. Divine simplicity means that the divine attributes are inseparable in God's actions. All divine actions reflect all the attributes. The "attributes" are only distinct in the discursive domain of theological discourse. A valid point. But then, rather than a conflict between love and justice, punishing the innocent Christ and vengeful wrath are not only consistent with but acts of love. Vidu states, "punishment is the form the holy love of God had to take, given the human condition of sin and liability to punishment." See Adonis Vidu, *Atonement, Law, and Justice: The Cross in Historical and Cultural Contexts* (Grand Rapids: BakerAcademic, 2014), 262 and 235–72. Thomas H. McCall earlier made a similar argument in *Forsaken: The Trinity and the Cross, and Why It Matters* (Downers Grove: IVP Academic, 2012), 73–86.

[37] For an unapologetic affirmation of the atonement as retributive justice, see Letham, *The Work of Christ*, 125–6. For a critique of retributive justice atonement theology, see Belousek, *Atonement, Justice, and Peace*, 24–58 and 434–60.

[38] Andrew Sung Park calls for the cross to be understood in the wider "context of [Christ's] entire work." He developed this idea on categories of trinitarian and liberation theology. See Park, *Triune Atonement: Christ's Healing for Sinners, Victims, and the Whole Creation* (Louisville: John Knox, 2009), x–xi. Hans Boersma also criticizes traditional Western atonement theology for an "inclination to de-historicize the cross." Boersma, *Violence, Hospitality, and the Cross*, 168.

particularity of Christ and the cross must be seen from the universal and perennial perspective of Pentecost. The Holy Spirit is the foundation of the universal and perennial human vocation to bear the divine image. What the Spirit was doing in and through the particular life of Christ reveals and fulfills the universal and perennial work of the Spirit. The mission of the Spirit of Pentecost, and thus also of Christ and the cross, begins with the Spirit of God's first stirring over the primal waters and the lifeless dirt in the Genesis creation stories. The Spirit of God creates a world of abundant life and breathes life into human beings to participate in the life of that world. The human vocation is to bear the Spirit-breathed divine image in all the dimensions of life in and for this world. This pneumatological purpose is fundamental to the narrative of redemption.

The work of the Holy Spirit in the life of Jesus Christ fulfills the pneumatological plot of human life. The penal view of the atonement makes suffering and death the apex of God's redemptive work. The primary work of redemption is penal death to pay for human sin. A pentecostal atonement theology frames Jesus' death on the cross in the wider narrative of the Spirit. The mission of the Spirit is to create a world of life and abundance: from Eden, where the Spirit animates human life so that it can flourish in relation with God, with each other, and with creation, to the Hebrew prophets where the Spirit of God renews the people and land and finally the new creation, where the Spirit raises the children of God to new life and "liberates creation from its bondage to decay" (Rom. 8:18-23). But sin and death are part of the narrative too. The Spirit animated human beings with the breath of life to flourish in relationship with God and with each other. Sin alienated people from that life. The result is death. The world is turned upside down. Human beings created for abundant life in Eden live in the parched reaches east of Eden. People are estranged from God and from each other. No longer naked, they live exposed and vulnerable before each other. It is a world where Cain murders Abel and crowds chant "crucify him!" (Mt. 27:11-26). Righteousness, life lived in fellowship with God and love toward others, becomes a threat. Righteousness is a spotlight that unveils the hypocrisies, corruptions, and double-dealings of the world. Christ's death on the cross makes sense in this stage of the history of redemption. He dies because he was faithful to God. The fallen condition of this world leads to the irony that Christ's fulfilling of Spirit-breathed life leads to the cross. Thus, Jesus' suffering and death are part of the mission of the Spirit of Pentecost to fulfill the nature and purpose of Spirit-breathed life. The next section provides a deeper account of the place of Christ's life and the cross in the mission of the Spirit of Pentecost.

Christ's Spirit-Breathed Life Fulfills Righteousness

The centrality of the cross in Christianity is paradoxical and ironic. On the cross, Jesus dies, but also fulfills his life as the Spirit-anointed messiah. What appears to be abject failure and denigrating death is the zenith of Christ fulfilling the human vocation to bear the Spirit-breathed divine image—to live in love and faithfulness toward God and all other human beings. Consideration of the cross necessarily requires thinking about

God's righteousness. The cross, atonement, righteousness, and the justice of God are inextricably bound. Jesus told John the Baptist that John must baptize him in order "to fulfill all righteousness" (Mt. 3:15). Immediately afterward, the Spirit of God descended upon Jesus, and God the Father pronounced his love and devotion to Jesus as the Son of God. What was the righteousness that Jesus Christ fulfilled as the Spirit-anointed messiah? Jesus' fulfillment of righteousness involves his life, death, and the Holy Spirit.

Matthew places Jesus in the context of his Israelite predecessors. Like Moses, he escapes politically inspired infanticide by hiding. He faces temptation in the desert and, unlike Israel, he remains faithful. Jesus, again paralleling Moses, ascends a mountainside and gives the people of Israel the laws of the kingdom of God. Jesus also stands in the line of promise and despair. He is the Son of Abraham and the Son of David, namesakes of the great covenants Yahweh made with his people. Fourteen generations separated Abraham from David and fourteen more David from the exile. Jesus comes fourteen generations after the exile to Babylon (Mt. 1:17). First-century Jews living in Palestine technically lived in the Promised Land. But they were not living the promise. They lived under occupation. The land of Israel was Rome's, not Israel's. They were exiles in their own homeland. Matthew's genealogy that connects Jesus with Abraham, David, and exile makes a point. The promise of Abraham and David was never fulfilled in the life of Israel. It ended in exile. Jesus, however, ends the exile by fulfilling "all righteousness." But how does he do it? He fulfills the promise of Israel and God's desires for creation because he is the Spirit-anointed messiah. Matthew transitions from Jesus' genealogy to his Spirit-breathed conception. The outpouring of the Spirit of God promised in Isaiah, Ezekiel, and Joel began in the womb of the Virgin Mary. God has come to dwell with his people. Immanuel is here (Mt. 1:18-23). The incarnate Son of God in Jesus Christ fulfills the Spirit-breathed purpose of human life. Chapter 2 on Pentecost showed that the gift of the Spirit of God was a defining feature of the eschatological expectation of Israel. As Jesus begins his public ministry, he receives the Spirit's anointing. That anointing finds fulfillment in his life, ministry, and death on the cross and finally in the outpouring of the Spirit of Pentecost. That is why John the Baptist declares that the coming messiah will "baptize you with the Holy Spirit" (Mt. 3:11). But before the outpouring of the Holy Spirit on "all people," Jesus fulfills "all righteousness" in his life and death (Mt. 3:14-16). The cross, atonement, and the righteousness and the justice of God are indissolubly bound. On the cross, God demonstrates justice. The death of Christ on the cross establishes the justice of God. But what kind of righteousness? A righteousness that is pneumatological and renewing.

First, Jesus manifests the justice and righteousness of God throughout his life and ministry because the Spirit of God is upon him. Jesus' healings of and compassion to people connect him to and demonstrate that he is the promised Spirit-anointed messiah. As the Spirit-anointed messiah, Jesus brings the anticipated hope of Israel—the outpouring of the Holy Spirit that will renew the people. Where his predecessors failed, Jesus succeeds. The outpouring of the Spirit of God, from Isaiah and Ezekiel to Joel, inaugurates the eschatological restoration of Israel and indeed the world. Jesus fulfills all righteousness by inaugurating this eschatological hope of renewal that would arise from the gift of God's Spirit. The Gospel of Matthew showcases the Spirit-anointed and righteous character of Jesus' life and work.

Matthew 12 consists of a sequence of dialogues and healings that identify Jesus Christ as the Spirit-anointed messiah who brings God's "justice to the nations" (Mt. 12:18). Matthew 12 links Jesus' work directly to the Spirit-anointed messiah of Isaiah.[39] The chapter opens with the Pharisees nit-picking with Jesus over Sabbath violations. The problem? His disciples dared to gather and eat heads of grain on the Sabbath. The next scene is in a synagogue. The Pharisees confront him with the question, "Is it lawful to heal on the Sabbath?" (Mt. 12:10). Jesus answers by healing a man with a "shriveled hand" (Mt. 12:9). Incredibly, the Pharisees turn to plot "how they might kill him" (Mt. 12:14). Jesus withdraws from the place, but he carries on healing the sick. At this point, Matthew says,

> this was to fulfill what was spoken through the prophet Isaiah: "Here is my servant whom I have chosen . . . I will put my Spirit on him and he will proclaim justice to the nations. . . . A bruised reed he will not break, and a smoldering wick he will not snuff out, till he leads justice to victory." (Mt. 12:17-20)

The story continues with the Pharisees confronting Jesus with a demon-possessed man who is blind and mute. Jesus heals him so that he can "talk and see" (Mt. 12:22). The people present ask, "Could this be the Son of David?" The Pharisees denounce Jesus and accuse him of healing by "Beelzebub, the prince of demons" (Mt. 12:23-24). Jesus retorts, "if I drive out demons by the Spirit of God, then the kingdom of God has come upon you" (Mt. 12:28). The answer to the people's question is yes, he is the Son of David, the Spirit-anointed messiah. How do we know? Because in the healing of the first man he saved the "bruised reed," and of the second man he rekindled the "smoldering wick." The passage shows him "proclaim[ing] justice to the nations . . . [and leading] justice to victory" (Mt. 12:18 and 20).

Matthew 12 highlights several vital elements about Jesus and his Spirit-anointed life and ministry. In terms of his perception of his relationship to the Holy Spirit, Jesus recognizes that his ministry derives from the presence of the Spirit of God. He declares, "if I drive out demons by the Spirit of God, then the kingdom of God has come upon you" (Mt. 12:28). Jesus heals these two people, thereby bringing justice to the nations, because "the Spirit [is] on him." The presence of the Holy Spirit is the foundation of Jesus' messianic identity and ministry. The story also indicates the type of justice Jesus brings—"I desire mercy, not sacrifice" (Mt. 12:7). Justice here is not the retributive and punitive justice that dominates Western atonement theology.

On the one hand, the focus of the atonement is not a dialectical tension between God's wrath and love toward human beings. The Spirit of atonement does not resolve a conflict in God. It fulfills God's dreams for the world God created. The narrative of the Spirit of Pentecost shows that atonement is the redemptive activity of God on behalf of creation. Classical theism's reliance on Platonic notions of perfection and aseity requires that everything that God does is about God and nothing in creation for fear of

---

[39] The Gospel of Luke does so as well. After self-identifying as the Spirit-anointed messiah of Isaiah in the synagogue, Jesus goes forth and frees a person tormented by an "evil spirit" and heals people suffering from various physical illnesses and infirmities (Lk. 4:31–5:26).

corrupting the immutability of the divine being. Applying this logic to the atonement means that the atonement is objective and for the purpose of demonstrating God's glory.[40] The result is a divine narcissist. Everything is always and ever about glorifying the divine ME, the divine Ego. The narrative of the Spirit of Pentecost, however, shows that atonement is the redemptive activity of God on behalf of creation. Indeed, Jesus taught and embodied that the nature of love is action on behalf of others—"Greater love has no one than this, that one lay down his life for his friends" (Jn 15:13). Love gives life. In creation, God's Spirit shares the divine life. Redemption is the story of God's Spirit to renew that shared life. The narrative of the Spirit of Pentecost is a love story. It is not a self-justifying and self-glorifying act of the divine Ego.

On the other hand, the justice of the Spirit-anointed Christ in Matthew 12 is the healing power that restores broken lives. It is also the courage that unmasks the hypocrisy and pretension of religious and cultural elites claiming to be on the side of the angels. Atonement, God bringing justice to the nations and to the lives of people, is holistic and material. It takes that which is broken and marginalized and heals and restores it. Western atonement theology has more in common with the carping Pharisees than Jesus in Matthew 12. They imagine that God is like them—draconian moral and religious bean counters.[41] More concerned with their straitjacket religious system that serves more to ensconce their cultural and political privileges than to improve the lot of their "lessers." Jesus shows that the purpose of the Sabbath, and therefore what God really cares about, is not fastidious rules but wholeness of life for human beings. Jesus cares about the justice and the righteousness of God that restores human life to its Spirit-breathed purpose. Thus, Jesus says to the Pharisees in the same story in Mark, "The Sabbath was made for man, not man for the Sabbath" (Mk 2:27). Jesus keeps the Sabbath, and displays that he is the Spirit-anointed messiah, the Son of David, by healing first a man with a shriveled hand and second a man blind and mute and possessed by a demon. In doing so, he was fulfilling "all righteousness" (Mt. 3:15).[42] His acts of restoring these two men were ways that he brought divine justice and the kingdom of God. They were ways that Jesus brought the Sabbath rest and restored goodness to creation (cf. Gen. 1:31–2:3). They were moments of atonement.

---

[40] For example, Anselm's satisfaction theory is distinct from the penal-substitutionary view that became popular in Protestant forms of Christianity. In his rehabilitation of Anselm's theory of the atonement that posits God's purposes for creation as the cause of atonement, Peter Schmiechen nonetheless argues that the world and human beings as such are not the "final end of atonement," but "revealing the glory of God." See Peter Schmiechen, *Saving Power: Theories of Atonement and Forms of the Church* (Grand Rapids: Eerdmans, 2005), 220. Thus, resolving an inner conflict between justice and mercy is a characteristic of objective theories, whether satisfaction or penal. For the distinction of Anselm's notion of satisfaction from the penal view, see Colin E. Gunton, *The Actuality of the Atonement: A Study of Metaphor, Rationality, and the Christian Tradition* (Grand Rapids: Eerdmans, 1989), 90–1.

[41] Darrin Belousek argues that Western atonement theologies assume that God acts according to "the common human understanding . . . that justice is based on the law of retribution." See Belousek, *Atonement, Justice, and Peace*, 434.

[42] For an excellent and succinct account of the way Jesus fulfills "all righteousness" throughout his life and death, see Marilyn McCord Adams, "12th January: The Baptism of the Lord. Matthew 3:13-17. Fulfilling all Righteousness," *The Expository Times* 125, no. 3 (2013): 127–9.

Second, a direct link exists between the righteousness that Jesus brings by the power of the Holy Spirit and his death. Because he is the Spirit-anointed messiah and the embodiment of divine justice, he is killed. After declaring himself "Lord of the Sabbath" and demonstrating that claim by bringing God's justice in the healing of "a man with a shriveled hand," "the Pharisees went out and plotted how they might kill Jesus" (Mt. 12:8, 10, and 14). His crucifixion, however, is not God the Father bringing down the gavel of justice on his Son. It is the zenith of Christ fulfilling the human vocation to bear the Spirit-breathed divine image, to live in love and faithfulness toward God and all other human beings. The Spirit enables Jesus to embody the fullness of the divine image—to fulfill "all righteousness." Because Christ is righteous, he becomes the object of hate, persecution, and finally political murder.

Although my focus here has been the Gospel of Matthew, the Apostle Paul affirms a similar theology of Jesus' life and death as the fulfillment of righteousness. In Romans, Paul proclaims that in Jesus Christ "a righteousness from God is revealed" (Rom. 1:17). Paul's emphasis at this point is the righteousness of Jesus Christ received in faith. But what is the nature of the righteousness of Christ? His life of devotion to God the Father that never strayed into sin and the eternal life that arises from it. Paul clarifies that "just as sin reigned in death, so also grace might reign through righteousness to bring eternal life through Jesus Christ our Lord" (Rom. 5:21). What was the righteousness that overcame sin and brought the grace of eternal life? Christ's life of obedience to God the Father. He refused to betray his devotion to God the Father even to the point of death. Sin did not reign in Christ, so death did not either. Indeed, his death was his final act of dying to sin (Rom. 6:10). Christ died to sin, so death died in him. Conversely, his death to sin was his life lived in devotion to God the Father. As Paul indicates, "the life he lives, he lives to God" (Rom. 6:10). How did Jesus die to sin and "live to God" (Rom. 6:10)? He lived according to the "law of the Spirit of life" that frees "from the law of sin and death" (Rom. 8:2). Since righteousness, not sin, reigned in Christ, "death no longer has mastery over him" (Rom. 6:9).

Third, Jesus Christ fulfilled righteousness by fully embodying the purpose and nature of Spirit-breathed life.[43] The paradox of the life of Jesus Christ is that his death on the cross signals his final victory over the death of sin; so, in death, Christ fulfills righteousness. Christ was "tempted in every way, just as we are—yet was without sin" (Heb. 4:14-15). He did not know "death" in the first way Adam experienced it. God told Adam that if he ate from the "tree of the knowledge of good and evil," he would "die" (Gen. 2:17). Adam's first taste of death was the shame of nakedness. The consciousness of alienation first from Eve and then from God because of sin. Adam knew what it means to live in fear. The fear that robs life of its safety and protection. The absolute experience of that "death" is the return to the dust when the Spirit no longer contends with human beings (Gen. 6:3). The Cain and Abel story shows that human beings are not mere victims and passive recipients but purveyors of death. The experience of "death"—alienation, envy, fear, bitterness—makes them dealers of death. The paradox for Adam and Eve is that while the Spirit continued to animate

---

[43] In a similar, but Christocentric, way, Belousek affirms that Christ fulfills righteousness and justice on the cross through covenant faithfulness (Belousek, *Atonement, Justice, and Peace*, 369–71).

their life, they were alienated from God. They lived according to what Paul calls "flesh" or the sinful nature, and what the Gospel of John calls the "world" (Rom. 8:5-11 and Jn 3:16). Jesus, however, was an Eden person living outside the Garden. He was "naked." He had no shame before God and other human beings. And yet, he lived east of Eden. He lived among people estranged from each other and their God and from the world God created for them. He lived with people trying to cover their shame and sin with whatever lay at hand—avarice, pride, position, power, religious ritual, self-righteousness. He lived among the dealers of death, the final trump card in the game of hiding shame and nakedness. As Paul S. Fiddes puts it, in Christ "God has never gone further . . . into the far country of our estrangement and despair."[44] Jesus entered into the world east of Eden in order to redeem it from death and fulfill "all righteousness." He did so in two ways.

On the one hand, he retained the integrity of his Spirit-breathed life even to death on the cross. On the cross, Jesus fulfills humanity's vocation to live in love and righteous relationship with God and other human beings. In doing so, Christ atones for human sin. Christ did what human beings could not do. In short, Jesus fulfills the pneumatological purpose of human life. The Spirit that breathed life into the dirt of Gen. 2:7 brings about the incarnate life of Jesus Christ, leads Jesus into the desert to undergo satanic trials, and sustains him in his faithfulness to the Father that culminates in agonizing death on the cross. Jesus remains faithful to the Father to the point of cruel suffering and death on the cross, and thereby fulfills humanity's vocation to image God. Hebrews indicates that "he learned obedience from what he suffered and once made perfect, he became the source of eternal salvation for all who obey him" (Heb. 5:8-9; cf. 2:10). In fulfilling the human vocation to bear the divine image, Christ's suffering and death on the cross is not punitive and penal, but eschatological. The cross is eschatological not because it brings the work of redemption to a sudden halt. But because the story of the Spirit that began in creation (e.g., Gen 2:7) reaches a pinnacle in the particular life of Christ—the presence of the Spirit-enabled Jesus Christ to "fulfill all righteousness" (Mt. 3:14-16). In Christ, the Spirit animated dirt embodied the fullness of the divine image. The Apostle Paul declares, "because through Christ Jesus the law of the Spirit of life set me free from the law of sin and death" (Rom. 8:2). Jesus "condemned sin in sinful man" by living in the righteousness of "the Spirit of life" (Rom. 8:2-3). He did this not primarily for a penal purpose, but so that people could once again live "according to the Spirit," just as he did and for which they were originally created (Rom. 8:2-4). For a pentecostal theology of the atonement, the justice of the cross resides in the renewal of life promised in Christ's fulfillment of the human vocation to bear the Spirit-breathed image of God.[45]

On the other hand, Jesus redeems human beings from their death by passing through the veil of death. On the cross, Jesus shares the nakedness and the shame of

---

[44] Fiddes, *Past Event and Present Salvation*, 109.
[45] From an ecumenical perspective, the pentecostal approach to the cross and atonement developed here shares affinities with the reading of Pauline atonement theology and justification as covenant faithfulness, new exodus, and fulfilling the human vocation to worship God proposed by N. T. Wright in *The Day the Revolution Began: Reconsidering the Meaning of Jesus' Crucifixion* (New York: HarperOne, 2016).

Adam and Eve and all their descendants. Unlike them, he cannot run and hide from God. God provides no animal skins for Christ on the cross. Even worse than Adam and Eve hiding from God in the Garden, Jesus is abandoned by God the Father. Jesus cries from the cross, "my God, my God, why have you forsaken me?" So, Jesus dies a shameful and solitary death to make his solidarity with human beings complete. He descends to the darkest depth of human despair—death, the absolute denouement of human life—without caving to the temptation to retaliate in kind. Christ shared the human condition of death and dejection so that he could "free those who all their lives were held in slavery by their fear of death" (Heb. 2:14-15). Jesus experiences death in order to redeem human beings from the fundamental condition of their lives as post-Eden people. "[H]e suffered death, so that by the grace of God he might taste death for everyone" (Heb. 2:9). Orthodox theologian Peter Bouteneff, quoting St. Basil the Great, puts it well, "'He gave himself as a ransom to *death*,' so that Christ's death makes 'a path to the resurrection of the dead.'"[46] As Paul affirms, "God demonstrates his own love for us in this: While we were still sinners, Christ died for us" (Rom. 5:8). God enters into the human condition of death. Not only the physical cessation of life, but the death of alienation from God, other people, and life in this world. Created for nakedness with each other, people vainly reach to protect their exposure from others with fig leaves and animal skins. So, Christ experiences the viciousness of human vitriol, when his people trade him for a criminal and clamor for his crucifixion. He descends into the darkest regions of human desolation in the experience of God-forsakenness on the cross, where he feels utterly abandoned by God the Father (Mt. 27:46 and Mk 15:34). The power of love revealed in the cross is that God in Christ endured the human tragedy in order to redeem people from it even while they are the source of his suffering.[47] But the suffering of God extends beyond, or "before," the cross. God suffers the Fall of creation.[48] Seeing creation abdicate and rebel against the gift of Spirit-breathed life is the genesis of God's suffering. That suffering reaches its nadir on the cross when God in Christ "with a loud cry . . . breathed his last" (Mk 15:37 and Lk. 23:46).

The key difference between Adam's and Christ's experience of death is that the Spirit of God does not leave Christ when he dies. The heirs of Adam, although still receiving life by the Spirit of God, live under the shadow of death all their days. When they finally pass through death, they stay dead. They are separated from the life of the Spirit. Their return to the dust is but the definitive experience of their "painful toil" by "the sweat of [their] brow" amid the "thorns and thistles" of life (Gen. 3:17-19). They live under the curse of death in the world outside the Garden. Death is the final and absolute experience of exile from Eden, from the life for which God created human beings. Death, in the Hebrew Bible, marks the loss of the breath of life (Gen. 6:3, 7:22-23 and Ps. 104:29). The Spirit of God ceases animating life and the human being returns to the

---

[46] Peter Bouteneff, "Christ and Salvation," in *The Cambridge Companion to Orthodox Theology*, ed. Mary B. Cunningham and Elizabeth Theokritoff (New York: Cambridge University Press, 2008), 98 (emphasis in original).

[47] Fiddes makes a similar argument in *Past Event and Present Salvation*, 157.

[48] "Before" is placed in quotes, to recognize that a common view is that God is timeless and simple, which means that God does not have a temporal experience. For this view and its implications for atonement, see Vidu, *Atonement, Law, and Justice*.

dust. That did not happen with Jesus Christ. Even on the cross, the Spirit of God never left Jesus, but Jesus "through the eternal Spirit offered himself unblemished to God" (Heb. 9:14). He died, but the Holy Spirit reinvigorated his life and raised him from the dead (1 Pet. 3:18). As Daniela C. Augustine highlights, in death and resurrection, Christ's hands take hold of Adam and Eve's and all their children's and so "his life becomes their life—the life for which they were created."[49] Jesus' experience of death and resurrection is the climax of his ministry of bringing the kingdom of God in the power of the Holy Spirit. Because Jesus lived according to the Spirit of life even unto death he fulfilled "all righteousness."

The Cross, Substitution, and Participation

That "Christ died for us" on the cross is fundamental to Christianity (Rom. 5:8). Christ substituted his life for ours. He died vicariously in our place. Classical Protestant theology emphasizes the substitutionary nature of Christ's death on the cross. That is not a problem as such. The problem is that crucicentric penal-substitutionary atonement theology abstracts the cross from the majority of Jesus' life and ministry.[50] Bruce Demarest argues that "Christ's example, teachings, and miracles must not be neglected by the inquirer into truth; but his atoning death is absolutely crucial. Scripture portrays the Savior's death as the basis of every spiritual blessing."[51] Really!? Nothing else that Christ did, never mind the Holy Spirit at this point, is the "basis" of Christian grace? His teachings that instruct on life in the kingdom of God, his healings that herald the kingdom of God, his ministry to the broken and marginalized have nothing to do with the atonement? Why does Demarest place everything on the cross? Because the essence of salvation consists in a legal pardon from sin and imputation of Christ's righteousness. One might object that Christ's life of perfect obedience is part of atonement. True. But it too relates to the judicial paradigm of penal-substitutionary atonement. God demands both moral perfection and punishment for human sin. Christ's moral perfection makes him a fitting penal substitute.

Penal-substitutionary atonement often uses the concepts of active and passive obedience to describe the relationship between Jesus' life and death. His life of faithfulness to God's law was his active obedience. His suffering and death on the cross to pay the penalty for human sin was his passive obedience. Although both his life and death relate to the fundamental judicial vision of God, they do so in different ways. His life satisfies God's need for perfect obedience. His death appeases God's need to punish lawbreakers. My point is that Jesus' death on the cross stands in continuity with his entire life. His death on the cross was not a passive act. The cross is Jesus' final act of

---

[49] Daniela C. Augustine, *The Spirit and the Common Good: Shard Flourishing in the Image of God* (Grand Rapids: Eerdmans, 2019), 177.

[50] I am not the first to note this tendency. E.g., see Dunning, *Grace, Faith, and Holiness*, 306 and Vladimir Lossky, *In the Image and Likeness of God* (1974; reprint, Oxford: A. R. Mowbray/Alden Press, 1975), 98–9; note also that Lossky critiques Western substitutionary atonement theology for making the Holy Spirit an "auxiliary" and "deputy of the Son" (see pp. 99 and 103).

[51] Demarest, *The Cross and Salvation*, 167.

faithful Spirit-breathed life. In penal substitution, however, Christ's work of atonement, whether his perfect obedience or penal suffering, is entirely taken up with appeasing the holiness and wrath of God. It is, moreover, objective, which means that it has nothing to do with the transformative experience of grace and participating in Christ's righteousness. Following Jesus' teachings and moral example relate to sanctification and the subjective aspect of grace, which is never the fulcrum of saving grace in the legal view of atonement. Following Jesus and being holy does not save anyone. That would be works righteousness. His obedience to God's law and penal death on the cross are all that matter for the atonement. This theology, in other words, empties the rest of Jesus' life and the Holy Spirit's work in it of significance for the atonement.

The argument here is that Christ's entire Spirit-breathed life, from conception to cross (and resurrection and ascension), is the work of atonement. Here a pentecostal theology of atonement agrees with Eastern Orthodoxy. As Peter Bouteneff maintains, Western substitutionary atonement theories "so stressed the sacrificial death of the Cross that they undermined the comprehensive work of God in Christ and the Spirit for the salvation of the world."[52] The cross stands in continuity with the entirety of Jesus' life and the Christian experience of redemption. The continuity moreover is not simply to qualify Jesus as the perfect penal sacrifice. Christ's whole life was cross bearing. The cross is Jesus' final act of faithful Spirit-breathed life. The problem with penal substitution is twofold: it is overly crucicentric and extrinsic. A pentecostal atonement theology is substitutionary and participatory. Substitutionary in the sense that Christ did through "the law of the Spirit of life" (Rom. 8:2) what human beings on their own could not. Participatory in the sense that he did it so that all people can participate in that death to sin and in that life lived in fellowship with God—that is precisely Paul's point in Rom. 8:1-4.[53] That life, moreover, includes the whole life of Christ, not only the cross. The purpose of Christ's life and ministry, which reaches its zenith on the cross, is not forensic and extrinsic. Christ died for us and, in that sense, the cross is objective. But Christ embodied Spirit-breathed life so that others could as well by receiving the Spirit of Pentecost. Christ becomes what we are so that we can become like him.[54] What is the path from a crucicentric to a wholistic pentecostal theology of atonement? Two steps: show that Christ's entire life is substitutionary and frame that substitution in terms of pneumatology.

First, the entirety of Jesus' Spirit-breathed life, which reaches its full display on the cross, is substitutionary. Philippians 2 places the Incarnation and the cross on a continuum. The kenosis (self-emptying) of the Son of God in Christ includes his Incarnation, life, and death on the cross. The Son, who was "in very nature God," was made "in human likeness," and was "found in appearance as a man" (Phil. 2:6-8). The

---

[52] Bouteneff, "Christ and Salvation," 98. Although my method of interpreting Christ and cross in terms of Pentecost reverses the direction of Orthodox theology.

[53] Paul S. Fiddes also recognizes that since union with Christ is central to Paul's theology of atonement, the latter includes "our sharing in Christ's own life of obedience before the Father." See Fiddes, *Past Event and Present Salvation*, 99.

[54] This point corresponds to a primary emphasis in Eastern Orthodox and patristic (i.e., Athanasius) soteriology and Christology. See Bouteneff, "Christ and Salvation," 104 and John Meyendorff, *Byzantine Theology: Historical Trends and Doctrinal Themes*, 2nd ed. (New York: Fordham University Press, 1979), 160 and 164.

Son of God in Christ came not to dazzle the world with displays of grandiosity but to be a humble "servant" and to be "obedient" to the Father "to death—even death on a cross" (Phil. 2:7-8). Paul presents Christ's incarnate life and eventual death as a continuum. They are not separate redemptive elements in an *ordo salutis*. As Susan Wood notes, "[t]he self-emptying begun in the incarnation reaches its consummation on the cross. These events represent the alpha and omega of the same continuum."[55] Paul sees the self-emptying of the Son in the Incarnation and his death on the cross as a whole. But does following Christ in self-abnegation legitimize victimhood and acquiescence to exploitation? No, because no one forced Christ to be a servant. He "humbled himself" in order to redeem people from their bondage to sin (Phil. 2:8). Indeed, using the servanthood and the self-sacrifice of Christ to condone oppression of any sort subverts Paul's essential point. Christ, who was God, used power for the benefit of others and not for selfish interest. Tyranny, however and wherever encountered, uses power and position for self-aggrandizement. But God does not.[56] As the Spirit-anointed messiah, Jesus touched lepers, healed the infirm, and befriended people society regarded as contemptible. Jesus healed the "bruised reed" and sheltered the "smoldering wick" because the Spirit of God was on him to "bring justice to the nations" (Isa. 42:1-4; cf. Mt. 12:18-21). Christ's death on the cross was the final and most vivid renunciation of the way the world uses power. As Wonhee Anne Joh argues, the cross was a "resistance against suffering and the structures of oppression."[57] The cross was not the divinization of the brutality of the world. Christ subjected himself to humiliation, torture, and death for the sake of others. The world uses power to emasculate, degrade, and destroy, and to preserve pride, position, and power. Christ's death on the cross was the final and definitive way he lived his life in faithfulness to God the Father. Again, as Joh, drawing on the theology of Leonardo Boff, argues, the suffering on the cross is "only redemptive when it is the result of struggle against suffering itself."[58] From a pneumatological perspective, the atonement is not about penal punishment and pardon. Atonement solves the fundamental human problem of alienation from Spirit-breathed life. Jesus fulfills the pneumatological purpose of human life. His death on the cross was his last and most absolute act of faithfulness to God the Father. Jesus' life, therefore, is vicarious.

Second, a pentecostal theology of the cross retains a substitutionary dimension of atonement but frames it pneumatologically. Hebrews describes Jesus taking on the vulnerabilities of human life in all its dimensions, from temptations to suffering and death. Because he did so, he can serve as the "merciful and faithful high priest . . . and . . . make atonement for the sins of his people" (Heb. 2:17). Christ's priestly service, however, is not retributive, but restorative. As Christopher D. Marshall points out, the

---

[55] Susan Wood, "Is Philippians 2:5-11 Incompatible with Feminist Concerns?" *Pro Ecclesia* 6, no. 2 (1997): 175.
[56] For a detailed account of the history of interpretation of Phil. 2:5-11, see N. T. Wright, "Earpagmos and the Meaning of Philippians 2:5-11," *The Journal of Theological Studies* 37, no. 2 (1986): 321–52, esp. 344–7 for Wright's view and that reflected in my argument.
[57] Wonhee Anne Joh, *Heart of the Cross: A postcolonial Christology* (Louisville: Westminster John Knox, 2006), 84.
[58] Joh, *Heart of the Cross*, 79.

righteousness of God revealed in the gospel is "God's work of justice-making."[59] He endures the weaknesses of "flesh and blood" to destroy the power of death, to restore people to the "family" of God, and to make them "holy" (Heb. 2:11-18). He becomes what human beings are in order to help them become what he is. Jesus was tempted but did not sin (Heb. 4:15). He died but rose again (Heb. 4:14). He empathetically intercedes on behalf of human beings because he knows the intensity of their struggle with temptation and the torment of death. In this sense, Jesus' life is substitutionary. But it was substitutionary for the sake of participation. To use traditional Western atonement terms and concepts, his "objective" life was for the purpose of helping human beings with their "subjective" sin. Hebrews recognizes a distinction between Christ's priestly service of offering his life (objective) and the renewal of grace (subjective). But the purpose of Christ's atonement is to make "men holy" and "free those who all their lives were held in slavery by their fear of death" (Heb. 2:11 and 15). Although the passage in Hebrews 2 does not reference the Holy Spirit's role in Christ's priestly service of identifying with those he considers his brothers and sisters, Heb. 9:14 does.[60] There the Holy Spirit is the source of Christ's life of impeccable holiness, resurrection, and ascent to priestly service before God. Vital to his service as priest and thus the atonement he provides is sharing his Spirit-empowered victory over sin and death with all those who become part of his family (Heb. 9:14 and 2:11-13). Jesus' blood of atonement purifies the human heart in Hebrews. Indeed, the interior sanctifying work of Christ's blood contrasts with the blood of "goats and bulls" (Heb. 9:13). The latter do nothing beyond symbolize external purification. Christ's blood, however, can "cleanse our consciences from acts that lead to death, so that we may serve the living God" (Heb. 9:14). In other words, the atonement offered by Christ is participation in the "unblemished" life and resurrection to new life and service before God that he achieved through the "eternal Spirit" (Heb. 9:14). Inclusion in the family of God and becoming children of God with the Son and the transformation of life through the Holy Spirit is the purpose of Christ's Spirit-anointed substitutionary life and the nature of atonement.

Sacrifice, Death, and Solidarity

Christ's death on the cross was a sacrifice for sin (Rom. 3:25). The purpose of sacrifice is to effect atonement. Sacrifices for sin (sin offerings) remove guilt, reconcile estranged parties, and release from judgment or consequence of sin.[61] The penal view of atonement affirms that God the Father sends the Son to bear the penalty of human sin. His substitutionary death propitiates (assuages) God the Father's wrath toward sinful human beings.[62] But, did God the Father demand and take satisfaction in the death of Christ as a propitiation for human sin? No. Christ's death, as a sacrifice for

---

[59] Christopher D. Marshall, *Beyond Retribution: A New Testament Vision for Justice, Crime, and Punishment*, Studies in Peace and Scripture (Grand Rapids: Eerdmans, 2001), 42 and 45–53.
[60] See Chapter 5 for the role of the Holy Spirit in the resurrection of Christ and the atonement in Hebrews 9:14.
[61] Fiddes, *Past Event and Present Salvation*, 64.
[62] Demarest, *The Cross and Salvation*, 172–4.

sin, is better understood in terms of expiation. God is not the object that receives the sacrifice of Christ on the cross. God is the agent that makes the sacrifice and effects the release from guilt and sin and reconciles estranged human persons.[63] This final section outlines a pentecostal way of understanding Christ's death as a sacrifice of atonement.

First, sacrifice was common in the ancient Near East. In that respect, Israel's sacrificial system was not unique. If the sacrifice of penal substitution is the "only means possible" for understanding Christian atonement, then that means that the religious practices of the ancient Near East were fundamentally correct.[64] Their errors lie in things such as their polytheism, idols, and sexual-fertility role-playing, but not in their basic way of understanding how to relate to God and what God requires. Bruce Demarest, for example, prefers the meaning of propitiation (*hilasterion*) used in the wider Greek world for understanding its application to Christ's atoning work.[65] Jesus and the Bible clearly spoke in language intelligible to their audiences. But they also offer something transformative. Jesus warned of trying to put the new wine in old wineskins (Mt. 9:17). Was Jesus just a new and improved, bigger and better sacrifice? It seems odd to reduce the story of Jesus Christ to a culmination of ancient Near Eastern sacrifice rituals.

Second, sacrifice seems to be God's concession to, not ideal for, the people of Israel. The prophet Hosea declares, "For I desire mercy, not sacrifice, and acknowledgment of God rather than burnt offerings" (Hos. 6:6). The Pharisees, assuming a penal view of God, object to Christ consorting with "tax collectors and 'sinners'" (Mt. 9:11). The holiness of a penal God cannot abide the presence of sinners, much less consorting with them in familiar and personal ways as Jesus did. But Jesus expresses a different view of holiness. He counsels the Pharisees to "learn" the meaning of "I desire mercy, not sacrifice" (Mt. 9:13). The Pharisees' demand for exacting and retributive justice diverges sharply from the mercy, compassion, and justice of the kingdom of God that Jesus Christ brings in the power of the Holy Spirit (Mt. 12:7 and 28). Jesus refuses to be forced into the Pharisees draconian moral legalism that requires judicial accounting and punitive action for any and every misdeed. Richard Rohr maintains that demanding sacrifice makes God like vindictive human beings.[66] Humans demand retribution. But on the cross, Christ asks the Father to forgive (Lk. 23:34). So, Christ's death as a sacrifice is not a propitiation offered to God to ameliorate divine wrath and thereby facilitate reconciliation.

Third, Jesus, as the Spirit-anointed messiah of God's coming kingdom, offers an alternative way of reconciling to God. The promise of eschatological renewal offered something new. The Spirit-anointed Christ was that new thing. But penal-substitutionary atonement theologies carry on the old way. They assume the commonplace expectation of retributive justice. A pentecostal theology of the atonement, however, if not fully embracing, sympathizes with Eastern Orthodox theologian Peter Bouteneff's conclusion that "Orthodox theology renounces not

---

[63] Fiddes, *Past Event and Present Salvation*, 71.
[64] Demarest, *The Cross and Salvation*, 188.
[65] Demarest, *The Cross and Salvation*, 179.
[66] Richard Rohr, "The Franciscan Option," in *Stricken by God? Nonviolent Identification and the Victory of Christ*, ed. Brad Jersak and Michael Hardin (Grand Rapids: Eerdmans, 2007), 207.

only their distortions but their foundational principle that the sacrifice of the Son is in any way demanded by the Father."[67] But then why does Jesus die? Paul S. Fiddes suggests that "when the judgment of God is understood as his personal consent to the natural outworking of people's estrangement from God and from each other, then we can think of Christ as participating in our experience of being 'accursed' without any suggestion that the Father is punishing the Son on our behalf."[68] Fiddes' point can leave the impression that Christ's death was happenstance; the general result of living under the human condition. But Christ's death is the consequence of his fulfillment of Spirit-breathed life. Christ fulfills righteousness by fulfilling the human vocation to embody the Spirit-breathed divine image. The Spirit's work in humanity that began in Gen. 2:7 finds its completion in the life of Jesus Christ. Christ fulfills righteousness on the cross, but he does not pay a penal price. Jesus Christ's death on the cross is the inevitable consequence of being the manifestation of God's righteousness and justice. Not a penal sort of justice, but a justice that sides with the marginalized and unmasks the conceit of the oppressors and victimizers. Christ is crucified because victimization, exploitation, and brutalization are the predictable outcomes when the righteous confront social, ethnic, and religious bigotries and establishment powers.[69] Refusing recourse to the vindictive violence of those he came to save, Jesus inevitably succumbs to their hands. God the Father takes no pleasure in Christ's death as such. God the Father accepts the death of Christ as the inevitable consequence of his Son embodying a Spirit-empowered life of righteousness (Acts 2:23 and 3:18). Christ offers his Spirit-breathed life as a sacrifice that expiates or removes both the reality and the guilt of sin, and thereby reconciles humanity to God. His cruciform life and crucifixion are substitutionary. But they are not simply a legal proxy. Christ lived in faithfulness to God and suffered the abuse and eventual martyrdom because of it so that he could offer that life to all people. Christ's atoning work becomes effective (expiates and reconciles) when, through the Spirit of Pentecost, people are engrafted into his cruciform life.

Fourth and following from the previous point, because Christ was the Spirit-anointed messiah, he dies because of human sin. Saying that Jesus died because of human sin strikes a discordant note in the ears of people conditioned by the therapeutic nature of Western culture. Westerners are shocked by the idea that God requires a penal payment for sin. Most people do not regard other people, let alone themselves, as sinners. We are basically good. Any aberration of human behavior is the result of mental illness or economic and political inequality. The problems human beings face

---

[67] Bouteneff, "Christ and Salvation," 98. Vladimir Lossky also gives unsparing critique of Western substitutionary atonement in *In the Image and Likeness of God*, 98–103. Although not renouncing substitutionary atonement theologies, John Meyendorff maintains that the Eastern tradition never developed them and, in contrast, emphasized God becoming incarnate to redeem the human condition from sin and death. See Meyendorff, *Byzantine Theology*, 160. In a similar tone and line of thought with Meyendorff's is Stephen Thomas' in *Deification in the Eastern Orthodox Tradition: A Biblical Perspective*, Gorgias Eastern Christian Studies, 2 (Piscataway: Gorgias, 2007), 22–3.

[68] Fiddes, *Past Event and Present Salvation*, 104.

[69] For similar accounts of the reason for Jesus' death, see Marshall, *Beyond Retribution*, 57; Donald Senior, *Why the Cross? Reframing New Testament Theology*, ed. Joel B. Green (Nashville: Abingdon, 2014), 32; and Michael M. Winter, *The Atonement*, Problems in Theology (Collegeville: Liturgical, 1995), 116–27.

can be ameliorated with the appropriate psychoactive prescription and enlightened social programs. The human problem is not sin. The contemporary revulsion to God's wrath toward human sin and the optimistic outlook on the human condition derives from self-delusion. We are insufficiently acquainted with our capacity for and practice of evil. We are dishonest. The horror of the Holocaust, for example, is not that those who perpetrated it or pretended to ignore it were insane monsters, but that they were ordinary people. No, the terrifying nature of the death camps is not their monstrosity but their banality—they functioned like any other industrial machine, except that they turned out corpses and ashes.[70] Although condemning the bombing of cities with the intent of inflicting civilian casualties when carried out by the Japanese and Germans, the American and British air forces would later reduce Japanese and German cities to vast funeral pyres with the intentional use of incendiary bombs. Commander of U.S. air forces against Japan Curtis LeMay described the deaths of 80,000 to 100,000 Japanese civilians in the March 9–10, 1945, firebombing of Tokyo as "scorched and boiled and baked to death."[71] Niall Fergusson provides statistics that between 167 and 188 million people died in the twentieth century due to organized human violence.[72] That does not happen because people are basically good or are just disgruntled by inequities in income distribution. Figures like those show that human evil is pervasive in scope and scale. Something is profoundly wrong with people. The Adam and Eve and Cain and Abel stories illustrate the human predicament. Humans accelerate from snatching the innocuous fruit from the tree of knowledge of good and evil to fratricide. Whatever one thinks about the historical accuracy of the Genesis creation stories, its portrayal of the human propensity for betrayal and violence is correct.[73] The Bible calls the problem sin. Given the depth and breadth of human sin, God cannot simply wish it away with fairy dust, give it a wink and a nod, and a tongue-in-check smile of forgiveness. That would be injustice. Whatever problems the penal-substitutionary view possesses, it gets the gravity of human sin correct and the cross deals with it. Its chief problem is to construe the remedy in terms of penal payment. The result is that the atonement, the chief work of Christ on the cross according to penal substitution, does nothing to deal with the fundamental problem of sin—the broken human condition.[74] As Paul S. Fiddes remarks, for a theology that allegedly "'takes sin seriously' . . . we would expect . . . that God would want to root sin out of the lives it infests."[75] Proponents of the penal view will no doubt object that sanctification heals the sinful human heart. True, but it has nothing to do with atonement.

---

[70] Daniel Jonah Goldhagen, *Hitler's Willing Executioners: Ordinary Germans and the Holocaust* (1996; reprint, New York: Vintage, 1997).
[71] John W. Dower, *War without Mercy: Race and Power in the Pacific War* (New York: Pantheon, 1986), 40–1 and 38–9.
[72] Niall Ferguson, *The War of the World: Twentieth-Century Conflict and the Descent of the West* (New York: Penguin, 2006), 649.
[73] Steven A. LeBlanc, with Katherine E. Register, *Constant Battles: Why We Fight* (New York: St. Martin's, 2004) and David Livingstone Smith, *The Most Dangerous Animal: Human Nature and the Origins of War* (New York: St. Martin's, 2007).
[74] Fiddes makes a similar point in *Past Event and Present Salvation*, 100–1.
[75] Fiddes, *Past Event and Present Salvation*, 101.

In the end, the death of Christ atones for human failure only when seen in the larger frame of resurrection and Pentecost. God chose to become a victim and to suffer *with* all those who suffer and from the depths of agony, despair, and death to bring new life. The life of Christ that ends on the cross cannot be isolated from his resurrection and the outpouring of the Spirit of Pentecost that makes the Spirit-breathed life of Christ available to all people, which are the subjects of the next two chapters. Any sense of satisfaction that the Father has in the death of Jesus Christ arises from Christ fulfilling the human vocation to bear the Spirit-breathed divine image even in the face of death and from the promise of the Spirit of Pentecost to give that life a universal horizon.

Conclusion

This chapter developed a pentecostal theology of the cross. Pneumatology usually has little to no role in traditional atonement theologies. Taking the Spirit of Pentecost as a point of orientation suggests that the cross is the culmination of Jesus Christ's Spirit-breathed life. The cross, therefore, is part of the wider mission of the Spirit of Pentecost. Although critiquing traditional Western atonement theologies at certain points, this chapter also provided a pentecostal rereading of key areas of atonement theology such as the substitutionary nature and the meaning of Jesus' death. This chapter provided the Spirit Christological categories of atonement that set the stage for the Spirit of Pentecost's participatory theology of the cross (Chapter 9). Christ fulfilled the Spirit-breathed divine image on the cross and the Spirit of Pentecost shares that fulfillment potentially with all people.

5

Resurrection

The resurrection is a key element of a pentecostal theology of the atonement that correlates with the holistic, transformative, and pneumatological character of pentecostal praxis (see Chapter 10). The resurrection takes part in a larger narrative of the Spirit that includes Incarnation and cross. Renewal and new life in Christ—correspondents with resurrection—are crucial to pentecostal praxis. The resurrection, however, is not central to most Western atonement theologies. Atonement theologies overwhelmingly focus on Christ's death on the cross.[1] The predominance of penal-substitutionary themes in Protestant theology in general and pentecostal theology in particular too often reduces the resurrection to a vindication of Christ's death for sin.[2] Resurrection, as such, is not part of the atonement.[3] Downplaying the resurrection is out of step not only with pentecostal experience, but also with the biblical narrative of the atonement considered from the perspective of the Spirit of Pentecost.[4] This chapter argues that the Spirit's resurrection of Christ contributes to the work of atonement. Death on the cross is not the telos of Christ's life and ministry. Christianity is not a

---

[1] J. Denny Weaver's work is an exception: see J. Denny Weaver, "The Nonviolent Atonement: Human Violence, Discipleship and God," in *Stricken by God? Nonviolent Identification and the Victory of Christ*, ed. Brad Jersak and Michael Hardin (Grand Rapids: Eerdmans, 2007), 316–55.

[2] I. Howard Marshall recognizes this problem with the traditional way of understanding the resurrection in the penal view of the atonement. He suggests understanding the resurrection as the expression or demonstration of God's pardon and release of Christ from the consequences of sin resulting from Christ's death on the cross. Marshall's view is better than reducing the resurrection to a vindicatory role, but he continues primarily to give the resurrection a forensic meaning, although the use of representative language and discussion of Romans 6 suggest that participation in Christ is also part of his vision of redemption. See Marshall, *Aspects of the Atonement: Cross and Resurrection in the Reconciling of God and Humanity* (London: Paternoster, 2007), 80–93.

[3] Indeed, Thomas R. Schreiner finds it possible to detail the penal-substitutionary view without even discussing the resurrection. See Schreiner, "Penal Substitution View," in *The Nature of the Atonement: Four Views*, ed. James Beilby and Paul R. Eddy (Downers Grove: IVP Academic, 2006), 67–98. Richard Gaffin's essay in *The Glory of the Atonement*, an apologetic for penal-substitutionary atonement, endeavors to give the resurrection equal role with the cross or the "renovative" and "forensic" elements of grace. In the end, however, it succumbs to the logic of the penal view—the resurrection relates not to "slavery to sin," the transformative dimension of grace, but to the guilt of sin. See Richard Gaffin, "Atonement in the Pauline Corpus: 'The Scandal of the Cross,'" in *The Glory of the Atonement: Biblical, Historical, and Practical Perspectives*, ed. Charles E. Hill and Frank A. James, III (Downers Grove: IVP Academic, 2004), 160–1.

[4] Including Christ's resurrection along with his death on the cross in atonement gives this pentecostal theology of atonement affinity with Eastern Orthodox soteriology. See James R. Payton, Jr., *The Victory of the Cross: Salvation in Eastern Orthodoxy* (Downers Grove: IVP Academic, 2019), 12.

death cult, but the promise of new life in the Holy Spirit.[5] Christ dies so that he can be raised in order to give hope and the promise of new life to all those who walk through the valley of the shadow of death. The Spirit of Pentecost makes his historical experience of death and resurrection available to all people. Although the cross is the climax of Jesus' faithfulness to the Father—his devotion to the Father and to all humanity takes its most absolute form when he dies, it is not the climax of the gospel. Death, the principal consequence of sin, is overcome only in Christ's resurrection.[6] The Holy Spirit is the vital agent of Christ's resurrection. The Holy Spirit, therefore, is key to the atonement.

This chapter continues the argument that the atonement takes in the totality of Christ's life, and the Holy Spirit is central to that work. The constructive part of this chapter has two goals. First, it argues that the Holy Spirit is the agent of the resurrection of Jesus Christ and that Christ's resurrection is integral to atonement. Second, it shows the resurrection's role in the wider narrative of the Spirit of Pentecost. Before turning to that constructive task, however, this chapter answers two questions: Why focus on the penal view and why does this atonement theology downplay the resurrection? Since penal atonement has been the subject of critiques in previous chapters, the argument here is briefer and focused on resurrection.

Penal Atonement and the Resurrection

Answering the first question is straightforward. The penal view of atonement is the default view of many Pentecostals and is prevalent in the wider Protestant traditions. Charismatic Baptist theologian Clark H. Pinnock effectively summarizes the problem: "Western theology has allowed itself to be dominated by a legalistic view of sin and a forensic model of atonement which leaves little room for resurrection."[7] But why does this atonement theology minimize the resurrection? Because atonement is a judicial proceeding between the Father and the Son and not a life-transforming and renewing experience of grace. Southern Baptist theologian Lee Tankersley recognizes the problem that the resurrection often has no clear role in penal-substitutionary atonement.[8] Tankersley affirms the traditional Protestant view that the resurrection vindicates that God the Father accepted Christ's vicarious life of obedience and penal death on behalf of human sin: "Christ's resurrection means that *Christ* has received a

---

[5] Eastern Orthodox theologian Alexander Schmemann also rejects Christianity as a "death-centered religion." The context of this statement is an implicit critique and rejection of Western atonement theology that focuses on Christ's death. Although focusing on Christ's death in his own way, Schmemann nevertheless puts the emphasis on Christ's life that is the source of the Christian life. See Alexander Schmemann, *For the Life of the World: Sacraments and Orthodoxy* (St. Vladimir's Seminary Press, 1973), 104.

[6] Georges Florovsky also argues that death is the fundamental problem resolved in the work of redemption, see Florovsky, *Creation and Redemption* (Belmont: Nordland, 1976), 109.

[7] Clark H. Pinnock, "Salvation by Resurrection," *Ex Auditu: An International Journal of Theological Interpretation of Scripture* 9 (1993): 2.

[8] Lee Tankersley, "Raised for Our Justification: The Resurrection and Penal Substitution," *The Southern Baptist Journal of Theology* 18, no. 4 (2014): 52–3.

legal sentence of justification" and, therefore, cross and resurrection are "two forensic acts."[9] The resurrection is the legal declaration that God the Father accepts Christ's obedience and death as the fulfillment of the law and the penalty for human sin.[10] Fleming Rutledge, although taking an apocalyptic view of *Christus Victor* as the primary atonement theme and not penal substitution, also sees the "crucifixion as the most important historical event that has ever happened."[11] The resurrection is "God's mighty transhistorical Yes to the historically crucified Son."[12] For Rutledge, the resurrection vindicates and "ratifies" Christ's crucifixion, which is "*the* defining feature of his entire life and mission."[13] She argues that "all the Evangelists . . . aim their Gospels toward the cross as the climax to the story of Jesus."[14] Christ's crucifixion is a pivotal moment in the history of redemption. But it is not the climax of redemption, either in the Gospels or the wider New Testament elaboration of the gospel. Peter's Pentecost sermon emphasizes Christ's death and resurrection and situates it within a broader history of redemption that culminates in the outpouring of the Holy Spirit (Acts 2:16-17 and 38-39). Given the history of Christocentrism and crucicentrism and the importance of the cross in the history of redemption, let me state what should be obvious: I am not downplaying the cross. I am making a case, however, that the other aspects of Christ's life, the resurrection in this chapter, and the Spirit of Pentecost are not less important than the cross.

Crucicentric readings of the gospel minimize the resurrection and the gift of the Spirit of Pentecost.[15] But why? Marginalizing the importance of the resurrection is the result of reading the gospel through the prism of a forensic theology of atonement and justification. In other words, atonement coordinates with the doctrine of justification. Human sinners stand guilty before the divine tribunal of God the Father, who acquits their debts and foregoes unleashing divine wrath on them because Christ offers his blood shed on the cross. Vindicating Christ's death on the cross for human sin is the primary role of the resurrection in this traditional atonement theology. The resurrection, as such, however, contributes nothing to the substance of the atonement. The atonement is entirely complete when Christ dies on the cross. The vindicatory function of the resurrection means that the resurrection signals that God accepts Christ's life of obedience as fulfilling the law and his death on the cross as the penal payment for sin. Since Christ's work fundamentally deals with legal and penal issues,

---

[9] Tankersley, "Raised for Our Justification," 59–63.
[10] Bruce Demarest details the "Big Idea of the Atonement" with no reference to the resurrection in *The Cross and Salvation*, Foundations in Evangelical Theology, vol. 1 (Wheaton: Crossway, 1997), 171–5.
[11] Fleming Rutledge, *The Crucifixion: Understanding the Death of Jesus Christ* (Grand Rapids: Eerdmans, 2015), 44 and 393.
[12] Rutledge, *Crucifixion*, 44.
[13] Rutledge, *Crucifixion*, 44 and 59 (emphasis in original).
[14] Rutledge, *Crucifixion*, 41.
[15] I am not the first to make the observation that traditional Protestant theology downplays the resurrection relative to the cross. Michael F. Bird, for example, notes the Protestant penchant for considering the cross in "isolation" from the resurrection. Bird, "Justified by Christ's Resurrection: A Neglected Aspect of Paul's Doctrine of Justification," *Scottish Bulletin of Evangelical Theology* 22, no. 1 (2004): 72; also see Morna D. Hooker, *From Adam to Christ: Essays on Paul* (New York: Cambridge University Press, 1990), 38–9.

resurrection has no role in it, except to demonstrate the Father's approval of Christ's judicial and penal work. Secondarily, resurrection serves as a symbol for Christian sanctification. Resurrection relates to sanctification and to the Spirit's inner renewal and growth in grace, but they are never the basis for standing before God as righteous. The resurrection, consequently, contributes nothing to the penal atonement as such. Keeping justification and sanctification distinct is meant to protect salvation by grace through faith in traditional Protestant theology. The result, however, is an atonement theology that renders Christ's resurrection subsidiary to the cross and excluded from the substance of the atonement. Having illustrated that traditional penal atonement sidelines the resurrection, the following sections build the case for the place of the resurrection in a pentecostal theology of the atonement.

The Spirit and the Resurrection of Christ

Romans is the place to go for the penal view of atonement. Romans contains the mother lode of the forensic Protestant theology of justification by faith. So, maybe a pentecostal theology of the atonement would be better off turning to Luke-Acts, after all, that is its locus classicus. Richard B. Hays, however, asks, has the "Protestant preoccupation with the question of justification created a certain hermeneutical distortion and occluded other significant theological themes in Romans?"[16] Hays argues that the Holy Spirit is prominent in the structure and thematic development of Romans—that is, Rom. 1:3-4, 5:5 and 8, 14:17, and 15:13.[17] In other words, reading Romans from the perspective of pneumatology is neither contrived nor imposing pentecostal predilections on Paul. Indeed, ignoring the Holy Spirit forces an overly forensic hermeneutic on Romans. The remainder of this chapter consists of two sections. The first section focuses on the Spirit in the resurrection of Christ. The key passages are Rom. 1:3-4 and 8:11, although 1 Tim. 3:16 is also covered. Although not part of Romans, the Spirit's role in the resurrection of Christ in 1 Tim. 3:16 corroborates the Spirit's role in Romans. The second situates Christ's resurrection in the wider biblical history of the Holy Spirit, which takes Pentecost as the climax of the biblical narrative of redemption.

First, the Spirit's role in the resurrection in Rom. 1:3-4 is foundational and, therefore, receives primary focus in this section. Paul opens the epistle to the Romans, declaring that he is an apostle of the gospel. He identifies the central content of the gospel: "regarding his Son, who as to his human nature was a descendant of David, and who through the Spirit of holiness was declared with power to be the Son of God by his resurrection from the dead: Jesus Christ our Lord" (Rom. 1:3-4).[18] Many scholars

---

[16] Richard B. Hays, "Spirit, Church, Resurrection: The Third Article of the Creed as Hermeneutical Lens for Reading Romans," *Journal of Theological Interpretation* 5, no. 1 (2011): 38. In this article, Hays conducts a reading of Romans through the third article of the Nicene-Constantinopolitan Creed.

[17] Hays, "Spirit, Church, Resurrection," 40.

[18] Michael Bird calls Rom. 1:3-4 one of the "most concise summaries of the gospel in the New Testament" (*The Saving Righteousness of God: Studies on Paul, Justification, and the New Perspective*, Paternoster Biblical Monographs [Milton Keynes: Paternoster, 2007], 69). Joshua W. Jipp argues

believe this statement is an early Christian hymn or creedal fragment and are mixed on its meaning in this passage.[19] Emphasizing Jesus' Davidic descent is unusual for Paul as is the phrase "Spirit of holiness." Some scholars also suggest that the Christology reflected in Rom. 1:4 is developmental (in later church history known as adoptionism) because Christ is only "declared" to be the Son of God at his resurrection. James M. Scott is surely correct when he surmises that if Paul did draw on an existing hymn or creed, he did so because he "stood in full agreement with it as a valid statement on the gospel."[20] Although highlighting Davidic descent is unusual for Paul, he uses the same pairing of Davidic descent and resurrection in 2 Tim. 2:8 and cites Isa. 11:10 to affirm Davidic lineage in Rom. 15:12.[21] Perhaps the reason is that Paul often addressed Gentile Christians. Underlining Jesus' Jewish background may not have been helpful, especially given the controversy and tension among Gentile and Jewish Christians communities (e.g., Acts 15 and the Jerusalem Council). The Roman Christian community, however, had a strong Jewish influence, so Paul opens his epistle in a way that connects with his audience. That he does not emphasize Davidic descent in other epistles addressed to more or less Gentile audiences does not mean he regards it as theologically unimportant; it just may have not served a pastoral purpose. As Richard N. Longenecker argues, Paul's writings are "circumstantial." They were tailored to the background and considerations of his audience.[22] In contemporary terms, they were missional.

Although New Testament scholars often see Paul contrasting Jesus' human nature, linked to Davidic descent, with his resurrection life, attributed to the Spirit of holiness, N. T. Wright argues that these two claims are the "core" content of Paul's gospel.[23] At this point, I will not enter into the larger debate in Pauline scholarship, but offer a reading that reflects my goal of understanding resurrection from the perspective of the Spirit of Pentecost. In light of this pentecostal consideration, two exegetical issues are important. First, the passage contains the parallelism of Jesus' human and divine natures (*kata sarx* and *kata pneuma*). Does this reflect an early developmental (later known as adoptionistic) Christology? Second, what, if anything, does the Spirit

---

that Rom. 1:3-4 "functions in a programmatic way" introducing "key themes that Paul will further develop" in "Ancient, Modern, and Future Interpretations of Romans 1:3-4: Reception History and Biblical Interpretation," *Journal of Theological Interpretation* 3, no. 2 (2009): 256. Frank J. Matera describes it similarly in *Romans*, Paideia Commentaries on the New Testament (Grand Rapids: BakerAcademic, 2010), 25-30. Also, Mehrdad Fatehi, *The Spirit's Relation to the Risen Lord in Paul: An Examination of Its Christological Implications*, Wissenschaftliche Untersuchungen zum Neuen Testament, 128 (Tübingen: Mohr Siebeck, 2000), 247-9.

[19] For discussion of the sources of Paul's phrase, see Christopher G. Whitsett who advances the argument that Rom. 1:3-4 and 15:12 are Paul's Christological exegesis of traditional messianic passages such as 2 Samuel 7 and Ps. 2:7 in "Son of God, Seed of David: Paul's Messianic Exegesis in Romans 1:3-4," *Journal of Biblical Literature* 119, no. 4 (2000): 661-81.

[20] James M. Scott, *Adoption as Sons of God: An Exegetical Investigation into the Background of "huiothesia" in the Pauline Corpus*, Wissenschaftliche Untersuchungen zum Neuen Testament, vol. 2 (Tübingen: Mohr Siebeck, 1992), 236.

[21] Whitsett, "Son of God, Seed of David," 674-8.

[22] Richard N. Longenecker, *The Epistle to the Romans: A Commentary on the Greek Text*, The New International Greek Testament Commentary (Grand Rapids: Eerdmans, 2016), 68.

[23] N. T. Wright, *The Resurrection of the Son of God*, Christian Origins and the Question of God, vol. 3 (Minneapolis: Fortress, 2003), 270, 242, 380-1, and 572.

contribute to the resurrection? Addressing these two points gets to the question of the Spirit's role in the resurrection of Christ and its meaning for a pentecostal theology of the atonement.

To begin, why does Paul parallel Jesus' human and divine natures in Rom. 1:3-4? This pairing of human nature/Davidic descent and resurrected life in/by the Spirit of holiness is usually taken to set up an antithetical parallelism that indicates a downplaying of Jesus' earthly or fleshly life relative to his resurrected spiritual life. James D. G. Dunn, for example, suggests that Paul's negative portrayal of Jesus' natural life as a descendant of David serves to accentuate Paul's emphasis on Jesus as the savior, the man of the Spirit, who "transcends the role of merely a Jewish Messiah."[24] Craig S. Keener puts less emphasis on the negative quality of Jesus' earthly life, but nonetheless argues that the contrast between Jesus' life prior to the resurrection and his resurrection by the Spirit—for example, life according to the flesh and to the Spirit—serves to relativize, without denigrating, Jesus' fleshly life prior to the resurrection to his spiritual resurrected life.[25]

The hermeneutic that contrasts Jesus' human Davidic descent and Spirit-resurrected life has two problems. The first problem is the assumption that the syntactical sequence of Davidic descendant according to his human nature and "through the Spirit of holiness was declared with power to be the Son of God by his resurrection from the dead" (Rom. 1:4) indicates a temporal and existential development in Jesus' life—that is, Jesus went from being primarily the earthly Davidic descendant to being the more significant and resurrected spiritual Christ.[26] Paul, however, identifies Jesus Christ according to the fundamental characteristics of the promised Messiah: "A shoot will come up from the stump of Jesse . . . [and] the Spirit of Lord will rest on him" (Isa. 11:1-2).[27] Paul is an apostle of the good news of the promised and long-awaited Spirit-anointed messiah.[28] The two characteristics function in tandem; they effectively form an *inclusio* of Jesus Christ's messianic qualifications.[29] Paul's emphasis on resurrection also sets Jesus Christ within the broader biblical narrative of the Spirit of Pentecost. It

---

[24] Dunn's emphasis on the negative nature of the flesh and spirit parallelism and Jesus' pre-resurrection and resurrection life seems to have evolved. His earlier interpretation emphasized the negative connotation more so than his later view; compare his "Jesus—Flesh and Spirit: An Exposition of Romans 1:3-4," *The Journal of Theological Studies*, n.s., 24, no. 1 (1973): 40–68 with James D. G. Dunn, *Romans 1-8*, Word Biblical Commentary, vol. 38 (Waco: Word, 1988), 13–15. For a similar view, also see Arland J. Hultgren, *Paul's Letter to the Romans: A Commentary* (Grand Rapids: Eerdmans, 2011), 45–9.

[25] Craig S. Keener, *Romans: A New Covenant Commentary* (Eugene: Cascade, 2009), 20.

[26] Whitsett makes a similar argument that the textual movement indicates two aspects, not historical periods, of "Jesus' messiahship" (see "Son of God, Seed of David," 681).

[27] Paul also may have in mind 2 Sam. 7:12-14 and Ps. 2:7; see Whitsett, "Son of God, Seed of David," 674.

[28] Gordon D. Fee, *Pauline Christology: An Exegetical-Theological Study* (Peabody: Hendrickson, 2007), 240–2; although Fee does not regard the Holy Spirit as the agent of the resurrection.

[29] Stanley E. Porter, *The Letter to the Romans: A Linguistic and Literary Commentary*, New Testament Monographs, 37 (Sheffield: Sheffield Phoenix Press, 2015), 46. Adolf Schlatter argues that "he would not be the promised Son of God if he did not share in the flesh and thus belong to Israel and to the family of David"; see *Romans: The Righteousness of God*, trans. Siegfried S. Schatzmann (Peabody: 1995), 9. Wright maintains that Paul's affirmation of Jesus Christ's identity as the Davidic messiah and divine Son "amount to the same thing" (*The Resurrection of the Son of God*, 270).

shows that the curse of death has been broken (cf. 1 Cor. 15:55, "Where, O death, is your sting?"). The Spirit of life does not abandon Jesus Christ to the dust but breathes new life into him. Even if a contrast between the life of flesh and the life of the Spirit is granted, the point is not to denigrate Christ's humanity.[30] Indeed, the resurrection validates the value of human life. Christ does not transcend and leave behind his earthly Davidic body in the resurrection. The Spirit resurrects his incarnate life as the first fruits of the new creation that includes the renewal of human beings and creation itself (Rom. 8:18-25).[31] In other words, God has provided a way out of the desert of Genesis 3 and into the new creation. That way out of the desert and the dust of death is by the same Spirit that first breathed life into human beings. Thus, the Spirit's raising of Christ is, within the wider narrative of redemption, an *inclusio*—the Spirit of life in Gen. 2:7 fulfills its work by raising Christ from the dead and sharing the resurrected life of the new Adam with all people as the Spirit of Pentecost (cf. 1 Cor. 15:45-49). Pairing the flesh/Davidic descent and the spirit/resurrection by the Spirit of holiness, Paul also provides a succinct framing of the totality of Jesus' incarnate life—Christ is the Spirit-anointed messiah.[32] For Paul, the entirety of Jesus' incarnate life is the foundation of the gospel.

The second problem is that the Gospels do not present an antithesis of human nature and Spirit raised life. The agency and activity of the Holy Spirit is the foundation of Jesus Christ's identity and work as the incarnate Son of God. In the conception narrative of the Gospel of Luke, the angel announces to Mary "[h]e will be great and will be called the Son of the Most High. The Lord God will give him the throne of his father David, and he will reign over the house of Jacob forever; his kingdom will never end . . . [and] the Holy Spirit will come upon you . . . so the holy one to be born will be called the Son of God" (Lk. 1:32-35). Luke's conception narrative links Christ's Davidic and pneumatological identity. When Jesus enters the synagogue to inaugurate his public ministry, he reads from the prophet Isaiah: "The Spirit of the Lord is on me, because he had anointed me to preach good news to the poor" (Lk. 4:18). The Gospel of Matthew also makes Jesus' Davidic descent and Spirit anointing foundational for his messianic identity (e.g., Mt. 1:1-17, 20-21 and 12:18-21 and 28). Although the common interpretation has been to see Paul contrasting Davidic descent and resurrection by or in the realm of the Spirit, my argument for continuity between Davidic descent and Spirit identity resonates with the work of James M. Scott and Nathan C. Johnson. They convincingly argue that the two identifiers work together. In contrast to antithetical parallelism, Scott argues for climatic and Johnson for dynamic equivalent parallelism, according to which the designation of Son of God elaborates or further identifies

---

[30] Matthew W. Bates also argues that highlighting Davidic descent and Jesus' human nature are not negative qualifiers in "A Christology of Incarnation and Enthronement: Romans 1:3-4 as Unified, Nonadoptionist, and Nonconciliatory," *The Catholic Biblical Quarterly* 77 (2015): 107–27.

[31] For resurrection as indicating the promise of new creation as well as its connection to Genesis 1 and 2 in Paul, see Wright, *The Resurrection of the Son of God*, 223–4, 334, and 353–5.

[32] Although not using the term "*inclusio*," Peter Stuhlmacher argues that Rom. 1:3-4 includes under the gospel the entire life of Jesus "from his birth to his exaltation." See Stuhlmacher, *Paul's Letter to the Romans: A Commentary*, trans. Scott J. Hafemann (Louisville: Westminster/John Knox, 1994), 19.

the messiah who is the descendant of David.³³ This line of interpretation stands in continuity with not only the Hebrew Bible prophetic expectations for messianic identity, but also the Gospels that portray Jesus Christ as the Spirit-anointed messiah and inaugurate his ministry with the promise of the outpouring of the Holy Spirit (e.g., Jn 1:32-34). So, whatever flesh and spirit mean in Rom. 1:3-4, they are not an antithesis. What then does flesh and spirit connote in respect of Jesus' pre- and post-resurrection life? Again, setting Jesus' life and ministry within the wider narrative of the Spirit of Pentecost and the history of redemption is important.³⁴ Jesus' life and ministry were his sojourn through the world of Genesis 3. The Son of God came to his people amid the world of "thorns and thistles," he lived among them by the "sweat of the brow," and, in the end, he suffers humiliating shame and death on their behalf (Gen. 3:17-19). The Spirit's raising Christ from the dead "declare[s] with power" (Rom. 1:4) that the eschatological consummation of the new creation has begun.³⁵

The next consideration is whether or not the "Spirit of holiness" in Rom. 1:4 is Paul giving the Holy Spirit agency in the resurrection of Jesus Christ. Dunn admits that "Spirit of holiness" refers to the Holy Spirit in Rom. 1:4, but he maintains that Paul remains "determined . . . to avoid attributing the resurrection of Jesus to the Spirit . . . [and] describing Jesus' resurrection life as dependent on the Spirit."³⁶ Dunn remarks that although in Rom. 1:4 Paul refers to the Holy Spirit, he "elsewhere . . . seems to go out of his way to avoid accrediting Jesus' resurrection to the Spirit."³⁷ New Testament scholars seem determined to avoid recognizing what Paul clearly affirms. For example, Colin G. Kruse argues that "Spirit of holiness" is "the Holy Spirit" or "Spirit of sanctification," but then insists that the Holy Spirit is "*never* the agent who raises Jesus from the dead." But immediately suggests that in Rom. 8:11 the Spirit is the "*means* by which God raised Jesus from the dead. In this case, we could interpret Romans 1:4 to mean that through the Spirit, by the resurrection, God appointed Jesus to be the Son of God with power."³⁸ Gordon D. Fee also maintains that the Holy Spirit is not

---

33 Scott, *Adoption as Sons of God*, 239–44 and Nathan C. Johnson, "Romans 1:3–4: Beyond Antithetical Parallelism," *Journal of Biblical Literature* 136, no. 2 (2017): 467–90, esp. 487. Although Longenecker regards the *kata* parallelism as antithetical he suggests they make an "inclusive christological affirmation" of Jesus' identity as Israel's promised Davidic Messiah and as God's Son. Longenecker, *The Epistle to the Romans*, 69 and 75.

34 According to Peter Stuhlmacher, "Verses 3 and 4 contain the history of Christ told in the Gospels in short form, and emphasize that the entire way of Jesus, from his birth to his exaltation, stands under the sign of the promises of God" (*Romans*, 19).

35 Dunn, *Romans 1–8*, 15–16 and Keener, *Romans*, 21.

36 Dunn, *Romans 1–8*, 15 and 433. He also affirms that Paul was reticent to attribute Christ's resurrection to the Spirit, although he indicates "it is the logical corollary of Rom. 8.11." See James D. G. Dunn, *Jesus and the Spirit: A Study of the Religious and Charismatic Experience of Jesus and the First Christians as Reflected in the New Testament* (1975; reprint, Grand Rapids: Eerdmans, 1997), 447n117.

37 Dunn, *Romans 1–8*, 15.

38 Colin G. Kruse, *Paul's Letter to the Romans* (Grand Rapids: Eerdmans, 2012), 44 and 46 (emphasis in original). Hultgren also admits that the Holy Spirit is "instrumental in the resurrection of Jesus from the dead," but then insists that "the work of the Spirit in this passage is not characteristic of Paul's own thinking" (*Paul's Letter to the Romans*, 45). The obvious question is why did he use the language, even if borrowed from the creed/hymn known to the Jewish Romans Christians, if it represented a Christology so at variance with his own? Fatehi also regards the Holy Spirit's role in

the means of the resurrection.[39] He suggests that "who through the Spirit of holiness was declared with power to be the Son of God by his resurrection from the dead" in Rom. 1:4 means "the Spirit in this passage probably has to do with the heavenly, eschatological sphere of life, into which Christ himself by resurrection has now entered and into which all who are his will finally enter."[40] I appreciate Dunn and Fee's concern, and what they perceive as Paul's motivation, to refrain from implying what would in later Christian theology be called adoptionistic Christology and casting Jesus as deficient and thus "dependent" on the Spirit.[41] Fee also rejects Spirit Christology, which he sees behind efforts to identify the Holy Spirit as the agent of resurrection.[42] But a trinitarian Spirit Christology does not deny the personal distinctions of the Holy Spirit and the Son or diminish the deity of the Son.[43] Paul links the resurrection by the Spirit with Jesus' life and death. The messiah's Davidic and pneumatological identity are not sequential but synchronous. In respect to the gospel, Paul does not consider the cross compartmentally as something distinct from Jesus' life and resurrection. The cross is a major moment in his life, but it is not the sum of the drama of redemption. This Spirit Christological understanding of Christ's life and resurrection is vital for a pentecostal theology of atonement. Highlighting the synergy between Christ and the Spirit in the resurrection has two results. It coheres with the Spirit's role in Jesus' life portrayed in the Gospels and the organic and paradigmatic relationship that Paul presents between the Spirit's raising of Christ and participation in Christ's resurrected life through the Holy Spirit (e.g., Rom. 6 and 8:11).[44]

Second, Rom. 8:11 ("if the Spirit of him that raised up Jesus from the dead") prima facie affirms that the Holy Spirit is the agent of the resurrection of Jesus Christ. Attributing the resurrection to the Holy Spirit is, nevertheless, a contentious issue among New Testament scholars.[45] To keep the discussion succinct, I focus on Gordon

---

the resurrection as instrumental, not agential—*The Spirit's Relation to the Risen Lord in Paul*, 256 and 284–85n36.

[39] Fee critiques the "mistaken notion that the Sprit is the agent of [Christ's] resurrection," in Gordon D. Fee, *God's Empowering Presence: The Holy Spirit in the Letters of Paul* (Peabody: Hendrickson, 1994), 808.

[40] Fee, *Pauline Christology*, 244. For similar readings, see Dunn, *Romans 1–8*, 15 and Longenecker, *The Epistle to the Romans*, 75.

[41] Dunn, *Romans 1–8*, 433.

[42] Gordon D. Fee, "Christology and Pneumatology in Romans 8:9–11—and Elsewhere: Some Reflections on Paul as Trinitarian," in Gordon D. Fee, *To What End Exegesis: Essays, Textual, Exegetical, and Theological* (Grand Rapids: Eerdmans, 2001), 218–23 [218–39].

[43] E.g., Myk Habets, *The Anointed Son: A Trinitarian Spirit Christology* (Eugene: Pickwick, 2010).

[44] Frank Matera and Wright also attribute the resurrection to the Holy Spirit (Matera, *Romans*, 30 and Wright, *The Resurrection of the Son of God*, 245 and 256). Note however that later Matera (following Fee's interpretation), in respect to Rom. 8:11, affirms that God, not the Spirit of God, raises Christ from the dead (*Romans*, 196).

[45] For others who argue that the Spirit is not the agent of resurrection, see Douglas J. Moo, *The Epistle to the Romans*, NICNT (Grand Rapids: Eerdmans, 1996), 493; Hultgren, *Paul's Letter to the Romans*, 305; Dunn, *Romans 1–8*, 433. Keener, *Romans*, 21 and 101 and Matera, *Romans*, 196, say that God raised Christ "through" the Spirit. Recognizing that Paul attributes the resurrection to the Holy Spirit are Trevor J. Burke, "Romans," in *A Biblical Theology of the Holy Spirit*, ed. Trevor J. Burke and Keith Warrington (London: SPCK, 2014), 131–4; Kruse, *Paul's Letter to the Romans*, 334; and Max M. B. Turner, "Significance of Spirit Endowment for Paul," *Vox Evangelica* 9 (1975): 56–69; see 64 and 66.

Fee, who denies that Paul gives the Holy Spirit agency in Christ's resurrection in Rom. 8:11.[46] Fee argues that "the Spirit . . . who raised Jesus from the dead . . . will also give life to your mortal bodies through his Spirit" does not indicate the Spirit's agency in the resurrection, but makes "the closest possible connection between Christ's resurrection and ours. For Paul the presence in our lives of the Spirit of God who raises the dead does not imply agency, but rather expresses certainty about our future."[47] First, that the Spirit "raises the dead" but has no agency in their resurrection is baffling.[48] The Spirit's presence cannot give certainty about the future, if the Spirit is not active in manifesting that eschatological new life that emerges from the resurrection of Christ. Second, if Paul's point is to accentuate the parallel between Christ's and the believer's resurrection (as Fee argues), then the Spirit's role in raising the dead in Christ should match the Spirit's role in raising Christ.[49] But Fee's argument undoes this parallel relationship. Again, Fee denies what Paul affirms—the Spirit raised Christ from the dead—because he fears "Spirit Christology," which for Fee "confuses . . . or somehow identifies [i.e., Son and Spirit] as one and the same reality."[50] The better course is to go with what Paul says and realize that although some forms of Spirit Christology may obscure the distinctions of the Son and Spirit, not all do so.[51]

Third, 1 Tim. 3:16 declares that Christ "appeared in a body, was vindicated by the Spirit." Two questions arise, what is the meaning of vindicate and what is the relationship between "body" and "Spirit"? Philip Towner argues that 1 Tim. 3:16 should be understood "through a christological lens, forcing the whole of salvation history, as well as the preceding 'mystery of godliness,' to be understood christocentrically."[52] He continues that "the crucifixion is to be understood as the ultimate purpose and climax of this stage of existence."[53] Thus, Towner takes the phrase "appeared in a body" as pointing primarily to the crucifixion. The crucifixion is clearly implied in 1 Tim. 3:16, but the resurrection or vindication by the Spirit receives the explicit emphasis. Gordon Fee also rejects regarding the Holy Spirit as the agent of resurrection in 1 Tim. 3:16. Articulating a common way of interpreting the relationship between "appeared in a body" and "vindicated by the Spirit," he suggests that "body" and "Spirit" indicate the difference between his natural and supernatural modes of existence, with the former referring to Christ's incarnate life and the latter to his resurrection life. Thus, Jesus is resurrected into the sphere of the Spirit, but the Spirit is not the agent of resurrection.[54]

---

[46] Fee, *God's Empowering Presence*, 552–4.
[47] Fee, *God's Empowering Presence*, 553.
[48] As Douglas A. Campbell points out, "Christ is not resurrected merely at the behest of the Father but by the Spirit." See Campbell, *The Quest for Paul's Gospel: A Suggested Strategy*, Journal for the Study of the New Testament Supplement Series, 274 (New York: T & T Clark, 2005), 78.
[49] Trevor Burke and James M. Scott also argue that the correspondence between the Spirit's raising of Christ and believers is precisely Paul's point. See Scott, *Adoption as Sons of God*, 256–7 and Burke, "Romans," 133.
[50] Fee, *God's Empowering Presence*, 554.
[51] E.g., again, Habets, *The Anointed Son*.
[52] Philip H. Towner, *The Letters to Timothy and Titus*, NICNT (Grand Rapids: Eerdmans, 2006), 278.
[53] Towner, *Letters to Timothy and Titus*, 280.
[54] Fee, *God's Empowering Presence*, 764–6; also, Towner, *Letters to Timothy and Titus*, 280–1. Fee does not denigrate the physical body but does draw a contrast between Christ's incarnate life as natural and resurrected life as supernatural life. Underlying this interpretation of 1 Tim. 3:16 seems to be

In other words, Fee posits contrast between his incarnate life and his resurrected life. But this dichotomy is unwarranted. Christ never had a purely natural existence. Jesus Christ was always the Spirit-anointed messiah. He was constituted the Christ, the incarnate Son of God, by the agency of the Spirit of God (Mt. 1:18 and Lk. 1:35). Although 1 Tim. 3:16 is less clear on the Holy Spirit's agency in the resurrection than is Rom. 1:4 and 8:11, it clearly affirms that the resurrection vindicates Christ. But, in what sense does the resurrection vindicate Christ? Coupling 1 Tim. 3:16 with the clear agency of the Holy Spirit in the resurrection of Christ in Rom. 1:4 and 8:11 suggests that the Spirit's raising of Christ vindicates him as the Spirit-anointed messiah.[55] The resurrection is not simply God the Father's approval of his Son's penal death on the cross.[56] Christ passes through death and is raised to new life because he was the culmination of the Spirit of life's stirring over the darkness of the deep, raising human life from the dirt, and renewing the people of God and their land (Ezekiel 36–37). Jesus Christ is "vindicated by the Spirit" because he was, from the moment of the Incarnation, the Spirit-anointed messiah. As such death was never the *telos* of the life of Jesus Christ. The work of God's Spirit does not end in death and darkness. The cross is a culminating moment in Christ's life, and resurrection marks a transition to his glorified existence, but the life of Christ, from the first moment of the Incarnation to glorification, embodies the Spirit's wider narrative of redemption.[57] Thus, understanding 1 Tim. 3:16 as the Spirit's raising of Christ from the dead is consistent with Rom. 1:4 and 8:11.[58] It also reflects continuity with the wider biblical story of the Holy Spirit.

Fee's rejection of Spirit Christology (see *God's Empowering Presence*, 484). He also rejects the Spirit as the agent of resurrection in his discussion of Romans 1:4; see *God's Empowering Presence*, 484. Fee is not alone in this interpretation of 1 Tim. 3:16. E.g., see Towner, *Letters to Timothy and Titus*, 280–1; Frank J. Matera, *New Testament Christology* (Louisville: Westminster John Knox, 1999), 162–3; David J. Macleod, "Christology in Six Lines: An Exposition of 1 Timothy 3:16," *Bibliotheca Sacra* 159, no. 635 (2002): 341–2; and William D. Mounce, *Pastoral Epistles*, Word Biblical Commentary, vol. 46 (Nashville: Thomas Nelson, 2000), 228.

[55] Although not emphasizing the Holy Spirit as I do here, I. Howard Marshall affirms that vindication means that "by his resurrection Jesus is confirmed to be what he gave himself out to be." Marshall, with Philip H. Towner, *A Critical and Exegetical Commentary on the Pastoral Epistles* (Edinburgh: T & T Clark 1999), 525.

[56] Drawing on the work of Richard Gaffin, Tankersley, for example, interprets Christ's death and resurrection in forensic terms—his death was the penal verdict for bearing human sin and his resurrection "the legal sentence of justification" (Tankersley, "Raised for Our Justification," 61). So, the meaning of the resurrection is primarily forensic, not participatory, only secondarily does it serve as a model for sanctification and transformation. Although Gaffin affirms the "forensic significance" of the resurrection, he emphasizes the participatory nature of union with Christ and the transformation of life signified by participating in Christ's resurrection. See Richard B. Gaffin, Jr., "Resurrection and Redemption: An Exercise in Biblical-Systematic Theology," *Themelios* 2, no. 2 (2002): 16–31. Michael F. Bird extends Gaffin's linkage of resurrection-participation and justification in *The Saving Righteousness of God*, 53–9.

[57] For the cross as "ultimate purpose and climax," see Towner, *Letters to Timothy and Titus*, 280.

[58] Wright directly affirms that the "phrase 'in the Spirit' . . . refer[s] to the *agency* of the Spirit in his resurrection" (*The Resurrection of the Son of God*, 271).

Resurrection and the Narrative of Pentecost

Christ's resurrection is part of the narrative of the Spirit of Pentecost.[59] Too often Christ's work is dissected into an *ordo salutis* that elevates the cross over all other aspects of Christ's work and the Spirit's too. Although not entirely de-historicizing because it connects the cross to Israel's sacrificial rites, penal and crucicentric atonement theology does not set Christ in relief to the wider history of redemption. Why is connecting Christ to the history of redemption important? Because Jesus Christ emerges within that longer history of redemption and carries it forward. The resurrection, moreover, is a turning point in that story. I am using a narrative and a biblical-theological approach. I situate Christ's resurrection in the wider biblical history of the Holy Spirit, which takes Pentecost as the climax of the biblical narrative of redemption (even though penultimate historically because eschatological consummation awaits). So, in that sense I am using a narrative approach. At the same time, my approach is biblical theology because I endeavor to uncover what the texts portray about the Holy Spirit, in other words, the narrative of the Holy Spirit emerges from the biblical accounts of the Spirit of God beginning with creation in Genesis 1 and culminating with Acts 2. Although agreeing with many narrative scholars that Paul's soteriology is participatory, Douglas A. Campbell critiques narrative approaches because they give too much attention to Paul's Jewish background. He argues that a Pauline hermeneutic should give priority to Paul's experience of Christ. Thus, for Campbell, the "pneumatological participatory martyrological eschatology model" takes precedence to a salvation-history model (as well as what he calls the justification by faith model).[60] Although I agree with Campbell that participation in Christ is central to Paul's soteriology, my point of orientation gives priority to pneumatology rather than participation. Giving precedence to pneumatology is methodologically sound because it is theologically—participation in Christ is made possible by the same Holy Spirit who was the foundation of Jesus Christ's life and ministry. But what is the place of Christ's resurrection in the narrative of the Spirit of Pentecost?

The Spirit's resurrection of Christ marks the definitive turn in the narrative of redemption from the world of Genesis 3 to the emergence of the eschatological new creation. For this reason, Paul identifies Christ as the second Adam (Rom. 5:12-21 and 1 Cor. 15:45). The work of Christ, atonement, answers the predicament of

---

[59] "Narrative" readings of Paul are many and contested. Narrative readings often mean the effort to interpret Paul in terms of his Jewish background. Examples include the following. Gorman sees Jesus Christ providing justification through covenantal faithfulness—*Inhabiting the Cruciform God: Kenosis, Justification, and Theosis in Paul's Narrative Soteriology* (Grand Rapids: Eerdmans, 2009), 45–63. Sylvia C. Keesmaat argues that the exodus tradition is the background for elements of Paul's theology in Romans and Galatians—*Paul and His Story: (Re)Interpreting the Exodus Tradition*, Journal for the Study of the New Testament Supplement Series, 182 (Sheffield: Sheffield Academic Press, 1999). James M. Scott argues that Paul's theology of divine adoption through Christ connects with Jewish eschatological expectation that the Messiah would "redeem his people from Exile in a Second Exodus"—*Adoption as Sons of God*, 268. N. T. Wright's use of exile and restoration as metanarrative and conversation around it in James M. Scott, ed., *Exile: A Conversation with N. T. Wright* (Downers Grove: IVP Academic, 2017).

[60] Campbell, *The Quest for Paul's Gospel*, 24–5 and 37.

Adam—separation from God in the world of Genesis 3.[61] Why is Christ the second Adam? Jesus Christ is the light that shined in the darkness (Jn 1:5). He was the life animated by the Spirit of God (Mt. 1:18-21 and Lk. 1:35) that overcame the darkness and death (Jn 1:9-13). On the cross "darkness came over all the land." Jesus cried "my God, my God, why have you forsaken me?" and then "he gave up his spirit" (Mt. 27:45, 46, and 50). The tomb of Jesus was dark and lifeless. But the dank and dark tomb gave way to the light and the life of the resurrected Christ (Lk. 24:5 and Mt. 28:2-3). Just as the movement of the Spirit brought forth creation in Genesis 1 and gave life to dirt in Genesis 2, so the Spirit raises Christ from the dead (Rom. 1:4 and 8:11). The same Spirit that raised Christ will resurrect the children of God and even "liberate creation from its bondage to decay" (Rom. 8:18-27). The parallel between the Holy Spirit's resurrection of Christ and the Spirit's work in creation is clear. The resurrection is vital not only to the story of Jesus Christ but to the wider narrative of redemption. The breath of life that animated the dust in Gen. 2:7 finds its most fecund manifestation when the Holy Spirit raises Christ from the dead. Leaving resurrection out of atonement theology, therefore, is like ending the creation stories with the "darkness . . . over the surface of the deep" and the lifeless dirt (Gen. 1:2 and 2:7). Just as the Genesis 1 creation story is only complete when God declares the world teeming with life "good" on the evening of the sixth day, so atonement includes resurrection, when Jesus Christ "through the Spirit of holiness was declared with power to be the Son of God by his resurrection from the dead" (Rom. 1:4).

The Spirit's resurrection of Christ also enables Christ to carry on his ministry of atonement. In fact, the Spirit's raising of Christ in Rom. 1:4 detailed earlier mirrors the Spirit's raising and transport of Christ to the Holy of Holies in Heb. 9:14.[62] Christ's work of atonement continues beyond the cross. David M. Moffitt argues that Hebrews includes resurrection in the work of atonement. Accordingly, Jesus' death on the cross is not the pivot point in history as often understood. In contrast, he maintains that focus on Jesus' death on the cross misses the point of atonement theology in Hebrews. Moffitt argues that sacrifice does not mean to "*slaughter* or *kill* something." Sacrifice refers to a complex and sequence of ritual acts. Moffitt points out that some atonement sacrifices do not include slaughtering an animal and none command inflicting suffering (whatever the animal does suffer is not part of the sacrifice and atonement), and the animal offerings are not objects of divine wrath for sin, even though their offering in the ritual can ameliorate God's wrath for human sin. The purpose of offering blood, moreover, is purification to gain access into divine presence.[63] Atonement in Hebrews

---

[61] This point provides another connective with the soteriology of Eastern Orthodox theology that emphasizes reconciliation through transformation in the image of Christ. E.g., see Peter Boutneff, "Christ and Salvation," in *The Cambridge Companion to Orthodox Theology*, ed. Mary B. Cunningham and Elizabeth Theokritoff (New York: Cambridge University Press, 2008), 104–5.

[62] For the Holy Spirit's role in Christ's resurrection and his enthronement in heaven and inauguration of the kingdom of God, see Timo Eskola, *A Narrative Theology of the New Testament: Exploring the Metanarrative of Exile and Restoration*, Wissenschaftliche Untersuchungen zum Neuen Testament, 350 (Tübingen: Mohr Siebeck, 2015), 365–9.

[63] See David M. Moffitt, "It Is Not Finished: Jesus's Perpetual Atoning Work as the Heavenly High Priest in Hebrews," in *So Great a Salvation: A Dialogue on the Atonement in Hebrews*, ed. Jon C. Laansma, George H. Guthrie, and Cynthia Long Westfall (New York: T & T Clark, 2019), 163–5.

is the result of the risen Christ offering his life to God the Father in heaven.[64] Thus, exclusively emphasizing Jesus' death is off balance. In the Levitical sacrificial system, the backdrop of Jesus' priestly role in Hebrews—the offering of blood, not death—is the central focus and it represents life and purity. The blood of the sacrifice, not death as such, "has the power *both* to redeem and to purify."[65] The risen Christ effects atonement when he presents his blood/life to God the Father in the heavenly tabernacle where God the Father accepted the resurrected and glorified Christ. What role does the Holy Spirit play in the atonement? The Spirit is the "power that enabled [Christ] to enter heaven and make his offering. In his resurrection the eternal transformed his mortal body into a glorified, indestructible body capable of entering God's heavenly presence."[66] Timo Eskola also argues that Christ's atonement is only complete when he "through the eternal Spirit" offers his blood in the heavenly Holy of Holies.[67] Eskola also argues that Rom. 4:25 reflects this dynamic process of atonement that moves from the cross to the resurrected Christ in heaven—"He was delivered over to death for our sins and was raised to life for our justification" (Rom. 4:25).[68] Pentecostal atonement does not marginalize Christ's death on the cross. But it connects the cross to the resurrection in the narrative of redemption. It also embraces a pneumatological and participatory theology of the atonement that extends beyond the Spirit-anointed life of Christ.

Christian A. Eberhart also maintains that death does not atone. The blood of the sacrifice atones because it purifies, not punishes. See Eberhart, "'The Lamb of God that takes away the Sin of the World': Reflections on Atonement in the New Testament," *Touchstone: Heritage and Theology in a New Age* 31, no. 2 (2013): 37–8. Eberhart and Moffitt reflect the theology of sacrificial offerings also in Jacob Milgrom, *Leviticus: A Book of Ritual and Ethics* (Minneapolis: Fortress, 2004), 17 and Jacob Milgrom, "Two Kinds of Hatta't," *Vetus Testamentum* 26, no. 3 (1976): 333–7. Of course, not everyone agrees with Moffitt. George H. Guthrie argues that while correctly emphasizing Christ's resurrection and exaltation, Moffitt nevertheless downplays his death by "refracting" it to thoroughly through the sacrifice of the Day of Atonement. See Guthrie, "Time and Atonement in Hebrews," in *So Great a Salvation: A Dialogue on the Atonement in Hebrews*, ed. Jon C. Laansma, George H. Guthrie, and Cynthia Long Westfall (New York: T & T Clark, 2019), 218–20. Cynthia L. Westfall also agrees with Moffitt that the atonement is a process completed in the heavenly tabernacle, but that Christ's death remains central to it. See "Space and Atonement in Hebrews," in *So Great a Salvation: A Dialogue on the Atonement in Hebrews*, ed. Jon C. Laansma, George H. Guthrie, and Cynthia Long Westfall (New York: T & T Clark, 2019), 243–7, esp. note 75.

[64] Marshall also sees the entry into heaven and high priestly offering of his sacrifice as entailed in the process of atonement, which means atonement is not complete on the cross (*Aspects of Atonement*, 76–9).

[65] David M. Moffitt, *Atonement and the Logic of Resurrection in the Epistle to the Hebrews*, Supplements to Novum Testamentum (Boston: Brill, 2011), 263.

[66] Moffitt, *Atonement and the Logic of Resurrection in the Epistle to the Hebrews*, 296 and 280; see esp. chapter 4, 215–96.

[67] Timo Eskola, *Messiah and the Throne: Jewish Merkabah Mysticism and Early Christian Exaltation Discourse*, Wissenschaftliche Untersuchungen zum Neuen Testament, 142 (Tübingen: Mohr Siebeck, 2001), 254–67.

[68] Eskola, *Messiah and the Throne*, 267. R. B. Jamieson agrees that the self-offering of Christ takes place in heaven, but also that he offers his death on the cross as the atoning work. See Jamieson, *Jesus' Death and Heavenly Offering in Hebrews*, Society for New Testament Monograph Series, 172 (New York: Cambridge University Press, 2019). Leithart also argues that the resurrection is a constituent part of Christ's sacrifice of atonement. Christ dies and rises to God the Father just as the sacrifices died and rose to God in smoke on the altar. Peter J. Leithart, *Delivered from the Elements of the World: Atonement, Justification, Mission* (Downers Grove: IVP Academic, 2016), 166–9.

How does atonement extend beyond the life of Christ? The Spirit of Pentecost offers all people the opportunity to participate in the resurrected life of Jesus Christ. Atonement, therefore, is not only an event in but also an ongoing feature of the narrative of redemption. Yes, atonement has fixed historical events. Jesus lived, died, and was raised to new life by the Spirit of God. But the Spirit of Pentecost extends the fullness of Spirit-breathed life realized in Christ across time and place to all people. Receiving the renewal of life brought by the Spirit of Pentecost is the fundamental purpose and experience of atonement. The gospel that Paul preaches is participation in the new life the Spirit brought first to Jesus Christ and then offers to all people as the Spirit of Pentecost. Thus, atonement, the theological category that understands the work of Christ in redemption, is not limited to the cross, but includes the totality of Christ's incarnate life and resurrection. The purpose, moreover, of what traditional theology calls Christ's objective work is participation in that Spirit-breathed life. Romans 8:11 links the Spirit's raising of Christ with the new life brought by the Spirit in grace. In short, Rom. 8:11 integrates Spirit Christology and atonement-justification. Paul, for example, in the Rom. 1:3-4 couplet of Davidic descent/human nature-Spirit-resurrected Son of God assumes the cross but accents the resurrection. This focus on the Holy Spirit and the resurrection of Christ in the opening of his letter is consistent with the climax Paul gives the gospel message in Romans 8, which emphasizes participation in the resurrection life of Christ by the indwelling Holy Spirit.[69] The cross is important, but in the summative statement of Rom. 1:3-4 Paul emphasizes Christ's incarnate life as the Son of God whom the Holy Spirit renews in resurrection. The gospel, moreover, is not ultimately about the death of Christ, but sharing in that new life that the Spirit of Pentecost offers to all people.[70]

Conclusion

Integrating resurrection with atonement from the perspective of the Spirit of Pentecost shows that atonement is ultimately about life, not death. The primary work of redemption is not the death of Christ, but the renewal of life that comes from his being raised to new life by the Spirit of God. Resurrection has priority in the narrative couplet of death-resurrection because it initiates the eschatological new creation. Death, cruel and degrading death on the cross, was God's way of entering into the black hole of

---

[69] Note that Mark A. Seifrid, although affirming a forensic theology of justification by faith in Romans, recognizes that Paul's full articulation of the gospel includes the transformative and pneumatological elements found in Romans 6-8. See Seifrid, *Justification by Faith: The Origin and Development of Central Pauline Theme*, Supplements to Novum Testamentum, 68 (New York: Brill, 1992), 226-7. Seifrid's later work continues to emphasize the comprehensiveness of the Pauline gospel, but gives more attention to the forensic aspect—see Seifrid, *Christ, our Righteousness: Paul's Theology of Justification*, New Studies in Biblical Theology, 9 (Downers Grove: InterVarsity Press, 2000). Timo Eskola also argues that the Spirit raises Christ from the dead and that this "ensures believers of their own resurrection." See Eskola, *A Narrative Theology of the New Testament*, 368.

[70] Douglas A. Campbell summarizes Paul's theology with "his atoning work is incarnational and reconstitutive in rationale, not penal . . . [and] the divine Spirit is an *irreducible* and *central* feature of this model, not an optional extra." See Campbell, *The Quest for Paul's Gospel*, 47.

human despair and suffering, and emerging through it as the light and life that renews the world. The renewal of the abundant life for which the Spirit of God created human beings is the *telos* of atonement. The resurrected life of atonement also reveals that the justice and righteousness of the atonement is not penal death for sin. The atonement is about the righteousness and the grace that brings "eternal life through Jesus Christ our Lord" (Rom. 5:21). The Holy Spirit, moreover, is the primary agent in the resurrection of atonement both for Christ and for all those who participate in his renewed life (Rom. 1:4 and 8:11). Christ passes through death, is raised by the Holy Spirit (Rom. 1:4), so that the Spirit of Pentecost, the Spirit who gave the breath of life, can share the resurrected life of Christ with all people and raise all life in new creation. Thus, the righteousness of atonement includes resurrected life. God's righteousness brings life (Rom. 8:10). The answer to God's wrath over sin is not the penal death of the innocent Christ, but the resurrection of Christ, the renewal of life, and bringing of light and life where there was darkness and death (see Chapter 10 for atonement as participation in the resurrection life of Christ).

6

Eschatology

Eschatology deals with the end of the world in traditional pentecostal theology. For most of its history, Pentecostals embraced a premillennial eschatology.[1] Animated by the conviction that they were living in the last days, they eagerly awaited Jesus' second coming to rapture them before the world descended into the clutches of the Antichrist and the great tribulation that culminates in the Battle of Armageddon and the great cosmic bonfire (e.g., 2 Pet. 3:10, "the earth . . . and the works . . . therein shall be burned up," KJV).[2] In that way, pentecostal eschatology was escapist and otherworldly.[3] At the same time, pentecostal eschatology was not entirely disembodied and spiritualized. When Pentecostals talked about mansions in glory, streets of gold, and jewels in their crowns, they were not simply talking poetically and metaphorically, but realistically. To a certain extent, they expected a real mansion in glory and jewels in their crown. The irony, given their Götterdämmerung eschatology, is that Pentecostals also affirm various degrees of the prosperity gospel. The prosperity gospel exists on a spectrum within the pentecostal movements. The explicit and crass forms of the prosperity gospel are rightly rejected—for example, if I tithe 10 percent, then God will return a hundredfold to my business. But the basic assumption that the grace of God transforms the material circumstances of a person's life is widespread and implicit to the pentecostal experience of the Spirit of Pentecost.[4] It is, moreover, correct. The materiality of pentecostal practice reflects the embodied eschatology of Scripture better

---

[1] Larry R. McQueen, *Toward a Pentecostal Eschatology: Discerning the Way Forward*, Journal of Pentecostal Theology Supplement Series, 39 (Blandford Forum: Deo, 2012), 57. McQueen proposes a rereading of the fivefold gospel from an eschatological perspective (pp. 219–84).

[2] Gerald T. Sheppard and Matthew K. Thompson argue that although Christ's imminent second coming was central to early pentecostal theology, the dispensational theology popular among Evangelicals and Fundamentalists did not become prominent until later in the 1920s as Pentecostals gravitated toward Evangelicalism during the Modernist and Fundamentalist controversies and divisions. See Sheppard, "Pentecostals and the Hermeneutics of Dispensationalism: The Anatomy of an Uneasy Relationship," *Pneuma: The Journal of the Society for Pentecostal Studies* 6, no. 2 (1984): 7–10 and Thompson, *Kingdom Come: Revisioning Pentecostal Eschatology*, Journal of Pentecostal Theology Supplement Series, 37 (Blandford Forum: Deo, 2010), 49–58.

[3] Although Jeffrey S. Lamp shows that some early Pentecostals affirmed a holistic soteriology and cosmic eschatology in "New Heavens and New Earth: Early Pentecostal Soteriology as a Foundation for Creation in the Present," *Pneuma: The Journal of the Society for Pentecostal Studies* 36, no. 1 (2014): 64–80.

[4] Harvey Cox, *Fire from Heaven: The Rise of Pentecostal Spirituality and the Reshaping of Religion in the Twenty-First Century* (Reading: Addison-Wesley, 1995), 263–80. Also see, Kimberly Ervin Alexander, *Pentecostal Healing: Models in Theology and Practice* (Leiden: Brill, 2006); Kate Bowler, *Blessed: A History of the American Prosperity Gospel* (Blandford Forum: Deo, 2006); and Katherine

than the dispensational eschatology of pentecostal rhetoric. This chapter develops the eschatological nature of the Spirit's work, especially as a dimension of atonement.[5] The first part establishes the eschatological nature of Pentecost—the Spirit telocity of the history of redemption. The second part sets forth the primary character of the Spirit of Pentecost's eschatological work of atonement—exodus from exile. The final section addresses the objection of the finality of the cross and continues the development of a pentecostal Spirit Christology with respect to the dynamic nature of atonement.

Spirit Telocity

The Holy Spirit has an end-time role in the history of redemption. The Day of Pentecost is an eschatological event. My primary use of eschatological indicates the Spirit's role in effecting God's purposes in the narrative of redemption. In other words, narrative and eschatological role are interrelated.[6] They are not simply synonymous. But a narrative, a story, is going somewhere and something takes it there. The somewhere and the something are eschatological.[7] The following charts the eschatological character of the Spirit of Pentecost. Saying that means (1) the Holy Spirit is central to not only the ministry of Christ but the entire history of redemption; (2) the Spirit of Pentecost fulfills the life and ministry of Jesus Christ; and (3) Pentecost inaugurates eschatological renewal.

First, the outpouring of the Holy Spirit on the Day of Pentecost stands in continuity with but also advances the narrative of redemption. At Pentecost, the Holy Spirit appeared with manifestations of the "blowing of a violent wind" and "what seemed to be tongues of fire" (Acts 2:2-3). Why were wind and fire signs of the Holy Spirit? Because wind and fire were ways that God manifested redemptive presence in the history of the people of Israel. From the wind that made a way through the sea in the exodus and the winds that would raise the dry bones of Israel in exile to the pillar of fire that marked God's presence among the people of Israel and consumed the sacrifice

---

Attanasi and Amos Yong, eds., *Pentecostalism and Prosperity: The Socio-Economics of the Global Charismatic Movement* (New York: Palgrave Macmillan, 2012).

[5] T. F. Torrance recognizes the eschatological nature of the atonement in the sense that Christ's work on the cross has the final redemption in the new creation as its ultimate goal. He also applies the term "telos" to atonement. Torrance emphasizes the role of the Holy Spirit in facilitating union with Christ that is the relational foundation for participating in Christ's atoning work on the cross. Thomas F. Torrance, *Atonement: The Person and Work of Christ*, ed. Robert T. Walker (Downers Grove: IVP Academic, 2009), 171–80 and 189–90.

[6] As Wolfgang Vondey points out, the conviction among Pentecostals that their movement was the latter rain to the former rain or outpouring of the Holy Spirit on the Day of Pentecost indicates that eschatological identity is essential to pentecostal theology. See Vondey, *Pentecostal Theology: Living the Full Gospel*, Systematic Pentecostal and Charismatic Theology, ser. ed. Wolfgang Vondey and Daniela C. Augustine (London: Bloomsbury, 2017), 133–4.

[7] Identifying Pentecost as the telos of redemption resonates with Eastern Orthodoxy's emphasis on Pentecost. But my proposal differs in the respect that I link Christ's and the Spirit's work in Incarnation and Pentecost more so than found in some Eastern Orthodox theology. See Georges Florovsky, *Creation and Redemption*, Collected Works, vol. 3 (Belmont: Nordland, 1976), 189 and Vladimir Lossky, *The Mystical Theology of the Eastern Church* (Crestwood: St. Vladimir's Seminary Press, 1976), 170.

on the altar (Exod. 3:1-3, 13:21-22, 14:21, 19:16-20; Lev. 9:24; 1 Kgs 18:38; and Ezek. 37:1-14). The manifestation of the Holy Spirit in wind and fire places Pentecost in this wider narrative of redemption. A narrative in which the Spirit of God is the central agent of God's redemptive activity in the world. The coming of the Holy Spirit in wind and fire indicates to the disciples that the God of Israel is present to redeem.[8] Just as God declared to Moses from the burning bush, "I have indeed seen the misery of my people in Egypt. I have heard them crying out because of their slave drivers, and I am concerned about their suffering. So I have come down to rescue them from the hand of the Egyptians and to bring them up out of that land into a good and spacious land" (Exod. 3:7-8), so God was coming down again to save his people. The descent of the Holy Spirit on the disciples on the Day of Pentecost parallels not only the movement of God in the burning bush narrative but also the life of Christ. The Holy Spirit descends upon Mary and later on Jesus at his baptism (I detail the significance of this in Chapter 3 on the Incarnation). Pentecost is part of but is also more importantly a pivot point that advances this wider biblical narrative of redemption. Pentecost was doing something more expansive and grander than these earlier works of redemption. In this respect, the Spirit of Pentecost has to be understood in terms of the Spirit-anointed life of Jesus Christ.

Second, Pentecost fulfills the life and ministry of Jesus Christ. When the disciples asked the resurrected Christ, if now was the time that he would "restore the kingdom of Israel," he deflected their question on a political kingdom and reiterated the purpose of his life and ministry—"you will be baptized with the Holy Spirit . . . you will receive power when the Holy Spirit comes on you" (Acts 1:5 and 8). Jesus Christ's life and ministry, having begun with the work of the Holy Spirit, found its telos in the gift of the Spirit of Pentecost. Peter's Pentecost sermon provides a condensed narrative of Christ's ministry (miracles, cross, resurrection) that concludes with the pouring out of the "promised Holy Spirit" (Acts 2:33). It confirms the pneumatological purpose of Christ. Recognizing the place of the Spirit of Pentecost does not displace Christ but binds Christ and the Spirit in a wider narrative of biblical redemption. The Spirit of Pentecost does not come alone but brings the resurrected life of Christ to the Christian community. In Acts 3, a physically disabled man asks Peter for money at the temple gate. Peter tells him, "Silver or gold I do not have, but what I have I give you. In the name of Jesus Christ of Nazareth, walk" (Acts 3:1-6). Peter gives the man renewal of life in Christ. Peter can do this because he has received the Spirit of Pentecost. The physical healing of the man is also significant. The Spirit of Pentecost does not come to renew "spiritual" but human life in all its embodied dimensions. The ministry of Christ and the Holy Spirit are synergistic. The Spirit of Pentecost, therefore, does not supplant Christ. Considering atonement from a pneumatological perspective integrates the work of the Holy Spirit and Jesus Christ in a common narrative of redemption. But it also means that atonement cannot be narrowly conceived as only a Christ and cross event.

---

[8] Blaine Charette argues that fire indicates that judgment is also one of the effects of the outpouring of the Holy Spirit. See Charette, "'Tongues as of Fire': Judgment as a Function of Glossolalia in Luke's Thought," *Journal of Pentecostal Theology* 13, no. 2 (2005): 173-86.

Third, Pentecost inaugurates eschatological renewal. According to Peter's Pentecost sermon, the eschatological outpouring of God's Spirit promised in Joel 2:28-32 began on the Day of Pentecost. What was the content of that eschatological expectation? The restoration of all people to their God and the life for which they were created. Through the Spirit of Pentecost, the gospel will go to "the ends of the earth" (Acts 1:8). The emphasis on "God-fearing Jews from every nation under heaven" correlates with Joel's promise that the Spirit is for "all people" and is the first step to the "ends of the earth" (Acts 2:5 and 17). The restoration of people from their exile from God and from each other and renewing their life is a foundational motif in biblical redemption. In the renewal of the Mosaic covenant, God ensures to "restore your fortunes and have compassion on you and gather you again from all the nations where he scattered you. Even if you have been banished to the most distant land under the heavens, from there the LORD your God will gather you and bring you back. He will bring you to the land that belonged to your fathers" (Deut. 30:3-5). The later Hebrew prophets gave that promise a universal scope (Isa. 42:6 and 65:17). The description of the first Christian community at the conclusion of Acts 2 begins the fulfillment of the promise of restoring the people of God: "All the believers were together and had everything in common. . . . They broke bread in their homes and ate together with glad and sincere hearts, praising God and enjoying the favor of all the people" (Acts 2:46-47). Pentecost is programmatic.[9] Acts 1-3 is not a systematic theology. It does not present an exhaustive theology of Pentecost and the Holy Spirit. But it does identify Pentecost as a culminating and an inaugurating event. Pentecost is the fulcrum in the history of redemption from exile in the world of Genesis 3 to the universal advent of the new creation.

Pentecost and Eschatological Exodus

What is a biblical motif for describing the character of the Spirit's eschatological work? Exodus or deliverance from exile is a central theme in the history of redemption. The Spirit of God, moreover, is the primary agent of redemption from exile in its various forms—for example, exiled from God, each other, and creation. Chapter 2 detailed the Holy Spirit's role in the exile-exodus theme in the history of redemption from creation to Pentecost. This section develops that theme in terms of the eschatological character of pentecostal atonement. To begin, four clarifications are in order. First, I am not being reductive with the exile-exodus motif as the "meta"-narrative for all redemptive history. Redemption is multifaceted. Second, I am not advocating an exile posture for Christian communities to live in opposition toward "empire" or for Christians living in post-Christendom.[10] Third, exile-exodus is a comprehensive redemptive theme.

---

[9] Hinne Wagenaar, "Babel, Jerusalem and Kumba: Missiological Reflections on Genesis 11:1-9 and Acts 2:1-13," *International Review of Mission* 92, no. 366 (2003): 414.

[10] Thus, I am not situating myself in the exile theology that has developed over the past several decades under the important influence of John Howard Yoder. For an excellent introduction to this trajectory and its literature, see Stephen B. Chapman, "The Old Testament and the Church after Christendom," *Journal of Theological Interpretation* 9, no. 2 (2015): 159-67.

For example, Rodrigo J. Morales argues that death replaces exile as the fundamental problem in Paul's soteriology.[11] Paul, moreover, enlarges the expectations associated with the outpouring of the Spirit and restoration from exile to the victory of life over death in the Spirit's raising of Christ. I agree with Morales that Paul's vision shifts from national exile from the land and restoration to the more fundamental redemption from death. But death in the history of redemption is exile. It is exile from the life for which God created human beings. Thus, Paul's emphasis on death does not transcend exile-exodus as such, although Morales is correct that it transcends the ethnic and nationalist vision of restoration. At the same time, the creational and political vision of redemption is not lost. Indeed, it expands to include all creation. So, yes, Paul does not regard redemption as recovering the fortunes of national Israel. But the exodus from exile motif remains helpful for understanding the nature of the Spirit's redemptive work. Fourth, exodus is primary in the exile-exodus motif. Exile is not the normative condition from the perspective of redemptive history. Exile happens, but the Spirit did not create human beings for life in exile. The Spirit works to redeem them from it. Similarly, Paul emphasizes death and resurrection. But the point is not to revel in death, but in resurrected life in Christ that is the victory over death in all its forms. The key to the eschatological nature of the Spirit of Pentecost and atonement is that Pentecost stands in the redemptive history of exodus from exile. The outpouring of the Holy Spirit on the Day of Pentecost is the eschatological threshold from the exile in the world of Genesis 3 to the new creation of Revelation 21 and 22 and Rom. 8:21. So in what ways does exodus and the eschatological Spirit of Pentecost relate to atonement?

First, atonement, as the reconciling act of God, is exodus from exile. The fundamental problem in the narrative of redemption is the expulsion from Eden. Atonement resolves this fundamental problem. Atonement is about regaining access to the life for which God created human beings.[12] Atonement enables people alienated from God to return to righteous relationship with God (here penal-substitutionary atonement is correct). Exodus from exile is a preeminent theme for portraying redemption and the Spirit of God is often the primary agent effecting this deliverance. Life in the world of Genesis 3 is life in exile. It is the place where human beings experience estrangement from God, from each other, and from the goodness of creation. Death characterizes the spectrum of life east of Eden. Living by the sweat of the brow amid thistles and thorns are incremental encounters with death. Heartache, exasperation, petty and great indignities, and futility are experiences of living in exile from the life for which God created human beings. The final return to the dust, the dissolution of the divine image, is the most absolute and definitive experience of this alienation. The final vision of redemption in Revelation 21 and 22 portrays the renewal of the earth (the new heaven and the new earth) and resurrected embodied life within it (the New Jerusalem) because it is the consummation of exodus from the world of Genesis 3 into the land

---

[11] Rodrigo J. Morales, *The Spirit and the Restoration of Israel: New Exodus and New Creation Motifs in Galatians*, Wissenschaftliche Untersuchungen zum Neuen Testament, 282 (Tübingen: Mohr Siebeck, 2010).

[12] Jacob Milgrom, *Leviticus: A Book of Ritual and Ethics* (Minneapolis: Fortress, 2004), 17.

of eschatological promise.¹³ The Spirit's work of bringing new life, in other words, remains earthy and embodied. This vision of human life and creation redeemed from death is consistent with the Holy Spirit's role in the narrative of redemption that begins in Genesis 1 and 2. The promise of the New Jerusalem and renewal of the nations of the earth in Revelation 21 and 22, moreover, is consistent with the Hebrew prophets' attributing the renewal of Israel's social life to the Spirit's outpouring, albeit the former is inclusive of all people and not limited to Israel. In other words, the scope, not the nature, of the promised renewal expands with the Spirit of Pentecost.

Second, atonement, as eschatological exodus from exile, also characterizes current life in the Spirit of Pentecost. Traditional theology calls it sanctification. It is not a punctiliar omega event. It is not, moreover, Pelagian or works righteousness because the newness of life derives from the Holy Spirit who unites the believer with Christ and empowers the transformation of the believer into the image of Christ. Liberation from the "sinful nature" to live by the "law of the Spirit of life" only happens when "the Spirit of him who raised Jesus from the dead is living in you" (Rom. 8:2-3 and 11).¹⁴ Paul implicitly recognizes the narrative sequence of Genesis 2 and 3 in Romans 8. The present world "was subjected to frustration" and suffers under its "bondage to decay" (Rom. 8:20-21). That it "was subjected" means that it was not always so. Given Paul's earlier reference to Adam and Christ as his successor, the suffering of creation and its "eager expectation" for renewal in Romans 8 alludes to the loss of Eden. Paul links together the resurrection of Christ, the saints, and creation. The Spirit that raised Christ "will also give life to your mortal bodies" and will liberate creation "from its bondage to decay" (Rom. 8:11 and 21). The Spirit's eschatological work of raising the children of God with the resurrected Christ and renewing creation assumes the Genesis creation and exile from Eden narrative. Romans 8 carries on the narrative of the Spirit of God that began in Genesis 1. The death that marks life in the world of Genesis 2 will be vanquished. The same Spirit that stirred over the swirling

---

13 Although not addressing the pneumatological foundation of the eschatological exodus, David Mathewson argues that Rev. 21:5 ("I am making everything new") is a direct allusion to Isa. 43:19 ("See, I am doing a new thing"), which promises a new exodus from exile. See Mathewson, *A New Heaven and a New Earth: The Meaning and Function of the Old Testament in Revelation 21:1–22.5*, Journal of the Study of the New Testament Supplement Series, 238 (New York: Sheffield Academic Press, 2003), 62–3.

14 The transformation from death to life that the Spirit brings (atonement) invites comparison with the Eastern Orthodox theology of *theosis* (deification). Vladimir Lossky argues that Eastern theology does not think in terms of Western merit, but cooperation between God's grace and human free will. He clarifies that "grace is not the reward for merit of the human will, as Pelagianism would have it; but no more is it the cause of the 'meritorious acts' of our free will." A pentecostal theology of the atonement can affirm common cause on the transformative and processive nature of theosis, but the last phrase that rejects that grace is the "cause" of the sanctified acts of free will is problematic, I think, for most Pentecostals. Human freedom to live in love and fellowship with God is a product of Spirit-breathed life. For my part, a pentecostal theology of atonement, as well as a pentecostal anthropology, will place priority on the Holy Spirit as the foundation and ultimate source of human life and acts that reflect Christlikeness. Lossky, however, in a previous chapter seems to suggest as much when he bases the divine image on the work of the Holy Spirit. For Lossky, see *The Mystical Theology of the Eastern Church*, 196–8 and 118. John Meyendorff also emphasizes the "divine 'energy'" or uncreated grace of God (e.g., the Holy Spirit) as the foundation of deification. See Meyendorff, *Byzantine Theology: Historical Trends and Doctrinal Themes*, 2nd ed. (New York: Fordham University Press, 1979), 164 and 170–3.

darkness of the deep and brought forth God's good world is now at work as the Spirit of Pentecost. The purpose of the Spirit, moreover, is the same. The Holy Spirit is creating a people that lives in loving fellowship with their God and each other and enjoys abundant life in God's creation. So, one dimension of eschatological is participating in the Spirit-empowered type of life God created for human beings—Spirit telocity. But participating in the eschatological nature of the atonement also means sharing in Christ's victory over death.[15] Like Christ, the Spirit will raise all those in Christ to immortal life. Participating in the eschatological resurrection is participating in the promise of Gen. 3:15—"he will crush your head, and you will strike his heel." The Holy Spirit will no longer leave the embodied divine image bearer to return to the dust. The Holy Spirit will effect in all the people of Pentecost the final exile from life lived under the "bondage to decay" and the "old order of things" and bring them "into the glory of the children of God" (Rom. 8:21 and Rev. 21:4).

Atonement from Spirit Baptism to Eschaton

Spirit baptism, the outpouring of the Spirit of Pentecost, is the transition from the particularity of Christ's fulfillment of Spirit-breathed life to its universal offer to all people. The outpouring of the Spirit initiates, consummates, and culminates in the eschatological new creation. Because the history of redemption is still in process, atonement is dynamic. Neither Christ's nor the Spirit's work is static or finished. Sharing the life that the Spirit brought about in Christ is ongoing and, therefore, the atonement is eschatological. In other words, since atonement is the transformation by the Spirit of Pentecost into the image of Christ, it is a dynamic process. It is dynamic, moreover, from the perspective of the Spirit, Christ, and all those who participate in atonement. This section first addresses the objection to dynamic atonement that on the cross Christ declared his work "finished." Second, it details the dynamic and convergent character of Christ's and the Spirit's work in a pentecostal theology of atonement.

First, the obvious objection to a dynamic theology of the atonement is that before he died on the cross Jesus declared "it is finished." The "it" must be his work of atonement, no? Well, no. Jesus' life of faithful service to God, his fulfillment of Spirit-breathed life came to a conclusion on the cross. Jesus' cry from the cross, "it is finished," does not signal that the work of redemption concludes in an act of death (Jn 19:30). The work of atonement includes but transcends the cross. Indeed, the scope of the work of atonement is not the particular life of Jesus Christ, but the outpouring of the Spirit that brings the resurrected life of Christ to all people and creation. The Spirit of atonement is about new life for all creation and not only the death of Christ on the cross. Chapter 4 discussed the relationship between the cross and Pentecost. It argued that the gift of the Spirit of Pentecost, not the cross, is the telos of the life of Christ. This

---

[15] According to Thomas D. McGlothlin resurrection is fundamental to Paul's soteriology and entails the "double conformity" of the Spirit enabling moral transformation in the image of Christ and being raised to new life with him. See McGlothlin, *Resurrection as Salvation: Development and Conflict in Pre-Nicene Paulinism* (New York: Cambridge University Press, 2018), 32–43.

chapter also critically engages the crucicentrism of traditional atonement theologies, but in a different direction. It argues that Pentecost is eschatological and that the new creation, not death on a cross, is the ultimate goal of the atonement. Recognizing the eschatological nature of the Spirit of Pentecost does not discount Christ and the cross. But the particularity of neither the cross nor Christ culminates the work of atonement. The Spirit's universal and perennial work of giving and renewing life is always the fundamental nature and goal of the Spirit's work of redemption. The Spirit of God was at work in Christ "to save the world" (Jn 3:17). The Spirit's anointing of Christ is for the renewal of all creation. Cross-centered atonement theologies, especially the satisfaction and penal-substitutionary traditions, often miss the eschatological nature of Christ and the atonement.[16]

Graham Ward uses the phrase "eschatological remainder" to indicate that the Christian life is an ongoing process of participating in the coming kingdom of God.[17] In an earlier work, I pentecostalized the concept with the "pneumatological remainder."[18] The point is that the character of Christian redemption and especially the theology of atonement indicate that the ministry of Christ and of the Holy Spirit continues. So, here, I propose a Spirit-Christ remainder. Atonement is dynamic. But that does not make what traditional atonement theologies regard as the finished work of Christ tenuous. Atonement is in one sense complete. The Spirit-resurrected Christ has entered heaven and offered his life of faithfulness to God and has received the promise of life. God accepts his offering and will extend the blessings of covenant faithfulness in the new creation to all those who call on his name (e.g., Heb. 9:14-15). But, the historical actualization of that new creation is outstanding. In that sense, atonement is a work in progress and not finished.[19] Thus, atonement, with respect to the fulfillment of Spirit-breathed life in Christ, is finished. But the Spirit-breathed life manifested in Christ was never the telos of the work of redemption. Sharing that life with all people and creation is. Atonement, therefore, is eschatological because its actualization by the Spirit of Pentecost is ongoing. Extending the Spirit-breathed life fulfilled in Christ with all the people of Pentecost is the Spirit-Christ remainder.

Pentecost, moreover, gives the cross and the entirety of Christ's Spirit-anointed life eschatological coherence in the wider history of redemption. The Spirit's role in raising Christ, "the firstborn among many" (Rom. 8:29), and its comprehensive consummation in the renewal of creation completes the Spirit's narrative arc. The Spirit's work in the Incarnation of the Son in Jesus Christ initiates the exodus of humanity from its exile from the life for which God created it. Thus, Paul portrays Jesus as the second Adam

---

[16] Peter Schmiechen argues that Anselm's satisfaction theory differs from the penal-substitutionary view because Christ dies not to pay a penalty for sin, but to achieve God's larger purpose of restoring creation. See Schmiechen, *Saving Power: Theories of Atonement and Forms of the Church* (Grand Rapids: Eerdmans, 2005), 194–221.

[17] For Graham Ward's development of the term, see *The Politics of Discipleship: Becoming Postmaterial Citizens*, The Church and Postmodern Culture, ser. ed. James K. A. Smith (Grand Rapids: BakerAcademic, 2009), 167–80.

[18] For my use of the pneumatological remainder, see *From Pentecost to the Triune God: A Pentecostal Trinitarian Theology* (Grand Rapids: Eerdmans, 2012), 88–94.

[19] See David M. Moffitt, *Atonement and the Logic of Resurrection in the Epistle to the Hebrews*, Supplements to Novum Testamentum (Boston: Brill, 2011), 284.

(Rom. 5:14). The first Adam led humanity out of Eden and into the world of Genesis 3 and to the reign of death. The first Adam, in other words, lost Spirit-breathed life. Jesus Christ, the Spirit-anointed messiah, redeems the children of the first Adam from the world of dust and death and leads them into the new creation. The Spirit of God is central to this biblical narrative of redemption. Adam's life begins with the Spirit's breath of life and ends when the Spirit departs (Gen. 6:3; also Job 33:4, 34:14-15). So also, the Holy Spirit catalyzes the Incarnation of the Son of God in Jesus Christ. The Spirit empowers Jesus' ministry (e.g., Mt. 12:28). And, when darkness appears to descend and death reign absolute, the Spirit raises Christ from the dead and into the glory of resurrected life. The risen Christ then sends the Holy Spirit, the Spirit of Pentecost, to share his Spirit-anointed life with all people in order to effect the end of exile and the renewal of all creation. The Spirit's raising of Christ begins the liberation of people from the condition of life in the world of Genesis 3 and the renewal of creation itself. The Spirit's raising of Christ means that exile from the life for which God created human beings is over. The world of dust and death has been overcome. The Spirit of life, not death, has triumphed.

Second, the dynamism of atonement includes Christological and pneumatological dimensions and convergence points. Indeed, the work of Christ and the Spirit retains their synergy developed in previous chapters. David M. Moffitt's work on Hebrews showcases Christ's ongoing work of atonement. Moffitt makes the provocative argument that Christ's work of atonement includes his life, death, resurrection, ascension to heaven, and ongoing intercession as high priest before God the Father.[20] Moffitt's work relies on Christ's priestly role in Hebrews. He argues that Hebrews emphasizes Jesus' deliverance as a righteous sufferer after having suffered death in obedience to the Father. The emphasis is not on Christ's death as such, but "that Jesus has been *delivered* from the realm of death. The suffering precedes the deliverance, but the deliverance is the focal point, not the suffering itself."[21] The death of Jesus is important, although not as a vicarious penalty for sin, but as the transition to heaven.[22] Christ's work of atonement, moreover, primarily relates to his intercessory role before God the Father. In Hebrews, atonement takes place when the resurrected Christ presents himself to the Father in heaven, the throne room, in order to mediate on behalf of his people

---

[20] Of course, not all agree with Moffitt's case for Christ's intercessory atonement in Hebrews. For example, Michael Kibbe argues that Moffitt (renewing a Socinian trajectory of atonement theology) is correct to emphasize the Hebrew Bible's ritual background and remind that the atonement is multifaceted, but is incorrect to downplay the centrality of the cross for accomplishing atonement. See Michael Kibbe, "Is It Finished? When did It Start? Hebrews, Priesthood, and Atonement in Biblical, Systematic, and Historical Perspective," *The Journal of Theological Studies* n.s. 65, no. 1 (2014): 25–61. Moffitt responds to Kibbe's (as well as Jeremy R. Treat's critical interaction in *The Crucified King: Atonement and Kingdom in Biblical and Systematic Theology* [Grand Rapids: Zondervan, 2014]) association of his view with Socinius by showing that interpreting Christ's atonement as a sequence that includes the post-crucifixion and the post-resurrection offering of himself as a sacrifice before the Father in heaven was present in the early church. See David A. Moffitt, "Jesus' Heavenly Sacrifice in Early Christian Reception of Hebrews: A Survey," *The Journal of Theological Studies* n.s. 68, no. 1 (2017): 46–71.

[21] Moffitt, *Atonement and the Logic of Resurrection*, 241 (emphasis in original).

[22] Christian A. Eberhart, "'The Lamb of God that takes away the Sin of the World': Reflections on Atonement in the New Testament," *Touchstone: Heritage and Theology in a New Age* 31, no. 2 (2013): 39.

(Heb. 10:10). Moffitt maintains that "heaven is the location of the offering of Jesus' body, not the earthly moment of his death on the cross."[23] He continues that "Jesus' life of faithful obedience enables his body to be offered to God as the sacrifice that fully satisfies what God desires."[24] Yet God does not desire sacrifices, but a life of faithfulness. Jesus lived as one with the law on his "heart" and "mind" (Heb. 10:16). Christ "was, in other words, the one qualified to be the mediator of the promised new covenant in which all members would have the Law written on their hearts."[25] One of Moffitt's key points is that Jesus continuously intercedes and provides "ongoing atonement" for his people (Heb. 8:1 and 7:25).[26] The resurrected Christ remains before the Father where his "sacrificial, atoning work is perpetual."[27] What is complete is Christ's entering the presence of God and initiating the sacrifice of ministering presence—it is perpetual until the final consummation of the heavenly kingdom, at which point his people will be made perfect and beyond the need of a high priest to intercede on their behalf.

Jesus' perennial priestly role in heaven also highlights the importance of the ascension for atonement. Douglas Farrow identifies the ascension as the "climax" of Jesus' ministry. He argues that "cross, resurrection, and finally the ascension, which is the proper outcome of his messianic career."[28] I argue that Pentecost is the "outcome" or telos of Christ's ministry. Farrow, nevertheless, raises an important reminder. The ascension is an important, although often overlooked, part of the story of Christ. Christ ascends to the Father to reconcile human beings to God. In other words, he returns to God the Father in order that all the people of Pentecost can return with him. As Farrow puts it, "Jesus' destiny is our destiny . . . he has reached it not only for himself but also for us."[29] Jesus ascends to the Father to intercede until the saints are perfected in grace and to prepare their eschatological home (Jn 14:2).[30] The ascension, moreover, is an activity of the triune God. Through the Holy Spirit Christ presents himself to the Father who in turn receives him and invites him to sit at his side. Atonement takes place when all the people united to Christ through the Holy Spirit join this heavenly fellowship.[31] Frank D. Macchia argues that Christ's ascension and exaltation before the Father "was not just for himself but for us. It was not just representative, but was a gift poured out and offered, reaching out to us and seeking to draw us in."[32] That drawing in

---

[23] Moffitt, *Atonement and the Logic of Resurrection*, 247. Timo Eskola also affirms "that atonement was obtained only in the Holy of Holies, and not at the moment . . . of Christ's death." See Timo Eskola, *Messiah and the Throne: Jewish Merkabah Mysticism and Early Christian Exaltation Discourse*, Wissenschaftliche Untersuchungen zum Neuen Testament, II/142 (Tübingen: Mohr Siebeck, 2001), 276—as quoted in R. B. Jamieson, *Jesus' Death and Heavenly Offering in Hebrews* (New York: Cambridge University Press, 2019), 13–14.

[24] Moffitt, *Atonement and the Logic of Resurrection*, 246.

[25] Moffitt, *Atonement and the Logic of Resurrection*, 252.

[26] David M. Moffitt, "It Is Not Finished: Jesus's Perpetual Atoning Work as the Heavenly High Priest in Hebrews," in *So Great a Salvation: A Dialogue on the Atonement in Hebrews*, ed. Jon C. Laansma, George H. Guthrie, and Cynthia Long Westfall (New York: T & T Clark, 2019), 168.

[27] Moffitt, "It Is Not Finished," 173.

[28] Douglas Farrow, *Ascension Theology* (New York: T & T Clark, 2011), 7–8.

[29] Farrow, *Ascension Theology*, 10.

[30] Farrow, *Ascension Theology*, 10–11.

[31] Farrow, *Ascension Theology*, 122.

[32] Frank D. Macchia, *Jesus the Spirit Baptizer: Christology in Light of Pentecost* (Grand Rapids: Eerdmans, 2018), 315.

occurs in the outpouring of the Spirit of Pentecost. As the ascended and exalted Lord, Jesus Christ's first and fundamental gift of redemption is to pour out the Holy Spirit.[33] Humanity's exile from relationship with God and the life for which God created it is overcome in the ascension. Jesus takes his sacred humanity before the Father, and the Father receives him in fellowship. Adam no longer hides from God in the Garden but goes to God. The eschatological work of the Holy Spirit in Christ's resurrection from the dead and ascension to heaven, therefore, fulfills the purpose of creation. It restores humanity to its relationship with God.

Atonement is eschatological because Jesus, the high priest, sanctifies his people until they are made perfect when they receive their inheritance in the everlasting kingdom.[34] But what is the Spirit's role in Christ's ongoing intercession? The Holy Spirit's dynamic role in the atonement has two facets. On the one hand, the Spirit's role in the Incarnation of Christ and empowering his ministry continues. Hebrews 9:14 declares Christ offered himself "through the eternal Spirit unblemished to God."[35] The enabling power of the Spirit in Christ's intercession for his people before the Father is consistent with the Spirit's role in the life of Christ in the narrative of redemption. Indeed, the ongoing synergy between the Spirit and Christ carries on the work of redemption until its full consummation in the everlasting kingdom of God. The Spirit was the foundation of Jesus' life of faithfulness. Through the Spirit, he fulfilled the human vocation to live in love and faithfulness to God. Jesus' offering of this life of faithful obedience to the Father is part of atonement. But the offering in heaven is not punctiliar, a one-off event. It is not the end of atonement. Christ came as the Spirit-anointed messiah in order to share his life of faithful obedience with all people. Not to establish a religion of morality, but a faith and a way of life that lives in loving fellowship and faithfulness with God. Yes, Christ's atoning work is objective and has a once-for-all dimension to it. He was a historical figure; his life of faithful obedience took place in a certain time and context. But his atonement, his life of Spirit-anointed faithfulness, was never meant to remain in the past as an objective historical event or even in heaven. Christ came to live Spirit-anointed life so that he could share that atoning life with all people. David M. Moffitt puts it this way: Christ "will one day return from the heavenly location to the earthly realm at the consummation of all things, the point at which all his siblings will join him in the inheritance of their eternal salvation" (cf. Heb. 10:36-39 and Rom. 8:17-27).[36] In the end, whether or not one agrees with Moffitt that Jesus' work of atonement includes perpetual intercession before God the Father, the Spirit's

---

[33] Macchia, *Jesus the Spirit Baptizer*, 313.
[34] Moffitt, "It Is Not Finished," 174.
[35] Hebrews 9:14 is the only verse that directly links the Spirit to the atonement. See Martin Emmrich, "'Amtscharisma': Through the Eternal Spirit (Hebrews 9:14)," *Bulletin for Biblical Research* 12, no. 1 (2002): 22–3. Grant Osborne, however, argues that Revelation opens with a trinitarian vision of the heavenly throne room where the Spirit, along with Christ, is before the Father (Rev. 1:4-5). Osborne maintains that "seven spirits before his throne" refers to the Holy Spirit. The number seven indicates the Spirit's "perfect carrying out of the work of God in this world." See Grant R. Osborne, *Revelation* (Grand Rapids: Baker Academic, 2002), 36–7. John Christopher Thomas also argues that the "seven spirits" in Rev. 1:4 indicate the Holy Spirit—see "Revelation," in *A Biblical Theology of the Holy Spirit*, ed. Trevor J. Burke and Keith Warrington (London: SPCK, 2014), 257–8.
[36] Moffitt, *Atonement and the Logic of Resurrection*, 284.

role in the offering of Christ (Heb. 9:14) indicates the Spirit's eschatological agency in the work of atonement because Christ's offering, the atoning sacrifice, takes place in and through the Holy Spirit.

On the other hand, the Holy Spirit's role in enabling Christ to offer his sacrifice is reciprocal with the Spirit's role in making atonement efficacious in the believer—that is, as the "heavenly gift" of grace (Heb. 6:4).[37] Christ's altar service before the Father comprehends his entire life and ministry. Christ's work of atonement began when the Holy Spirit catalyzed the Incarnation. By the same Spirit, Christ "[offers] himself . . . to God" (Heb. 9:14). Atonement began through and continues through the Holy Spirit. Where traditional atonement theology, moreover, separates Christ's work and the application or benefit of atonement (i.e., justification), a pentecostal theology of the atonement coordinates them.[38] Christ offers himself to God so that all those united to him as co-heirs, as his brothers and sisters, can "cleanse [their] consciences from acts that lead to death, so that [they] may serve the living God" (Heb. 9:14). Christ lives and offers himself to God through the Holy Spirit so that he can offer that same Spirit-breathed life to all people so that they can join him at the altar before God the Father.[39] How do people share in the Spirit-breathed life fulfilled in Christ? The answer is by receiving the Spirit of Pentecost. Spirit baptism is the promise announced in the Gospels at the opening of Jesus' ministry when he was baptized by John the Baptist. Jesus confirms this promise of the gift of the Spirit when he urges his disciples to wait in Jerusalem until they receive the promise of the Father. The promise of the Father, the promise of the Holy Spirit that would renew the people of God and empower faithfulness to God. When the Gentile household of Cornelius received the gospel, signaling the inclusion of "all people" in the promise of the gospel, Peter summarizes it pneumatologically—"the Holy Spirit came on them as he had come on us at the beginning. Then I remembered what the Lord had said, 'John Baptized with the water, but you will be baptized with the Holy Spirit'" (Acts 2:17 and 11:15-16).

So, atonement has two Spirit Christological dimensions and the Holy Spirit is foundational to them. First, the Spirit is the foundation of Jesus Christ's life and ministry—from Incarnation to resurrected high priest interceding before the Father (Lk. 1:3 5 and Heb. 9:14). Second, the Holy Spirit unites people to Christ and brings the renewal of resurrected Christ-like life. These two dimensions are a unified work of atonement grounded in the outpouring of the Holy Spirit first on Christ and then on "all people" (Acts 2:17). The Holy Spirit is eschatological because the gift of the

---

[37] Allen also affirms that the Spirit's work in grace parallels the Spirit's work in Christ; see David M. Allen, "'The Forgotten Spirit': A Pentecostal Reading of the Letter to the Hebrews?" *Journal of Pentecostal Theology* 18, no. 1 (2009): 62. Allen also argues that receiving the Holy Spirit, the "heavenly gift," is equivalent with conversion and "demarks an eschatological conclusion for its recipients"; it marks the "new covenant dispensation" ("The Forgotten Spirit," 57–8 and 63).

[38] Alan K. Hodson also argues that Heb. 9:14 shows the Holy Spirit's involvement in the work of atonement, especially when Heb. 9:14 is coordinated with the Spirit anointing of the servant of Isa. 42:1 and Isa. 53:10-12. See Hodson, "Hebrews," in *A Biblical Theology of the Holy Spirit*, ed. Trevor J. Burke and Keith Warrington (London: SPCK, 2014), 231–2.

[39] Christian A. Eberhart argues that atonement relates to an offering presented to and before God for "purification and consecration" in order to "encounter God." See Eberhart, "The Lamb of God that takes away the Sin of the World," 43 and 36.

Spirit entails tasting the "the powers of the coming age" that were first on display in Christ (Heb. 6:4-5). In sum, human life begins with the breath of life from God's Spirit. Atonement is the return of God's Spirit to redeem human life from death, to rescue it from its descent into dust, and to restore it to the life for which God created it. Jesus Christ is the Spirit-anointed messiah that restores humanity from its exile from creation. Jesus fulfilled Spirit-breathed life; the human vocation to bear the Spirit-breathed divine image. The Holy Spirit redeems Christ from death. Christ sends the Spirit of Pentecost to share his Spirit-breathed life with all people, thus providing atonement. Pentecost, moreover, is eschatological because it makes the exile overcome in the Incarnation a universal opportunity for all people. Exiled from the life God created for them, the Spirit of Pentecost reconciles people to their relationships with the triune God, with each other, and with creation.

Conclusion

The Spirit of Pentecost opens the door to the new creation. The outpouring of the Holy Spirit on the Day of Pentecost inaugurates the eschatological exodus. The Spirit of Pentecost leads the people of God from darkness and death into the horizon of the liberated life of the kingdom of God. Doing so reconciles the "all people" of Pentecost to the life for which God created them (Acts 2:17). This eschatological journey to the new creation is the substance of the experience of atonement and of the Spirit of Pentecost. Characterizing atonement as the dynamic experience of life in the Spirit of Pentecost on the way to the new creation and situating atonement in terms of the history of redemption requires a reinterpretation of the finality of cross. The cross becomes part of the wider drama of redemption and the narrative of the Spirit of God that stretches from creation to Pentecost and new creation.

Part Two

Practicing Atonement

7

Empowering All People

The promise of the Spirit of Pentecost is power. Jesus declared to his disciples "do not leave Jerusalem, but wait for the gift my Father promised . . . you will receive power when the Holy Spirit comes on you" (Acts 1:4 and 8). But what is the purpose of the power of the Spirit of Pentecost? To take the Gospel to the "ends of the earth" so that "all people" can be reconciled and included in the community of the Spirit of Pentecost (Acts 2:17). This empowered witness that fosters redemptive communities of inclusive diversity—ecclesial, social, and civil—is the praxis of atonement that participates in the Spirit of Pentecost. Essential to the inclusive community of the Spirit of Pentecost is diversity. The unique ways that human beings bear the Spirit-breathed divine image compose the tapestry of the community formed by the Spirit of Pentecost. The many tongues of Pentecost, the manifold gifts of the Holy Spirit constitute the redemptive community of the Spirit. The Spirit of Pentecost comes in power to reconcile "all people" to each other and their God. The many tongues of Pentecost are a sign of the Spirit-created community. Too often, however, Pentecostals have sought the signs of tongues and spiritual gifts, but not the signified.

This chapter begins Part Two of this book. Part Two transitions to pentecostal praxis of atonement. It does not, however, leave behind pentecostal theology. On the contrary, the chapters of Part Two give a theological account of pentecostal praxis based on the constructive theology of Part One. The task is twofold. On the one hand, they interpret pentecostal experience in terms of the theology of Part One. On the other hand, they illustrate ways that the pentecostal experience of grace embodies the theology of atonement presented in Part One. Each chapter in Part Two corresponds to its theological companion in Part One. They treat the same consecutive theological categories of Part One—"Pentecost," "Incarnation," "Crucifixion," "Resurrection," and "Eschatology"—but they focus on their meaning for pentecostal practice of atonement. So like the first chapter of Part One, this chapter centers on Pentecost. It first looks at two people in pentecostal history—Pandita Ramabai and William J. Seymour—and the ways they endeavored to practice the promise of the Spirit of Pentecost. Early pentecostal preaching and ministry was politically and socially subversive: gender and racial mixing in altar prayer; black men and women preaching to white people; the socially marginalized carrying the banner of renewal. Early pentecostal praxis manifested the promise of Pentecost—the outpouring of the Spirit on "all people." As the pentecostal churches developed institutionally, however, they tended to lose their subversive elements. In doing so, they also lost something essential to the Spirit of Pentecost. The final section considers a contemporary pentecostal church—Valley Gate Vineyard. The church and its ministries display the many tongues of Pentecost and the manifold gifts of the Holy Spirit that constitute the redemptive community of the Spirit. Embodying inclusive community is not only a prominent feature of the promise of Pentecost but a pressing need for contemporary society. The movement of multiculturalism endeavors but often fails to achieve inclusive communities. Valley Gate Vineyard provides a concrete example of embodying the promise and power of the Spirit of Pentecost and as such a public witness to a type community life sorely needed in contemporary society. Together these historical and current examples point the way to recovering the empowered witness and practice of the many tongues of Pentecost.

Pandita Ramabai and the Mukti Mission

At the turn of the year in 1905, Pandita Saraswati Ramabai (1858–1922) along with other women at the Mukti Mission began praying for an outpouring of the Holy Spirit. Ramabai's early morning prayer group, which eventually grew to 500 women, received their request six months later in June 1905. The outpouring of the Holy Spirit brought revival that lasted for eighteen months and led to numerous conversions, over one thousand baptisms, extended prayer meetings, and ministry teams being sent out into the regions around the Mukti Mission. The pentecostal revival at Mukti, "Pentecost in India," is important because it supports the case for the global emergence of the pentecostal movements rather than privileging Azusa Street as the origin of Pentecostalism, and it also counters the case for tongues as the exclusive sign of Spirit baptism.[1] Yan Suarsana argues that taking the Mukti Revival as a pentecostal predecessor to Azusa Street is a historical construction governed by multicultural political motivations as much as the preference for Azusa Street as the origin of the pentecostal movement was driven by ecclesial needs of self-legitimacy. Both views, according to Suarsana, marginalize the nationalist and anti-colonial narrative of the revival put forth by Ramabai.[2] The Mukti Mission under Ramabai's leadership also eventually dissociated from the influx of Western pentecostal church missionaries and their movements.[3] Litigating the debate over which came first, Mukti or Azusa and

---

[1] Allan Anderson, *Spreading Fires: The Missionary Nature of Early Pentecostalism* (Maryknoll: Orbis, 2007), 77–89 and Gary B. McGee, "'Latter Rain' Falling in the East: Early-Twentieth-Century Pentecostalism in India and the Debate over Speaking in Tongues," *Church History* 68, no. 3 (1999): 648–56. Note that other pentecostal-type revivals took place independently from both Mukti and Azusa in the Khassia Hills in northeast India, China, Korea, and Australia. For "Pentecost in India," see *The Apostolic Faith* 1, no. 3 (November 1906): 1. Also, note that this brief report does not mention Western missionaries as bringing the revival, but says the people "are simply taught of God."

[2] Yan Suarsana, "Inventing Pentecostalism: Pandita Ramabai and the Mukti Revival from a Postcolonial Perspective," *PentecoStudies* 13, no. 2 (2014): 173–96.

[3] Michael Begrunder, *The South Indian Pentecostal Movement in the Twentieth Century*, Studies in the History of Christian Missions (Grand Rapids: Eerdmans, 2008), 24–5.

whether or not Mukti remained "pentecostal" is not my concern.[4] Both revivals are part of the history of the global pentecostal movements.[5] But what was the driving source of the Mukti Mission pentecostal revival and how does it relate to pentecostal atonement theology?

The common view holds that Ramabai's contacts with the Holiness and Reformed revival movements in England (e.g., the Keswick movement) and in parts of America (e.g., Rochester, NY, and the holiness movement) provided the background for the revival at the Mukti Mission.[6] Protestant missionaries in India and Minnie Abrams, a key leader and support person at the Mukti Mission, came with backgrounds in the Higher Life and holiness movements that included preaching on and the anticipation of experiencing Spirit baptism. The aspiration for revival, however, needs to be set in the context of Ramabai's deeper motivations for social and religious liberty. The holiness and Higher Life connections are vital, but Ramabai's search for, in modern terms, social liberation precedes it. Indeed, before becoming a Christian she established the Arya Mahila Samaj society to promote the "emancipation of women," which situates Ramabai in the emerging movement of Indian nationalism and independence.[7] Ramabai believed that Christianity could provide freedom from the Hindu caste and the colonial hierarchies.[8] Her quest for social and economic freedom for Indian women and for an authentic indigenous Indian expression of Christianity preceded the pentecostal revival at the Mukti Mission (*Mukti* means "liberty"). The pentecostal revival and social liberation, moreover, were a common cause for Ramabai. They should be understood on a continuum of participating in the Spirit of Pentecost.[9] Throughout her spiritual quest she saw religious salvation as the source for "women's

---

[4] Indeed, Michael J. McClymond argues for historical and theological reasons that the scholarly discussion of pentecostal origins should move beyond the binary polygenesis (global origins) or monogenesis (Azusa Street) debate and understand the emergence of Pentecostalism in terms of "inclusive origins." See McClymond, "'I Will Pour Out of My Spirit Upon All Flesh': An Historical and Theological Meditation on Pentecostal Origins," *Pneuma: The Journal of the Society for Pentecostal Studies* 37, no. 3 (2015): 356–74.

[5] Edith L. Blumhofer also makes this argument even though Ramabai refused to insist on speaking in tongues as the sign of Spirit baptism and so distanced herself from early Pentecostalism. See Blumhofer, "Consuming Fire: Pandita Ramabai and the Early Pentecostal Impulse," in *Indian and Christian: The Life and Legacy of Pandita Ramabai*, ed. Roger E. Hedlund, Sebastian Kim, and Rajkumar Boaz Johnson (Delhi: MIIS/CMS/ISPCK, 2011), 127–54.

[6] For Ramabai's connection to the holiness movement, see Anderson, *Spreading Fires*, 78; McGee, "Latter Rain," 651–3 and 658; and Howard A. Snyder, "Holiness Heritage: The Case of Pandita Ramabai," *Wesleyan Theological Journal* 40, no. 2 (2005): 30–51.

[7] Antoinette M. Burton, *At the Heart of the Empire: Indians and the Colonial Encounter in Late-Victorian Britain* (Berkeley: University of California Press, 1998), 80–3 and Robert Eric Frykenberg, "The Legacy of Pandita Ramabai: Mahatma of Mukti," *International Bulletin of Mission Research* 40, no. 1 (2016): 61–2.

[8] Robert Eric Frykenberg, "Pandita Ramabai Saraswati: A Biographical Introduction," in *Pandita Ramabai's America: Conditions of Life in the United States*, ed. Robert Eric Frykenberg, trans. Kshitija Gomes (Grand Rapids: Eerdmans, 2003), 7–14.

[9] Robert Eric Frykenberg describes her experience of the outpouring of the Holy Spirit and the "Great Revival" at Mukti as the fourth major turning point in her Christian life. See Frykenberg, "Pandita Ramabai Saraswati: A Biographical Introduction," 49–53. Also see Frykenberg's account of Ramabai in *Christianity in India: From Beginnings to the Present*, Oxford History of the Christian Church, ed. Henry Chadwick and Owen Chadwick (New York: Oxford University Press, 2008), 382–411.

emancipation."[10] The outpouring of the Spirit and the pentecostal revival that took place at the Mukti Mission is the culmination and the confirmation of her heart opening up to, and of her life and practice of being empowered by, the Spirit of Pentecost. That means regarding Ramabai and the Mukti Mission as the Indian Pentecost is correct, but also misleading. The outpouring of the Holy Spirit at Mukti sparked religious revival and as such it was part of the emergence of global Pentecostalism. Understanding the Mukti Revival primarily as a "religious" event, however, obscures both Ramabai's life and ministry and the nature of Pentecost. The outpouring of the Holy Spirit and the revival at Mukti was the culmination of Ramabai's longer and ongoing life and ministry that resisted and transcended gender and cultural chauvinism. Yes, the Mukti Revival participated in the charismatic renewal of the church that today is called global Pentecostalism. But Ramabai's Mukti Mission and global Pentecostalism are more than "religious" phenomena.

The chief background for understanding Ramabai's turn to the Christian faith and search for an outpouring of the Holy Spirit was the Hindu caste system and English colonialism and their respective chauvinisms.[11] Ramabai converted to Christianity while studying in England in 1883. She became convinced that the "egalitarian principles of Christianity" supported social liberation from the caste and colonial forms of inequality.[12] But the escape she sought was not "spiritual." Ramabai wanted freedom from the caste hierarchy that subordinated women. She believed that education and skills training would empower women to gain economic freedom and security.[13] Patriarchy however was not only a product of the Hindu social hierarchy. Ramabai encountered it in England too in two ways. First, she went to England in 1883 to pursue a medical education. She studied at the Anglican Cheltenham Ladies College. But disagreement over doctrine and the hierarchy of the Anglican church led to her departure. Part of the tension was Ramabai's resistance to "her [English] benefactor's attempts to make her an evangelical missionary to India."[14] The problem she encountered in the Anglican church was patriarchal prejudices that artificially limited the educational and professional opportunities of women.[15] She wanted to study medicine. But due to a hearing disability, her church superiors steered her to become a missionary. Second, she was not content to be a missionary supervised and

---

[10] Ram Bapat, "Pandita Ramabai: Faith and Reason in the Shadow of the East and West," in *Representing Hinduism: The Construction of Religious Traditions and National Identity*, ed. Vasudha Dalmia and Heinrich von Stietencron (New Delhi: Sage, 1995), 248. Bapat argues, however, that Ramabai's focus on spiritual salvation stalled her development of thoroughgoing social reform for women. See Bapat, "Pandita Ramabai," 250–1.

[11] For Ramabai's reform initiatives in the Hindu caste context, see Meera Kosambi, "Introduction: Situating Pandita Ramabai's American Encounter," in *Pandita Ramabai's American Encounter: The Peoples of the United States (1889)*, trans. and ed. Meera Kosambi (Bloomington: Indiana University Press, 2003), 10–17.

[12] Anderson, *Spreading Fires*, 76.

[13] Anderson, *Spreading Fires*, 77–8.

[14] Burton, *At the Heart of the Empire*, 3–4, 72, 85–7, and 92–107.

[15] R. S. Sugirtharajah argues that Ramabai developed her method of Bible translation and biblical hermeneutics as a response to this infantilizing patriarchy and as such it should be understood as "resistance hermeneutics." See Sugirtharajah, *The Bible and the Third World: Precolonial, Colonial, and Postcolonial Encounters* (Cambridge: Cambridge University Press, 2001), 98 and 104.

controlled by the graces of her Western and, ultimately male, superiors. The issue was not only patriarchy but also colonial chauvinism. Ramabai wanted to develop indigenous Indian-Christian reform initiatives.[16] She did not want to serve at the tutelage and leave of self-appointed Western church "superiors."[17] Antoinette M. Burton points out "British imperial power and colonial Christianity were not just contiguous, but completely coincidental."[18] At the same time, witnessing the work of the Sisters of Wantage (the Community of Saint Mary the Virgin) among English "orphans, widows, and prostitutes became the model of Ramabai's work and words in India."[19] Dorothea Beale, principal of the Cheltenham Ladies College was a "champion of women's education" and provided her with inspiration and support to pursue education.[20]

Disaffected with England, Ramabai left for America in 1886. She spent two and half years there raising funds for her social and mission work in India. Her speaking and fundraising itinerary in America was brisk and successful. Her time in America also introduced her to the abolitionist movement and social and civil rights leaders such as William Lloyd Garrison, Harriett Tubman, and Abraham Lincoln. She encountered figures in what today is called first wave feminism, which inspired and encouraged her vision for civil and economic freedom for Indian women.[21] In general, she received more support from American reformers for her Indian initiatives. She was nevertheless appalled no less at the tendency to subordinate women to men and to exclude women from certain professions, especially preaching, in the American churches.[22] Ramabai's international travel to England and America itself was a controversial form of social liberation. Traveling overseas to gain education, although common for her male counterparts, was "heretical" and socially subversive behavior for "high-caste Hindu women" that left them open to public shaming and even violence upon their return to India.[23]

Ramabai returned to India (1889) and eventually established the Mukti Mission (1895). Its purpose was to provide a haven and training school for impoverished girls and young women (especially widows of child marriages). The mission grew from a few dozen in 1895 to nearly 2,000 in 1905. Her conviction that Indian (Hindu) women could gain genuine freedom only through Christianity and economic independence was

---

[16] For Ramabai's quest for an indigenous expression of Christianity appropriate for India, see Paul Joseph Bhakiaraj, "Forging an Identity Fit for God and Country: Pandita Ramabai as a Pioneer of Indigenous Christianity," in *Indian and Christian: The Life and Legacy of Pandita Ramabai*, ed. Roger E. Hedlund, Sebastian Kim, and Rajkumar Boaz Johnson (Delhi: MIIS/CMS/ISPCK, 2011), 279–306.
[17] Frykenberg, "Pandita Ramabai Saraswati: A Biographical Introduction," 18–24.
[18] Burton, *At the Heart of the Empire*, 95.
[19] Rajkumar Boaz Johnson, "The Biblical Theological Contribution of Pandita Ramabai: A Neglected Pioneer Indian Christian Feminist Theologian," *Ex Auditu* 23 (2007): 114–15; Frykenberg, "Pandita Ramabai Saraswati: A Biographical Introduction," 16–17; and Meera Kosambi, *Pandita Ramabai's Feminist and Christian Conversions: Focus on Stree Dharma-Neeti* (Bombay: Research Centre for Women's Studies, S.D.N.T. Women's University, 1995), 183–5.
[20] Frykenberg, "Pandita Ramabai Saraswati: A Biographical Introduction," 18–19.
[21] Especially important was the help and the influence offered by Dr. Rachel L. Bodley, president of the Woman's Medical College of Pennsylvania. See Frykenberg, "The Legacy of Pandita Ramabai," 64 and Frykenberg, "Pandita Ramabai Saraswati: A Biographical Introduction," 24–30.
[22] Snyder, "Holiness Heritage," 35.
[23] Burton, *At the Heart of the Empire*, 73–4.

foundational to the mission.[24] Although initiated to rescue destitute women from social depredations, additional ministries were established for the sick and elderly, orphaned boys, and the blind.[25] Chapter 2 charted key features of the narrative of redemption (e.g., Eden as the proto-charismatic community and exile-exodus) and argued that they anticipate and set the stage for the promise of the Spirit of Pentecost. The argument here is that Ramabai's quest for social liberation that came to fruition at Mukti was the manifestation of the power of the Spirit of Pentecost and practices of atonement.

First, the Mukti Mission's effort to transcend Hindu patriarchy and Western colonial and ecclesial bigotry is Spirit-empowered exodus from exile.[26] The quest for the outpouring of the Holy Spirit and revival and the consequent renewal of Christian practices in the Indian churches arose in part from Ramabai's opposition to the colonizing attempts and ethnocentric attitudes of Western church leaders. Allan Anderson suggests that Ramabai's desire for an indigenous Indian expression of pentecostal Christianity shows the influence of Ramabai's background in "philosophical Brahmanism" and Indian nationalism.[27] Without questioning the philosophical and nationalist influences on Ramabai, her aspiration for an experience of the Holy Spirit adapted to Indian culture can also be understood as a manifestation of the Spirit of Pentecost. In other words, resisting Western missionaries as agents of chauvinist colonialism partly animated her search for an outpouring of the Holy Spirit. Ramabai's search for an Indian expression of Christianity was a quest for the many tongues of Pentecost. Ramabai's resistance to the doctrine and practice of speaking in tongues as initial evidence of Spirit baptism may be an example of her opposition to ecclesial colonialism. She believed that the Spirit would inspire "a contextual form of Indian Christianity."[28] American pentecostal missionaries showing up and demanding that Indians speak in tongues to legitimize their experience of the Holy Spirit was simply another colonial boot. Her resistance can be understood as the empowerment of one of the many tongues of Pentecost. The Spirit of Pentecost empowers a return to life unburdened from oppression. The many tongues of Pentecost recognize the integrity of human diversity and freedom.

Second, Ramabai's life and ministry at the Mukti Mission are examples of atonement because they participated in the perennial purpose of the outpouring of the Spirit of Pentecost—to prepare a place for people to flourish in their Spirit-breathed life. Ramabai declared that Isa. 61:1 was central to the gospel for India—"The Spirit of the Sovereign Lord is on me, because The LORD has anointed me to preach good news to the poor."[29] One of the central features of the Spirit's work in the narrative of redemption is the creation and the provision of land, a place, for flourishing. In creation, the Spirit of God separates the land from the waters of the deep and brings forth life on the land. In the

---

[24] Anderson, *Spreading Fires*, 78.
[25] Frykenberg, "Pandita Ramabai Saraswati: A Biographical Introduction," 37–43 and Frykenberg, "The Legacy of Pandita Ramabai," 66.
[26] Situating Ramabai's spiritual journey and social reforms in the context of nascent Indian nationalism, Hinduism, early feminism, British colonial rule, Western Christianity, and Pentecostalism is complicated. For a nuanced analysis of these factors in Ramabai, see, Bapat, "Pandita Ramabai," 224–52.
[27] Anderson, *Spreading Fires*, 84–5.
[28] Anderson, *Spreading Fires*, 85.
[29] Boaz Johnson, "The Biblical Theological Contribution of Pandita Ramabai," 123.

exodus, the Spirit makes the way through the sea and eventually brings the people of Israel into the land across the Jordan. Restoration to and renewal in the land is central to the promises of the exilic prophets. The renewal of the land, indeed of all creation, finds its fullness in the promised new heaven and new earth in Revelation 21. The promise of land is not about dirt and geography per se (although the land of promise was a specific place). It is the promise of a place for life to flourish—"I will . . . bring you back into your own land . . . I will put my Spirit in you and . . . you will be my people and I will be your God . . . this land . . . has become like the garden of Eden" (Ezek. 36:24-35). Ramabai's Mukti Mission provided a "land," a place, for dispossessed and discarded people. It gave them a place to flourish in community and to achieve economic sustainability. It made a way out of exile to the life for which God created them.

Third, the outpouring of the Holy Spirit and the revival it started at the Mukti Mission stands in continuity with the redemptive narrative of the Spirit of Pentecost— the Spirit that delivered the earth from the primal abyss, the Spirit that animated human beings for edenic life, the Spirit of Pentecost that comes to raise up and speak in the tongues of "all people," and the Spirit that will liberate creation in the new heaven and the new earth. Situating Ramabai and the Mukti Mission within the ongoing history of redemption is consistent with her Indian biblical hermeneutic. She regarded the Bible as a history of redemptive testimonies and "the 'liberty' of the Indian woman and outcaste . . . as a continuation of the wonderful testimonies, the salvation testimonials of the biblical texts."[30] The biblical narrative of the Spirit became the narrative of redemption at Mukti. Ramabai's quest for gender equality, economic security, and indigenous and contextualized expressions of the Christian life honored and participated in the sacredness of the diverse fecundity of Spirit-breathed life. They participated in the Spirit of atonement. They were eruptions of Spirit-breathed life and empowering experiences of the Spirit of Pentecost. The Spirit renews and empowers the lives of "all people"— sons and daughters, young and old, "and even . . . my servants"—who speak in the many tongues of Spirit-breathed divine image bearers. Atonement reconciles people to the life for which God created them. Ramabai's Mukti Mission created a community in which women could experience freedom from the oppression and poverty of their patriarchal society, the dignity of living in fellowship with others, and an authentic expression of their relationship with God. It was the Holy Spirit speaking in the many tongues of Pentecost. Every time a widowed bride escaped the funeral pyre, a daughter from a child-marriage or temple prostitution, or a baby girl from infanticide was an experience of the Spirit of Pentecost, the Spirit of atonement.

William Seymour and the Azusa Street Revival

The Azusa Street revivals sprouted in prayer meetings, first in the home of Edwards S. Lee and then in Richard and Ruth Asberry's home at 214 North Bonnie Brae Street.[31]

---

[30] Boaz Johnson, "The Biblical Theological Contribution of Pandita Ramabai," 125.
[31] For a detailed account of the people and the events of the Azusa Street Revival, see Cecil M. Robeck, Jr., *The Azusa Street Mission and Revival: The Birth of the Global Pentecostal Movement* (Nashville: Thomas Nelson, 2006), 53–186.

On April 9, 1906, Edward Lee spoke in tongues while William J. Seymour prayed for him. Afterward Seymour rushed to the Asberry's Bonnie Brae Street home to report the news and soon after seven others spoke in tongues. A week later, the Azusa Street Mission opened. News of the revival spread rapidly, and it soon became a clearinghouse for pastors, evangelists, and missionaries seeking spiritual revival.[32] The first period of revival lasted until 1908. A second revival and surge in attendance took place in 1911–1912. Debate continues over whether or not Azusa is the catalyst for the modern pentecostal movement. The numbers present at the Azusa Street Mission fluctuated from a few dozen during the lulls of revival to upward of fifteen hundred during peak periods.[33] What is clear is that many of the key leaders responsible for leading the early pentecostal revivals and churches (denominations) passed through the Azusa Street Mission.

What characterized the pentecostal revival at the Azusa Street Mission? Introduction to pentecostal experiences, from Spirit baptism and speaking in tongues to divine healing, was a hallmark and explicit purpose of many pilgrimages to Azusa. But another, although less enduring, experience of the Spirit of Pentecost was also on display at Azusa. Whites, blacks, Hispanics, and Asians came together to worship.[34] *The Apostolic Faith* reported that "The work began among the colored people. God baptized several sanctified wash women with the Holy Ghost. . . . God makes no difference in nationality, Ethiopians, Chinese, Indians, Mexicans, and other nationalities worship together."[35] The *Los Angeles Daily Times* described the Azusa Street Mission as a

> tumble-down shack. . . . Colored people and a sprinkling of whites . . . fanatics. . . . STONY OPTIC DEFIES. . . . An old colored exhorter, blind in one eye, is the major-domo of the company . . . pandemonium breaks loose, and the bounds of reason are passed by those who are "filled with the spirit," whatever that may be. . . . "You-oo-oo gou-loo-loo" . . . shouts an old colored "mammy."[36]

The rhetoric is racist, but it also exposes class bigotry. Early-twentieth-century LA was, relative to other places in America, progressive on race relations. LA had a thriving middle- and upper-middle class African American community. It seems unlikely that the reporter would have used such derogatory terms to describe the celebratory service of the new African Methodist Church on March 6, 1904. The new church seated 700 people and LA's mayor, Meredith P. Snyder, was a featured speaker at its opening

---

[32] Gastón Espinosa, *Latino Pentecostals in America: Faith and Politics in Action* (Cambridge, MA: Harvard University Press, 2014), 45–7.

[33] Anderson, *Spreading Fires*, 49. For detailed accounts of William Seymour, see Gastón Espinosa, *William J. Seymour and the Origins of Global Pentecostalism: A Biography and Documentary History* (Durham: Duke University Press, 2014) and Robeck, *The Azusa Street Mission and Revival*.

[34] Gastón Espinosa demonstrates that Latino Pentecostalism traces its roots to the Azusa Street revivals, but most of the history of the movement concentrates on the black-white origins of the revival. Although this chapter focuses on Seymour, it does not discount or intend to contribute to this imbalance in the research on pentecostal origins and Azusa Street. See Espinosa, *Latino Pentecostals in America*, 35–6.

[35] "The Same Old Way," *The Apostolic Faith* 1.1, September 1906 (p. 3, col. 2).

[36] "Weird Babel of Tongues," *Los Angeles Daily Times*, April 18, 1906 (p. 1).

event.[37] The Azusa Street Mission, however, was primarily a congregation of LA's new population of working- and lower-class African Americans. William Seymour was the son of former slaves and a holiness preacher with minimal education. He had recently arrived in LA to pastor a small African American Holiness church. A church of and for the new working- and lower-class African Americans. The problem with the Azusa Street revival, in other words, was not only the color of its leader and its primary congregants but also their class. They were uneducated, poor, and given to emotional excess. Even the middle- and upper-middle classes of the mainline black churches repudiated the early black Pentecostals as uneducated fanatics. Seymour and the people of the Azusa Street Mission represented a lower-class black "folk religion" that they repudiated for the economic benefits of assimilating to the cultural standards of white middle- and upper-middle-class society.[38] The rhetoric of the Azusa participants also exhibits class consciousness and antimony.[39] The Azusa Street Mission, nevertheless, was exceptional because it was "interracial and intercultural."[40] One report in *The Apostolic Faith* declared

> it is noticeable how free all nationalities feel. If a Mexican or German cannot speak English, he gets up and speaks in his own tongue and feels quite at home. . . . No instrument that God can use is rejected on account of color dress or lack of education. This is why God has so built up the work.[41]

In other words, the author identifies the revival's egalitarianism and inclusion of people from diverse ethnic and social backgrounds as the basis for receiving God's blessing. The Azusa Street Mission also stood out because it shared leadership not only among whites and blacks but also among women, who comprised more than half of the leaders of the ministry.[42]

Unfortunately, charismatic phenomena soon eclipsed the social transcending character of the outpouring of the Holy Spirit at Azusa Street. As the pentecostal denominations emerged and defined their characteristics, social transcending

---

[37] Cecil M. Robeck Jr., "The Azusa Street Mission and the Historic Black Churches: Two Worlds in Conflict in Los Angeles' African American Community," in *Afro-Pentecostalism: Black Pentecostal and Charismatic Christianity in History and Culture*, ed. Amos Yong and Estrelda Y. Alexander (New York: New York University Press, 2011), 26.

[38] Robeck argues that the African American community was divided between middle- and upper-middle-class blacks who attended mainline churches and adapted to the symbols and practices of affluent white culture and the lower-class blacks who attended "folk churches," which carried on traditional black religious practices (Robeck, "The Azusa Street Mission and the Historic Black Churches," 31–5).

[39] The *Apostolic Faith* describes the revivalists being expelled from other churches: "we may be turned out of the big wood and brick structures," *Apostolic Faith* 1.2, October 1906 (p. 4, col. 2). One account revels in not needing "song books of earth" or "organs and pianos" because the Holy Spirit gives "anthems from the paradise of God." That is making a virtue out of a necessity, since they probably could not afford these instruments of worship found in the middle- and upper-middle-class churches. See *Apostolic Faith* 1.4, December 1906 (p. 2, col. 5).

[40] Anderson, *Spreading Fires*, 48.

[41] "Bible Pentecost: Gracious Pentecostal Showers Continue to Fall," *The Apostolic Faith* 1.3, November 1906 (p. 1, col. 1).

[42] Anderson, *Spreading Fires*, 50.

community and inclusive diversity were not included in their doctrinal statements or their practices. The development of the pentecostal denominations paralleled, indeed perpetrated, the wider racial prejudices and segregation of early-twentieth-century American culture.[43] The result was that the doctrine and experience of Spirit baptism and speaking in tongues became the trademarks of Pentecostalism (along with entire sanctification for Holiness Pentecostals).

Why is Azusa's social transcending community of "all people," even if it was short lived, so important for a pentecostal theology of the atonement (Acts 2:17)? The outpouring of the Holy Spirit on the Day of Pentecost was a pivotal moment in the history of redemption. It reveals and advances the perennial and universal work of the Spirit of God in the history of redemption. Creating a social transcending community by virtue of the empowerment of the Holy Spirit was central to the promise of Pentecost and it was a fundamental feature of William Seymour's pentecostal revival at Azusa Street. Frank Bartleman declared that "the color line was washed away in the blood."[44] This statement links the egalitarian nature of the Azusa revivals with the atonement. Experiencing the Spirit of Pentecost empowered the people at the Azusa Street Mission to transcend the racism and social segregation of their culture. The Spirit-empowered transcendence of social and ethnic bigotries shows that Pentecostalism "has at its heart the dynamics of conscientization," according to Cheryl Bridges Johns.[45] The Spirit of Pentecost, in other words, empowers people to discern and overcome racism, chauvinism, classism.

The Azusa Street revival embodied the two elements of the outpouring of the Holy Spirit announced in Acts: the inclusion of diverse people in the community of Pentecost and charismatic manifestations. For the most part, pentecostal churches have focused on the latter and dropped the former. That is a problem because charismatic manifestations without the formation of the inclusive community of the Spirit of Pentecost are "clanging cymbals" (1 Cor. 13:1-13). I am reluctant to prioritize the elements of Pentecost. But the account of Pentecost and Peter's sermon seem to do so. The point of the charismatic many tongues is that the Spirit has been poured out on "all people." The ongoing narrative focus of Acts reinforces that point. The gospel moves from Jerusalem and Samaria to the ends of the earth. Acts is not primarily a story of charismatic experiences, but the Spirit's inclusion of "all people" in the Spirit-

---

[43] Allan Anderson, "The Dubious Legacy of Charles Parham: Racism and Cultural Insensitivities among Pentecostals," *Pneuma: The Journal of the Society for Pentecostal Studies* 27, no. 1 (2005): 51–64 and Derrick R. Rosenior, "The Rhetoric of Pentecostal Racial Reconciliation: Looking Back to Move Forward," in *The Liberating Spirit*, ed. Michael Wilkinson and Steven M. Studebaker (Eugene: Pickwick, 2010), 53–84. The segregation of black and white Pentecostals along denominational lines is more pronounced than mainline Protestant churches. This division likely derives from the formation of the Assemblies of God along racial lines and, after being excluded from the former, the formation of the black Church of God in Christ. See Michael O. Emerson with Rodney M. Woo, *People of the Dream: Multiracial Congregations in the United States* (Princeton: Princeton University Press, 2006), 49–50 and Joe Newman, *Race and the Assemblies of God Church: The Journey from Azusa Street to the "Miracle of Memphis"* (Youngstown: Cambria, 2007), 65–87.

[44] Frank Bartleman, *How Pentecost Came to Los Angeles*, citied in McClymond, "Historical and Theological Meditation," 369.

[45] Cheryl Bridges Johns, *Pentecostal Formation: A Pedagogy among the Oppressed*, Journal of Pentecostal Theology Supplement Series, 2 (Sheffield: Sheffield Academic Press, 1993), 65.

baptized community of God's people. Charismatic gifts, the tongues of Pentecost, were not an end in themselves, but the sign that the Holy Spirit was gathering "all people" and reconciling them to each other and to their God. The Spirit of Pentecost is a Spirit of atonement because the Spirit resolves the fundamental rupture in the history of redemption—the alienation from God and from each other indicated in the expulsion from Eden. The Holy Spirit draws "all people," Jew and Gentile, into the community of Pentecost and together in their manifold diversity, their many tongues, they constitute the body of Christ. Experiencing the Spirit of Pentecost, participating in the Spirit of atonement, means to "wash away" the "color line" and all the other bases for bigotry and alienation that prevent the embrace of the "all people" of Pentecost.[46]

Pentecostal churches have too often missed this essential element of Pentecost. One objection is that Pentecostals have been at forefront of missions in the twentieth century. They have taken the gospel to the ends of the earth so that "all people" might come to Christ. That is true. But too often that was understood as converting people to the missionary's brand of pentecostal Christianity (e.g., Ramabai resisted this pressure from pentecostal missionaries in India) and treating their converts according to Western racial and cultural bigotries.[47] The history of missions, however, is not a simple one of white racists going forth to save what they perceived as their racial inferiors. Gary B. McGee argues that training indigenous church leaders to lead self-sustaining indigenous churches arose early and, in time, became the central vision of Assemblies of God foreign missions.[48] Angela Tarango, moreover, shows that Assemblies of God (AG) missionary and missiologist Melvin Hodges' indigenous principle became the basis for American Indians to resist and subvert the ethnocentric bigotry of the AG denominational bureaucracy. The indigenous principle affirms the integrity of other cultures and the Spirit-empowered life brought forth within them. The irony is that the AG had to be cajoled over decades "to let" American Indian Pentecostals apply it. The pentecostal leaders of the AG who claimed to represent the Spirit of Pentecost, who proclaimed that the Spirit can empower "all people," were parsimonious in recognizing that Spirit's power in other people. They eventually nevertheless did. The history of the American Indian AG Pentecostals also showcases another dimension of the Spirit-empowered community of Pentecost—"Your . . . daughters will prophesy" (Acts 2:17). Women, such as Alma Thomas and Alta "Sister" Washburn, were in the vanguard of advocating for American Indian Pentecostals' autonomy and self-governance. And, at the risk of piling up ironies, ministry to American Indians was a way to evade the restrictions placed on women and give them "more autonomy, room to innovate, and freedom than would have been the case for a conventional pastor or world missionary."[49] The purpose here is not to blight the AG. I became a Christian through the ministry

---

[46] Frank Bartleman, *How Pentecost Came to Los Angeles*, cited in McClymond, "Historical and Theological Meditation," 369.
[47] Anderson, *Spreading Fires*, 249–56. The history of missions, however, is not a simple one of white racists going forth to save what they perceived as their racial inferiors.
[48] Gary B. McGee, "Assemblies of God Mission Theology: A Historical Perspective," *International Bulletin of Missionary Research* 10, no. 4 (1986): 166–9.
[49] Angela Tarango, *Choosing the Jesus Way: American Indian Pentecostals and the Fight for the Indigenous Principle* (Chapel Hill: The University of North Carolina Press, 2014), 11 and 1–12.

of a Bible Study sponsored by Forest Grove AG Church (Forest Grove, OR). The point to highlight, however, is that Pentecostals have a mixed history in experiencing and practicing the central purpose of Spirit-empowered life. Pentecostal churches, for the most part, have not carried on the inclusive community forming power of the Spirit of Pentecost; they have focused on saving souls and experiencing spiritual gifts. They did not lose everything that arises from the Spirit of Pentecost (which subsequent chapters detail), but the inclusive community that is a core promise of Pentecost has not been a hallmark of many pentecostal churches. Pentecostals have spoken in tongues, but have they experienced the many tongues of Pentecost and the pentecostal community of "all people"?

Indeed, the most popular view of Pentecostalism among contemporary scholars is that charismatic experience characterizes the movement rather than a particular theology.[50] I am sympathetic with the motivation of this view to recognize the legitimacy of the diverse global points of origin and forms of Pentecostalism and to thwart the denominational hegemony of classical pentecostal groups, but it has two problematic consequences—it reduces theology to an epiphenomena of Pentecostalism and it overlooks the social transcending character of Pentecost in Acts 2 (and the remainder of Acts) and the outpouring of the Holy Spirit at Azusa Street.[51] Engaging the debate on pentecostal origins, Michael J. McClymond argues in this direction as well. He suggests a theology of inclusive origins for Pentecostalism. Rather than picking one person and doctrine (e.g., Parham and speaking in tongues), or one tradition (e.g., black origin), or one person and place (e.g., Seymour and Azusa Street), or polygenetic points of origin (e.g., Azusa and Mukti), he argues for putting the focus on the message of Pentecost in Acts 2. Peter declared the words of Joel, "I will pour out my Spirit on all flesh" (Acts 2:17). Creating inclusive communities that harbor the "poor, the weak, and the marginalized" and transcend race, ethnic, class, gender, and political bigotries is the message of Pentecost.[52] McClymond calls this "*empowering inclusion.*"[53] Ironically, although McClymond calls for inclusive origins, Seymour and Azusa Street stand out because they embodied the message of Pentecost—empowering inclusion. Seymour's emphasis on love and social inclusion captured the essence of the promise of Pentecost.[54] One of the primal experiences of the pentecostal movements embodied a primary promise of the Spirit of Pentecost. Cheryl Bridges Johns calls on contemporary Pentecostals to recover this earlier experience for contemporary

---

[50] For examples, see Allan Anderson, *Pentecostalism: An Introduction* (New York: Cambridge University Press, 2014), 9–15 and 60; Mark J. Cartledge, *Encountering the Spirit: The Charismatic Tradition* (Maryknoll: Orbis, 2007), 19–32; Harvey Cox, *Fire from Heaven: The Rise of Pentecostal Spirituality and the Reshaping of Religion in the Twenty-First Century* (Reading: Addison-Wesley, 1995), 81–3; and Keith Warrington, *Pentecostal Theology: A Theology of Encounter* (New York: T & T Clark, 2008), 18–27.

[51] I have addressed at length the problem that this approach has for pentecostal theology in *From Pentecost to the Triune God: A Pentecostal Trinitarian Theology* (Grand Rapids: Eerdmans, 2012), 11–52.

[52] McClymond, "I Will Pour Out of My Spirit Upon All Flesh," 374.

[53] McClymond, "I Will Pour Out of My Spirit Upon All Flesh," 370 (emphasis in original).

[54] McClymond, "I Will Pour Out of My Spirit Upon All Flesh," 371.

Spirit-empowered life.⁵⁵ The final section highlights a church's effort in Kentville, Nova Scotia, to practice atonement by embodying the inclusive community of Pentecost.

Searching for the Community of Pentecost

As the pentecostal denominations consolidated their identities around the doctrines of Spirit baptism and speaking in tongues and as charismatic experience and spiritual gifts became the defining features of the movement, the social transcending community of the Spirit of Pentecost was largely lost in the churches that practiced, if not explicit, then de facto, segregation.⁵⁶ Class segregation also characterized pentecostal experience. Pentecostals predominantly came from the urban and rural poor during the first decades of the movement. Their churches, consequently, comprised that demographic for many years.⁵⁷ The social deprivation and lower-class poor of pentecostal demographics has been the subject of criticism over recent years. It, nonetheless, captures something true about the movement in the United States (Chapter 10 discusses this topic at length). Pew Research indicates that just under half of Pentecostals "report annual household incomes of less than $30,000, and 27% say they have attained less than a high school education," compared to evangelicals with 34 percent in the respective income and 16 percent in the education levels.⁵⁸ In the last two decades of the twentieth century, pentecostal churches increasingly became middle- and upper-middle class and like most churches in North America, they are mostly demographically homogenous.⁵⁹ At the same time, American Pentecostals are more racially diverse than evangelical churches. According to Pew Research, among pentecostal churches 67 percent are white, 19 percent are Latino, and 7 percent are black, where 81 percent are white and 7 percent are Latino in evangelical churches (Pew does not list ethnic identities for the remaining 12%).⁶⁰ The wider social world in North America is increasingly divisive and polarized into partisan political camps.⁶¹

---

⁵⁵ Johns, *Pentecostal Formation*, 70 and 100–1.
⁵⁶ The inability of Pentecostals to actualize the equality intrinsic to the Spirit of Pentecost is an ongoing problem. The problem is not only a North American one. Weng Kit Cheong shows that although Chinese pentecostal women exercise leadership in certain church contexts and functions, they are nonetheless constrained within an overriding patriarchal culture. See Cheong, "The Attenuation of Female Empowerment among Three Pentecostal-Charismatic Chinese Churches in Malaysia and Singapore," *Pneuma: The Journal of the Society for Pentecostal Studies* 41, nos. 3–4 (2019): 477–99.
⁵⁷ Robert Mapes Anderson, *Vision of the Disinherited: The Making of American Pentecostalism* (New York: Oxford University Press, 1979).
⁵⁸ "Palin V.P. Nomination Puts Pentecostalism in the Spotlight," Pew Research Center, September 12, 2008. https://www.pewforum.org/2008/09/12/palin-vp-nomination-puts-pentecostalism-in-t he-spotlight/
⁵⁹ Gerardo Marti notes that about 8 percent of churches in America are multiracial. Although not specifically data drawn from pentecostal churches, it seems unlikely, given their histories, that pentecostal churches, whether white or black, would register a higher percentage. See Gerardo Marti, "When Does Racial Integration 'Count?' A Caution about Seeking Ideal Ethnographic Cases," *Journal for the Scientific Study of Religion* 49, no. 2 (2010): 227.
⁶⁰ "Palin V.P. Nomination Puts Pentecostalism in the Spotlight."
⁶¹ Shanto Iyengar and Masha Krupenkin, "The Strengthening of Partisan Affect," *Advances in Political Psychology* 39, suppl. 1 (2018): 201–18.

The social and political divides are stark. Political and cultural differences almost immediately escalate into zero-sum battles.[62] Mainstream institutions from media to public education maintain that multiculturalism is the solution to this culture of toxic tribalism. Multiculturalism endeavors to overcome differences by advocating inclusiveness and celebrating diversity. The result, however, is often the replacement of one worldview and its morality with a new multicultural one. Multiculturalism tolerates its own secular and politically correct ideology and denigrates the ideological other. The aspiration of multiculturalism is correct. Indeed, the goals of multiculturalism to transcend bigotries and to create inclusive and diverse communities stand in continuity with the Spirit of Pentecost. Unfortunately, bereft of the Holy Spirit that empowers the many tongues and the social transcending communities of Pentecost, it leads to ideological intolerance and social ghettoes. What is the pathway forward? What is the answer to church communities marked by histories of racial and class segregation and a wider society riven socially, politically, and economically? The diverse community of people brought together in the fellowship of the Spirit of Pentecost. This final section puts forward an example of a church community living in the power of the Holy Spirit to create the social transcending community of Pentecost. First, however, I want to describe and interact with an ecclesial movement that parallels the multiculturalism movement.

Multicultural, multiethnic, and multiracial churches parallel the multiculturalism movement in the wider culture. A multicultural or interracial church is one in which a minority racial/ethnic group/s comprise/s a significant percentage of the congregation (20% minority attendance is the common standard for research on multiracial churches) and no one group consists of 80 percent or more.[63] They make up a small percentage (about 7%) of churches in America but are an important effort to integrate diverse people in a faith community.[64] Multiracial churchgoers tend toward more progressive social, moral, and political views than do people "who attend racially homogenous congregations."[65] The vision that motivates the multiracial church reflects the diverse tongues of Pentecost, but the reality that people often experience in them does not. Gerardo Marti points out that the danger of multiethnic churches is the eclipse of actual ethnic diversity with a new "inclusive religious identity."[66] The result is that the church's religious inclusiveness identity takes precedence to the diverse ethnic identities of their members. The new religious identity is not based on "ignoring distinctives [such

---

[62] For the increasing economic and political segregation in America and its consequences, see Bill Bishop with Robert G. Cushing, *The Big Sort: Why the Clustering of Like-Minded America Is Tearing Us Apart* (Boston: Houghton Mifflin, 2009); Richard Florida, *The New Urban Crisis: How Our Cities are Increasing Inequality, Deepening Segregation, and Failing the Middle Class—and What We can do About It* (New York: Basic, 2017); and Robert D. Putnam, *Our Kids: The American Dream in Crisis* (2015; reprint, New York: Simon and Schuster, 2016).
[63] Emerson and Woo, *People of the Dream*, 35.
[64] Samuel L. Perry, "Racial Diversity, Religion, and Morality: Examining the Moral View of Multiracial Church Attendees," *Review of Religious Research* 55, no. 2 (2013): 356–7.
[65] Perry, "Racial Diversity, Religion, and Morality," 357.
[66] Deborah L. Berhó, Gerardo Martí, and Mark T. Mulder, "Global Pentecostalism and Ethnic Identity Maintenance among Latino Immigrants: A Case Study of a Guatemalan Neo-Pentecostal Congregation in the Pacific Northwest," *Pneuma: The Journal of the Society for Pentecostal Studies* 39, no. 1 (2017): 11.

ethnic and/or racial backgrounds] but rather on accentuating an alternative identity rooted in the ecclesial community."[67] The "color line" washed away by the Spirit of Pentecost, however, does not transcend individuality, ethnic identity and difference, and sociopolitical class status for the sake of a new colorless pentecostal religious identity. The many tongues are not surpassed in a new mono-tongue of Pentecost. They are, rather, brought together in the chorus of the "all people" of Pentecost. At the same time the "many" of the many tongues of Pentecost should not be so stressed as to enforce ethnic or racial essentialism.[68] The solution is an ecclesial practice that celebrates actual diversity, not merely a rhetorical and putative ideological one, and that can integrate it with shared life in community.

Gerardo Marti and Gladys Ganiel developed the term "pluralist congregations" to describe the churches they encountered in their research on the Emerging Church Movement. They describe pluralist congregation as "rare examples of religious institutions that try to facilitate rather than fail to recognize or try to suppress diversity. *We define pluralist congregations as social spaces that permit, and even foster, direct interaction between people with religiously contradictory perspectives and value systems.*"[69] Pluralist congregations combine the tension, and at times contradictory impulses, between individualism and community.[70] They combine emphases on the radical integrity and autonomy of the individual and the necessity of life in community. The fulfillment of the individual Christian life requires shared life in community with others, others that are different. In this sense and paradoxically, the diverse life of community is the necessary incubator of the individual's relationship with God and their spiritual development.[71] This insistence on individualism and community life can more effectively achieve ecclesial communities of inclusive diversity—the many tongues of Pentecost—than the alternatives of ethnic churches (whether culturally dominant white or minority and immigrant congregations) and the multicultural, multiethnic, multiracial churches that transcend ethnic particularity for the sake of an inclusive religious identity. One caveat is in order, however. Although multicultural/racial churches often do not realize their vision of embodying actual multiculturalism, their motivating vision stands more in continuity with the Spirit of Pentecost than the widely influential Homogenous Unit Principle of the Church Growth Movement.[72] One shortcoming of pluralist congregations investigated by Marti and Ganiel is that

---

[67] Gerardo Marti, "Fluid Ethnicity and Ethnic Transcendence in Multiracial Churches," *Journal for the Scientific Study of Religion* 47, no. 1 (2008): 14. Note also that interracial churches often struggle to overcome dominant white culture preferences and assumptions and to achieve actual interracial church experiences. See Korie L. Edwards, *The Elusive Dream: The Power of Race in Interracial Churches* (New York: Oxford University Press, 2008).

[68] Gerardo Marti makes the case that racial-essential presuppositions can forestall recognizing the reality of ethnic fluidity among people—that racial and ethnic identity is both fungible and secondary to other identity markers for some people. See Marti, "Fluid Ethnicity and Ethnic Transcendence in Multiracial Churches," 11–16.

[69] Gerardo Marti and Gladys Ganiel, *The Deconstructed Church: Understanding Emerging Christianity* (New York: Oxford University Press, 2014), 34 (emphasis in original).

[70] Marti and Ganiel, *The Deconstructed Church*, 35.

[71] Marti and Ganiel, *The Deconstructed Church*, 35 and 190–2.

[72] Gerardo Marti, "The Religious Racial Integration of African Americans into Diverse Churches," *Journal for the Scientific Study of Religion* 49, no. 2 (2010): 209.

although they promote and experience diversity across the spectrum of Christian thought and practice (e.g., they are highly ecumenical and eclectic in respect to ecclesial practices), demographics (economic and age diversity), and life styles, they are less successful at achieving racial and ethnic diversity. Pluralist congregations, nevertheless, offer an example of the empowered diversity and ministry of the Spirit of Pentecost. I suggest, however, for theological reasons, switching "pluralist" for "pentecostal." The Holy Spirit, the Spirit of Pentecost, is the power that enables people to embody the inclusive and diverse communities achieved in pluralist congregations and sought for in multicultural churches and society.[73]

My research with Lee Beach on alternative churches in Canada took us to many churches that reflected the ethos and practices of pluralist congregations.[74] I focus here on one of them—Valley Gate Vineyard in Kentville, Nova Scotia—because it is a pentecostal congregation that embodies the multicultural promise of Pentecost. Valley Gate's home is a renovated theatre in downtown Kentville. The church is demographically diverse—professional and working classes, mental health patients, people recovering (or not) from substance abuse. They describe their worship as postmodern and influenced by an artistic mindset. Sunday morning worship services are the product of team collaboration and are rarely the same. They integrate multimedia, arts, music, dialogue, and various traditions of Christian liturgy. Teaching is part of the worship experience, but not a didactic sermon from the pastor. Their worship and church community arise from the diversity of its participants, the diverse tongues of Pentecost.

Valley Gate's organic approach to ministry also reflects the many tongues and the radiating orientation of the Spirit of Pentecost's empowered witness. They are organic in two ways. They arise from the vision casting and brainstorming of people in the church and from the needs of the community. While renovating the theatre, they noticed that a commuting workforce makes downtown Kentville bustle with life during the day but leaves it deserted in the evening. They also "got to know the kids" in Kentville. Connecting with these people led them to open an ice cream parlor for the kids that evolved into a café for the commuters. People in the church with relevant skills and background assumed leadership, and they hired local young people to staff the parlor and café. Kentville is also home to youth and adult correctional centers, social assistance agencies, and a regional hospital. The café led to building relationships with the professionals who work for these social and health services. Church members also became aware that people leaving the correctional facilities

---

[73] Nimi Wariboko's proposal of pentecostal cosmopolitan communities also offers an example of Spirit-empowered pentecostal communities. See Nimi Wariboko, *The Charismatic City and the Public Resurgence of Religion: A Pentecostal Social Ethics of Cosmopolitan Urban Life* (New York: Palgrave Macmillan, 2014).

[74] A Lilly Collaborative Research Grant provided funding for this project. The majority of our research took place from 2012 to 2014. The Lilly Grant enabled us to investigate alternative and emerging churches across Canada in British Columbia, the Prairie Provinces, Ontario, Quebec, and the Maritimes. For more on this project, see Steven M. Studebaker and Lee Beach, "From Monks to Punks: Emerging Christianity in Canada," in *The Emerging Church, Millennials, and Religion*, ed. Randall Reed and G. Michael Zbaraschuk, vol. 1, Prospects and Problems (Eugene: Cascade, 2018), 84–107.

needed support transitioning to a stable and healthy life. In response, the church initiated the Refuge. It provides transitional housing for up to ten men (from three months to three years) and social skill development. Members of the Refuge usually are people at risk of homelessness due to complications from substance abuse and/or discharge from a correctional facility. Vital for Valley Gate's development of the Refuge, moreover, were the relationships they formed with people working in the various social and health services agencies. These connections provided networks to partner with government agencies in supporting men transitioning from life on the streets and in correctional facilities. In short, Valley Gate's ministries arise from being attentive to the social circumstances of its community. They adapt their ministries to their community and connect their people's gifts and talents to those ministry opportunities. Valley Gate Vineyard is an example of the empowerment of the many tongues of Pentecost and of the outpouring of the Spirit on "all people . . . sons and daughters . . . young men . . . old men . . . even on my servants, both men and women" (Acts 2:17-18). The diverse people of Valley Gate, the many tongues of Pentecost, are not transcended in a new mono-community of the Spirit. Valley Gate embodies actual diversity, especially class and demographic. The many tongues of Pentecost arise from the Spirit. They find their unity in and from the Spirit. They are gifts of the Spirit to create human flourishing in community with each other—in this case, Kentville, Nova Scotia.

Finding inspiration for pentecostal renewal within a Vineyard congregation is fitting. Renewal is intrinsic to the pentecostal movements. They began as renewal movements within the wider Christian churches. The Vineyard churches are a charismatic renewal within the wider pentecostal renewal movements—it is a renewal within a renewal! The place and people of Valley Gate Vineyard are also significant. The outpouring of the Spirit is taking place with those just out of prison and others escaping the bondage of substance abuse and life on the streets. It includes nurses, social workers, and small business owners empowered by the Spirit of Pentecost to embody the gospel at the "ends of the earth" far removed from the world's centers of power and influence (Acts 1:8). Valley Gate Vineyard stands in continuity with the social transcending and empowering community that the Spirit of Pentecost brought to Pandita Ramabai's Mukti Mission, William J. Seymour's Azusa Street Revival, and to Jesus' forlorn disciples on the Day of Pentecost.

Churches like Valley Gate Vineyard point the way forward for Christian life and ministry in the increasingly post-Christian world of North America. Current cultural forces in North America threaten the formation of redemptive communities of inclusive diversity. Political and social partisanship assume differences are insoluble. Fear demonizes religious and cultural differences. The inclusive diversity created by the Spirit of Pentecost is contrary to forces and movements of nativism, ethnocentrism, and political partisanship. An important implication of the Spirit of Pentecost and the eschatological vision of the new creation is that the pentecostal community of inclusive diversity not only is ecclesial but also includes civil, social, and even national communities. But it also critiques reductionistic forces within multiculturalism that strip away cultural particularities and impose a common culture in the name of social unity. In practice, multiculturalism can move toward a secular monoculture that excludes religion for the sake of tolerance and a "safe" secular space. Pentecost promotes the manifold diversity that arises from human beings bearing the Spirit-breathed divine image. The praxis of pentecostal atonement means public witness that advocates on behalf of the "all people" of Pentecost. Valley Gate Vineyard's worship and shared church life and their ministry in the community of Kentville embody the organic emergence of the diverse tongues of the Spirit of Pentecost. Congregations empowered by God's Spirit to embrace others in love, moreover, can foster authentic multicultural communities and practices. Indeed, U.S. pentecostal churches, despite a history of at best ambiguity on racial issues, are more diverse than their evangelical counterparts. Pew Research shows that black pentecostal churches "are more racially diverse compared with the historically black church tradition overall. Roughly two-thirds of those who belong to historically black pentecostal denominations are black (68%), compared with 92% of members of these churches overall. Together, white (14%) and Latino (13%) Pentecostals account for more than one out of every four members of historically black churches."[75] This suggests that the Spirit of Pentecost, the Spirit poured out at Azusa, is still being poured out and animating the many tongues of Pentecost.

But one may object, why is Spirit-empowered community so important? Does it shortchange atonement? After all, it seems less momentous than penal-substitutionary atonement that puts at bay the wrath of God with Christ's death on the cross. Discounting the importance of inclusive and diverse communities of the Spirit of Pentecost can only happen when ignoring history and current events. Over the past one hundred years, between 167 and 188 million people perished as the result of organized human violence (or approximately 5% of deaths).[76] Consider the world today. Does it need more bloodletting? Does it need more redemptive violence? If the Spirit-empowered community of the many tongues and the "all people" of Pentecost were actualized across the world and in the heart of every person today, AK-47s and M1 Abrams tanks would be "beat . . . into plowshares . . . and pruning hooks" (Isa. 2:4). Receiving and living in the power of the Spirit of Pentecost, practicing atonement, is to walk in the way of, to participate in, and to embody the Spirit-anointed life brought about in Jesus Christ. It is to dwell in the nexus of the triune God's redemptive work in the world. A redemptive work that leads to the redemption of the nations in the new heaven and the new earth. So, yes, embodying the social transcending community of the Spirit of Pentecost is central, not peripheral, to participating in the reconciling and redemptive work (atonement) of the Holy Spirit.

---

[75] "Palin V.P. Nomination Puts Pentecostalism in the Spotlight."
[76] Niall Ferguson, *The War of the World: Twentieth-Century Conflict and the Descent of the West* (New York: Penguin, 2006), 649. Although the rate of violent deaths dropped in recent years (from 540,000 in 2004–7 to 508,000 in 2007–12), the rates remain high. For statistics, see Geneva Declaration Secretariat, *Global Burden of Armed Violence 2015: Every Body Counts*, Geneva, 2015. http://www.genevadeclaration.org/measurability/global-burden-of-armed-violence/global-burden-of-armed-violence-2015.html. The twentieth century also saw a rise in the role of civilians in armed conflicts. See Andreas Wenger and Simon J. A. Mason, "The Civilianization of Armed Conflict: Trends and Implications," *International Review of the Red Cross* 90, no. 872 (2008): 835–52.

Conclusion

Empowered witness, speaking in tongues, and operating in the spiritual gifts have been hallmarks of Pentecostalism. This emphasis, however, misses the central character of Pentecost—Spirit-created and -empowered social transcending communities of inclusive diversity. The early pentecostal revivals led by Pandita Ramabai and William J. Seymour embodied this essential feature of Pentecost. But as the pentecostal denominations formed, they, for the most part, lost this essential element of Pentecost. Pentecostal churches too often reflect the ethnic and class divisions and gender hierarchies of society. They need to recover the full experience of Pentecost. The Spirit of Pentecost is a Spirit of atonement because "all people" and their many tongues are brought together as one people of Pentecost. Differences are not transcended. The diversity of Pentecost, the many tongues, are empowered by the Holy Spirit and are the foundation of the community of "all people." A contemporary Vineyard church in Kentville, Nova Scotia, one of the "ends of the earth," points the way toward recovering the full experience of the Spirit of Pentecost.

8

Renewing Embodied Life

Pentecostals believe in the Incarnation. They confess that Christ is God and has the power to perform miracles. Traditional pentecostal theology, however, focuses on functional Christology. Consider the hallmark of pentecostal theology—the Full Gospel. It spotlights ways that Christology relates to redemption—Christ is savior, sanctifier, healer, Spirit baptizer, and soon coming king. But the Incarnation, as such, plays little role in pentecostal theology.[1] This is a problem because the Incarnation is the basis for everything else that can be said of Christ. For that reason, Chapter 3 developed a pentecostal Spirit Christology of the Incarnation that lays the foundation of the atonement. This chapter integrates that Spirit Christology with the pentecostal praxis of social mobility for an embodied theology of pentecostal atonement. Before launching into the Incarnation and the embodied experience of atonement, defining "embodied" is important. I use "embodied" in a comprehensive manner. It entails what Amos Yong describes as the multidimensionality of a pneumatological and holistic theology of salvation. It includes the transformation of the physical/biological and psychological dimensions of bodily life, interpersonal and community relations, and the "social, political, and economic structures that shape all of our interactions."[2] Embodied life includes essentially everything in life that would not be considered part of "spiritual" matters. I am not the first to propose the embodied and material nature of pentecostal praxis.[3] But the materiality of pentecostal atonement stands in tension with the popular view that primarily regards Pentecostalism "as a form of . . . Christian spirituality."[4] In other words, although an embodied or holistic vision of grace is implicit to the pentecostal experience of grace, it has not been an overt emphasis of traditional pentecostal theology. Mark Cartledge proposes that pentecostal healing can indicate a more holistic vision of redemption that includes the personal, physical, communal, and social. He suggests that the traditional Christological and cross-centered theology "can

---

[1] An effort to redress this problem is Frank D. Macchia's *Jesus the Spirit Baptizer: Christology in Light of Pentecost* (Grand Rapids: Eerdmans, 2018).

[2] Amos Yong, *Theology and Down Syndrome: Reimagining Disability in Later Modernity* (Waco: Baylor University Press, 2007), 248–58.

[3] E.g., Miroslav Volf, "Materiality of Salvation: An Investigation in the Soteriologies of Liberation and Pentecostal Theologies," *Journal of Ecumenical Studies* 26, no. 3 (1989): 447–67 and Wolfgang Vondey, *Pentecostal Theology: Living the Full Gospel*, Systematic Pentecostal and Charismatic Theology (New York: Bloomsbury, 2017), 119.

[4] Daniel E. Albrecht and Evan B. Howard, "Pentecostal Spirituality," in *The Cambridge Companion to Pentecostalism*, ed. Cecil M. Robeck, Jr. and Amos Yong (New York: Cambridge University Press, 2014), 235–42.

be further strengthened ... by emphasizing not only the work of Christ upon the cross but also the assumption of humanity in the incarnation. Christ is the healer not just because of his act of atonement but because he embodied in himself the one who is the healer of Israel."[5] Cartledge is correct on the holistic nature of redemption. Cartledge links cross, healing, and atonement and recommends adding the implications of the Incarnation to a holistic pentecostal theology of grace. But this recommendation seems to separate the cross and atonement from the Incarnation (e.g., "emphasizing not only ... cross but also ... incarnation"). The "not only ... but also" indicates the need to integrate Incarnation and atonement. The Incarnation is the ground of atonement—the reconciliation and renewal of human life with God. Healing, which signals the materiality of pentecostal grace, arises from the Incarnation. The most fundamental theological claim about Jesus Christ is that he was the Incarnation of the Son of God. God took on flesh. God became embodied as a human being in the Incarnation of Jesus Christ. The Spirit of Pentecost, therefore, cannot be primarily an experience of charismatic/spiritual experiences and giftings. The Spirit of Pentecost does not come simply to heal the soul, but to renew the fullness of human life. The Spirit's incarnation of the divine Son in Jesus Christ corresponds to and fulfills the Spirit of God's breath of life that animated human beings in the Garden of Eden. The Spirit-breathed life fulfilled in Christ was embodied life. The work of the Spirit of Pentecost stands in continuity with this wider narrative of redemption. Lisa P. Stephenson puts it well: "where the Spirit once brought forth promise in the midst of the chaos in creation, the Spirit once again is bringing forth promise in the midst of chaos in the new creation."[6] The Incarnation informs the very nature of the atonement—the Holy Spirit's redemption and renewal of embodied life.

This chapter argues that the pentecostal praxis of social mobility exhibits that the fundamental subject matter of the Incarnation and the Spirit of atonement is embodied life in and for this world. This chapter has three sections. The first section is a critical analysis of the social deprivation theory and the otherworldly character of pentecostal rhetoric, both of which obscure the materiality and holistic character of the pentecostal experience of grace. The second section illustrates the holistic theology of grace implicit among Pentecostals in Cameroon and Vietnam. The third section proposes making the embodied character of the Incarnation, implicit in pentecostal praxis, explicit in a pentecostal theology of atonement.

From Otherworldly Rhetoric to Embodied Praxis

Pentecostal praxis, the way Pentecostals experience the grace the Spirit brings to their lives, transforms their lives in this world. But they are not known for that. Why? Two factors have inhibited the recognition of the embodied character of pentecostal praxis.

---

[5] Mark J. Cartledge, *Testimony in the Spirit: Rescripting Ordinary Pentecostal Theology* (New York: Routledge, 2010), 126.
[6] Lisa P. Stephenson, *Dismantling the Dualisms for American Pentecostal Women in Ministry: A Feminist Pneumatological Approach*, Global and Charismatic Studies, 9 (Boston: Brill, 2012), 128.

These are the popularity of the social deprivation theory for explaining Pentecostalism and the otherworldly rhetoric and doctrinal definitions self-selected by Pentecostals. This section treats each of these in turn to set the stage for investigating the embodied nature of the pentecostal praxis of the Spirit of atonement.

Social Deprivation: Holy Rollers on Shinbone Ridge[7]

Uncouth, uneducated, and unhinged hicks are common caricatures of Pentecostals. They are the reddest of Red State Christians. Desperate poor people driven to extremes of emotion and fanaticism and easily manipulated by con-pastors and duplicitous evangelists. Thomas Alfred Tripp expressed this social view of Pentecostals in a 1938 article in the *Christian Century*. Although sympathetic to Pentecostals, he warned of a "serious dilemma for rural Protestantism as represented by the older, more rational and 'respectable' denominations. . . . [They] are not proving very effective in holding poor farmers, low income renters, sharecroppers, rural relief clients and village 'slum' dwellers. Meanwhile, the new 'holy roller' sects are springing up and growing rapidly among these disadvantaged folk everywhere."[8] Tripp effectively expresses what later scholarship calls the social deprivation theory of Pentecostalism. Robert Mapes Anderson's *Vision of the Disinherited* is a key work in this trajectory of interpreting earlier Pentecostals.[9] According to this view, Pentecostalism emerged as a dysfunctional reaction among uneducated and poor farmers, immigrants, urban dwellers, and black Americans. Pentecostalism's otherworldly and anti-worldly preaching and ecstatic worship practices reinforced their social marginalization. The social deprivation theory, nevertheless, is problematic as a primary explanatory account of Pentecostalism for several reasons.[10]

First, in North America, where the perspective developed, it does not accurately account for the spectrum of people who participated in pentecostal churches. Grant Wacker argues that Pentecostals came from "a cross section of the American population."[11] Wacker details that the pentecostal movement's early leaders primarily

---

[7] Allene M. Sumner, "The Holy Rollers on Shin Bone Ridge," *The Nation*, July 29, 1925: 137–8, referenced in Grant Wacker, *Heaven Below: Early Pentecostals and American Culture* (Cambridge, MA: Harvard University Press, 2001), 303n7.

[8] Thomas Alfred Tripp, "Shall the Holy Rollers Win the Farmers?" *The Christian Century* 55, no. 34 (1938): 1009. Tripp calls for the churches to renew their efforts, not only for the sake of buttressing their numbers, but because bringing together people of all classes is part of "essential Christianity" (p. 1010).

[9] Robert Mapes Anderson, *Vision of the Disinherited: The Making of American Pentecostalism* (New York: Oxford University Press, 1979).

[10] For a review of additional problems with the social deprivation theory not detailed here, see Peter Althouse, "Waxing and Waning of Social Deprivation as a Model for Understanding the Class Composition of Early American Pentecostalism," in *A Liberating Spirit: Pentecostals and Social Action in North America*, ed. Michael Wilkinson and Steven M. Studebaker (Eugene: Pickwick, 2010), 113–29 and Adam Stewart, "Re-Visioning the Disinherited: Pentecostals and Social Class in North America," in *A Liberating Spirit: Pentecostals and Social Action in North America*, ed. Michael Wilkinson and Steven M. Studebaker (Eugene: Pickwick, 2010), 136–57.

[11] Wacker, *Heaven Below*, 199.

came from the middle class and upper-middle class.¹² Kate Bowler shows that the prosperity gospel held strong popularity with the "upwardly mobile and middle class, rather than the working class."¹³ It was essentially "preaching prosperity to the prosperous."¹⁴ Scholars that reject the deprivation theory, nevertheless, recognize the attractiveness that Pentecostalism holds for lower-class people living outside the economic and social mainstream of North American culture. Wacker notes that pentecostal churches have always consisted of "a small but significant minority" of poor and marginalized people.¹⁵ Yet, other research raises questions on Wacker's case for a demographic cross spectrum comprising pentecostal church attendance. Philip Schwadel argues that social class levels among American white Evangelicals and Pentecostals relative to other religious and church groups match Niebuhr's church-sect theory. Although change across birth cohorts is evident, white Evangelicals and Pentecostals come from the lower classes and "are relatively likely to have low levels of education, family income, and occupational prestige."¹⁶ Pew Research also shows that roughly half of Pentecostals are in low-income households and one in four have less than a high school education. About 12 percent have graduated from college compared to a national average of about 27 percent.¹⁷ Of course, these statistics mean that half of Pentecostals are in middle- and higher-income households and three of four have a high school education or higher. Yet, less than one in five Pentecostals earn incomes of $75,000 or more, making them the "second poorest" group in the United States.¹⁸ Half of Americans, moreover, live in middle-income households, about 20 percent in higher-income households, and only about 30 percent in lower incomes ones, which means that Pentecostals disproportionally have lower income relative to other Americans.¹⁹ Or as Harvey Cox puts it, "the people who attend pentecostal churches tend to be from

---

[12] Wacker, *Heaven Below*, 202–5. Heidi Dahles' study shows that Pentecostalism is the favored religion of the new middle-class Chinese in Malaysia. See Dahles, "In Pursuit of Capital: The Charismatic Turn Among the Chinese Managerial and Professional Class in Malaysia," *Asian Ethnicity* 8, no. 2 (2007): 89–106.

[13] Kate Bowler, *Blessed: A History of the American Prosperity Gospel* (New York: Oxford University Press, 2013), 233.

[14] Bowler, *Blessed*, 233. Although not in the form of the prosperity gospel, Pentecostalism grew among the urban and "emerging elite of mixed and social and ethnic backgrounds" in Ethiopia in the late 1960s. See Tibebe Eshete, "Persecution and Social Resilience: The Case of the Ethiopian Pentecostals," *Mission Studies* 34, no. 3 (2017): 312.

[15] Wacker, *Heaven Below*, 216.

[16] Philip Schwadel, "Are White Evangelical Protestants Lower Class? A Partial Test of Church-Sect Theory," *Social Science Research* 46 (2014): 101 and 100–16. Nathan L. Gerrard's account of Pentecostals in southern Appalachia also coheres with the deprivation theory. See Gerrard, "The Holiness Movement in Southern Appalachia," in *The Charismatic Movement*, ed. Michael P. Hamilton (1975; reprint, Grand Rapids: Eerdmans, 1977), 159–71.

[17] "Palin V.P. Nomination Puts Pentecostalism in the Spotlight," Pew Research Center, September 12, 2008. https://www.pewforum.org/2008/09/12/palin-vp-nomination-puts-pentecostalism-in-the-spotlight/

[18] See Bowler, *Blessed*, 233 and David Leonhard, "Is Your Religion Your Financial Destiny?" *The New York Times*, May 11, 2011. https://www.nytimes.com/2011/05/15/magazine/is-your-religion-your-financial-destiny.html

[19] Richard Fry and Rakesh Kochhar, "Are You in the American Middle Class? Find Out with Our Income Calculator," Pew Research Center, September 6, 2018. https://www.pewresearch.org/fact-tank/2018/09/06/are-you-in-the-american-middle-class/

the same population that plays the lottery."[20] Even if Wacker is correct with respect to twentieth-century North American Pentecostalism, from a global perspective, Pentecostalism is primarily a religion of the poor and not just dispossessed but never-possessed.[21] Painting Pentecostals, nevertheless, with a monochromatic cultural brush as poor, illiterate, and gullible bumpkins grossly oversimplifies Pentecostals and their demographic range and their relation to mainstream culture both yesterday and today.[22] At the same time, Pentecostalism has been and is popular among poor and culturally marginal people.

Second, the social deprivation theory arises from cultural and religious chauvinism. It assumes the church-sect categories of Max Weber, Ernst Troeltsch, and later H. Richard Niebuhr, which in turn assume the reciprocal relationship between the established Christendom churches and modernism and its culture. Pentecostalism is a sect because it is a religious protest movement of people on the margins of mainstream society and the established churches. They fit neither the socially acceptable churches nor respectable society. It is a theory of the culturally privileged to explain what they do not like about the culturally un-privileged. But as Peter Althouse points out, although the sect is an aberration from the perspective of the culturally advantaged, it can be the "prophetic voice that calls into question the dehumanizing powers of the state" from the perspective of the culturally marginalized.[23] The social deprivation theory can also reflect a Marxist theory that regards Pentecostalism as a dysfunctional religious reaction by people excluded from and powerless to respond to the forces of urban industrialization and capitalism (e.g., Robert Mapes Anderson). In other words, ecstatic pentecostal spirituality sublimates social and economic marginalization. But William J. Seymour's Azusa Street Revival, for example, can be understood in terms of Althouse's

---

[20] Harvey Cox, *Fire from Heaven: The Rise of Pentecostal Spirituality and the Reshaping of Religion in the Twenty-First Century* (Reading: Addison-Wesley, 1995), 271.

[21] E.g., see the popularity of Pentecostalism among the poor in Latin America and India in Martin Lindhardt, "Introduction," in *New Ways of Being Pentecostal in Latin America*, ed. Martin Lindhardt (Lanham: Lexington, 2016), vii–viii and V. V. Thomas, *Dalit Pentecostalism: Spirituality of the Empowered Poor* (Bangalore: Asia Trading, 2008), 353–9.

[22] Donald E. Miller and Tetsunao Yamamori, *Global Pentecostalism: The New Face of Christian Social Engagement* (Berkeley: University of California Press, 2007), 21. Also, even while showing signs of social deprivation, pentecostal churches promote practices that support mainstream cultural engagement (Stephen J. Hunt, "Deprivation and Western Pentecostalism Revisited: 'Classical' Pentecostalism," *PentecoStudies* 1, no. 1 [2002]: 16–17). As Dahles shows, Chinese Pentecostals in Malaysia effectively use social and cultural capital to advance economically, "In Pursuit of Capital: The Charismatic Turn Among the Chinese Managerial and Professional Class in Malaysia," 102–5. Calvin L. Smith provides a superb survey of political, social, and economic engagement among global Pentecostals in "The Politics and Economics of Pentecostalism: A Global Survey," in *The Cambridge Companion to Pentecostalism*, ed. Cecil M. Robeck, Jr. and Amos Yong (New York: Cambridge University Press, 2014), 175–94. For the diverse and complex relationship of Pentecostals to culture and politics, see the essays in Martin Lindhardt, ed., *New Ways of Being Pentecostal in Latin America* (Lanham: Lexington, 2016) and Néstor Medina and Sammy Alfaro, *Pentecostals and Charismatics in Latin America and Latino Communities*, Charis: Christianity and Renewal—Interdisciplinary Studies (New York: Palgrave Macmillan, 2015).

[23] Althouse, "Waxing and Waning of Social Deprivation as a Model for Understanding the Class Composition of Early American Pentecostalism," 116. For a review and analysis of the social deprivation theory and Pentecostalism, see Stephen Hunt, "Sociology of Religion," in *Studying Global Pentecostalism: Theories and Methods*, ed. Allan Anderson, Michael Begrunder, and Andre Droogers (Berkeley: University of California Press, 2010), 180–4.

prophetic paradigm.²⁴ Here pentecostal eschatology, often maligned as evidence of social deprivation and escapism, was a source of Seymour's countercultural vision and practice. Anticipating the imminent return of Christ, Seymour worked to prepare a multicultural/ethnic and gender integrated church fit for his return.²⁵ Pentecostalism, moreover, is less Anderson's protest of the powerless and more a religious movement that empowers the powerless. Pentecostals do not regard themselves as hapless victims of larger and malignant social and economic forces.²⁶ They regard themselves as people empowered by God's Spirit to change their lives and the world around them.

Third, and most importantly for considering a pentecostal theology of the atonement, the social deprivation theory misses the theological meaning of pentecostal experience and practice. Yes, Pentecostals engaged in socially indecorous worship practices, but for the people who took part in them they were spiritual experiences that empowered their lives in this world. They opened their lives to the primal piety of the Spirit of Pentecost so that they could lay hold of what they perceived as a better life.²⁷ That better life, moreover, often included better social and economic conditions for themselves and their children. In other words, the experience of the Spirit of Pentecost was implicitly a quest for enhanced embodied life. V. V. Thomas shows, for example, that among the Dalit's of Kerala, the turn to Pentecostalism was always grounded in "existential needs" and "related to the life in the here and now. Their concerns included . . . financial and economic problems . . . need for a house . . . [and] the desire for social mobility."²⁸ Although the rhetoric of pentecostal preaching often focused on heaven and spiritual matters, the actual experience of transformed life indicates the implicit affirmation of embodied life in pentecostal praxis. Donald E. Miller and Tetsunao Yamamori assume elements of the social deprivation theory, but nevertheless their assessment of social mobility among Pentecostals dovetails with the implicit affirmation of embodied life in Pentecostalism. Miller and Yamamori argue that although early Pentecostals mostly came from the lower classes, today more and more are "affluent and educated" and they are "'homegrown' [and] their embrace of the Pentecostal ethic and lifestyle has resulted in upward social mobility."²⁹ Social mobility also characterizes pentecostal ecclesial

---

²⁴ Amos Yong also uses the terminology of "prophetic politics" to describe pentecostal social protest. Althouse and Yong seem to have come independently to this common terminology as both of their publications appeared in 2010. For Yong, see *In the Days of Caesar: Pentecostalism and Political Theology—The Cadbury Lectures 2009*, Sacra Doctrina: Christian Theology for a Postmodern Age series (Grand Rapids: Eerdmans, 2010), 11-14.

²⁵ Althouse, "Waxing and Waning of Social Deprivation as a Model for Understanding the Class Composition of Early American Pentecostalism," 129-32.

²⁶ Cox, *Fire from Heaven*, 173.

²⁷ Cox, *Fire from Heaven*, 182. Martin Lindhardt calls the connection between pentecostal piety and social uplift the instrumentalist view, according to which pentecostal churches and the practices they encourage yield positive social benefits for people. See Lindhardt, "Introduction: Presence and Impact of Pentecostal/Charismatic Christianity in Africa," in *Pentecostalism in Africa: Presence and Impact of Pneumatic Christianity in Postcolonial Societies*, ed. Martin Lindhardt, Global Pentecostal and Charismatic Studies, 15 (Leiden: Brill, 2015), 6-7.

²⁸ Thomas, *Dalit Pentecostalism*, 349.

²⁹ Miller and Yamamori, *Global Pentecostalism*, 21. In Argentina, for example, Pentecostals are an increasing minority middle class. See Jens Koehrsen, *Middle Class Pentecostalism in Argentina: Inappropriate Spirit*, Religion in the Americas Series, 15 (Boston and Leiden: Brill, 2016). The class distribution is complex in Latin and South American Pentecostalism. For a survey of the

life. Pentecostals traded the storefront mission and the camp meeting's sawdust trail for the suburban church.[30] The middle class and upper-middle class megachurch, the evangelicalized pentecostal churches, are the product of the implicit life and social transforming nature of experiencing the Spirit of Pentecost.[31]

Understood theologically, pentecostal experience of the Holy Spirit correlates with the fundamental nature of the Incarnation of Jesus Christ—the fulfillment of Spirit-breathed embodied life in and for this world. The experience of the Holy Spirit that enabled Pentecostals to enjoy a fuller and richer life in this world and to pass that on to their children was a fundamental way of participating in the atoning work of the Spirit of Pentecost. The Incarnation, the embodied life of the Son of God, mediated and instantiated in Jesus Christ by the Holy Spirit is fundamental to atonement. The Incarnation is not a steppingstone to the cross. It is not a prelude to the real work of dying on the cross. The Holy Spirit's union of the Son of God with the humanity of Jesus Christ is the ground and the primary datum of the atonement. The life the Spirit breathed into the dirt of Gen. 2:7 finds is fullest expression in the embodied Spirit-breathed life of Jesus Christ. The pentecostal experience of personal life transformation that empowers social, cultural, and economic achievement is a praxis of pentecostal atonement because it participates in the Spirit-breathed life incarnated in Jesus Christ.

Otherworldly Rhetoric: Riding the Glory Train

Two ways of defining Pentecostalism are popular: doctrinal and experiential. Both approaches focus pentecostal rhetoric on otherworldly spiritual experience/s. In doing so, they obscure the importance of the Incarnation for redeeming embodied life and its implicit recognition in pentecostal praxis. Otherworldly means an emphasis on spiritual matters and experiences. Prayer, church activities, saving souls, for example, all happen in this world, but they do not have this world as such as their subject matter. Pentecostal otherworldly rhetoric is often eschatological in nature, but not necessarily so. Otherworldly rhetoric includes a spirituality focused on going to heaven, but also refracts everything in this life through a "spiritual" prism. The "gospel" becomes almost entirely about "spiritual" matters and the pedestrian activities in this world become a distraction and/or impediment to pentecostal spirituality. Otherworldly rhetoric and the way Pentecostals define their movement can obfuscate the renewal of embodied life intrinsic to pentecostal praxis. This section takes the Full Gospel as the most comprehensive and common doctrinal definition of Pentecostalism (especially among classical pentecostal groups). Defining Pentecostalism in terms of charismatic

---

distribution, see Koehrsen, *Middle Class Pentecostalism in Argentina*, 2–20 and David Martin, *Pentecostalism: The World Their Parish* (Malden: Blackwell, 2002), 77–115.

[30] Evangelist Billy Sunday used "Sawdust Trail" in his autobiography, but it is also used to characterize Pentecostals and Charismatics. See the unflattering and condescending account by Larry L. King, "Prophets of the Sawdust Trail," *New York Times*, August 5, 1973. https://www.nytimes.com/1973/08/05/archives/the-preachers-by-james-morris-illustrated-by-tom-huffman-418-pp-new.html

[31] Miller and Yamamori argue that social mobility was a by-product of pentecostal preaching, worship, and spirituality. Economic success may not be the explicit goal of people who turn to pentecostal churches, but it is the outcome of their life-transforming experience in the churches (*Global Pentecostalism*, 168–71).

experience emerged as the major and, in recent years, the most popular, at least among scholars, alternative to the doctrinal definition.

First, the Full Gospel illustrates the explicit otherworldly nature of pentecostal doctrinal rhetoric. Christ the savior provides forgiveness of sins so that a person can go to heaven. Christ the sanctifier often meant participating in a pentecostal negative-positive spirituality. Negatively, not participating in the world—for example, not smoking, not drinking, not dancing, and not going to movies—is the measure of pentecostal spirituality. Positively, taking part in personal acts of devotion, such as Bible reading and personal prayer time, and participating in church-based worship and prayer services define the Christian life. Spirit baptism and speaking in tongues provide the initiation into pentecostal experience as such, at least in the classical pentecostal churches. Spirit baptism also empowers to win souls for Christ. Spirit baptism, consequently, was almost entirely understood as a personal spiritual experience that provided a gateway to evangelism and further charismatic experiences and spiritual gifts. Divine healing is the exception to the implicit embodiment of pentecostal spirituality. Pentecostals believe that Christ's atonement on the cross provides freedom from sin, which includes the healing of the physical body. Admittedly anecdotal, I have never witnessed even a hint of irony when a preacher in a pentecostal service proclaims, on the one hand, a desire to escape this evil world and the temptations and weakness of the body for a heaven paved with streets of gold and, on the other hand, that Christ's blood not only frees the soul from the guilt of sin, but the body from its curse of disease and sickness. The final element of the Full Gospel is Christ the soon coming king. Pentecostals preached that history is perennially on the cusp of the Second Coming of Christ. Jesus would return, not to renew the earth, not to an earth made fit for him by dedicated Christians, but to rapture the faithful to a heavenly paradise so that they would escape the coming tribulation and Battle of Armageddon. The rhetoric of this type of pentecostal eschatology is otherworldly. It assumes that society is corrupt and demonic and will only go from bad to worse until Jesus returns to transport faithful Christians to a better place in heaven.

Wolfgang Vondey's argument for "Spirit baptism and human embodiment" is an important corrective to the otherworldly accent of pentecostal rhetoric. Vondey highlights the implicit-explicit nature of pentecostal rhetoric and theology of sanctification. He shows that the experience of Spirit baptism "marks the transformative moment between coming to the altar and going into the world ... [and that] Spirit baptism must therefore possess implications for the physical, biological, and social embodiment of human beings."[32] Vondey's contribution is to make this essential nature of the experience of Spirit baptism and sanctification explicit. In other words, he provides a theological excavation of the foundation of the rhetorical and visible structure of pentecostal theology and spirituality. No one has to be told that ecstatic experiences of the Holy Spirit and manifestations of spiritual gifts characterize pentecostal spirituality, but they do need the embodied nature and social consequences of those experiences articulated. This chapter argues that the transformation of

---

[32] Vondey, *Pentecostal Theology*, 185–6.

embodied life in pentecostal praxis indicates participation in the Spirit-breathed life incarnated in the life of Jesus Christ.

Second, defining Pentecostalism in terms of charismatic experience has become increasingly popular. Its strength is that it showcases something essential to Pentecostalism and is more inclusive than the doctrinal approaches, such as Classical Pentecostalism's doctrine of Spirit baptism and speaking in tongues. Arelene M. Sánchez Walsh, for example, defines Pentecostalism as "a movement within Christianity that emphasizes an active presence of the Holy Spirit in the lives of its adherents" and the experience of spiritual gifts such as speaking in tongues, healing, and prophecy.[33] Allan Anderson also illustrates this trend among scholars when he defines Pentecostalism as "globally all churches and movements that emphasize ... the *experience* of the working of the Holy Spirit and the *practice* of spiritual gifts. Because Pentecostalism has its emphasis in experience and spirituality rather than in formal theology or doctrine."[34] I agree with scholars like Sánchez and Anderson who reject a narrow classical pentecostal definition of the pentecostal movements. Defining Pentecostalism in terms of charismatic experience, rather than a particular doctrine/s, is more inclusive. But even the classical pentecostal doctrinal definition of Spirit baptism accompanied by speaking in tongues highlights a certain category of spiritual experience as the defining feature of the movement—namely, the experience of Spirit baptism and speaking in tongues. The Full Gospel, moreover, centers on spiritual experiences. The emphasis is on being saved, sanctified, healed, empowered for witness, and preparing for Jesus to come. In other words, although Classical Pentecostalism and the Full Gospel have formal doctrinal definitions, their focus is on spiritual experience/s. In the end, moreover, both approaches to Pentecostalism accentuate rhetorical otherworldliness. Why? Because they center Pentecostalism on spiritual experience. Embodied life in this world is not central to these definitions, even though often implicit in pentecostal praxis.

Third, these approaches to defining Pentecostalism are problematic and ironic for two reasons. On the one hand, even though the doctrinal definitions of Pentecostalism and the explicit rhetoric of their spiritualities are Christological, even Christocentric, and make the experience of the Holy Spirit paramount, they do not arise from the fundamental work of God in Christ and the Spirit's role in it—the Incarnation. Salvation comes from the cross, sanctification and Spirit baptism from the power of the risen Christ. Healing is a benefit of the cross. The imminent return of Christ assumes his divine status, but the Incarnation as such plays no significant, if any, part in it. One might object that sanctification ties in with the Incarnation. But not really. When Pentecostals emphasize Jesus' moral example as the model for the Christian life, they typically suggest that as Christ in his humanity emptied himself of divine prerogatives and relied on the Holy Spirit to overcome sin, so Christians should follow his example

---

[33] Arlene M. Sánchez Walsh, *Pentecostals in America* (New York: Columbia University Press, 2018), 1–13.

[34] Allan Anderson, *An Introduction to Pentecostalism: Global Charismatic Christianity* (New York: Cambridge University Press, 2004), 13–14 (emphasis original).

and rely on the power of the Holy Spirit.[35] But the point is that as God, Christ did not need the power of the Holy Spirit. The Spirit's empowerment of Christ is not intrinsic to the Incarnation, but a concession the Son of God makes to provide a moral example to his followers. In short, pentecostal theology does not link sanctification to the Spirit's work in incarnating the Son of God in Jesus Christ. Despite the emphasis on Christ and the Spirit in pentecostal rhetoric, the fundamental work of the Incarnation is not a primary matter in traditional pentecostal theology. The Incarnation and the Spirit's work in it remain implicit in pentecostal preaching, doctrine, and spiritual experience, much like the embodied nature of their experience of the Holy Spirit remains implicit.

On the other hand, the irony of pentecostal rhetoric and praxis is that the common theological descriptions of Pentecostalism (whether doctrinal or more inclusive experiential) highlight experiential spirituality, yet the consequence of pentecostal experience is not spiritual, but transformed life in this world. In other words, otherworldly pentecostal rhetoric ignores Christianity's central claim and its implications—that God was in Christ to renew the world, but pentecostal praxis embodies them. Miller and Yamamori are correct when they point out that positive social results are not explicit and overt "goals" in traditional Pentecostalism, but they are its "*indirect* results . . . [and] latent corollaries."[36] They identify four types of pentecostal churches: "legalistic and otherworldly," the "Prosperity Gospel or health-and-wealth churches," "Progressive Pentecostalism," and "routinized Pentecostalism."[37] I have been interacting for the most part with their "legalistic and otherworldly" type. Their assessment of these churches reflects the irony of pentecostal rhetoric and praxis. Miller and Yamamori doubt that "legalistically oriented Pentecostals will do much more than save their own souls."[38] But the moral lives of legalistic Pentecostals make them "upright citizens, disciplined employees, and honest business people."[39] So, although the message heard in legalistic pentecostal churches focuses on Jesus' imminent return, the eschatological destruction of the world, and going to heaven, the resulting life practices, nevertheless, yield economic benefits and social mobility or at

---

[35] Warrington articulates this vocational view of the Spirit's relation to Christ and also critiques its use as a basis for carrying on Jesus' healing ministry. See Keith Warrington, "The Role of Jesus as Presented in the Healing Praxis and Teaching of British Pentecostalism: A Re-Examination," *Pneuma: The Journal of the Society for Pentecostal Studies* 25, no. 1 (2003): 88–92.

[36] Miller and Yamamori, *Global Pentecostalism*, 34 (emphasis in original). Earlier David Martin made this point that Pentecostalism is "a movement of spiritual renewal with economic and social implications" (Martin, *Pentecostalism*, 78). Also see Daniel Míguez, "Exploring the Argentinian Case: Religious Motives in the Growth of Latin American Pentecostalism," in *Latin American Religion in Motion*, ed. Christian Smith and Joshua Prokopy (New York: Routledge, 1999), 213–25 and for the social and economic uplift inspired by Pentecostalism among lower-caste Indians, see Chad M. Bauman, *Pentecostalism, Proselytization, and Anti-Christian Violence in Contemporary India* (New York: Oxford University Press, 2015), 81–2.

[37] Miller and Yamamori, *Global Pentecostalism*, 28–31.

[38] Miller and Yamamori, *Global Pentecostalism*, 31.

[39] Miller and Yamamori, *Global Pentecostalism*, 31. At the same time, the negative and otherworldly worldview of more conservative Pentecostals is real and warn against a pollyannaish perspective on pentecostal social mobility. Research conducted by Joseph Clark and Samuel Stroope show a "decrease in upward mobility" among Pentecostals. See Clark and Stroope, "Intergenerational Social Mobility and Religious Ecology: Disaggregating the Conservative Protestant Bloc," *Social Science Research* 70 (2018): 250.

least maintenance and functional living in the world. In other words, the emphasis on following the narrow path to heaven has positive social and economic consequences. The legalistic pentecostal rhetoric is world denying, but the Spirit praxis of transformed life indicates the world affirming, embodied nature, and material consequences of experiencing the Spirit of Pentecost, the Spirit that fulfilled human embodied life in the Incarnation of the Son of God in Jesus Christ.

Embodied Pentecostal Atonement in Cameroon and Vietnam

The previous section critiqued the otherworldly descriptions of Pentecostalism. But recent sociological and theological work on Pentecostalism argues for its holistic vision of redemption.[40] Sociological research on Pentecostals shows that, intentional or not, becoming a pentecostal Christian is transformative for the non-"spiritual" areas of life in the world. The holistic experience of redemption among Pentecostals, moreover, connects directly with the Incarnation. The Incarnation affirms, indeed fulfills, the embodied life of the Spirit-breathed divine image. Holistic redemption is the correspondence of Spirit Christology and the Spirit of Pentecost. The Holy Spirit's work in the Incarnation of Christ is manifest in the "all people" of Pentecost (Acts 2:17). The Spirit of Pentecost offers all people the opportunity to participate in Christ's fulfillment of embodied life.

Although this chapter argues for an embodied emphasis that ties in with the Incarnation, pentecostal religious experience should not be discounted or disconnected from embodied life. Defining Pentecostalism as a genre of religious experience, such as charismatic experience, can decoy from the embodied outcomes of the pentecostal experience of grace. My point, however, is not to dismiss the importance of the charismatic character of pentecostal experience, but to avoid overlooking the embodied nature of that experience. Pentecostal practices include spiritual gifts and experiences, but also personal and social transformation. Pentecostal churches in Africa are a case in point. Pentecostal Christianity has grown significantly over the past two decades in Africa. For example, between 1996 and 2001, pentecostal churches grew by 50 percent (from 4.6 million to 6.8 million) in South Africa and comprised 15 percent of the population.[41] The churches emphasize experiencing God and self-empowerment. One of the consequences of their spiritual experience is a deeper sense of personal initiative to address the material circumstances of their lives. *Under the*

---

[40] For an example of theological, see Daniela C. Augustine, *Pentecost, Hospitality, and Transfiguration: Toward a Spirit-Inspired Vision of Social Transformation* (Cleveland: CPT, 2012) and for sociological David Maxwell, *African Gifts of the Spirit: Pentecostalism and the Rise of a Zimbabwean Transnational Religious Movement* (Athens: Ohio University Press, 2006) and Miller and Yamamori, *Global Pentecostalism*.

[41] Lawrence Schlemmer, *Dormant Capital: The Pentecostal Movement in South Africa and Its Potential Social and Economic Role* (Johannesburg: The Centre for Development and Enterprise, 2008), 75. This report is also available online as "Under the Radar: Pentecostalism in South Africa and Its Potential Social and Economic Role," Centre for Development and Enterprise, March 6, 2008. https://www.cde.org.za/under-the-radar-pentecostalism-in-south-africa-and-its-potential-social-and-economic-role/

Radar, the Centre for Development and Enterprise report on Pentecostalism in South Africa, suggests this fusion of spiritual experience and proactive engagement with the world invites comparison with Max Weber's description of the "this-worldly asceticism" of early modern Calvinists.[42] Although *Under the Radar* does not quantify the economic impact of Pentecostalism, it does show that many Pentecostals anticipate and experience economic and social benefits as a result of their faith and the new life that it enables. These benefits are consistent with David Maxwell's account of the Zimbabwe Assemblies of God Africa churches experience of "redemptive uplift." As their new moral life frees them from drug addictions, alcoholism, and promiscuity, Pentecostals become more attractive employees that facilitates their promotion to better employment opportunities.[43] The church's message inspires hope and a sense of personal empowerment to combat poverty and social marginalization "that arise from structural conditions that are beyond the power of individuals to alter and which their political leaders are unable or unwilling to change."[44] The church also provides a network of social support that helps individuals overcome the isolating forces of neoliberal economics. But perhaps most important is "Pentecostalism's capacity to redeem, restore and re-pattern the family as the primary defence against the destructive effects of neo-liberalism."[45] The remainder of this section considers in more detail the holistic redemption and embodied effects of experiencing the Spirit of Pentecost among Pentecostals in Cameroon and Vietnam.

First, Tomas Sundnes Drønen's research on the pentecostal churches of Ngaoundéré in northern Cameroon showcases that pentecostal faith can promote embodied life in the world. A majority Muslim region since the mid-nineteenth century, the area also came under first German and then more importantly after the First World War French colonial rule. Norwegian Lutherans first (1925) and then Catholics (1946) brought Christianity to Ngaoundéré and the surrounding region. During the second half of the twentieth century, Christian missionaries made inroads among certain ethnic groups, but Islam remained the majority religion. In recent decades, economic migrants from southern Cameroon and more liberal social policies enacted by the government have transformed the social space of Ngaoundéré. A key part of this change has been the growth of pentecostal churches.[46]

Drønen's research focuses on Iya Moussa's Living Faith Church (Eglise de la Foi Vivante) in Ngaoundéré, Cameroon. Moussa personifies the pentecostal message popular in Ngaoundéré. He left Ngaoundéré for university in Germany. Paying his own way through school, he also took part in pentecostal crusades in Eastern Europe. Completing his education, he returned to join the faculty of the University of Ngaoundéré. He also established the Living Faith Church. Although emphasizing an "economic theology," Living Faith Church does not emphasize the prosperity gospel,

---

[42] Schlemmer, *Dormant Capital*, 81.
[43] Maxwell, *African Gifts of the Spirit*, 202.
[44] Maxwell, *African Gifts of the Spirit*, 209.
[45] Maxwell, *African Gifts of the Spirit*, 210.
[46] Tomas Sundnes Drønen, *Pentecostalism, Globalisation, and Islam in Northern Cameroon: Megachurches in the Making?* Studies of Religion in Africa, 41 (Boston: Brill, 2013), 7–9.

which is commonplace in African pentecostal churches.⁴⁷ Rather than preaching seed of faith gifts to the church and miraculous blessings, the church emphasizes hard work, discipline, and advancement through higher education. Moussa encourages church members to practice what Drønen describes as pentecostal entrepreneurship.⁴⁸ But this entrepreneurship takes place in government jobs, multinational companies, and education. Why does this "entrepreneurship guided by the Spirit" take place in these unusual venues and not the more common ones of small businesses?⁴⁹ The answer is context.

Since French colonial rule, the Muslim community has controled and restricted access to the local business markets. Legacy educational and healthcare institutions ran by Lutherans and Catholics, moreover, have dominated Ngaoundéré's social space, but recent decades have seen the erosion of their overseas financial support and the quality of their services. Emphasizing achievement through education, discipline, and strategic work has be an effective adaptation to this social context. Education provides a pathway to serve in government, multinational companies, and the local universities and schools. This strategy enables pentecostal believers to achieve "economic development without challenging the Muslim monopoly of the local business market."⁵⁰ It is entrepreneurial because it is the creative and adaptive behavior that enables pentecostal believers to overcome economic disadvantages and achieve upward mobility.⁵¹

A second group that reflects holistic redemption is Vietnamese Pentecostals. They are primarily poor ethnic minorities of the Central and Northwest Highlands and migrant urban workers. They are not part of the majority and socially dominant Viêt ethnic group. Consequently, they do not have access to political power, state economic development programs, and privileges of patronage from the Communist Party of Vietnam. They also face economic exploitation (e.g., land grabbing) and religious persecution.⁵² Pentecostalism has become increasingly popular for these

---

⁴⁷ Drønen, *Pentecostalism, Globalisation, and Islam in Northern Cameroon*, 186.
⁴⁸ The pentecostal churches in Ngaoundéré appear to be an exception to Paul Gifford's criticism of African forms of Pentecostalism. Gifford maintains that despite promoting individual advancement, entrepreneurial activity, and hard work and personal discipline, African pentecostal churches still perpetuate anti-modern beliefs and practices, such as the prosperity gospel, which attributes success to faith and divine favor and blessing from the man of God rather than work and education and misfortune to the power of evil spirits. Consequently, Gifford disagrees with scholars such as Peter Berger who regard African Pentecostalism as a contemporary embodiment of Max Weber's Protestant ethic. See Paul Gifford, *Christianity, Development, and Modernity in Africa* (New York: Oxford University Press, 2016), 48–68 and Peter L. Berger, "Max Weber is Alive and Well, and Living in Guatemala: The Protestant Ethic Today," *The Review of Faith and International Affairs* 8, no. 4 (2010): 3–9 and "Under the Radar: Pentecostalism in South Africa and Its Potential Social and Economic Role."
⁴⁹ Drønen, *Pentecostalism, Globalisation, and Islam in Northern Cameroon*, 190.
⁵⁰ Tomas Sundnes Drønen, "Material Development and Spiritual Empowerment: Pentecostalism in Northern Cameroon," *PentecoStudies* 14, no. 2 (2015): 215. Also see, Drønen, "'Now I Dress Well. Now I Work Hard': Pentecostalism, Prosperity, and Economic Development in Cameroon," in *Pastures of Plenty: Tracing Religio-Scapes of Prosperity Gospel in Africa and Beyond*, ed. Andreas Heuser, Studies in the Intercultural History of Christianity, vol. 161 (New York: Peter Lang, 2015), 249–63.
⁵¹ Drønen, *Pentecostalism, Globalisation, and Islam in Northern Cameroon*, 191–9.
⁵² See "Losing the Plot: Land Grabs in Vietnam," *The Economist*, March 16, 2013: 42–3; James Lewis, "The Evangelical Religious Movement among the Hmông of Northern Vietnam and the

people disenfranchised from the dominant culture and its economic benefits. The explosive growth of Pentecostalism in Vietnam is a development from the evangelical and holiness Christianity brought to Vietnam by Christian and Missionary Alliance missionaries in 1911.[53] Vince Le's *Vietnamese Evangelicals and Pentecostalism: The Politics of Divine Intervention* argues that the pentecostal "belief in divine intervention" is fundamental for Pentecostalism's appeal to the poor and ethnic minorities. They turn to Pentecostalism because it offers hope that God can intervene to deliver them from their desperate social conditions and provide material blessings that will alleviate their poverty and suffering.[54] The following discussion highlights ways that the Vietnamese pentecostal practice of worship and apocalyptic imagining empowers the renewal of embodied life. Why focus on worship and eschatology? Because they are two areas that sociologists regard as dysfunctional reactions among Pentecostals to their concrete social disadvantages. They are essential to the pentecostal deprivation theory. Rather than joining trade unions and self-advocating through political and cultural institutions, they retreat to the spiritual narcotic of ecstatic worship and the emolument of hope for heaven.[55] Worship and apocalyptic imagining among Vietnamese Pentecostals, however, inspire hope and a vision for the improvement of their lives in this world.

Pentecostal worship opens people's lives to an encounter with God that reassures them that they are not alone. They may be marginalized by social and political circumstances, but God stands with them. This experience of divine presence inspires hope and confidence to overcome social disadvantages. The pentecostal confidence in divine intervention, moreover, is not simply a belief in magical power that undermines proactive personal and group initiative. Pentecostals anticipate that the Holy Spirit will guide, direct, and empower their lives in ways that will enable them to overcome their problems, both personal and social. The encouragement they receive from experiencing the Holy Spirit in worship, in other words, does not sublimate their need for social transformation in a spiritual and otherworldly ghetto. Pentecostal worship also inspires people to imagine new ways of living that transcend their "negative life experiences of marginalization, oppression, and abuse."[56] Le continues that this Spirit-inspired imaginative space facilitated by pentecostal worship is not irrational. On the contrary, it takes place within a theological horizon of Spirit-enabled new life, transformation, and empowerment. In this respect, testimonies are vital. Members of pentecostal churches hear other believers testify to overcoming debilitating circumstances and are in turn inspired to imagine their "particular vision of an enhanced and better life."[57]

Government's Response: 1989–2000," *Crossroads: An Interdisciplinary Journal of Southeast Asian Studies* 16, no. 2 (2002): 79–112; and Tam T. T. Ngo, "Protestant Conversion and Social Conflict: The Case of the Hmong in Contemporary Vietnam," *Journal of Southeast Asian Studies* 46, no. 2 (2015): 274–92.

[53] Vincent Le, *Vietnamese Evangelicals and Pentecostals: The Politics of Divine Intervention*, Global Pentecostal and Charismatic Studies, 29 (Leiden: Brill, 2018), 13.
[54] Le, *Vietnamese Evangelicals and Pentecostals*, 122.
[55] E.g., see Anderson, *Vision of the Disinherited*, 229.
[56] Le, *Vietnamese Evangelicals and Pentecostals*, 133.
[57] Le, *Vietnamese Evangelicals and Pentecostals*, 134.

Apocalyptic theology also enables Vietnamese Pentecostals to imagine a transformed world in which their lives prosper.[58] The apocalyptic character of traditional (classical) pentecostal eschatology starts with the profound truth that the concrete and material world is problematic. Apocalyptic theology appeals to people suffering under the conditions of a dysfunctional society. A society that ensures privileges for elites and favored groups and oppresses, exploits, or otherwise marginalizes other people. Apocalyptic theology is a protest from the margins in a religious register. At root, therefore, the problem is not apocalyptic theology, but the social and cultural forces that do not create opportunities for all people to flourish. Apocalyptic theology also contains hope for the disruption of the injustice of this world and its replacement with a better world. In traditional pentecostal eschatology, hope for freedom from life's travails meant going to heaven, being enraptured at Christ's Second Coming, and the advent of the peace and justice of God's kingdom after the Battle of Armageddon. Recognizing that pentecostal eschatology runs the risk of spiritualizing and offering little explicit hope for changing the current world, Le argues, nevertheless, that apocalyptic theology is "an invitation to imagine a new, improved condition of life . . . for Vietnamese [pentecostal] evangelicals . . . a settled life . . . a rooted life in a relatively peaceful, undisputed land, with a just social structure and good social and economic conditions to support human flourishing."[59] Vietnamese Pentecostals dream less for transport to an off-world heavenly space than restoration to a prosperous, peaceful, and abundant land. Their apocalyptic aspirations emerge from the Spirit of Pentecost whose outpouring makes the "land that was laid waste . . . like the garden of Eden" (Ezek. 37:35).

Although Pentecostals can seem as world denying as they turn to charismatic spirituality, their "iconoclastic" attitude is not toward the world as such, but to the oppressive status quo they encounter in Vietnamese society. They protest against a system that demeans and marginalizes them. They turn to "faith as a liberating force that is able to free people from cultural elements that impede their . . . flourishing."[60] The irony of Vietnamese Pentecostals, given their marginal social location and their "message which prioritizes care for the socially disadvantaged," is that they stand in continuity with the earlier twentieth-century Vietnamese communist leaders "who sought to dismantle colonial exploitation."[61] So, far from being a movement fixated on escaping the world for spiritual succor, they are "socially disadvantaged" people relying on God for social transformation and liberation from the social inequities fostered by

---

[58] David Smilde uses the term "imaginative rationality" to describe ways that converting to evangelical (pentecostal) Christianity provides concepts for renewing their economic and social prospects. Although based on sociological research in Latin America, Smilde's imaginative rationality captures the personal-social transformation that I am describing theological terms as the fruit of the Spirit of Pentecost. Smilde also argues that the social enhancements accruing from conversion are not by-products, but intentional aspirations among the converts. See David Smilde, *Reason to Believe: Cultural Agency in Latin American Evangelicalism* (Berkeley: University of California Press, 2007), 13.

[59] Le, *Vietnamese Evangelicals and Pentecostals*, 27 and 31.

[60] Le, *Vietnamese Evangelicals and Pentecostals*, 89–90.

[61] Le, *Vietnamese Evangelicals and Pentecostals*, 82.

the current "Vietnamese communist tradition."[62] That would-be liberators turn tyrants is prosaic, but the worldly orientation of pentecostal apocalyptic imagination offers an alternative to the social deprivation theory. Apocalyptic imagination inspires not simply or even primarily hope for an off-world heaven, but a vision for life in this world that subverts and disrupts abusive hierarchies and systemic inequities and replaces them with life structured according to the peace and justice of God's kingdom.[63] Thus, pentecostal beliefs, such as eschatology, are not necessarily ineffectual sops for addressing the material conditions of life. Indeed, Vietnamese government efforts to stop the spread of Christianity among ethnic minorities indicate that it regards the pentecostal and evangelical message possessing potential to foment political unrest, instability, and even transformation.[64]

Cameroonian and Vietnamese Pentecostalism are examples of atonement that correlate with the redemptive work of the Spirit-anointed Christ. Jesus healed the sick, he fed the hungry, he lifted up the broken hearted. Consider the man Jesus healed of leprosy in Mt. 8:1-4 (and Lk. 5:12-16). A leper in first-century Palestine was an extreme outcast. They existed on the physical margins of society; "they had to wear torn clothes, let their hair be unkempt, cover the lower part of their faces and shout 'Unclean! Unclean.'"[65] No one would touch them, and they could not participate in any social activities. Yet, Jesus "reached out his hand and touched the man" and healed him. Jesus' healing of the leper was a redemption of embodied life and of social renewal. The man could now reintegrate with society and his personal, family, and occupational connections. The leper's healing illustrates the nature of embodied redemption. Not only because Jesus healed the man's body. Embodied and holistic redemption is more than healing for body and soul. It includes all the dimensions of life. The point is that social, physical, economic, personal, and familial facets of this healing were not incidental to, but the substance of atonement. Jesus' acts of physical healing were not simply demonstrations of power to prove his divinity. They indicate the nature of his redemptive work. Jesus, as the Spirit-anointed messiah, has come "to preach good news to the poor . . . recovery of sight for the blind, to release the oppressed, to proclaim the year of the Lord's favor" (Lk. 4:18-19). The "year of the Lord's favor" that the Spirit-anointed messiah brings entails the renewal of human dignity and the social conditions of life (see Isa. 61:1-7). In John 10, Jesus likens himself to a "gate" and a "shepherd" that leads his sheep to verdant pastures. The sheep-pasture image indicates a holistic and embodied redemption. Jesus promises to give his life so that his sheep can have abundant life. That is why, moreover, his Spirit-empowered followers healed the sick, shared their resources, and "there were no needy persons among them" (Acts 3:1-10, 4:32-37, and 5:12-16). Renewing and restoring abundant life in this world is central to the atonement. As Ogbu Kalu argues that the expectation in African Pentecostalism for abundant life—"material, physical, and psychic"—is not primarily the import of American consumerism transposed in the religious key of the prosperity gospel, but

---

[62] Le, *Vietnamese Evangelicals and Pentecostals*, 82.
[63] Le, *Vietnamese Evangelicals and Pentecostals*, 27.
[64] Le, *Vietnamese Evangelicals and Pentecostals*, 87.
[65] Francois P. Viljoen, "Jesus Healing the Leper and the Purity Law in the Gospel of Matthew," *In die Skriflig* 48, no. 2 (2014): 5.

a continuation of the wholistic redemptive vision of the Hebrew Bible prophets.[66] It is the substance of the life the Holy Spirit brought about in Jesus Christ and of Christ's Spirit-empowered ministry. The traditional association of forgiveness of sins and atonement is also important. Forgiveness of sins and personal healing from guilt and reconciliation with other people are vital to the atonement. But forgiveness of sins is not the end of atonement. Forgiveness frees from debilitating guilt. It frees a person to soar in a life graced and renewed by the Spirit of Pentecost. So, even the traditional forensic account of atonement and forgiveness of sins entails holistic and embodied ramifications of grace.

From By-Products to the Purpose of Pentecost

What can North American Pentecostals learn from their Cameroonian and Vietnamese co-religionists? Pentecostal preaching and ministry rooted in a vision of the Holy Spirit's renewal of embodied life in the incarnate Christ and offered to all people in the gift of the Spirit of Pentecost can offer a pathway to personal and social transformation. Pentecostal worship can provide space for people to imagine new possibilities of life in the Spirit. This section considers the question of personal and social transformation and argues that personal-social transformation is intrinsic to a pentecostal theology of atonement rooted in the Spirit-incarnated life of Jesus Christ. It begins, however, with the bleak social conditions faced by many people in North America and a pentecostal imagining of a pathway to renewed life.

First, Robert D. Putnam's *Our Kids* and David Brooks' *The Social Animal* on a broad sociological scale, and J. D. Vance's *Hillbilly Elegy* on a more personal level describe the hopeless and harrowing experiences of people living on the margins of American society: Children of substance abuse parents, growing up in family conditions of chronic poverty, and the stultifying limitations of simply not knowing the means to participate in educational and career opportunities that are self-evident to the upper classes.[67] The bi-partisan report *Opportunity, Responsibility, and Security: A Consensus Plan for Reducing Poverty and Restoring the American Dream*, published by the American Enterprise Institute for Public Policy Research and the Brookings Institution shows that children of single-parent families are more likely to grow up in poverty and low-income households with long-term negative consequences for their education and economic achievement. "Two obvious consequences of the increasing number of children in single-parent families, 77 percent of which are headed by mothers, are lower income and higher poverty rates as compared to married-couple

---

[66] Ogbu Kalu, *African Pentecostalism: An Introduction* (New York: Oxford University Press, 2008), 255–63.
[67] Robert D. Putnam, *Our Kids: The American Dream in Crisis* (New York: Simon & Schuster, 2015); David Brooks, *The Social Animal: The Hidden Sources of Love, Character, and Achievement* (New York: Random House, 2012); and J. D. Vance, *Hillbilly Elegy: A Memoir of a Family and Culture in Crisis* (New York: HarperCollins, 2016).

families."⁶⁸ The poverty rate for children in single-mother families is "four and five times higher than the poverty rate of married-couple families; in 2013, the poverty rate for children in single-mother families was 45.8 percent, compared with 9.5 percent for children in married-couple families."⁶⁹ The report also advocates marriage and responsible parenting as key foundations for addressing this social issue. Not because they are retrograde "family values" conservatives, but because children raised by two parents exceed children raised "in a single-parent family on key developments, educational, behavioral, and employment-related outcomes."⁷⁰ The report shows that economic mobility is far more likely for children of two-parent families than their single-parent counterparts. For example, "four out of five children who started out in the bottom quintile [of income], but who were raised by parents married throughout their childhood, rose out of the bottom quintile as adults." *The New York Times* piece is correct that single mothers should not be shamed but ignoring or at least downplaying the consequences of single-parent families and seeing more government programs as the only solution is less than helpful.⁷¹ Government programs offer solutions. But so does strengthening families as, primarily, fathers become responsible husbands and parents to their children.

Pentecostals provide an example of the way that experiencing the Spirit of Pentecost can transform families. The Holy Spirit transforms (mostly) men from lives of debauchery and licentiousness and empowers them to be responsible husbands and parents, which fortifies their families and promises a better future for their children. Working-class kids can imagine escaping poverty, excelling in school, going to university, and becoming a nurse, a doctor, or a software engineer. For people coming from a middle-class or upper-middle-class family, such imaginings are pedestrian and a matter of course. But for young people growing up in families without parents, relatives, and neighborhood adults having gone to university and with school experiences where only the very smart and "rich" get to go to college, this type of Spirit and church community inspired social imagination is potent and life transforming. Overcoming debilitating feelings of personal inadequacies and a lower-class social world that artificially restricts the horizon of possibilities for a young person can be a way of experiencing the empowerment of the Spirit of Pentecost. It can be an experience of atonement that reconciles a person to the type of life God created for them. Pentecostals believe in the power of the Spirit of Pentecost. The same Spirit that raised Christ from the dead can raise people to new life (Rom. 8:11).

Second, some may wonder, if I am perpetuating the individualism and anti-worldliness or, at least, the pentecostal tendency to not give proper attention to changing social structures and systemic injustice. No. Pentecostals need to engage transforming wider social injustices through their individual lives and at more macro political and social levels. The way forward, however, is not to move away from the importance of

---

[68] *Opportunity, Responsibility, and Security: A Consensus Plan for Reducing Poverty and Restoring the American Dream* (AEI/Brookings Working Group on Poverty and Opportunity, 2015), 21.
[69] *Opportunity, Responsibility, and Security*, 22.
[70] *Opportunity, Responsibility, and Security*, 32.
[71] David Brady, Ryan M. Finnigan, and Sabine Hübgen, "Single Mothers are Not the Problem," *The New York Times*, February 10, 2018.

individual transformation, but to add an awareness and advocacy for social renewal. Indeed, discounting personal transformation as a vehicle for social change is facile. As Amos Yong insists, "Pentecostalism provides one avenue for the liberation of the poor, although such uplift involves at its core a Christian conversion, biblical spirituality, and charismatic piety."[72] Bernice Martin argues that Latin American Pentecostals "intend to improve social conditions. They conduct vigorous campaigns against 'the vices' and all the disorder they foster, and they deliberately try to strengthen and stabilize the family . . . [i]n this sense, they directly address the social . . . but with the primary purpose of healing and restoring individual souls."[73] In this respect, Salvatore Cucchiari points out, in a study on Sicilian Pentecostalism, that personal conversion is "not merely inner transformation per se but transformation directed toward more integrative systems of meaning, personal autonomy, and moral responsibility."[74] In her study of Pentecostals in Brazil, Cecília Loreto Mariz argues that people turn to religion because it provides meaning for their life, but also that "all religious groups that are popular among the poor are materially useful."[75] Individuals transformed into the image of Christ by the Spirit of Pentecost transform their social context. Recognizing that point does not abrogate the importance of addressing systemic social problems.

The Spirit of Pentecost brings the life of the incarnate Christ to transform human beings so that they can live in the fullness of Spirit-breathed life. Social structures often prevent people from flourishing and so need to be incorporated in a vision for participating in Spirit-baptized life. Pamela P. Martin, Tuere A. Bowles, LaTrese Adkins, and Monica T. Leach argue that although some black megachurches encourage personal spiritual transformation and "transforming oppressive systems within the USA," if the church is pentecostal it tends to focus on first order moral and spiritual transformation rather than higher orders of systemic social change.[76] This is a problem that calls for concerted attention.[77] Pentecostals can learn from liberation theology that the Holy Spirit "is also at work in political, economic, and social liberation, and not merely

---

[72] Yong, *In the Days of Caesar*, 36.
[73] Bernice Martin, "From Pre- to Postmodernity in Latin America: The Case of Pentecostalism," in *Religion, Modernity, and Postmodernity*, ed. Paul Heelas and David Martin (Malden: Blackwell, 1998), 128 and Virginia Nolivos and Eloy H. Nolivos, "Pentecostalism's Theological Reconstruction of the Identity of the Latin American Family," in *Pentecostal Power: Expressions, Impact and Faith of Latin American Pentecostalism*, ed. Calvin L. Smith, Global Pentecostal and Charismatic Studies, 6 (Boston: Brill, 2011), 221–4. The positive social impact of restoring families is common among global Pentecostals (see Martin, *Pentecostalism*, 140 and 171–2).
[74] Salvatore Cucchiari, "'Adapted for Heaven': Conversion and Culture in Western Sicily," *American Ethnologist* 15, no. 3 (1988): 418.
[75] Cecília Loreto Mariz, *Coping with Poverty: Pentecostals and Base Communities in Brazil* (Philadelphia: Temple University Press, 1994), 155.
[76] Pamela P. Martin, Tuere A. Bowles, LaTrese Adkins, and Monica T. Leach, "Black Mega-Churches in the Internet Age: Exploring Theological Teachings and Social Outreach Efforts," *Journal of African American Studies* 15, no. 155 (2011): 159, 167–8, and 172.
[77] For example, Frederick L. Ware recognizes the need for family restoration among black communities but also argues that black Pentecostals need an alternative eschatology that can facilitate "analysis of processes and systems" that can promote "the radical restructuring of society and redistribution of power and wealth." See Ware, "On the Compatibility/Incompatibility of Pentecostal Premillennialism with Black Liberation Theology," in *Afro-Pentecostalism: Black Pentecostal and Charismatic Christianity in History and Culture*, ed. Amos Yong and Estrelda Y. Alexander (New York: New York University Press, 2011), 199.

in spiritual liberation."⁷⁸ The social inclusive and transcending nature of the Spirit of Pentecost disrupts hierarchies of social inequity. Jonathan Langston Chism argues that too often pentecostal experience of the Holy Spirit has been too individualized and spiritualized. But the problem is not the experience of the Spirit of Pentecost as such, but a truncated vision of the meaning of the power of Pentecost. Theologies, spiritualities, and experiences of the Spirit of Pentecost that do not lead to a critical social consciousness are inadequate.⁷⁹ Pentecost is intrinsically an experience of critical social consciousness—"I will pour out my Spirit on all flesh ... sons and daughters ... young ... old ... even on my servants, both men and women" (Acts 2:17-18). Losing the importance of individual renewal, however, would be a mistake. As Martin Lindhardt shows in his research on Chilean Pentecostals, personal transformation that arises from pentecostal experience "enables congregants to defy the logic of a dominant sociocultural system, to construct new and meaningful biographies and to symbolically appropriate world history and make it their own."⁸⁰ The point of this chapter is that these social empowering and transforming benefits accruing from experiencing the Spirit of Pentecost are not by-products, but the substance of atonement. They are ways that the Holy Spirit reconciles people to embodying their Spirit-breathed life.⁸¹

Third, personal-social transformation is intrinsic to a pentecostal theology of atonement rooted in the Spirit-incarnated life of Jesus Christ. This point invites revisiting my earlier reference to Max Weber's Protestant ethic and its new manifestation in the pentecostal ethic. These two views maintain that social benefits can accrue as by-products of certain religious beliefs and practices. After experiencing life transformation in pentecostal churches, people embrace a stricter moral life that leads to stable families and increases the likelihood that their children will go on to higher education. They are more dependable in the workplace, which leads to career advancement. Rather than spending surplus income on various forms of moral dissipation, they save and invest it and increase their financial security.⁸² Dena Freeman shows that a variation of Weber's Protestant ethic is evident in African pentecostal

---

78 Brandon Kerston, "Latin American Liberation and Renewal Theology: A Pneumatological Dialogue," in *Pentecostals and Charismatics in Latin America and Latino Communities*, ed. Néstor Medina and Sammy Alfaro, Charis: Christianity and Renewal—Interdisciplinary Studies (New York: Palgrave Macmillan, 2015), 193.
79 Jonathan Langston Chism's work introduced me to the term "Pentecostal critical consciousness." Chism, "'The Saints Go Marching': Black Pentecostal Critical Consciousness and the Political Protest Activism of Pastors and Leaders in the Church of God in Christ in the Civil Rights Era," *Pneuma: The Journal of the Society for Pentecostal Studies* 35, no. 3 (2013): 424-43.
80 Martin Lindhardt, *Power in Powerlessness: A Study of Pentecostal Life Worlds in Urban Chile*, Religion in the America Series, 12 (Leiden: Brill, 2012), 248.
81 David Smilde's sociological work among Latin Americans confirms that economic and social benefits are explicit motives for people converting to evangelical (pentecostal) Christianity. See Smilde, *Reason to Believe*.
82 For examples, see Dena Freeman, ed., *Pentecostalism and Development: Churches, NGOs and Social Change in Africa* (New York: Palgrave Macmillan, 2012); Martin, *Pentecostalism*, 72-4 and 87; Bernice Martin, "New Mutations for the Protestant Ethic among Latin American Pentecostals," *Religion* 25, no. 2 (1995): 107-17; Eloy H. Nolivos, "Capitalism and Pentecostalism in Latin America: Trajectories of Prosperity and Development," in *Pentecostalism and Prosperity: The Socio-Economics of the Global Charismatic Movement*, ed. Katherine Attanasi and Amos Yong (New York: Palgrave Macmillan, 2012), 87-105.

churches. Indeed, she argues that pentecostal churches in Africa are more effective in promoting upward social mobility among their congregants than are NGOs.[83] Cecília Loreto Mariz's description of the relationship that Brazilian Pentecostals see between healthy spiritual life and relative economic success is consistent with Weber's thesis.[84] This chapter highlighted the economic and social benefits among Cameroonian and Vietnamese Pentecostals. I am not questioning the utility of the Weberian thesis as a sociological descriptor. This chapter, however, argues for a theological account of this phenomenon. Describing social benefits as by-products of religious experience assumes that redemption is "spiritual" and not primarily about life in this world. Indeed, this Weberian-esque view seems to assume a stark modernist division between spiritual and material. Religion is a personal spiritual matter. Grace saves the soul for heaven. It has nothing to do with the material world of politics and economics. In contrast, this chapter argues that these social benefits are not side-effects of experiencing the Spirit of Pentecost and reconciliation with God and with the life God desires for people (atonement).[85] They are part of the substance of atonement. They are ways that the Holy Spirit empowers people to participate in the incarnated life of Jesus Christ. Although I do not endorse the crass materialism of the prosperity gospel, its basic conviction that God desires for people to live in abundance is consistent with a biblical vision of Spirit-breathed life that was fully realized in the Incarnation of Jesus Christ.[86] Nothing in the biblical narratives of redemption makes ascetic austerity and grinding poverty a normative human aspiration.[87] Pentecostal praxis, moreover, suggests that the renewal of embodied life in and for this world is essential to the experience of the Spirit of Pentecost.

---

[83] Dena Freeman documents similar effects among African Pentecostals in "The Pentecostal Ethic and the Spirit of Development," in *Pentecostalism and Development: Churches, NGOs and Social Change in Africa*, ed. Dena Freeman (New York: Palgrave Macmillan, 2012), 15–26.

[84] Mariz, *Coping with Poverty*, 69–71.

[85] David Martin makes a similar observation that Pentecostalism in Latin America, drawing on "indigenous Amerindian and black spiritual currents . . . assumes no great distinction between spiritual, physical, and material well-being. Salvation consists in reintegrating these three dimensions and returning human life to the properly benign state which God intended." See Martin, *Pentecostalism*, 75.

[86] Although I agree with Cheryl J. Sanders critique that the prosperity gospel too easily can trade in the "worldly consumerism" of American capitalism and lose sight of systemic injustices, the desire for abundant life, which includes material well-being, should not be discounted as inconsistent with participating in the Spirit of Pentecost, which fulfills the Hebrew Bible prophets' vision of justice. See Cheryl J. Sanders, "Pentecostal Ethics and the Prosperity Gospel: Is There a Prophet in the House?" in *Afro-Pentecostalism: Black Pentecostal and Charismatic Christianity in History and Culture*, ed. Amos Yong and Estrelda Y. Alexander (New York: New York University Press, 2011), 146–50.

[87] The expectations for "self-betterment" and nascent "social engagement" initiatives among African Diaspora Pentecostal churches in the UK are instructive examples of the embodied nature of pentecostal atonement. See Mark J. Cartledge, Sarah L. B. Dunlop, Heather Buckingham, and Sophie Bremner, *Megachurch and Social Engagement: Public Theology in Practice*, Global Pentecostal and Charismatic Studies, 33 (Boston: Brill 2019), 213–14, 228, and 249–51.

Conclusion

Why does the Incarnation relate to the atonement? Because the Incarnation fulfills the Spirit-breathed divine image. The fundamental problem that atonement resolves is alienation from the life for which God created human beings. Christ was the fullest embodiment of the divine image. He fulfilled the divine image because he was anointed by the Holy Spirit. The Spirit of Pentecost shares the life realized in Christ with all people (potentially). Sharing in the life the Spirit empowered in Christ reconciles human beings to their fundamental calling—to embody the Spirit-breathed divine image. This chapter showed that the renewal of embodied life is essential to pentecostal practice. Although classical pentecostal rhetoric was often otherworldly, this chapter highlighted the embodied and social transforming potential of pentecostal praxis among African and Vietnamese Pentecostals. They provide a corrective to the social deprivation theory and examples of the embodied nature of the pentecostal praxis of atonement. This chapter also argued that social and personal transformation is intrinsic to the experience of pentecostal atonement.

9

Living in the Way of the Cross

A pentecostal theology of the atonement fundamentally means participating in the Spirit-anointed life of Jesus Christ by receiving the Spirit of Pentecost. This chapter contributes to that larger argument by showing that cruciform living is central to the life of Christ and thus to atonement. The argument here assumes the theological foundation set forth in Chapter 4—a Spirit Christological theology of the cross. It extends that theology first by critically engaging the traditional pentecostal theology of healing in the atonement and the rhetoric of prosperity in light of the pentecostal praxis of suffering and death. It then turns to develop the case for a pneumatological and participatory theology of the cross and atonement. Finally, it presents a pentecostal theology of the cross that recognizes the place of god-forsakenness but contextualizes it in terms of Pentecost and the wider narrative of redemption.

Healing and the Atonement

Pentecostal theology grounds healing in the atonement. Divine healing is part of the traditional pentecostal Full Gospel.[1] Jesus Christ is savior, sanctifier, Spirit baptizer, healer, and soon coming king.[2] Indeed, healing may be more of a pentecostal hallmark than speaking in tongues, despite the latter being the distinctive doctrine of classical pentecostal denominations.[3] Healing was also part of pentecostal mission. Signs and wonders, with divine healing paramount, drew people to faith in Christ. Although less

---

[1] The core teaching that healing is in the atonement was popular in certain Holiness and Reformed Higher Life predecessors of Pentecostalism. See Jonathan R. Baer, "Redeemed Bodies: The Functions of Divine Healing in Incipient Pentecostalism," *Church History* 70, no. 4 (2001): 735–71; Donald W. Dayton, *Theological Roots of Pentecostalism* (Grand Rapids: Francis Asbury/Eerdmans, 1987), 127–30; Vinson Synan, "A Healer in the House? A Historical Perspective on Healing in the Pentecostal/Charismatic Tradition," *Asian Journal of Pentecostal Studies* 3, no. 2 (2000): 190–201; and Joseph W. Williams, *Spirit Cure: A History of Pentecostal Healing* (New York: Oxford University Press, 2013), 3–7.

[2] Wolfgang Vondey, *Pentecostal Theology: Living the Full Gospel*, Systematic Pentecostal and Charismatic Theology, ser. ed. Wolfgang Vondey and Daniela C. Augustine (New York: Bloomsbury T & T Clark, 2017), 116.

[3] Candy Gunther Brown, "Pentecostal Power: The Politics of Divine Healing Practices," *PentecoStudies* 13, no. 1 (2014): 37. For the history of pentecostal healing and the gradual move from outright rejection of modern medicine to its embrace along with natural and psychological and mental health methods, see Williams, *Spirit Cure*.

prevalent in the pedestrian pentecostal churches of North America, healing remains a key driver in the growth of Pentecostalism around the world.[4] Pentecostal doctrine grounds healing in the atonement.[5] Number twelve of the Sixteen Fundamental Truths of the Assemblies of God USA states that divine healing is available to all Christians because it is central to the gospel and a provision of Christ's atonement.[6] Pentecostal systematic theologian Wolfgang Vondey states, "God's remedy for sickness and suffering is the atonement."[7] Pentecostals connect healing to atonement because they regard disease and death as a result of the Genesis 2 Fall. They are consequences of sin. Atonement is the antidote to sin. As Randall Holm puts it, "sin and sickness ... [are in] a kind of co-dependent relationship. As such, the cure for one was the cure for the other."[8] Christ's death on the cross—the work of atonement—delivers from the "penalties of sin" and its consequences.[9] Although the focus here is on physical healing of the body, pentecostal healing theology is holistic. It emphasizes the healing of the inner person, the spiritual relationship with God, and reconciliation with other people. The healing of physical sickness is part of this broader vision for renewed life in the Spirit. While early Pentecostals, moreover, may have rejected modern medicine, most Pentecostals today believe that healing can come from God through a miracle or medical interventions.[10] Furthermore, taking healing as a part of atonement is not a "naïve" belief that everyone will be healed of anything and everything.[11] Pentecostals base healing in the atonement theology on several biblical passages.[12] Isaiah 53:3-12 is a key passage, declaring that "he was pierced for our transgressions ... the punishment that brought us peace was upon him, and by his wounds we are healed." Matthew 8:16-17 applies this passage in Isaiah to Jesus. It links his healing ministry with his suffering and death on the cross, thus establishing the connection between Jesus' work of atonement and physical healing. 1 Peter 2:24 also plays an important role in tying

---

[4] For example, according to Oblau, "at least half of" Chinese Protestants "became Christians because they were motivated by a healing experience, either a personal one or one observed in the family." See Gotthard Oblau, "Divine Healing and the Growth of Practical Christianity in China," in *Global Pentecostal Charismatic Healing*, ed. Candy Gunther Brown (New York: Oxford University Press, 2011), 313; also see Brown, "Pentecostal Power," 51.
[5] Note that for Third Wave leader John Wimber, healing is not in the atonement, but comes through it. Using "in" means that healing is equivalent with salvation. James Wright, "Profiles of Divine Healing: Third Wave Theology Compared with Classical Pentecostal Theology," *Asian Journal of Pentecostal Studies* 5, no. 2 (2002): 275.
[6] https://ag.org/Beliefs/Statement-of-Fundamental-Truths#12
[7] Vondey, *Pentecostal Theology*, 116.
[8] Randall Holm, "Healing in Search of Atonement: With a Little Help from James K. A. Smith," *Journal of Pentecostal Theology* 23, no. 1 (2014): 57.
[9] William W. Menzies and Stanley M. Horton, *Bible Doctrines: A Pentecostal Perspective* (1993; reprint, Springfield: Logion, 2000), 195-7; Vernon L. Purdy, "Divine Healing," in *Systematic Theology: Revised Edition*, ed. Stanley M. Horton (1995; reprint, Springfield: Logion, 1998), 490-1; and Vondey, *Pentecostal Theology*, 116.
[10] Margaret M. Poloma, "Divine Healing, Religious Revival, and Contemporary Pentecostalism: A North American Perspective," *The Spirit in the World: Emerging Pentecostal Theologies in Global Contexts*, ed. Veli-Matti Kärkkäinen (Grand Rapids: Eerdmans, 2009), 27-39.
[11] Vondey, *Pentecostal Theology*, 116.
[12] I outline the most common biblical support for healing in the atonement but for the connection in the Gospel of John, see John Christopher Thomas, "Healing in the Atonement: A Johannine Perspective," *Journal of Pentecostal Theology* 14, no. 1 (2005): 23-39.

healing to the atonement: "He himself bore our sins in his body on the tree, so that we might die to sins and live for righteousness, by his wounds you have been healed."[13] Christ's suffering and death are also substitutionary and vicarious. Christ "carries our burdens of sin and sickness. In an act of transference, whereby that which afflicts us was historically in a once-for-all act carried by Christ by for us."[14] What are the implications of pentecostal healing for atonement theology?

First, pentecostal atonement theology that sees healing as a benefit of Christ's death on the cross reflects the influence of the legal-exchange (forensic) view of the atonement.[15] Whether or not pentecostal theology self-identifies with penal-substitutionary atonement, its logic mirrors this view: Christ's death pays the price for sin and thereby secures the benefits of redemption, which are received by the person of faith. For example, Assemblies of God theologians William W. Menzies and Robert P. Menzies explicitly reject a purely forensic view of atonement, which limits atonement to imputation of righteousness. They nonetheless regard "physical healing, like all of the benefits of salvation, flow[ing] from the cross."[16] Although they adopt a more holistic vision of the grace of atonement, they retain traditional Protestantism's legal transferal theology.[17]

This influence can be highlighted by comparing pentecostal healing theology and prosperity theology. Although the historical work of Christ on the cross is the foundation of healing, Pentecostals regard healing as a proleptic participation in the eschatological kingdom of God. Pentecostals regard Jesus' healing as an "anticipation" of the kingdom of God rather than a normative "paradigm."[18] Pentecostals believe that healing is a participation in the promise of redemption from the curse of death that takes place in the material and eschatological resurrection of the body.[19] But they live in the tension between eschatological participation and fulfillment. Christ's death and resurrection provide the solution to the tension between expectation for healing and the reality of death. Christ died and rose again. He bears the enormity of the fallen condition and overcomes it by the Spirit's resurrection to new life. "Christ bridges the existential tension between God and creation in the struggle that leads to his own death and the victory over death in his resurrection."[20] Anticipation rather than expectation distinguishes pentecostal theology from prosperity theology. They both affirm that

---

[13] William W. Menzies and Robert P. Menzies, *Spirit and Power: Foundations of Pentecostal Experience* (Grand Rapids: Zondervan, 2000), 166–7.

[14] Mark J. Cartledge, *Testimony in the Spirit: Rescripting Ordinary Pentecostal Theology* (New York: Routledge, 2010), 126. For pentecostal criticisms of interpreting these passages as teaching healing is in the atonement, see Graham Hill, "The Atonement and Healing: Wrestling with a Contemporary Issue," *The Pacific Journal of Baptist Research* 8, no. 1 (2013): 10–15; David Petts, "Healing and the Atonement," *EPTA Bulletin* 12, no. 1 (1993): 24–9; and Keith Warrington, "The Role of Jesus as Presented in the Healing Praxis and Teaching of British Pentecostalism: A Re-Examination," *Pneuma: The Journal of the Society for Pentecostal Studies* 25, no. 1 (2003): 79–84.

[15] E.g., see Menzies and Horton, *Bible Doctrines*, 195.

[16] Menzies and Menzies, *Spirit and Power*, 160–2.

[17] Menzies and Menzies, *Spirit and Power*, 163 and 166. Also see Menzies and Horton, *Bible Doctrines*, 198 and Purdy, "Divine Healing," 489 and 507.

[18] Vondey, *Pentecostal Theology*, 117.

[19] Vondey, *Pentecostal Theology*, 119.

[20] Vondey, *Pentecostal Theology*, 116.

"Christ's work on the cross earned not only redemption from sin but also deliverance from its penalties."[21] Pentecostals, however, are less likely to regard faith as a causal agent for unlocking the "power of the cross" and the benefits of the atonement.[22] In prosperity theology healing becomes like any of the other benefits Christ achieved on the cross—for example, justification and the forgiveness of sins.[23] The efficacy of the benefits is not in question. Christ secured them on the cross. When they are not forthcoming, the person's sin and/or lack of faith and spiritual ardor against demonic forces are the culprits.[24] The grace of atonement can easily lapse into a quid pro quo and, in the absence of healing, produce guilt and shame.[25] Rather than a message of comfort and grace, the gospel becomes bad news that accuses and condemns until the blessings manifest.[26] The basic logic of the prosperity gospel is widespread. Although most North American Christians may never attend a prosperity church, nearly half of them believe that God grants health and wealth to the faithful.[27] For Pentecostals of all kinds, healing, whether understood as an anticipation or a guarantee, is a product of Christ paying the price for sin on the cross. My critique of the transferal or exchange theology of healing in the atonement is not a rejection of healing as such. Healing now, however partial, and final resurrection to new life are gifts of the Spirit of Pentecost sharing the Spirit-anointed life of Christ. Divine healing is also often the last resort of the poor who are marginalized from the modern medical interventions taken for granted by people in Western societies.[28] The point, in terms of this project, is that this logic of atonement and healing whether in the form of pentecostal or prosperity theology is the result of being colonized by the Protestant and more or less Reformed evangelical tradition of atonement theology. The solution is to move from a crucicentric and forensic exchange to a participatory theology of the cross.[29]

Second, what is the role of the Holy Spirit in healing and atonement? Healing is the physical manifestation of the Holy Spirit enacting Christ's work on the cross. By bearing the penalty of sin, Christ secures freedom from sin, death, and the demonic. The Holy Spirit actualizes the spectrum of benefits earned by Christ on the cross.

---

[21] Kate Bowler, *Blessed: A History of the American Prosperity Gospel* (New York: Oxford University Press, 2013), 141.
[22] Allan Anderson, "Pentecostal Approaches to Faith and Healing," *International Review of Mission* 91, no. 363 (2002): 530 and 532 and Bowler, *Blessed*, 141.
[23] Cartledge, *Testimony in the Spirit*, 111.
[24] William K. Kay also makes this point in "Approaches to Healing in British Pentecostalism," *Journal of Pentecostal Theology* 7, no. 14 (1999): 116–17.
[25] Petts, "Healing and Atonement," 34.
[26] Shane Clifton, "The Dark Side of Prayer for Healing: Toward a Theology of Well-Being," *Pneuma: The Journal of the Society for Pentecostal Studies* 36, no. 2 (2014): 213–18; Holm, "Healing in Search of Atonement," 66; Jacques P. J. Theron, "Towards a Practical Theological Theory for the Healing Ministry in Pentecostal Churches," *Journal of Pentecostal Theology* 7, no. 14 (1999): 55, 57, and 61. Ian Stackhouse argues that the quid pro quo logic of faith-blessings is also operative more generally in pentecostal revival theology. Indeed, he describes its effect on pentecostal ministry leaders and parishioners as pathological. See Ian Stackhouse, *The Gospel-Driven Church: Retrieving Classical Ministries for Contemporary Revivalism* (Milton Keynes: Paternoster, 2004), 3–71.
[27] Bowler, *Blessed*, 6.
[28] Brown, "Pentecostal Power," 40-2 and Oblau, "Divine Healing and the Growth of Practical Christianity in China," 315–21.
[29] John Christopher Thomas also makes this recommendation in his research on healing and atonement in the Gospel of John. See Thomas, "Healing in the Atonement," 38.

Traditional Protestant atonement theology highlights the forgiveness of sins and the imputation of Christ's righteousness (i.e., justification) as the primary benefits of atonement. The Spirit plays no role in Christ's provision of atonement but inspires the faith that enables a person to receive remittance of sins and the imputed righteousness of Christ. Pentecostal atonement theology has a holistic rather than strictly forensic view of the atonement but retains the basic roles of Christ and the Holy Spirit. Healing is, in brief, the Holy Spirit's application of one of the benefits of Christ's atonement. Mark Cartledge summarizes a synthesis of popular and theological pentecostal healing and atonement theology as "by means of pneumatology, the benefits of Christ on the cross are made real to these Pentecostals."[30] This traditional pentecostal theology of atonement divides the work of Christ and the Holy Spirit into objective and subjective dimensions.[31] Christ objectively achieves the historical work of atonement on the cross and the Holy Spirit subjectively applies the benefits of that work—for example, healing.

Finally, is healing really in the atonement? Yes and no. First, healing is not a benefit that Christ bought with his suffering and death on the cross. So, in the sense of the penal and legal transference whereby Christ pays the price of human sin and infirmity, healing is not in the atonement. But healing is part of the redemptive work of the Spirit of Pentecost. Healing and resurrection are the telos of the Spirit that stirred over the primal waters of creation, that breathed life into the womb of Mary and brought about the Incarnation of the Son of God, that anointed and empowered his ministry, and that raised the crucified Christ from the dead. Healing is the proleptic participation in the final consummation of the promise of resurrected life in the new creation, the new heaven, and the new earth. So "yes," healing is in the atonement. But it is an atonement theology that arises from the biblical narrative of the Spirit of Pentecost. Leaving behind the legal-penal logic of atonement opens up space for an alternative theology of the cross. A theology of the cross that is pneumatological, participatory, and organic. Healing can be part of the experience of atonement and the new life brought by the Spirit of Pentecost, but Christ's suffering and death are participatory and organic rather than forensic transference of disease and suffering that exempts Christians from the same (also, Chapter 10 grounds healing in the Spirit's resurrection of Jesus Christ).

Pentecostal Participation in the Cross

Participation in the cross of Jesus Christ is central to pentecostal atonement. Paul declares that "those who belong to Christ Jesus have crucified the sinful nature.... Since we live by the Spirit, let us keep in step with the Spirit" (Gal. 5:24-25, cf. Gal. 6:14 and Rom. 6 and 8). For Paul, the cross is participatory, personal, and organic. Affirming cruciform living is not remarkable in Christian theology. But including it in atonement

---

[30] Cartledge, *Testimony in the Spirit*, 126.
[31] For extended discussion of the Christ the achiever-Spirit the applier paradigm, see Steven M. Studebaker, "Pentecostal Soteriology: Overcoming the Ecumenical Impasses of Classical Pentecostalism and Charismatic Experience," in *Pentecostal Theology and Ecumenical Theology: Interpretations and Intersections*, ed. Peter Hocken, Tony L. Richie, and Christopher A. Stephenson (Boston: Leiden, 2019), 287–99.

is. This section develops a pentecostal theology of atonement as participation in the cruciform life of Jesus Christ.

First, the cross is a participatory symbol of redemption. The cross symbolizes Christ's life of self-sacrificial service. As such, the cross, or Christ's cruciform life, began with the Incarnation. The triune God's most radical gift of self and love for the world was the Son of God becoming incarnate in Jesus Christ through the agency of the Holy Spirit. The self-offering that took place in the Incarnation was the ongoing nature of Christ's life that took its most absolute form in his suffering and death on the cross. Christ's life, from Incarnation to Golgotha, is a continuum of cruciform living. Although focusing here on the cross, Spirit Christology remains foundational for understanding Jesus Christ. The Holy Spirit catalyzed the Incarnation of the Son of God in Jesus Christ and remained fundamental for his life and ministry. Jesus Christ's cruciform way of life was the product of his Spirit-anointed messianic identity. In this sense, the traditional language of "objective" work makes sense. Christ was a historical person. The Son of God took on flesh in Jesus Christ as the Spirit-anointed messiah, lived, carried out his ministry of enacting the kingdom of God, and was crucified and raised from the dead. But that objective or historical work of Christ cannot be fully apprehended when understood only or even primarily in terms of Christology. Jesus Christ was the Spirit-anointed messiah. The entirety of his life, from Incarnation to cross (indeed even his resurrection), can only be understood in terms of Spirit Christology. The key for pentecostal atonement is that the same Spirit that empowered Christ's cruciform life empowers it in the "all people" of Pentecost (Acts 2:17).

As a symbol of participatory redemption, the cross indicates the way of discipleship. It stands for participation in the life of Christ. Paul's kenosis Christology in Philippians 2 expresses a participatory vision of the Christian life as walking in the way of Christ's cross. Paul parallels Christ's and the Christian's life (Phil. 2:1-5 and 12-18). Although affirming the deity of Jesus Christ, Paul's overall point in Philippians 2 is that because Christians are united to Christ, they can be "like-minded" with him and share "the same love . . . spirit and purpose" with him (Phil. 2:1-2). Christ's Incarnation and life of service to humanity that concludes with his death on the cross is not simply the object of faith, but the path of the faithful. Paul urges the Philippian Christians that their "attitude should be the same as that of Christ Jesus" (Phil. 2:5). After describing Christ's self-giving love, Paul continues that because Christ did this, they should too. They are to "work out [their] salvation with fear and trembling . . . do everything without complaining or arguing, so that [they] may become blameless and pure, children of God" (Phil. 2:12-15). I. Howard Marshall argues that Philippians 2 is not about salvation as such but the "exemplary" role of Christ's suffering and death.[32] In other words, Philippians 2 deals with sanctification, not atonement and justification. And yet, the passage specifically identifies this passage as soteriological—"therefore, . . . work out your salvation with fear and trembling" (Phil. 2:12). Marshall reads the meaning of the cross in Philippians 2 through the traditional Protestant paradigm that separates redemption into objective-forensic-Christological and subjective-transform

---

[32] I. Howard Marshall, *Aspects of the Atonement: Cross and Resurrection in the Reconciling of God and Humanity* (London: Paternoster, 2007), 72.

ational-pneumatological categories.³³ Paul, however, sees the cruciform Christian life arising from being "united with Christ" and sharing "fellowship with the Spirit" (Phil. 2:1). The verses in Philippians 2 that set forth what is traditionally called kenosis Christology sit within a context of Paul's call to be "like-minded" with Christ. In other words, Phil. 2:8 presents the cross as an example of service for others. It is not a penal punishment. It is a way of life for Christians to follow as they are "like-minded" with Christ. How can Christians follow in the way of the cross with Jesus Christ? As Christ was the Son of God through the "fellowship of the Spirit," so Christians are children of God through the same Spirit that was the foundation of Jesus' life and ministry. In other words, being like-minded with Christ means to share in his Spirit-empowered cruciform life.

Second, walking in the way of the cross is central to the experience of Christian atonement. The cross, in other words, is not a symbol of penal payment for sin, but a sign of faithful devotion to God. Jesus was killed because he remained faithful to God the Father. He was willing to lose the world for the sake of fidelity to the Father. He calls his disciples to do the same. Just after Peter declares Jesus "The Christ," Jesus warns his disciples that following him means self-sacrifice and suffering (Lk. 9:20-22). He said to them: "Whoever wants to be my disciple must deny themselves and take up their cross daily and follow me. For whoever wants to save their life will lose it, but whoever loses their life for me will save it. What good is it for someone to gain the whole world, and yet lose or forfeit their very self?" (Lk. 9:23-25). "Come suffer with me" is hardly an inspiring rallying cry. Indeed, it repelled Peter. Adding depth to the story, the Gospel of Matthew records that after Jesus announced his impending death at the hands of "the elders, chief priests, and teachers of the law," Peter "rebuked" Jesus (Mt. 16:21-22). But Jesus doubled down and insisted that "If anyone would come after me, he must deny himself and take up his cross and follow me" (Mt. 16:24). Jesus equates his cross bearing with his life of selfless service and with following him despite the costs. Here Christ portrays the cross not as penal punishment but as the way of discipleship. The cross, in other words, was the way of Spirit-breathed life. Jesus' call to "take up" the cross means that atonement includes following him in cruciform living. The cross was his way of life and, therefore, the way of life for those who follow him. Participating in the atonement of carrying the cross means saying no to bigotry, fear, hate, and indifference and suffering for doing so. The cross is denying the cravings of the flesh.³⁴ The irony for Jesus Christ is that he, who was there and participated in the creation of the world, could have gained the world. But that would have meant acting in the way of the world. Jesus chose the way of the cross. He remained sanctified to his mission from the Father. His life was a defiant "no" to the sinful way of the world. The way of the world is the use of power, in whatever form and in the name of whatever cause, for self-aggrandizement. Satan offered Jesus bread, wealth, and the vanity of authority over the kingdoms of the world (Luke 4:1-13). Yielding to those temptations, however, would have abdicated his life "full of the Holy Spirit" (Luke 4:1). Christ offers

---

[33] Marshall, *Aspects of the Atonement*, 10.
[34] Peter J. Leithart, *Delivered from the Elements of the World: Atonement, Justification, Mission* (Downers Grove: IVP Academic, 2016), 115.

to his followers the same sanctified life he fulfilled. Life lived in the abundance and righteousness of Spirit-breathed life.

Third, participation in the cross is personal and organic. Personal, because foundational to the Christian life is the Holy Spirit mediating the presence of Christ, which necessarily draws the believer into the fellowship of the triune God and, by extension, into fellowship with all other people who have received the Spirit of Pentecost. The mutual indwelling and personal fellowship that is fundamental to redemption is at once triune and ecclesial. Organic, because through personal union with Christ the Spirit of Pentecost activates in the believer the same power that fulfilled Spirit-breathed life in Christ. Walking in the way of Christ and of the cross emerges from the Holy Spirit's union of the believer with Christ, and by virtue of that union the same Spirit that empowered Christ's fulfillment of Spirit-breathed life enables the believer to walk in the way of the cross. The Gospel of John's Farewell Discourse (chapters 13/14–17) highlights the relational (triune and ecclesial) and organic nature of redemption. Jesus promises that he and his Father will come and make their home with his followers. Indeed, they will share an intimacy of personal fellowship and mutual indwelling that mirrors his loving relationship with the Father. He identifies the Holy Spirit, moreover, as the one who facilitates this fellowship between the triune God and Christ's followers (Jn 14:17, 16:15, and 17:20-26). This fellowship with God includes following in the way of Christ. The believer's life in the world parallels Christ's. Jesus prays that the Father will "sanctify them" as Jesus was sanctified. And, as the Father sent Christ into the world, so Christ has "sent them into the world" (Jn 17:17-19). Thus, the Spirit of Pentecost shares not only the power of Spirit-breathed life but the living presence of the one in whom it was fulfilled. Being sanctified in the world as Christ was is the substance of atonement and emerges from the fellowship with Christ and the Father facilitated by the Spirit of Pentecost.

Fourth, I want to address two objections. Does participating in Christ's cruciform life mean Christians have an intrinsic righteousness or an imputed righteousness and does participatory atonement reduce Christ and the cross to moral exemplarism? In respect to the first question, does righteousness inhere in Christians, thus giving them a claim on grace? Does sharing in the righteousness of Christ subvert salvation by faith and revert to works righteousness? These questions assume the legalistic view of penal substitution and what the Protestant reformers perceived as (and rejected) the merit and intrinsic righteousness system of the medieval church. But this theology of atonement misses the fundamental nature of the atonement and the narrative of redemption. The plotline of the history of redemption is not a wrathful divine judge getting his pound of flesh. God endeavoring to redeem his people (potentially "all people," Acts 2:17) and restore them as children of God is the lodestar. As Michael J. Gorman argues, the participatory nature of atonement presented in Romans 6 is not a "supplement to 'justification by faith'" found in Rom. 3:21-26, but its complement.[35] In other words,

---

[35] Michael J. Gorman, *Becoming the Gospel: Paul, Participation, and Mission* (Grand Rapids: Eerdmans, 2015), 278 and 283 and Michael J. Gorman, *Inhabiting the Cruciform God: Kenosis, Justification, and Theosis in Paul's Narrative Soteriology* (Grand Rapids: Eerdmans, 2009), 73. For interpreting Romans 3 and 6 as two distinct facets of redemption (penal-legal/justification and

being "justified... through the redemption that came by Christ Jesus," by his "sacrifice of atonement," is being "united with him in his death... [and] united with him in his resurrection" (Rom. 3:24-25 and Rom. 6:5). Romans 6 shows that the entire historical life of Christ, not only the cross, is his sacrifice of atonement. Peter J. Leithart makes this point well: "the whole movement of Jesus' life, death, resurrection and ascension is a single sacrificial sequence, and *that* is the sacrifice necessary to save."[36] The narrative of Christ, which is also the narrative of the Spirit of Pentecost, is the soteriological narrative for everyone united to him through faith. Being justified by God through faith in Christ takes place by participating in his life, death, and resurrection through the same "Spirit... who raised Jesus from the dead" (Rom. 8:11; development of the pneumatological nature of participation in Christ comes later in this chapter).[37] On the second question, does a pentecostal and participatory theology of the atonement reduce Christ and the cross to a moral exemplar of the Christian life? No. Christ is a moral example. That is why he told his disciples to take up their crosses and follow him. He expects his followers *to follow* him. But participation in Christ's cruciform life is more fundamental than moral role playing. The cross as a way of life does not reduce to moral exemplarism because the capacity and ability to bear the cross derives from the same Spirit that enabled Jesus to bear the cross even unto death. The life of the cross emerges from the foundation of triune fellowship just as it did in Christ. The Spirit of Pentecost brings people into fellowship with the Father through their union with the Son of God. Cruciform living is the manifestation of the love and relational power that arises in human life as it participates in the triune fellowship of God.

Fifth, a participatory theology of the cross means that the justice of the atonement is the holistic renewal of life. Isaiah declares that the Spirit-anointed messiah will "bring justice to the nations" (Isa. 42:1). Isaiah describes that justice in terms of the renewal of relationship with God and other human beings as well as the renewal of embodied life (Isa. 61:1-9). Jesus embodied that Spirit-anointed justice from healing lepers and the sick and dignifying the social deplorables to remaining faithful to God the Father to the point of death on the cross. Jesus' ministry reflects the promise of Isaiah. The Spirit-anointed activities of the messianic figure described in Isaiah and embodied by Christ cannot be separated from the experience of atonement. To do so is to lapse into an extrinsicism of grace. What Christ does and effects are distinct from each other, but they are not separate. The Spirit anoints the messiah to bring justice. The justice brought consists in the renewal of people's relationship with God and each other and their life in this world. Without the Spirit of Pentecost, Jesus' life and death on the cross remain extrinsic. They are a historical example of the righteous martyr or a punitive sacrifice offered to a God enraged at humans for transgressing divine law. But the Holy

---

transformational/sanctification), see Douglas J. Moo, *The Epistle to the Romans*, NICNT (Grand Rapids: Eerdmans, 1996), 350–2.

[36] Leithart, *Delivered from the Elements of the World*, 115.

[37] In a similar line, Douglas A. Campbell argues that participating in Christ is not "mere *imitation Christi*" because through the Spirit of God Christians "inhabit or... indwell" Christ, which reshapes them "into the likeness of Christ." See Campbell, *The Quest for Paul's Gospel: A Suggested Strategy*, Journal for the Study of the New Testament Supplement Series, 274 (New York: T & T Clark, 2005), 93.

Spirit who was the foundation of Christ's faithful life comes to share that life with "all people" as the Spirit of Pentecost. Pentecost liberates Christ and the cross from moral exemplarism and punitive sacrifice. A pentecostal theology of the atonement affirms the participatory nature of the Spirit-breathed life fulfilled in Jesus Christ. As the Spirit-anointed messiah, Jesus overcame sin and death—exemplified on the cross. In that sense, his life and ministry were vicarious; he did it for us—*pro nobis*. But Christ achieved the fullness of Spirit-breathed life so that he could share that life with "all people" through the Spirit of Pentecost. Seeing atonement from the perspective of Pentecost reveals that the righteousness of Christ is not for satisfying an intra-divine demand for retributive justice. Neither his life nor his death on the cross is an objective drama carried out before the Father's heavenly courtroom. The life and death of Christ are not a quid pro quo in a legal compact between the Father and the Son. But rather, the justice of the cross resides in offering the opportunity for all people to participate in Christ's fulfillment of the human vocation to bear the Spirit-breathed image of God.[38]

Pentecostal Theology of the Cross

Pentecostal atonement as participation in the way of the cross calls for a revised pentecostal theology of the cross. The irony is that god-forsakenness, although Christ's lot on the cross, is not a normative paradigm for a traditional pentecostal theology of the cross and the Christian life it inspires. Pentecostals, especially prosperity gospel Pentecostals, proclaim that since Jesus paid the price for their sin on the cross, they are set free from its curse and can receive the blessings of health and wealth. The logic is: he suffered, so we do not need to. Despite this rhetoric, many Pentecostals identify with the marginalized and abused people of Jesus' ministry. The pentecostal praxis of suffering and death stands in tension with pentecostal prosperity rhetoric. Pentecostal praxis includes the god-forsaken experience of Christ, but pentecostal rhetoric can tend toward triumphalism. At the same time, a pentecostal theology of the cross contextualizes Christ's solidarity with the god-forsaken in light of Pentecost.

First, a participatory theology of the cross critiques the exuberant triumphalism that often characterizes pentecostal rhetoric.[39] Pentecostal rhetoric may declare "healing in the atonement," but pentecostal pastors preside over the funerals of faithful pentecostal believers. Pentecostals experience poverty, their businesses go bankrupt, and they are overlooked for promotions. In other words, despite pentecostal rhetoric, they do not always live on, what the old hymn describes as, "The Hallelujah Side" of life. Pentecostal praxis, in other words, indicates that walking in the way of the cross is more than a metaphor of selfless service. The Spirit of Pentecost that catalyzed the life of Christ remained with him until he died, but Christ did die. His Spirit-breathed

---

[38] Holiness Pentecostalism better incorporates the cross into the vision of sanctified life. For example, see R. Hollis Gause, "Pentecostal Understanding of Sanctification from a Pentecostal Perspective," *Journal of Pentecostal Theology* 18, no. 1 (2009): 95–110.

[39] David Courey develops and evaluates the distance between the triumphal rhetoric and the too often-pedestrian experience and practice of Pentecostals in *What Has Wittenberg to do with Azusa? Luther's Theology of the Cross and Pentecostal Triumphalism* (New York: Bloomsbury, 2015).

followers die too. Participating in the narrative of Spirit-breathed life embodied in Jesus Christ includes personal dissolution in this world.[40] Profound irony, even sometimes perversion, characterizes the triumphalism of the theology of healing in the atonement. For sick people who do not receive their healing, Christ and the cross become the basis for shame and guilt.[41] They endure the guilt of not confessing sufficient faith in Christ and his work and so are abandoned by him to wither and die. This theology perverts the meaning of Christ and the cross. The crucified Christ, the god-forsaken Christ, is the preeminent embodiment of the God who suffers with the suffering. The gospel of Christ is good news to the poor and broken. But this theology of atonement makes it bad news. It makes the cross a message of condemnation. Over and against the championed healing in the atonement and victory in Jesus is the sick person, who can only conclude they have disappointed God, they have failed in faith, and are receiving the reward for their faithlessness. They have reached out but failed to touch the hem of his garment (Mt. 9:20).

Second, the cross signifies Christ's solidarity with the poor and suffering. I am not the first pentecostal theologian to make this point, but I want to articulate its significance in terms of a pentecostal theology of the atonement.[42] The basic point is that the cross stands not only for death, but for all the ways Christ co-suffered with and stood on the side of the poor, the outcast, and the weak throughout his life. As Amos Yong points out, "Jesus' life cannot be disconnected from his death, and a theology of the cross sees the entirety of the life of Christ as lived for others in anticipation of and shaped by the cross."[43] Pentecostal praxis correlates with this more expansive theology of the cross, both in the sense that the "cross" takes in the entirety of Christ's life and that, at least, one dimension of its redemptive nature is Christ's identification with broken and hurting people. Suffering and persecution are not new for Pentecostals. Early Pentecostals were maligned and excluded from the established churches and denominations (not uncommon for reformers, e.g., the Wesleys). Indian Pentecostals suffering persecution today are predominately rural poor, lower-caste, and female. These social factors make them easy targets for religious persecution.[44] Sometimes, nevertheless, healing in the atonement theology and the triumphal rhetoric it promotes among Pentecostals obscure the significance of the solidarity that Christ embodied with marginal and suffering people throughout his life and most dramatically on the cross. Harvey Cox's reflection on his visit to the

---

[40] Keith Warrington also points out the problem that Pentecostals do not escape death despite the quality of their faith in "The Role of Jesus as Presented in the Healing Praxis and Teaching of British Pentecostalism," 84.

[41] Warrington also draws this conclusion in "The Role of Jesus as Presented in the Healing Praxis and Teaching of British Pentecostalism," 80.

[42] E.g., in historical order, Samuel Solivan, *The Spirit, Pathos, and Liberation: Toward an Hispanic Pentecostal Theology*, Journal of Pentecostal Theology Supplement Series, 14 (Sheffield: Sheffield Academic Press, 2000), 59–60; Amos Yong, *Theology and Down Syndrome: Reimagining Disability in Late Modernity* (Waco: Baylor University Press, 2007), 174–5; and Daniela C. Augustine, *Pentecost, Hospitality, and Transfiguration: Toward a Spirit-Inspired Vision of Social Transformation* (Cleveland: CPT, 2010), 59.

[43] Yong, *Theology and Down Syndrome*, 177.

[44] Chad M. Bauman, *Pentecostalism, Proselytization, and Anti-Christian Violence in Contemporary India* (New York: Oxford University Press, 2015), 81–3.

Assemblies of God Sheffield Family Life Center in Kansas City, Missouri, illustrates the problem. Cox attended an evening service. It had hallmarks of large and successful pentecostal churches: full worship band, two "glamorous" worship leaders, two choirs illuminated with "spots and footlights," a dynamic pastor and, on this night, a high-powered visiting missionary.[45] During a transition in the worship, a band member gave a "staccato burst of glossolalia." Cox reports being "disturbed" and "annoyed." Because it came across not as "glossolalia as protest or as prophecy" from the heart of the congregation, but "glossolalia as performance, and—at least to me—it sounded counterfeit."[46] Why was Cox so upset? He wonders, through the eyes of the young black woman he met before the service, what this "glitz and glamor" means? The worship team repetitively sang "Whose Report Do You Believe?" What is the report she is to believe, the bawdy, boisterous, and bouffant "spectacle" on display in the church or the gospel, which was scarcely mentioned in the service?[47] Later during the service, when the young woman went forward

> to accept the Lord, what did she think she was accepting? If it is true that in most religion, and in Pentecostalism in particular, the medium is the message, exactly what *was* the message of this throbbing display of youthful energy and opulent beauty, especially to an auditorium filled with people who clean office buildings and shop at yard sales?[48]

The "glitz and glamor" of the pentecostal worship team and the "melodramatic evangelist" make no room for people in desperation, the people Cox saw in the congregation.[49] But these people, the "uprooted, neglected, the also-rans in the fierce American battle for success and security . . . brought the real pain and longing—the sense of the reality of God—to pentecostal worship."[50] Pentecostal theology needs a more robust theology of the cross. Not a theology that promises escape from difficulties because Jesus paid the price for them on the cross. But a theology that recognizes that struggle, suffering, disease, and ultimately death are part of life on this side of the eschaton. Because Jesus was anointed by the Spirit of the Lord, he became the god-forsaken on the cross and, thereby, identified with all the god-forsaken people of this world. A theology of the cross that recognizes Christ's solidarity with the suffering and not only his triumph over sin, disease, and death can inform church praxis and rhetoric that does not leave people feeling alienated from the grace of God.

Third, solidarity with the oppressed should be contextualized in light of the Spirit of Pentecost. Jesus Christ becomes the god-forsaken with the god-forsaken to redeem them to fellowship and life with God, not to wallow with them in misery. Some

---

[45] Harvey Cox, *Fire from Heaven: The Rise of Pentecostal Spirituality and the Reshaping of Religion in the Twenty-first Century* (Reading: Addison-Wesley, 1995), 269–70. The church still seems to be flourishing, now with multiple sites. See the church website, https://sflc.net/about/
[46] Cox, *Fire from Heaven*, 270–1.
[47] Cox, *Fire from Heaven*, 270 and 272.
[48] Cox, *Fire from Heaven*, 272–3 (emphasis original).
[49] Cox, *Fire from Heaven*, 272.
[50] Cox, *Fire from Heaven*, 272 and 280.

spiritualities seem to valorize suffering, marginality, and persecution. Pastor Jack Wellman, writing for *Patheos*, emphatically states that "persecution is a good thing." Why is it good? Because it leads to church growth and it is a blessing from God.[51] This view romanticizes persecution—a sort of Currier & Ives vision of persecution. Wishing for persecution is irresponsible and naïve at best. Do we really want to see people in our churches imprisoned and killed? Do we want to see our children excluded from career opportunities *because* they are Christians?[52] This optimistic view of persecution is also historically false. Gordon L. Heath charts a series of cases where persecution nearly led to the regional extermination of the church.[53] It is also theologically misguided. Christ does not valorize suffering. Indeed, Christ's agony in the Garden of Gethsemane repudiates this triumphalism. Christ came to bring the kingdom of God in the power of the Holy Spirit (Mt. 12:28). Indeed, when he arrived and offered his hand of healing and friendship and his words of forgiveness and compassion, people were no longer god-forsaken. God-forsakenness is not an aspirational paradigm for the Christian life, but a consequence of participating in the Spirit-empowered righteousness of Christ. Pentecostal prosperity rhetoric correctly captures the point that the Spirit-anointed Christ comes to deliver human beings from a world broken by sin, but it ignores that prior to the eschaton there is a cross to bear. Suffering, in other words, is not a sign of deficient faith in God, but a consequence of living in the way of the Spirit-anointed Christ in the midst of a world marred by evil.

Recognizing that participation in the cross, a life marked by suffering and death, is part of the Christian life does not deny the power of Pentecost. It does, however, call for a cross-conditioned understanding of pentecostal power. Following Christ in the way of the cross depends on the power of the Spirit of Pentecost. Christians rely on the Spirit of Pentecost in the same way that Christ did. Jesus was the Spirit-empowered messiah. He walked on water, fed the five thousand, and healed the sick. But he was also ridiculed by the religious and political elites, betrayed, and eventually killed by them. All of this, from the taunts of his ministry to his crucifixion, was cross bearing. It was, moreover, the result of his Spirit-anointed life. This understanding of pentecostal power differs from the triumphalism of pentecostal rhetoric that declares healing in the atonement and that the victorious overcoming life is just one prayer-of-faith away. In the pentecostal church where I became a Christian, we often sang, usually in Sunday evening services, the old-time hymn, "there is power, power, wonderworking power in the precious blood of the Lamb." I loved it. It was inspiring. I felt that with God on my side I could do anything. I left the church feeling empowered. Everything was possible.

---

[51] Jack Wellman, "Why Persecution Is a Good Thing," *Patheos*, June 26, 2017. https://www.patheos.com/blogs/christiancrier/2017/06/26/why-persecution-is-a-good-thing/

[52] Patrick Wintour, "Persecution of Christians 'coming close to genocide' in Middle East – Report," *The Guardian*, May 2, 2019 (https://www.theguardian.com/world/2019/may/02/persecution-driving-christians-out-of-middle-east-report). For the full report on religious persecution, see *Bishop of Truro's Independent Review for the Foreign Secretary of FCO Support for Persecuted Christians: Final Report and Recommendations*, 2019. https://christianpersecutionreview.org.uk/storage/2019/07/final-report-and-recommendations.pdf

[53] Gordon L. Heath, "When the Blood of the Martyrs Was Not Enough: A Survey of Places Where the Church Was Wiped Out," in *The Church, Then and Now*, Bingham Colloquium Series, ed. Stanley E. Porter and Cynthia Westfall (Eugene: Pickwick, 2012), 97–13.

That is the positive nature of pentecostal experience. And Pentecostals should not lose it. The Holy Spirit brings the presence of Christ to heal broken lives. But, like the people Jesus healed in the Gospels, life eventually falls apart again. At some point, Lazarus went back to his tomb and stayed there. Even if suffering is only the deterioration of aging and not the ravages of persecution, we will suffer and fade away. But the Spirit of the crucified Christ will remain with us just as the Spirit remained with Christ and eventually resurrected him. Again, the problem with pentecostal triumphalism is not that it affirms that Christ overcame sin and death. The problem is an over-realized eschatology. It does not recognize our place in the narrative of redemption. Death and suffering are not the final word. Even though Christians undergo pain and suffering, they are neither theologically normative nor aspirational spiritualities because the Spirit of Pentecost that is ever present with the god-forsaken will eventually raise them to new life in the everlasting kingdom of God.

Conclusion

Healing is a potent part of pentecostal preaching and experience. Pentecostals believe that healing of the body and the provision of prosperity are part of the benefits of the atonement that Christ earned on the cross. At the same time, many Pentecostals worldwide are poor and suffer disease and death. They never receive their healing and prosperity in the atonement. According to pentecostal rhetoric, they failed in faith. This chapter presented an alternative understanding of the cross and atonement. It called for a move away from the legal-exchange healing in the atonement theology to a participatory, organic, and personal paradigm of the cross and atonement. The cross is less about Christ suffering in the place of sinners and more about establishing solidarity with them and providing a pathway to faithfulness to God in a world marked by sin and suffering. Walking in the way of the cross is one of the ways the Spirit of Pentecost enables people to participate in Christ's Spirit-anointed life.

10

Waking to New Creation

Pentecostal praxis displays the renewal of life brought by the Spirit of Pentecost. The holistic experience of grace, however, is not peculiar to Pentecost. It is the wider testimony of the New Testament vision of redemption. Jesus described salvation as being "born again" and "born of the Spirit" (Jn 3:7-8). The Apostle Paul uses resurrection imagery to characterize salvation—"if anyone is in Christ, he is a new creation; the old has gone, the new has come!" (2 Cor. 5:17). He also describes the experience of new life in organic and pneumatological terms—"if the Spirit of him who raised Christ from the dead is living in you, he who raised Christ from the dead will also give life to your mortal bodies through his Spirit that lives in you" (Rom. 8:11). The Holy Spirit's resurrection of Jesus Christ is the foundation for these themes and images of renewal and new birth. Participating in the new life of the Spirit-resurrected Christ is a primary experience of the pentecostal praxis of atonement. Pentecostal atonement, in other words, includes forgiveness of sins and the hope of the everlasting kingdom, but no less so the transformation and renewal of this life. The constructive argument in this chapter relies on the Spirit's role in the resurrection and its paradigmatic function for the experience of grace in Romans 6 and 8. Why focus on Romans? Because Romans has been central to the Christian doctrine of grace, and especially to the Protestant theology of atonement and justification. Romans, moreover, is the most extended account of a Pauline theology of grace. Romans, for example, states in more breadth and detail the pneumatological and participatory vision of grace set forth in Galatians. Paul regards redemption as dying and rising with Christ—cross and resurrection—and since he does so, atonement includes resurrection. Several pentecostal theologians have also proposed moving away from exclusive reliance on penal-substitutionary atonement and toward a more transformational theology of the atonement.[1] Relying on Romans 6, Hollis Gause, for example, directly correlates Christ's crucifixion and atonement with the renewal of grace. Although he retains a Christocentric view of atonement and portrays the Holy Spirit's role as "an application of the atonement

---

[1] Sammy Alfaro, *Divino Compañero: Toward a Hispanic Pentecostal Christology* (Eugene: Pickwick, 2010), 5 and 147–8; Mark J. Cartledge, *Testimony in the Spirit: Rescripting Ordinary Pentecostal Theology* (New York: Routledge, 2010), 126–7; William W. Menzies and Robert P. Menzies, *Spirit and Power: Foundations of Pentecostal Experience* (Grand Rapids: Zondervan, 2000), 161; Wolfgang Vondey, *Pentecostal Theology: Living the Full Gospel*, Systematic Pentecostal and Charismatic Theology (New York: Bloomsbury T & T Clark, 2017), 52 and 116–17; and Amos Yong, *The Spirit Poured Out on All Flesh: Pentecostalism and the Possibility of Global Theology* (Grand Rapids: BakerAcademic, 2005), 112–20.

provision of Christ's death and resurrection," he endeavors to recognize the holistic and transformative nature of grace—atonement.[2] My goal in this chapter is to develop and expand these pentecostal instincts by proposing a pneumatological and transformational atonement theology based on the Holy Spirit's role in the resurrection of Jesus Christ. First, however, I want to revisit the healing in the atonement theology of the previous chapter and suggest both re-situating healing in the resurrection rather than the cross and expanding healing to embrace the holistic renewal of life that emerges from the Spirit's resurrection of Jesus Christ.

Healing and Resurrection

A pentecostal theology of the atonement correlates healing with the Holy Spirit's raising of Jesus Christ in new resurrected life. Classical pentecostal theology (esp. Finished Work traditions such as the Assemblies of God) sees healing arising from Christ's death on the cross; although Holiness Pentecostals, with their emphasis on sanctification, seem more likely to integrate healing with resurrection and include resurrection with the cross as part of the atonement.[3] As detailed in the previous chapter, for traditional pentecostal theology, healing is a legal and contractual entitlement provided by the blood of Christ. Christ's sacrificial death on the cross provides healing because it is the penal payment for sin. The cross liberates people from the consequences of sin. Pentecostal theology, arising historically from the Protestant evangelical traditions, emphasized that the cross provides forgiveness of and release from the guilt of sin. But they also affirmed that the cross frees the Christian from the physical consequences of sin. The logic was that the cross is sufficient for dealing with all the consequences of sin. Since illness and ultimately death are consequences of sin, physical healing now (for those with sufficient faith), just as the eschatological resurrection of the body, is a benefit of the cross—by "his stripes we are healed" (Isa. 53:5 and 1 Pet. 2:24). Affirming healing is not the problem. Healing is central to pentecostal experience and to a pentecostal theology of the atonement. The problem is locating it in the logic of penal exchange. The solution is twofold: situate healing in the context of the Spirit's resurrection of Christ and embrace a holistic theology of healing as participation in the manifold dimensions of the new life of the Spirit of Pentecost. The reframing of healing and resurrection among American Indian and Latin American Pentecostals provides a basis in pentecostal praxis for these two theological tasks.

First, Angela Tarango documents that American Indians reconceived divine healing as overcoming hatred for white injustices and embracing a spirit of reconciliation. She argues that this transformation of pentecostal healing displays the American Indian practice of the indigenous principle. Indigenizing the pentecostal message was necessary because the white pentecostal missionaries often carried with them the racial prejudices toward American Indians and their culture that were characteristic

---

[2] R. Hollis Gause, *Living in the Spirit: The Way of Salvation*, Revised and Expanded Edition (Cleveland: CPT, 2009), 100 and 95–101.
[3] Gause, *Living in the Spirit*, 74–5 and 95–6.

of the broader culture. American Indian Pentecostals transformed this theology and practice of healing to match their circumstances.[4] Angela Tarango summarizes that "their understanding of healing gave an American Indian flavor to Pentecostal restorationism; it was not just signs and wonders but a form of healing that could be shaped by a particular ethnic group's own experience of colonization and abuse."[5] The transformation of healing to include overcoming the debasing effects of racism, however, is not only an indigenous adaptation of pentecostal healing to the American Indian experience but a restoration of an indigenous promise of the Spirit of Pentecost to bring the new life of the resurrected Christ. As the Apostle Paul points out "we regard no one from a worldly point of view. . . . Therefore, if anyone is in Christ, he is a new creation: the old has gone, the new has come! All this is from God who reconciled us to himself through Christ and gave us the ministry of reconciliation" (2 Cor. 5:16-18). New creation is the fruit of resurrection. Healing in all its manifold dimensions arises from the resurrection of new life. American Indian Pentecostals adapted the pentecostal message to their racial circumstances and in doing so recovered the holistic character of the new resurrection life brought by the Spirit of Pentecost.

Second, Pentecostalism in Latin America offers people a new vision of God and of their own identity in the world. The legacy of Spanish colonialism informs the default worldview of many people. God is a "tyrant" and life is fatalistic and determined—for example, if you are born poor, you die poor.[6] The *Mestizo* cultural history also shapes the Latin American vision of God as an overbearing and uncaring overlord. The Spanish portrayal of Christ "through their words and actions was that of a suffering and defeated victim."[7] The God (Father) that punishes his Son on a cross (comparing culturally to the experiences of many *Mestizo* children and their Spanish fathers) "reinforces the view of an oppressive God."[8] The result is a widespread self-perception among people that they are victims with little to no control over their lives. The pentecostal message in contrast offers people the hope of the resurrected Christ. Not a hapless victim of abuse and shame, but the living Christ who conquers death and the grave. It encourages them to read Scripture and imagine the living God they find in its pages acting in their own lives. The pentecostal message proclaims the power of the Spirit of Pentecost to bring the new life of the resurrected Christ.[9] Pentecostalism also leads to the healing of dysfunctional and abusive family relationships. Husbands (for the most part) become more responsible spouses and parents by avoiding the dissipation of philandering, alcohol and drug abuse, and gambling. Jens Köhrsen calls

---

[4] Angela Tarango, *Choosing the Jesus Way: American Indian Pentecostals and the Fight for the Indigenous Principle* (Chapel Hill: University of North Carolina Press, 2014), 95–103.
[5] Tarango, *Choosing the Jesus Way*, 102.
[6] Virginia Nolivos and Ely H. Nolivos, "Pentecostalism's Theological Reconstruction of the Identity of the Latin American Family," in *Pentecostal Power: Expressions, Impact and Faith of Latin American Pentecostalism*, ed. Calvin Smith (Boston: Brill, 2011), 210.
[7] Nolivos and Nolivos, "Pentecostalism's Theological Reconstruction of the Identity of the Latin American Family," 212.
[8] Nolivos and Nolivos, "Pentecostalism's Theological Reconstruction of the Identity of the Latin American Family," 212.
[9] Nolivos and Nolivos, "Pentecostalism's Theological Reconstruction of the Identity of the Latin American Family," 217–19.

it the "self-disciplining effects" of Pentecostalism that lead to more stable families, financial security, and upward social mobility.[10] Pentecostalism offers positive personal and social alternatives for many people. It presents a new vision of God and self that empowers a new and proactive life.[11] The resurrected Christ is a key factor of pentecostal theology in Latin America.[12] It replaces the identity of a defeated and passive victim with a hope-inspired identity. Shifting from the crucified to the resurrected Christ is a "paradigm shift from victim to victor."[13] It empowers not only new personal habits but also the corporate ethos of the church. Praise and "celebration" replace the more customary apathy, gloom, and sadness in church services.[14] One may object that the crucified Christ was never meant to justify and fortify an oppressive colonial social structure. Fair enough. But that is beside the point. The resurrection of Christ and the power of the Spirit of Pentecost provide Latin American Pentecostals with a paradigm for transforming their personal lives and empowering an improved life in this world.

American Indian and Latin American Pentecostals indicate that transcending social injustices such as racism, ethnocentrism, classism, and poverty are intrinsic to the pentecostal praxis of grace. My argument is that these types of experiences are forms of healing that arise from participating in the resurrection life of the Spirit of Pentecost. The promise of the Spirit of Pentecost in Acts (and the Spirit's role in the longer history of the redemption) corroborates the pentecostal praxis of renewed life. People searching to escape from dehumanizing racism, poverty, and social marginalization find hope in the Spirit of Pentecost and quite often the empowerment to achieve their aspirations. Healing as personal renewal and social transcendence may not fit the more sensational paradigm of physical healing. The liberation of lives broken by sin and atrophying from hopelessness and despair, nevertheless, are ways that the Spirit of Pentecost actualizes the resurrection life of Christ in people's lives.

Summarizing the argument at this point, I propose shifting from a crucicentric basis for physical healing to a holistic one based on Christ's resurrection for two reasons. First, connecting experiences of renewal to resurrection dislodges healing from the attenuated and legal-contractual theology of atonement and frames it in the wider and pneumatological narrative of redemption. Giving and renewing life is a key plotline in this wider narrative of the Spirit. The pentecostal experience and anticipation of healing, renewal, and liberation participates in the Spirit's story of redemption that

---

[10] Jens Köhrsen, "Pentecostal Improvement Strategies: A Comparative Reading of African and South American Pentecostalism," in *Pastures of Plenty: Tracing Religio-Scapes of Prosperity Gospel in Africa and Beyond*, ed. Andreas Heuser, Studies in the Intercultural History of Christianity, vol. 161 (New York: Peter Lang, 2015), 53–4.

[11] Dena Freeman documents similar effects among African Pentecostals in "The Pentecostal Ethic and the Spirit of Development," in *Pentecostalism and Development: Churches, NGOs and Social Change in Africa*, ed. Dena Freeman (New York: Palgrave Macmillan, 2012), 9–15.

[12] Nolivos and Nolivos argue that Latin American Pentecostalism proclaims a "holistic five-fold encounter" with the "written Word of God, the incarnate Word of God, the Spirit of God, the community of God, and the *Missio Dei*" (Nolivos and Nolivos, "Pentecostalism's Theological Reconstruction of the Identity of the Latin American Family," 217).

[13] Nolivos and Nolivos, "Pentecostalism's Theological Reconstruction of the Identity of the Latin American Family," 218.

[14] Nolivos and Nolivos, "Pentecostalism's Theological Reconstruction of the Identity of the Latin American Family," 218.

begins in creation and reaches its most punctuated expression in raising Jesus from the dead. The Spirit's raising of Christ and then sharing that life in the renewal of grace carries on the life-giving role of the Spirit in the drama of redemption. Second, situating pentecostal healing in the wider story of the Spirit of Pentecost recognizes the legitimacy, even normativity, of liberation in pentecostal experience and practice. The Spirit of Pentecost brings the power of new life that raised Christ from the dead. Thus, rejecting the classical pentecostal rhetoric of atonement (healing as contractual entitlement of the cross), this project affirms the pentecostal praxis of transformation, which can and sometimes does include physical healing, by framing it within a wider pneumatological theology of atonement as participation in the resurrected life of Christ.

Resurrection and Righteousness

The Apostle Paul fuses Christ's death and resurrection in a participatory vision of redemption.[15] Indeed, Paul's couplet of death-resurrection expresses the fundamental nature of the atonement—organic participation in Christ through the presence and life-giving power of the Holy Spirit.[16] The Spirit brings to the lives of people the life that the Spirit brought about in Jesus Christ (of course, always retaining the sui generis

---

[15] A significant trajectory in Pauline scholarship sees Paul's soteriology as participationist, indeed with some describing it as deification/theosis. E. P. Sanders was a major catalyst for this trajectory of scholarship; although as Douglas A. Campbell points out, Sanders carried on an earlier German mystical interpretation of Paul—see Sanders, *Paul and Palestinian Judaism* (Minneapolis: Fortress, 1977), 522–3; for the scholarly background to Sanders, see Campbell, *The Deliverance of God: An Apocalyptic Rereading of Justification in Paul* (Grand Rapids: Eerdmans, 2009), 176–7. Other key contributions to Paul's participationist soteriology are Campbell, *The Quest for Paul's Gospel: A Suggested Strategy*, Journal for the Study of the New Testament Supplement Series, 274 (New York: T & T Clark, 2005) and *The Deliverance of God*; Richard B. Hays, *The Faith of Jesus Christ: An Investigation of the Narrative Substructure of Galatians 3:1–4:11*, SBL Dissertation Series, 56 (Chico: Scholars Press, 1983), 248–54; Morna D. Hooker, *From Adam to Christ: Essays on Paul* (New York: Cambridge University Press, 1990); and Michael J. Gorman, *Becoming the Gospel: Paul, Participation, and Mission* (Grand Rapids: Eerdmans, 2015). M. David Litwa argues that deification clarifies the content of Paul's theology better than participation in *We Are Being Transformed: Deification in Paul's Soteriology*, Beihefte zur Zeitschrift für die neutestamentliche Wissenschaft und die Kunde der älteren Kirche, 187 (Boston: Walter De Gruyter, 2012). Michael F. Bird argues that in Paul Christ's death and resurrection are "one redemptive event" and that "juridical and participationist categories" are connected (Bird, *The Saving Righteousness of God: Studies on Paul, Justification, and the New Perspective*, Paternoster Biblical Monographs [Milton Keynes: Paternoster, 2007], 57–8). Ben C. Blackwell also argues that Paul's soteriology is a form of deification in which the Spirit conforms believers to the image of Christ—Christosis. Similar to Bird, Blackwell sees the forensic and participatory elements as complementary in Paul's theology. See Blackwell, *Christosis: Pauline Soteriology in Light of Deification in Irenaeus and Cyril of Alexandria*, Wissenschaftliche Untersuchungen zum Neuen Testament, 314 (Tübingen: Mohr Siebeck, 2011), 117–35.

[16] Campbell also uses the term "organic" to indicate that the nature of participation in Christ is pneumatological, personal (even proto-trinitarian), and relational. See Campbell, *The Quest for Paul's Gospel*, 60–1. Udo Schnelle, in a similar way, argues that the point of justification is making the righteousness of God displayed in Christ a "concrete" experience in the life of believers and thus "justification . . . is organically connected with . . . transformation and participation." See Schnelle, *Apostle Paul: His Life and Theology*, trans. M. Eugene Boring (Grand Rapids: Baker Academic, 2005), 451 and 466.

nature of Christ as the Incarnation of the Son of God). Atonement consists in this Spirit-catalyzed participation in Christ because it makes people children of God. It reconciles to them to their God, each other, and the life for which they were created. The remainder of this chapter shows that the Spirit's raising of Christ is a participational paradigm for setting people free from sin and empowering their new life in Christ as God's children. To do so, it turns to Romans 6 in this section and Romans 8 in the final section of the chapter. But before I develop that material, why Romans 6 and 8?

Romans 6 and 8 showcase the pneumatological and participatory nature of grace.[17] But what about Romans 1–4, which Douglas J. Moo calls "The Heart of the Gospel" and is the locus classicus for the Protestant theology of atonement and justification?[18] Am I privileging the participatory vision of grace in Romans 6 and 8 over the justification by faith not by works of the law account in Romans 1–4? No. My focus on Romans 6 and 8 follows from two reasons. First, the development of the theological argument in Romans reaches its highpoint in Romans 8, according to which pneumatological participation in the resurrection of Christ is the essence of redemption. Second, Romans 6 and 8 develop several motifs for describing redemption that connect with the narrative of the Spirit of Pentecost. N. T. Wright, for example, places the death of Christ in Romans 6 and 8 in the larger context of the Passover and the return from exile.[19] Passover because freedom from sin and death correlates with redemption from Pharaoh and slavery. Exile because the people went into new bondage in Babylon due to their sin and covenant unfaithfulness and thus, needed forgiveness for their sins.[20] Richard B. Hays also situates Paul's theology of the Spirit and resurrection in the wider narrative of God and Israel: the Spirit's role is "leading the children of God out of slavery and into freedom (Rom. 8:14-15, echoing the language of Exod. 13 and Deut. 32). This same Spirit bears witness with our spirit that we too, like Israel, are 'children of God' (8:15b-16)."[21] Hays continues that Romans 8 "remind[s] us that the work of the Spirit cannot be understood properly apart from the story of Israel."[22] I agree with Wright and Hays and other scholars that exile and new exodus themes provide theological background for redemption in Romans. Nevertheless, the Spirit's role in raising Christ and giving new life to all those united to Christ in Romans calls for a wider pneumatological narrative frame. Why? Because the Spirit of God is the agent that redeems from exile in the biblical narrative of redemption (exodus from Egypt,

---

[17] See, for example, Schnelle, *Apostle Paul*, 478–85.
[18] Douglas J. Moo, *The Epistle to the Romans*, The New International Commentary on the New Testament (Grand Rapids: Eerdmans, 1996), 90.
[19] "Forced migration," rather than "exile," has become popular to describe the removal of the people of Israel and Judah by the Assyrians and Babylonians because it connects better with contemporary migration and emigration studies. See James M. Scott, ed., *Exile: A Conversation with N. T. Wright* (Downers Grove: IVP Academic, 2017), 5. Recognizing the more expansive meaning of the Hebrew term *"golah"* to cultivate connections with modern migration crises is worthwhile. The term "exile," however, captures the theological significance associated with the forced migration to Babylon and any unresolved sense of national debasement that persisted in Second Temple Judaism and beyond.
[20] N. T. Wright, *The Day the Revolution Began: Reconsidering the Meaning of the Crucifixion* (New York: HarperCollins, 2016), 276–9.
[21] Richard B. Hays, "Spirit, Church, Resurrection: The Third Article of the Creed as Hermeneutical Lens for Reading Romans," *Journal of Theological Interpretation* 5, no. 1 (2011): 45.
[22] Hays, "Spirit, Church, Resurrection," 46.

Babylon, and the final eschatological exodus to the new creation).²³ The Spirit's role in bringing renewed life to Christ, believers, and creation carries on the narrative of the Spirit that began in the Genesis creation stories and reaches its consummation in the new heaven and the earth. This section develops four points that contribute to the place of the resurrection in a pentecostal theology of the atonement: (1) the Christian life parallels the death and resurrection of Christ; (2) baptism symbolizes the organic and participatory nature of atonement; (3) participation in Christ's death and resurrection stand in continuity with the Holy Spirit's work in the history of redemption; and (4) the Holy Spirit's resurrection of Christ has eschatological priority over his death.

First, in Rom. 6:1-14, Paul parallels the Christian life with the death and resurrection of Christ. In doing so, Paul shows that Christ's life, death, and resurrection are a participatory paradigm of redemption (atonement). Christians are baptized into Jesus' death so that "just as Christ was raised from the dead through the glory of the Father, [they] too may live a new life" (Rom. 6:4). Paul continues that "united with him in his death, we will certainly also be united with him in his resurrection" (Rom. 6:5). The participation in Christ's death envisioned here characterizes life in the eschatological already and not yet. In Rom. 6:6, Paul says "our old self was crucified with him so that the body of sin might be rendered powerless, that we would no longer be slaves to sin." Paul concludes, "[i]n the same way count yourselves dead to sin but alive to God in Jesus Christ. Therefore do not let sin reign in your mortal body so that you obey its evil desires. . . . For sin shall not be your master, because you are not under law, but under grace" (Rom. 6:11-12). The righteousness of grace—atonement—is being united to Christ by the Holy Spirit in his death and resurrection and thereby dying to sin and rising to new life. Justification and the forgiveness of sins are integral elements of being "untied with" and "in Christ" (Rom. 6:5 and 8:10).²⁴ Those who the Spirit unites to Christ and enables to participate in Christ's life, death, and resurrection are considered one with Christ and, therefore, they share his righteousness.²⁵ But the righteousness Paul indicates is intrinsic, not forensic. Christians are "dead to sin" and "alive to God" because, like Christ and because they are united to him, they live in righteousness and faithfulness to God.

---

[23] For a detailed account of the correspondences between the themes of new exodus/creation and the outpouring of the Spirit in the Hebrew Bible prophetic literature, Second Temple Judaism, and Galatians, see Rodrigo J. Morales, *The Spirit and the Restoration of Israel: New Exodus and New Creation Motifs in Galatians*, Wissenschaftliche Untersuchungen zum Neuen Testament, 282 (Tübingen: Mohr Siebeck, 2010).

[24] For the history of interpretation of union with Christ, see Constantine R. Campbell, *Paul and Union with Christ: An Exegetical and Theological Study* (Grand Rapids: Zondervan, 2012), 31–64. Campbell retains the distinction between judicial justification and the transformational elements of redemption but regards them all as benefits of union with Christ. See Campbell, *Paul and Union with Christ*, 388–405. For further explorations of the meaning of "in Christ" in Paul and especially its significance for a participatory soteriology, see Michael J. Thate, Keven J. Vanhoozer, and Constanine Campbell, eds., *"In Christ" in Paul: Explorations in Paul's Theology of Union and Participation*, Wissenschaftliche Untersuchungen zum Neuen Testament, 384 (Tübingen: Mohr Siebeck, 2014).

[25] Gorman develops a similar view of participatory and relational righteousness and justification with what he calls "justification by co-crucifixion." See Michael J. Gorman, *Inhabiting the Cruciform God: Kenosis, Justification, and Theosis in Paul's Narrative Soteriology* (Grand Rapids: Eerdmans, 2009), 45.

Second, baptism symbolizes the death-to-sin and new-life-in-Christ pattern of salvation in Romans 6.[26] Going down into the waters of Christian baptism signifies participation in Jesus' life of death to sin and the absolute expression that takes on the cross. Rising from the waters of baptism represents participation in Jesus' life of faithfulness to and fellowship with God the Father, which was supremely manifest in his resurrection. Paul's language, moreover, is organic and participatory. He first connects Christ's death to the Christian life. He says, "[t]he death he died, he died to sin once for all" (Rom. 6:10). Paul points out that Jesus died *to*, not only *for*, sin (Rom. 6:10). Christ died to sin because he never succumbed to temptation. The Crucifixion was the final and absolute manifestation of Christ's ongoing life of dying to sin and living "to God." But dying to sin is only half of the good news. Paul says of Christ, "the life he lives, he lives to God" (Rom. 6:10). Death and new life are the negative and positive images of his comprehensive righteousness—his work of atonement. Christ's righteousness consists not only in the absence of evil, but also in the active pursuit of God throughout his life. Christ's death on the cross is the highest expression of his "death to sin" because death to sin becomes literal and absolute. His death to sin is not only an objective event in history but a way of life for Christians. But notice that Paul does not mention forgiveness of sin/s, which traditional atonement theology associates with Christ's death on the cross. Paul's couplet of dying to sin-rising to new life with Christ emphasizes being liberated from the power of sin and empowered to live in new resurrection life.[27] Participating in Christ's atonement provides the power to "[die] to sin . . . [and live] to God" (Rom. 6:10). In other words, the emphasis is, to use the traditional terms, subjective, not objective, and participatory, not forensic.

Taken together, dying and rising with Christ are the way Christians participate in the righteousness of Christ. That is why Paul says, "[i]n the same way, count yourselves dead to sin but alive to God in Jesus Christ" (Rom. 6:11). What is the "same way" that Paul calls Christians to share with Christ? The previous verse answers that question: "The death he died, he died to sin once and for all; but the life he lives, he lives to God" (Rom. 6:10). Notice again that Paul does not say, "died for sin," but "to sin." For the proponent of penal-substitutionary atonement that is arresting language. In what sense can Jesus die *to* sin? Jesus died *for* sin! And yet, Jesus dying to sin coheres with the participatory point Paul makes in Romans 6 (as well as in Romans 8). Arland J. Hultgren recognizes the threat this participatory language and imagery has for the traditional forensic way of understanding Christ's death *for* sin and so interprets it to

---

[26] Richard N. Longenecker, *The Epistle to the Romans: A Commentary on the Greek Text*, The New International Greek Testament Commentary (Grand Rapids: Eerdmans, 2016), 612–15. Baptism and the incorporation into Christ's death and resurrection that it signifies is the central category for Paul's soteriology, according to Schnelle (see *Apostle Paul*, 479–82). Note that not all scholars see Paul emphasizing the current function of the resurrection as paradigmatic for the experience of grace (e.g., moral life), but emphasize the believer's current identification with Christ's death and hope for the future resurrection; see Frank J. Matera, *Romans*, Paideia: Commentaries on the New Testament (Grand Rapids: Baker Academic, 2010), 150–1. I agree with Wright that Paul has in mind participation in resurrection life now and in its future consummation. See N. T. Wright, *The Resurrection of the Son of God*, Christian Origins and the Question of God, vol. 3 (Minneapolis: Fortress, 2003), 251.

[27] Hays, "Spirit, Church, Resurrection," 43.

conform to a forensic understanding.[28] The problem is that doing so evacuates Romans 6 of its primary point—the Christian life is participation in the life of Christ with his death and resurrection representing the fundamental nature of his life.[29] Jesus died to sin because, facing abandonment by his friends and agonizing death, he remained faithful to the Father, neither shirking his mission to embody the righteousness of God in the world nor lashing out in vengeance toward his tormentors. The cross was the ultimate and absolute way that Christ died to sin and lived in faithfulness to God the Father. The Christian life parallels the death and resurrection of Christ. Water baptism is a central rite for Christians because it publicly enacts their participation in the death and life of Christ. How does the Christian die and rise to new life with Christ? In the same way Christ did—"through Christ Jesus the law of the Spirit of life set me free from the law of sin and death" (Rom. 8:2).

Third, the from-death-to-life imagery of baptism and the historical experience of Christ's crucifixion and resurrection fit the broader canonical frame of the Spirit's redemptive work. Genesis 1 begins with "darkness over the surface of the deep" (Gen. 1:2). It is a place of menace and lifelessness. The hovering Spirit initiates the transition from doom and darkness to the light and life of the days of creation. The breath of God makes dust a living human being in Genesis 2. The floodwaters return the world to a murky state. God's Spirit makes the floodwaters flee from the face of the earth and restores life to its surfaces and spaces. Facing annihilation from Pharaoh's army, the Spirit of God makes a way for the people of Israel.[30] The bleaching bones scattered in the valley in Ezekiel 37 come alive again when God's Spirit blows on them. The same Spirit of life brings forth the Incarnation of the Son of God and raises Jesus from the tomb. What is more, Paul specifically situates the Spirit's role in the death-resurrection of Christ in the larger history of redemption. He presents Jesus Christ as the second Adam (Rom. 5:12-21). The first Adam abdicates his Spirit-breathed life. The second Adam embraces it and is "through the Spirit of holiness . . . declared with power to be the Son God by his resurrection from the dead" (Rom. 1:4). Thus, Paul places Christ within a narrative of the Spirit that reaches back to Genesis. Christ is the second Adam who fulfills Spirit-breathed life and is now raised by the Spirit in order to share that life with others. The Spirit brings life where there is death, light to dark places, hope where despair reigns, and prosperity in places of scarcity. The Spirit of God takes the world that is an empty black void and shapes it into a world full of life and vitality. The Spirit comes to human lives broken with and from sin, and heals and transforms

---

[28] Arland J. Hultgren, *Paul's Letter to the Romans: A Commentary* (Grand Rapids: Eerdmans, 2011), 251. Morna D. Hooker interprets Christ's dying to sin and its participatory purpose as I do, although without the emphasis on the Holy Spirit (Hooker, *From Adam to Christ*, 44–5 and 60).

[29] Moo retains the phrase Jesus died "to sin" because it is consistent with the parallel Paul draws between Christ's death on the cross and the rejection of sin in the Christian life—note that Moo sees Christ's dying to sin as equivalent with the cross, and does not, at least explicitly, extend it to his entire life of faithfulness to the Father as I do in this section. Moo also interprets Romans 6 in terms of justification and sanctification. Romans 1–4 deal with justification and deliverance from the penalty of sin and Romans 6 covers sanctification and deliverance from the power of sin. Moo, *The Epistle to the Romans*, 350–2, 356–9, and 378–80.

[30] The exodus was the backdrop of Paul's emphasis on resurrection in Romans 6 and 8, according to Wright (*Resurrection of the Son of God*, 248 and 253).

them in righteousness. The Spirit cultivates the life of Christ in "[e]veryone who calls on the name of the Lord" (Rom. 10:13). Being like Jesus is not an exercise in Christian moralism. It is not tacking on spiritual disciplines to an otherwise secular life. The essence of the Christian life is not religious calisthenics and moral asceticism. Being like Jesus is being the place where the Holy Spirit brings human life into union with the eternal Son of God and fellowship with the Father.[31] The gospel is the promise that through participation in Jesus Christ we may know the fellowship he shares with the Father ("that the love you have for me may be in them," Jn 17:26). The Spirit of Pentecost makes available to all people God's dream for human life that began with the Spirit's first stirring over the primeval waters and reached its fullness in the Spirit's resurrection of Jesus Christ. Atonement is participating in a relational and personal way in the Spirit's resurrection of Jesus Christ.

Fourth, situating the cross and the resurrection in the wider narrative of the Spirit of Pentecost indicates that the resurrection has the priority in Paul's couplet of death-resurrection. It does so because it signals the abiding nature of Christ as the glorified Son of God and the promise that the faithful will share his resurrected life as coheirs and children of God (Rom. 8:17). Douglas A. Campbell argues that participating in Christ's crucifixion and the weakness of the human condition became paramount for Paul rather than the transforming power of the resurrection. Campbell suggests that as Paul faced struggle and suffering, he came to identify more with the cross, although without losing hope for a final resurrection in Christ.[32] Paul's experience of cruciformity, however, does not obviate the theological primacy of the resurrection. Indeed, for all people, dying with Christ ultimately becomes definitive for life on this side of the consummated new creation. Yet, death is not the final word. And so eschatologically, the resurrection is primary for redemption. The initiation rite of baptism also highlights the principal place of resurrection in atonement. Going into the water and dying with Christ and rising with him are a set-piece. From the perspective of the Spirit of Pentecost, the cross leads to resurrection. Rising from the waters of baptism represents the Christians' participation in Jesus' life of faithfulness and fellowship with God the Father and in the life of eschatological promise.

Atonement and the Spirit of Resurrection

Spirit-empowered participation in Christ's death-resurrection is the basic content of Paul's theology of grace. Building on the resurrection theology of Romans 6, Romans 8 shows that the Holy Spirit is the foundation for the theology of atonement as participation in the resurrected life of Christ.[33] Romans 8:1-17 is Paul's promised

---

[31] My argument for Paul's pneumatological and participatory theology shares similarity with Douglas A. Campbell's description of being in Christ—for example, "this is no mere imitation; Paul is not just following Christ's example. He is finding in his own life the experience and life of Christ figuring forth. He is *participating* in Christ" (*The Quest for Paul's Gospel*, 54).

[32] Campbell, *The Quest for Paul's Gospel*, 52–4 and 60.

[33] Gordon D. Fee argues that Romans 6 and 8 articulate a common vision of newness of life, the former on Christological and the latter on pneumatological bases. Gordon D. Fee, *God's Empowering*

"spiritual gift" to the Romans (cf. Rom. 1:11). In other words, it is the "high-water mark" of Paul's gospel message to the Roman Christians, which is a "personal, relational, and participatory" vision of grace.[34] Richard N. Longenecker emphasizes that Romans 8, with its message of personal participation and transformation in Christ through the Holy Spirit, is the "essence" and "apex" of Paul's gospel of grace.[35] He regards Rom. 1:16–4:25 as Paul's effort to establish points of agreement with the Jewish Christians in Rome—for example, righteousness comes by faith and not by works of the law. This material is Paul's "first step" that sets forth "what he believed both they and he held in common" and that prepares them to hear his more comprehensive and deeper participational and personal vision of grace—I add pneumatological to the personal and participational categories.[36] Having established common ground on the gospel, Paul then develops "what he calls 'my gospel' in 2:16 and 16:25."[37] Romans 8 functions as the pinnacle of the summative section of Paul's theology of grace and the Holy Spirit plays a leading role in it.[38] Three initial observations are in order. First, Christocentric readings of Romans—indeed, of Paul for that matter—are inadequate. Second, the traditional Protestant reading of Romans makes primary what Paul considers preliminary. In other words, integrating Christ and the Spirit, Paul emphasizes the participational and transformational and not the forensic nature of grace. Third, either atonement, which the traditional forensic reading associates with Paul's preliminary stage setting in Rom. 1:16–4:25, is not Paul's primary concern (i.e., it is not his "spiritual gift" and the core of his gospel) or the traditional reading of Romans has misunderstood Paul by artificially limiting the nature of the atonement to forensic categories. The latter option is correct. Atonement deals with the fundamental nature of grace encountered in Jesus Christ. Traditional forensic views of the atonement, however, unnecessarily restrict it by overlooking the pneumatological and participational nature of the atonement that Paul develops in Romans 6 and 8. The following paragraph highlights Paul's integration of Christ and the Spirit and the transformational nature of grace and Pauline atonement theology.

First, Paul opens Romans 8 declaring that "there is no condemnation for those who are in Christ Jesus, because through Christ Jesus the law of the Spirit of life set me free from the law of sin and death" (Rom. 8:1-2). As in Romans 6, Paul uses death and resurrection/new life to describe the fundamental nature of participating in Christ. Those who are in Christ no longer face judgment because they share in the

---

Presence: The Holy Spirit in the Letters of Paul (Peabody: Hendrickson, 1994), 499–501.

[34] Longenecker, *The Epistle to the Romans*, 679–80 and 707–8. Michael J. Gorman makes a similar argument in "Romans: The First Christian Treatise on Theosis," *Journal of Theological Interpretation* 5, no. 1 (2011): 14. Also see Campbell, *The Quest for Paul's Gospel*, 56n1 and 74–89.

[35] Longenecker, *The Epistle to the Romans*, 679 and 708; for this argument, also see William E. W. Robinson, *Metaphor, Morality, and the Spirit in Romans 8:1–17*, Early Christianity and Its Literature (Atlanta: SBL Press, 2016), 9.

[36] Longenecker, *The Epistle to the Romans*, 149, 145–6, and 149–50.

[37] Longenecker, *The Epistle to the Romans*, 149.

[38] Florin T. Cimpean makes the argument for the centrality of chapter 8 and the Holy Spirit in Romans in "From Margins to Center: Pentecostal and Orthodox Readings of Romans 8 in Romania," in *Navigating Romans through Cultures: Challenging Readings by Charting a New Course*, ed. Yeo Khiok-khng, Romans Through History and Cultures: Receptions and Critical Interpretations (New York: T & T Clark, 2004), 42–7.

life of the resurrected Christ—they are liberated by "the Spirit of life . . . from the law of sin and death" (Rom. 8:2). Why are they no longer condemned? Paul states that Christ "condemned sin in sinful man" (Rom. 8:3). What does it mean that he condemned sin? He condemned it by saying "no" to it even unto death. Sin had no dominion over him. He rendered sin powerless, and so he was unshackled from its consequences—alienation from God and death. Christ condemning sin in Rom. 8:3 parallels his dying to sin in Rom. 6:10. He condemned sin by refusing to yield to it. Being free from condemnation corresponds to being set free from "the law of sin and death" (Rom. 8:2). In other words, real, not forensic, righteousness and new life frees the believer from condemnation and death. Why did Christ condemn sin? Reinforcing a pneumatological and transformational vision, Paul says that Christ came "in order that the righteous requirements of the law might be fully met in us, who do not live according to the sinful nature but according to the Spirit" (Rom. 8:3-4). Roger L. Hahn concludes that "[t]he Spirit internalizes the Law so that its righteous requirement may be fulfilled."[39] Although this pneumatological and participatory language may be inconsistent with the extrinsic theology of imputed righteousness, it is consistent with the biblical promise of redemption. Ezekiel declares that "I will give you a new heart and . . . I will put my Spirit in you and move you to follow my decrees and be careful to keep my laws" (Ezek. 36:26-27; cf. Jer. 31:32-33). Divine indwelling through the Spirit of God and the transformation of life it empowers, moreover, was fundamental to the covenantal promise of redemption (Isa. 63:11-14 and Hag. 2:1-5).[40]

Second, Paul reinforces the pneumatological condition of the Christian life when he insists that "if anyone does not have the Spirit of Christ, he does not belong to Christ" (Rom. 8:9). In other words, the "Spirit of life" (Rom. 8:2) is the basis for relationship with Christ and participation in his righteousness. Why is the Holy Spirit the foundation of participating in freedom from sin and the new creation, indeed, the resurrection life of Christ? Because the Spirit was the constitutive agent in the Incarnation of the Son of God and his life of faithfulness that led to cross and resurrection (e.g., Mt. 1:18-20 and Lk. 1:35).[41] Ben C. Blackwell is correct to highlight the "Christo-telic" nature of the believer's experience of the Holy Spirit.[42] But he does not develop the pneumatological basis for soteriological Christo-telocity. The Holy Spirit was the foundation of Jesus' life of faithfulness to the Father and the agent of his resurrection (e.g., Mt. 12:28, Lk. 4:18, and Rom. 8:11). Since the Spirit was the foundation of Christ's life of righteousness, so

---

[39] Roger L. Hahn, "Pneumatology in Romans 8: Its Historical and Theological Context," *Wesleyan Theological Journal* 21, nos. 1–2 (1986): 77.

[40] For the connection between the Spirit of Yahweh and the Holy Spirit sealing God's "covenant ownership" through divine indwelling in Romans, see Mehrdad Fatehi, *The Spirit's Relation to the Risen Lord in Paul: An Examination of Its Christological Implications*, Wissenschaftliche Untersuchungen zum Neuen Testament, 128 (Tübingen: Mohr Siebeck, 2000), 209–12.

[41] Here my view seems to diverge from Blackwell's and Fatehi's. They regard the Spirit's role as mediating the presence of Christ. My argument gives the Spirit agency in both Incarnation and grace, which includes mediating the presence of the risen Christ but goes beyond that by also constituting in believers the life the Spirit brought about in Jesus Christ. In other words, the Spirit's soteriological role derives from and reflects the Spirit's role in the Incarnation, life, death, and resurrection of Christ. See Blackwell, *Christosis*, 253–67 and Fatehi, *The Spirit's Relation to the Risen Lord in Paul*, 21–25 and 229.

[42] Blackwell, *Christosis*, 256–7 and 264–5.

also for believers.⁴³ Paul cements the organic and the participatory relationship between the Spirit's work in Christ and believers in Rom. 8:11—"if the Spirit of him who raised Jesus from the dead is living in you, he who raised Christ from the dead will also give life to your mortal bodies through his Spirit, who lives in you." The future resurrection life and the proleptic participation in that new creation by living "according to the Spirit" in the here and now stand in continuity (Rom. 8:4).⁴⁴ From beginning to end, the renewal of life that constitutes atonement derives from the Holy Spirit. As Paul declares in Gal. 6:8, "whoever sows to please the Spirit, from the Spirit will reap eternal life." Identifying the Holy Spirit as the "Spirit of life" also echoes the Spirit's role as a source of life in Genesis 1 and 2. The Spirit of God liberating creation from its bondage to decay (Rom. 8:21) and raising the children of God to resurrected life (Rom. 8:11 and 17) solidifies the narrative continuity of the Spirit's role as the source of life and its renewal. In raising Christ, the Spirit guarantees the telos of redemption. The Spirit's raising of Christ is the seed from which grows the final consummation of the new creation (Rom. 8:22-23).

Third, Romans 8 does not reflect the neat distinctions between justification and sanctification that emerged in Protestant systematic theology. Paul clearly indicates that those who are in Christ face no condemnation because "the law of the Spirit of life set [them] free from the law of sin and death" (Rom. 8:1-2). Moo's argument, for example, that Rom. 8:1-2 refers to justification and freedom from the penalty of sin is the result of reading Paul through the categories of Protestant systematic theology.⁴⁵ Indeed, he cites the Westminster Confession's distinction between justification (Christ imputes righteousness) and sanctification (the Holy Spirit infuses grace) to elaborate Paul's discussion of participation in Christ's death and resurrection in Romans 6.⁴⁶ Moo reads Romans 8 through Westminster's extrinsic-forensic-justification-crucicentric and intrinsic-transformation-sanctification-pneumatological categories. Moo no doubt believes that the Westminster Confession reflects Paul's theology. Unfortunately, Paul's pneumatological and participatory soteriology in Romans 8 does not fit the distinctions between justification and sanctification that Protestants developed in

---

⁴³ Describing the relationship between Christ and the Spirit, James D. G. Dunn says "Paul implies that the Spirit of God is now to be characterized and identified as the Spirit of Christ, as that power which determined Christ in his ministry and in so doing provided a pattern of life in the Spirit." James D. G. Dunn, *Romans 1-8*, Word Biblical Commentary, vol. 38 (Waco: Word, 1988), 446; also see Dunn, *Jesus and the Spirit: A Study of the Religious and Charismatic Experience of Jesus and the First Christians as Reflected in the New Testament* (1975; reprint, Grand Rapids: Eerdmans, 1997), 325.

⁴⁴ Dunn, *Romans 1-8*, 432 and 445. My argument that the Spirit replicates the life of Christ (death and resurrection) in Christians corresponds with Morna D. Hooker's case that "interchange in Christ" characterizes Paul's theology of atonement. My contribution highlights the Holy Spirit's role in this dynamic and personal experience of grace. See Hooker, *From Adam to Christ*, 18–25. Thomas D. McGlothlin's work on the reception of Paul's resurrection theology in the early church makes the case that Christ's resurrection is the paradigm of moral transformation in the present and of future glorification of the body, and the Holy Spirit is its effecting agent. See Thomas D. McGlothlin, *Resurrection as Salvation: Development and Conflict in Pre-Nicene Paulinism* (New York: Cambridge University Press, 2018), 32–43.

⁴⁵ Moo, *The Epistle to the Romans*, 471–3 and 476–7; cf. 352.

⁴⁶ Moo, *The Epistle to the Romans*, 350.

contradistinction to Roman Catholic theology.[47] Cross and resurrection are not a binary forensic and transformational couplet. Romans 8:1-2 expands on Rom. 7:6—"dying to what once bound us, we have been released from the law so that we serve in the new way of the Spirit."[48] Justification, facing "no condemnation," derives from the Holy Spirit's uniting believers to Christ and transforming them in the image of Christ, not on an extrinsic and imputed righteousness that covers sin. Atonement is participating in Christ's condemnation of sin, his rendering sin powerless—thus Paul affirms that believers "do not live according to the sinful nature but according to the Spirit" (Rom. 8:4). The death and resurrection of Christ are not forensic events in the long past, although they are objective historical events. But they were never meant to remain objective and historical. Mark A. Seifrid, for example, is correct to note that Christ's Incarnation, crucifixion, and resurrection were "accomplished outside of us." He also regards the Christian life of obedience as the fruit of being united with Christ's death and resurrection. He nonetheless maintains that Christ's righteousness "stands outside the believer which the believer is to serve and obey, rather than some quality imparted to the believer." But that extrinsicism is unwarranted. Paul's point is that atonement entails participating and sharing in the righteousness of Christ through personal union and identification with Christ and the emergence of his Spirit-anointed life—for example, dying to sin, living to God. Seifrid's rejection of obedience as a "quality imparted to the believer" suggests that he reads Paul through the lens of Protestant-Catholic theological disputes and differences.[49] Yet, the language and imagery of Rom. 8:1-11 is "relational, personal, and participatory."[50] Christ died and rose to new life to share his righteousness (his righteousness includes both dying to sin and living to God) for ever after with all people.[51] The Holy Spirit, the Spirit of Pentecost, moreover, is the animating source both of Christ's resurrected life and for potentially "all people" to participate in it (Acts 2:17).

Conclusion

The Spirit's raising of Jesus Christ from the dead is a participatory paradigm (like the cross) of atonement. Resurrection indicates the new life brought by the Holy Spirit. The Spirit comes to vanquish the power of sin and death and empower life in the Spirit-

---

[47] Although affirming that justification is legal, Peter Stuhlmacher argues that justification entails new creation; thus, the distinction between "justification" and "sanctification" in systematic theology is an "unbiblical abstraction." Peter Stuhlmacher, *Paul's Letter to the Romans: A Commentary*, trans. Scott J. Hafemann (Louisville: Westminster/John Knox, 1994), 63–4.

[48] Fatehi also argues that Romans 8 is as an elaboration of Romans 6 in *The Spirit's Relation to the Risen Lord in Paul*, 208 and Gorman, *Inhabiting the Cruciform God*, 73–4.

[49] Mark A. Seifrid, *Christ, Our Righteousness: Paul's Theology of Justification*, New Studies in Biblical Theology, 9 (Downers Grove: InterVarsity Press, 2000), 71 and 74.

[50] Longenecker, *The Epistle to the Romans*, 539. Roger Hahn makes a similar point, although he uses the traditional language of the Spirit applying the work of Christ; see "Pneumatology in Romans 8," 77–8.

[51] Although Dunn denies that Paul attributes Christ's resurrection to the Spirit, he maintains that through the Spirit the historical event of the resurrection remains an "active force in shaping human destiny" (Dunn, *Romans 1–8*, 433).

breathed divine image. What penal atonement theology refers to as the objective work of Christ for human beings becomes the organic and participatory paradigm for the traditional subjective work in grace. Christ's death is not an objective legal transaction with the Father and his resurrection is not primarily a divine verdict of vindication and secondarily a pattern for sanctified life. Participating in the new resurrection life of the Holy Spirit is the basic content of Paul's theology of grace. The Spirit that catalyzes the Incarnation and baptizes Jesus Christ as the Spirit-anointed messiah also raises him from dead. Resurrection is part of the ongoing story of the Spirit of Pentecost. Resurrection reflects the tangible transformation of life that many Pentecostals not only anticipate, but experience when they encounter the Spirit of Pentecost.

11

Going Home

This chapter completes a pentecostal atonement theology by recommending a shift from the escapist and otherworldly eschatology of Classical Pentecostalism to a realized and participatory eschatology of the Spirit of Pentecost. Participating in the Spirit of Pentecost is not about going to heaven but coming home to the life for which God created human beings. Throughout this book, I have used the terms "narrative" and "story" of the Spirit to give the atonement a wider (than crucicentric) pneumatological frame of reference. The dynamic and progressive nature of the Spirit's work indicates the narrative (i.e., eschatological) character of the history of redemption. Chapters 2 and 6 presented a theology of Spirit telocity that showcases the Holy Spirit's purposeful agency in the narrative of redemption. But what is the telos of the Spirit? What is the Spirit that first stirred over the darkness trying to achieve over the course of the history of redemption? What does the eschatological Spirit of Pentecost have to do with atonement? Atonement addresses the problem of the Fall. In the biblical Fall narrative of Genesis 3, human beings are alienated from their God and from each other, they are exiled from Eden, their primal home, and they are alienated from abundant life in this world. Atonement deals with the theological predicament of the human condition. The Spirit of Pentecost reconciles human beings to the life for which they were created; thus, the Spirit of Pentecost is a Spirit of atonement. The Spirit of Pentecost, moreover, is eschatological. Not because the Spirit brings the history of the world crashing down in an apocalyptic mega-battle, but because receiving the Spirit of Pentecost is participating in the emergence of the new creation that transforms human life in an eschatological arc toward the justice of God's kingdom. This chapter presents three features of the eschatological Spirit of Pentecost that overcome the human condition of alienation from God, from each other, and from the world of abundant life: becoming children of God, going home, and green cosmopolitanism. First, however, a reconsideration of traditional pentecostal eschatology and the social deprivation theory is important. This critical interaction provides the segue to the constructive and eschatological content that completes this pentecostal theology of atonement.

Pentecostal Eschatology and Social Deprivation

Connecting the outpouring of the Holy Spirit to eschatology has been a central feature of Pentecostalism from the beginning.[1] The early Pentecostals believed that their revivals

---

[1] D. William Faupel argues that eschatology was the central and organizing theological category of early Pentecostalism in *The Everlasting Gospel: The Significance of Eschatology in the Development*

and Spirit baptism empowered witness and spiritual gifts were part of the Latter Rain outpouring of the Holy Spirit that would usher in the Second Coming of Christ. Where the Day of Pentecost was the early rain that established the church, the pentecostal revivals were the latter rain that signaled the return of Christ and the end of the age.[2] The pentecostal revivals were the last great push of the Holy Spirit to evangelize the world before Christ's returned to rapture his church.[3] Although the Pentecostals were primitivistic or restorationist in their effort to restore the experience of Acts 2 to the church, they were not ahistorical.[4] They saw their movement standing not only in continuity with Acts 2 but also with God's raising up Luther to recover justification by faith and Wesley to restore sanctification to the church.[5] Thus, the experience of Spirit baptism and of signs and wonders is inextricably eschatological. Although Pentecostals are fairly critiqued for their otherworldly spirituality and eschatological escapism, they nonetheless believed they were playing a lead role in the closing scenes of this world.[6] Allan Anderson describes this as a "tension between the negative view of the world and the very positive view of their place in it."[7] So, ironically, while they looked for Jesus to return and take them out of the world, they believed they were principal actors in the final scenes of world history.[8]

The social deprivation theory takes pentecostal apocalyptic rhetoric as a sign of social dysfunction. It is the desperate, but ineffectual, religious response of Pentecostals to their adverse social situations and locations. A final consideration of this view is important. Robert Mapes Anderson argues that Pentecostalism emerged from a "radical" working class "protest against a social system that victimized them,

---

of Pentecostal Thought, Journal of Pentecostal Theology Supplement Series, 10 (Sheffield: Sheffield Academic Press, 1996), 18 and 20–43.

[2] Donald W. Dayton, *Theological Roots of Pentecostalism* (Grand Rapids: Francis Asbury, 1987), 26–8 and Larry R. McQueen, *Toward a Pentecostal Eschatology: Discerning the Way Forward*, Journal of Pentecostal Theology Supplement Series, 39 (Blandford Forum: Deo, 2012), 63–4.

[3] Peter Althouse, *Spirit of the Last Days: Pentecostal Eschatology in Conversation with Jürgen Moltmann*, Journal of Pentecostal Theology Supplement Series, 25 (New York: T & T Clark, 2003), 18–19.

[4] Daniel D. Isgrigg argues that the "latter rain" themes of restoring healing, prophecy, spiritual and ministry gifts and linking their restoration to the renewed work of the Holy Spirit was not unique to Pentecostals but central to the revival movements of the nineteenth century. See Daniel D. Isgrigg, "The Latter Rain Revisited: Exploring the Origins of the Central Eschatological Metaphor in Pentecostalism," *Pneuma: The Journal of the Society for Pentecostal Studies* 41, nos. 3–4 (2019): 439–57.

[5] Daniel E. Albrecht and Evan B. Howard, "Pentecostal Spirituality," in *The Cambridge Companion to Pentecostalism*, ed. Cecil M. Robeck, Jr. and Amos Yong (New York: Cambridge University Press, 2014), 246–7 and Donald W. Dayton, "The Limits of Evangelicalism: The Pentecostal Tradition," in *The Variety of American Evangelicalism*, ed. Donald W. Dayton and Robert K. Johnston (Knoxville: University of Tennessee Press, 1991), 45–7.

[6] For example, Calvin L. Smith argues that the premillennial and dispensational eschatology held by Nicaraguan Pentecostals forestalled their participation in the Sandinista revolutionary movement in "Revolutionaries and Revivalists: Pentecostal Eschatology, Politics, and the Nicaraguan Revolution," *Pneuma: The Journal of the Society for Pentecostal Studies* 30, no. 1 (2008): 55–82.

[7] Allan Anderson, *Spreading Fires: The Missionary Nature of Early Pentecostalism* (Maryknoll: Orbis, 2007), 220.

[8] As Wonsuk Ma puts it, the Pentecostals went "from being marginalized to being conspicuously 'called' for God's ministry." See Ma, "'When the Poor are Fired Up': The Role of Pneumatology in Pentecostal/Charismatic Mission," in *The Spirit in the World: Emerging Pentecostal Theologies in Global Contexts*, ed. Veli-Matti Kärkkäinen (Grand Rapids: Eerdmans, 2009), 43.

but it functioned in a way that perpetuated that very system. A potential challenge to the social system was transformed into a bulwark of it."[9] Recognizing a degree of validity in Anderson's assessment does not require accepting in toto his argument that Pentecostalism is a lower-class social protest sublimated in ecstatic religion. The pentecostal revival at Azusa Street was subversive to the mainstream order. The Spirit-empowered ethnic, racial, and gender diversity represented in Azusa's leadership was an intentional protest to the reigning racist and patriarchal social order.[10] The end-time eschatology and political separatism of early Pentecostalism, however, muted and, over time, supplanted its social protest.[11] As dispensational premillennialism became increasingly popular, saving souls became the preoccupation of pentecostal ministries.[12] Social justice ministries were often regarded as either perfunctory platforms to gain an audience for evangelism or distractions to winning soul for Christ.[13] The involvement of Black Pentecostals in the mid-twentieth-century civil rights movement is an exception to this overall trend among Pentecostals.[14] The tension, however, is that while their formal eschatology and preaching rhetoric became more otherworldly, they practiced social mobility. The question is, was the move to the middle class a pentecostal sellout of their original social protest and advocacy for the marginalized?

Anderson's argument that the Pentecostals were duped, co-opted, or complicit in the system against which they raged misunderstands their desire and the purpose of the Spirit of Pentecost. Anderson argues that the Pentecostals left behind their social protest instincts as they transitioned to the middle class.[15] Donald Dayton also laments the tendency toward the *embourgeoisement* of evangelical renewal movements (e.g., holiness and pentecostal churches). Churches that began as social protests on the margins lose their message of "faith-motivated social transformation" as they enter and

---

[9] Robert Mapes Anderson, *Vision of the Disinherited: The Making of American Pentecostalism* (New York: Oxford University Press, 1979), 222.
[10] Zachary Michael Tackett, "As a Prophetic Voice: Liberationism as a Matrix for Interpreting American Pentecostal Thought and Praxis," *Journal of the European Pentecostal Association* 33, no. 1 (2013): 42.
[11] Frederick Ware's critique of premillennialism and its tendency to discourage analysis of social "processes and systems" among African American Pentecostals equally applies to this eschatology's influence among white Pentecostals. See Frederick Ware, "On the Compatibility/Incompatibility of Pentecostal Premillennialism with Black Liberation Theology," in *Afro-Pentecostalism: Black Pentecostal and Charismatic Christianity in History and Culture*, ed. Amos Yong and Estrelda Y. Alexander, Religion, Race, and Ethnicity Series (New York: New York University Press, 2011), 198–202.
[12] Gerald T. Sheppard, "Pentecostals and the Hermeneutics of Dispensationalism: The Anatomy of an Uneasy Relationship," *Pneuma: The Journal of the Society for Pentecostal Studies* 6, no. 2 (1984): 5–33.
[13] Murray W. Dempster, "Christian Social Concern in Pentecostal Perspective: Reformulating Pentecostal Eschatology," *Journal of Pentecostal Theology* 1, no. 2 (1993): 52–4.
[14] Cheryl J. Sanders, *Saints in Exile: The Holiness-Pentecostal Experience in African American Religion and Culture* (New York: Oxford University Press, 1999), 122.
[15] Anderson, *Vision of the Disinherited*, 229. Anderson is not alone in critiquing pentecostal success in advancing to middle- and upper-middle classes as an enervating sellout to North American consumer and capitalist society; for example, see Harvey Cox, *Fire from Heaven: The Rise of Pentecostal Spirituality and the Reshaping of Religion in the Twenty-first Century* (Reading: Addison-Wesley, 1995), 317–18.

acquiesce to middle-class society.¹⁶ Making a similar critique, Cheryl J. Sanders states that "those Sanctified churches that have succeeded as vehicles of upward mobility need to be challenged to decide whether the goal of ministry is spiritual formation or socialization to the middle class."¹⁷ But becoming middle class is not antithetical to spiritual formation. That viewpoint seems to reflect a classism at variance with the inclusive nature of the many tongues and "all people" of Pentecost. In other words, becoming middle class was not a pentecostal sellout of their past. The Pentecostals did not protest against injustice and turn to the power of the Holy Spirit so that they could stay poor and dispossessed. They may not have had recourse to social and political methods for redressing economic grievances, such as trade unions and political parties, but they did, in spite of the otherworldly rhetoric of their eschatology, seek and expect the power of the Holy Spirit to change their lives in the here and now.¹⁸ And, that is what happened. Pentecostal believers and their churches increasingly became culturally successful in twentieth- and early-twenty-first-century North America. The eschatological rhetoric of the early Pentecostals protested the prejudices and inequalities of their cultural dislocation and projected an "alternative, a heavenly city to replace the earthly one."¹⁹ The pentecostal economically poor, ethnic minority, and socially disenfranchised pining for escape from this world for a heaven of streets paved with gold is a cry and longing for liberation from the adversity of their concrete circumstances.

Anderson is correct to critique the early pentecostal rejection of social and political means of alleviating their social grievances. Later Pentecostals, however, what Donald E. Miller and Tetsunao Yamamori call "Progressive Pentecostals," have begun to correct this problem.²⁰ Indeed, while North American Pentecostals were still debating with Evangelicals over speaking in tongues and the hermeneutics of Paul versus Luke-Acts, Argentine Church of God leader Lidia Susana Vaccaro de Petrella was calling for Spirit-empowered social justice ministries and activism to transform systemic

---

¹⁶ Donald Dayton, "The Embourgeoisement of a Vision: Lament of a Radical Evangelical," *Other Side* 23, no. 8 (1987): 19.
¹⁷ Sanders, *Saints in Exile*, 130. Note that Sanders' work is among African American Holiness and Pentecostal churches. But my overall point on social mobility and participating in the new life of the Spirit of atonement applies to white and black Pentecostals.
¹⁸ A similar dynamic is underway among Latin American Pentecostals, see David Martin, *Pentecostalism: The World Their Parish* (Malden: Blackwell, 2002), 114. Although embracing a holistic vision of salvation and not an otherworldly spirituality, African Pentecostals are more successful at promoting economic upward mobility because they emphasize personal transformation where secular NGOs emphasizing structural changes often fail. See Dena Freeman, "The Pentecostal Ethic and the Spirit of Development," in *Pentecostalism and Development: Churches, NGOs and Social Change in Africa*, ed. Dena Freeman (New York: Palgrave Macmillan, 2012), 24–5. Dalit Pentecostals, although emphasizing hope for eternal life, expect their faith to transform and improve their life in the "here and now." Their vision of salvation incorporates "'this worldliness' and 'other-worldliness.'" See V. V. Thomas, *Dalit Pentecostalism: Spirituality of the Empowered Poor* (Bangalore: Asia Trading, 2008), 349.
¹⁹ Cox, *Fire from Heaven*, 117.
²⁰ Donald E. Miller and Tetsunao Yamamori, *Global Pentecostalism: The New Face of Christian Social Engagement* (Berkeley: University of California Press, 2007), see chapter 2's title, "Progressive Pentecostals: Ministries, Beliefs, and Motivations."

structures of injustice.[21] Change, moreover, is underway. American Pentecostals today "are more likely than other evangelicals to prefer a bigger government providing more services over a smaller government providing fewer services."[22] Consider pentecostal Abiy Ahmed, Prime Minister of Ethiopia. He received the 2019 Nobel Peace Prize for leading an international peace agreement with Eritrea that ended bloody border fighting and fostered peaceful reconciliation among Muslim and Orthodox Christians.[23] The pentecostal focus on personal spirituality, moreover, can include a vision for social transformation. Annelin Eriksen, for example, argues that belief in personal transformation from the old to the new life in the Spirit catalyzes social change among Pentecostals on the island nation of Vanuatu. Vanuatuan Pentecostals pray for trade agreements, bills before parliament, and corrupt government bureaucrats. Although the strategy is spiritual, "prayer intercession," the aspiration for change is social. These Pentecostals, therefore, do not fit the pattern that Pentecostals use religion to palliate their marginal status while remaining oblivious to the larger social structures that cause it. At the very least, these Pentecostals believe that their faith has a direct contribution to make on the formation of their society and its policies.[24] Wonsuk Ma, moreover, contends that eschatology among Asian Pentecostals has shifted from its early Western missionary "otherworldly" character to indigenous "this-worldly concerns."[25] Néstor Medina and Sammy Alfaro's and Martin Lindhardt's recent work also showcases the political and social activities of Latin American Pentecostals.[26] Indeed, Pentecostals, in every country surveyed by Pew, are more inclined than other Christians to believe that Christians should help the poor.[27] In other words, Pentecostals both around the world and in the United States show that experiencing the power of the Spirit and advocating for social transformation can be common pursuits.

Harvey Cox, however, notes the loss of eschatological fervor among contemporary American Pentecostals. On the one hand, he regrets it. The expectation of the end-

---

[21] Lidia Susana Vaccaro de Petrella, "The Tension between Evangelism and Social Action in the Pentecostal Movement," *International Review of Mission* 75, no. 297 (1986): 34–8.
[22] "Palin V.P. Nomination Puts Pentecostalism in the Spotlight," Pew Research Center, September 12, 2008.
[23] The Nobel Peace Prize 2019. NobelPrize.org. Nobel Media AB 2019. Monday October 21, 2019. https://www.nobelprize.org/prizes/peace/2019/summary/
[24] Annelin Eriksen, "'New Life': Pentecostalism and Social Critique in Vanuatu," *Ethnos* 74, no. 2 (2009): 191–4. Spiritual intercession for social and political change also characterizes Pentecostalism in Africa. See Ogbu Kalu, *African Pentecostalism: An Introduction* (New York: Oxford University Press, 2008), 218–21.
[25] Wonsuk Ma, "Pentecostal Eschatology: What Happened when the Wave Hit the West End of the Ocean," *Asian Journal of Pentecostal Studies* 12, no. 1 (2009): 102–5. Calvin L. Smith maintains a similar transformation is underway among Latin American Pentecostals in "Pneumapraxis and Eschatological Urgency: A Survey of Latin American Pentecostal Theology and Its Outworking," in *Pentecostal Power: Expressions, Impact and Faith of Latin American Pentecostalism*, ed. Calvin L. Smith, Global Pentecostal and Charismatic Studies, 6 (Leiden: Brill, 2011), 181–203.
[26] Néstor Medina and Sammy Alfaro, *Pentecostals and Charismatics in Latin America and Latino Communities*, Charis: Christianity and Renewal—Interdisciplinary Studies (New York: Palgrave Macmillan, 2015) and Martin Lindhardt, ed., *New Ways of Being Pentecostal in Latin America* (Lanham: Lexington, 2016).
[27] See *Spirit and Power: A 10-Country Survey of Pentecostals*, The Pew Forum on Religion and Public Life (October 2006), 31. https://www.pewresearch.org/wp-content/uploads/sites/7/2006/10/pentecostals-08.pdf.

of-the-world catalyzed pentecostal hope and mission. Now, "middle-class pentecostal congregations appear very much at ease with the status quo. Now they seem confident not that Jesus is coming soon, but that He probably isn't, and that therefore nothing will interrupt their pursuit of success and self-indulgence."[28] On the other hand, he is glad to see it go because its end-of-the-world apocalypticism subverts meaningful concern and action on behalf of society and the environment.[29] But the middle-class success of Pentecostals is not something to be critiqued. I appreciate and sympathize often with Cox's "ambivalent" experiences with Pentecostalism, but for a professor at one of the most elite universities in the world to mock middle-class Pentecostals for their social grasping—"pursuit of success and self-indulgence"—is condescending cant. Cox is correct to critique the gaudy and bouffant materialism of the prosperity gospel, but not the aspiration and achievement of upward social and economic mobility of many Pentecostals and their churches. Why? Because this mobility was the result of the life-transforming experience of the Holy Spirit for many of these Pentecostals. Personal life transformation, experiencing the goodness of a stable and nurturing family, and the relative abundance and leisure of middle-class life can be gifts of the Spirit of Pentecost. They can be the concrete and material manifestations of atonement; ways the Holy Spirit reconciles people to the life for which they were created.

The social deprivation theory critiques pentecostal eschatology as a dysfunctional response to social circumstances. The fundamental problem here, however, is not pentecostal eschatology. The dysfunctional personal, social, political, and economic circumstances that Pentecostals encounter are. Why deprivation? Why racism, chauvinism, exploitive class hierarchies, and ecological degradation? Why do social systems that empower and enrich the few and sideline and despoil the rest exist? In other words, why are there social systems that exile people from the life for which God created them? Because cultural elites, adept in social functionality, use it to gain and to preserve privileges at the expense of others. The social deprivation of Pentecostals is a sign that human beings, perpetrators and victims, are estranged from God, from each other, and from the purpose of their Spirit-breathed life. Pentecostal eschatology has too often failed to address matters of social injustice, even though its message of release and redemption often arises directly from these injustices. Pentecostal praxis, whether intentionally or indirectly, has nevertheless counteracted many, although not all, social inequities. Social redress usually arises from personal moral and spiritual transformation. Pentecostal experience of the Holy Spirit, moreover, displays a quest for the renewal of all dimensions of life. From its beginning, in other words, pentecostal eschatology has been a theology of personal and social liberation.

"I Was in the Spirit, and There Before Me . . ." (Rev. 4:2)

The challenge facing pentecostal eschatology is twofold. First, reframe eschatology so that it drops escape to heaven and withdraw from the world apocalypticism. Second,

---

[28] Cox, *Fire from Heaven*, 317–18.
[29] Cox, *Fire from Heaven*, 318.

embrace an eschatology that empowers an explicit orientation to the renewal of life in this world as anticipation and participation in the one to come. The purpose here is not setting forth specific social policies. But proposing the contours of a pentecostal eschatology that reflects the pentecostal praxis of liberation and inspires more explicit social and public initiatives for the renewal of all dimensions of life.[30] Why is addressing social injustice germane to pentecostal eschatology and atonement? Because the theories and policies, the motivations and actions that give rise to injustice are contrary to the nature and purpose of Spirit-breathed life. Renewing the earth and its people in the justice of the new heaven and new earth and the New Jerusalem is the core vision of biblical eschatology, the telos of the Spirit of Pentecost, and the consummation of atonement.[31] The following sections tie together these themes in three features of the eschatological Spirit of Pentecost: becoming children of God, going home, and green cosmopolitanism.

Becoming Children of God

Although adoption and becoming children of God are usually treated under the doctrine of salvation, this chapter locates them in eschatology. Why? Eschatology deals with the telos of redemption. It addresses the purpose and goal of redemptive history. Since this project is pentecostal, it considers eschatology from the perspective of Spirit telocity—the purpose of the Spirit of God in the eschatological nature of the history of redemption. What is the telos of the Spirit of God? The Spirit animated dirt so that it could bear the divine image as God's children and live in fellowship with God.[32] Expelled from Eden, human beings did not lose their identity as God's image bearers and children, but they were alienated from it. They became estranged from their fellowship with God, from each other, and from their relationship with the world. The history of redemption is the Spirit of God's endeavor to reconcile God's children to their identity as Spirit-breathed divine image bearers.

Recovering identity as God's children is the centerpiece of redemptive history and fundamental to the atonement. The history of redemption is the economic sharing

---

[30] The first pentecostal liberation theologies were Eldin Villafañe, *The Liberating Spirit: Toward an Hispanic American Pentecostal Social Ethic* (Lanham: University Press of America, 1992) and Samuel Solivan, *The Spirit, Pathos, and Liberation: Toward an Hispanic Pentecostal Theology*, Journal of Pentecostal Theology Supplement Series, 14 (Sheffield: Sheffield Academic Press, 1998). More recently, Sammy Alfaro proposes a Hispanic Pentecostal Liberation theology in a Christological key in *Divino Compañero: Toward a Hispanic Pentecostal Christology*, Princeton Theological Monograph Series, 147 (Eugene: Pickwick, 2010).

[31] Other Pentecostal scholars emphasizing that eschatology entails the renewal of embodied and material life are Althouse, *Spirit of the Last Days*, 186–92; Matthew K. Thompson, *Kingdom Come: Revisioning Pentecostal Eschatology*, Journal of Pentecostal Theology Supplement Series, 37 (Blandford Forum: Deo 2010), 148–51; McQueen, *Toward a Pentecostal Eschatology*, 214–84; A. J. Swoboda, *Tongues and Trees: Towards a Pentecostal Ecological Theology*, Journal of Pentecostal Theology Supplement Series, 40 (Blandford Forum: Deo 2013), 192–237; and Nimi Wariboko, *The Charismatic City and the Public Resurgence of Religion: A Pentecostal Social Ethics of Cosmopolitan Urban Life*, Charis: Christianity and Renewal—Interdisciplinary Studies (New York: Palgrave Macmillan, 2014), 198–200.

[32] The creation of human beings in the likeness and image of God parallels human procreation (Gen. 5:1-3).

of the love and fellowship of the triune God. The Spirit of God gives life to human beings so that they can participate in and manifest in their lives the community that characterizes the triune God. Adam and Eve are collectively designated "man" or "Adam" to indicate that their familial relationship with God is inclusive and not based on gender (Gen. 5:1-3). The Spirit-breathed divine image bearers are not only sons but God's children. The emphasis on becoming God's children is also a reminder of why the Incarnation is so vital. Most fundamentally, Christ is the incarnate Son of God. Everything that Christ does—his life, ministry, death, resurrection, and ascension; his work of atonement—emerges from his incarnate identity as the Son of God, an Incarnation catalyzed and sustained by the Holy Spirit (see Chapter 3). The Spirit-anointed Christ fulfills his identity as the incarnate Son of God. Then through the Spirit of Pentecost, Christ offers "all people" the opportunity to recover their identity as God's children, to reconcile and to renew their fellowship with God the Father (Acts 2:17). The eschatological process of becoming children of God ties together the Christological and participatory nature of the atonement. By uniting people to Christ, the Spirit of Pentecost reconciles them to fellowship with the triune God and their identity as God's children. Spirit baptism, therefore, is the foundation for experiencing atonement. The most fundamental and enduring purpose of Spirit baptism is to reconcile human beings to their familial relationship with God. The Spirit of Pentecost draws "all people" into the fellowship of the triune God and brings forth the faithful and loving fellowship that the Spirit displayed in the life of Jesus Christ.[33] The Spirit of Pentecost reconciles people to their identity as God's children and in doing so the Holy Spirit is an agent of atonement. But why is the Spirit the source of identity as children of God?

First, becoming children of God parallels Christ's identity and life as the Son of God.[34] In other words, what traditional atonement theology separates into objective and subjective aspects of atonement, a pentecostal theology integrates. In Rom. 8:14-16, Paul connects the Sonship of Christ with Christian identity as children of God the Father: "because those who are led by the Spirit of God are sons of God. . . . For . . . you received the Spirit of sonship. And by him we cry, 'Abba, Father.' The Spirit himself testifies with our spirit that we are God's children." Christians are children of God—that is, partakers in "sonship."[35] Their "sonship," moreover, partakes in the Sonship of

---

[33] Frank D. Macchia also proposes a more expansive and eschatological vision of Spirit baptism in *Justified in the Spirit: Creation, Redemption, and the Triune God*, Pentecostal Manifestos (Grand Rapids: Eerdmans, 2010), 93–9.

[34] Trevor J. Burke also argues for a correlation and inseparable relationship between the Spirit's role in the Sonship of Christ and in Christian's becoming children of God (although he does not develop this point on the categories of Spirit Christology as I am doing here, but the exegesis of Rom. 8:14 and Gal. 4:6). See Trevor J. Burke, *Adopted into God's Family: Exploring a Pauline Metaphor*, New Studies in Biblical Theology, ser. ed., D. A. Carson, 22 (Downers Grove: InterVarsity Press, 2006), 125–43.

[35] "Sonship" is put in quotes because that is the term Paul uses. "Sonship" sounds exclusive, but the wider context of Paul's theology makes it clear that the term is inclusive and means "children of God." In Romans, Paul emphasizes the inclusion of Gentiles in God's grace. In Gal. 3:26-28, using the same image of Christians as "sons of God," Paul clarifies the gender inclusiveness of Christian identity as children of God—"There is neither Jew nor Greek, slave nor free, male nor female, for you are all one in Christ Jesus." I believe Paul uses the term "sonship" to accentuate the connection

Christ. For that reason, they can call their Father, "Abba." That the Spirit, not Christ, is the source of their "sonship" is notable. The Spirit makes Christians children of God. Connecting the Spirit to Christian identity as children of God is not limited to Pauline theology, however. The prologue of the Gospel of John defines the gospel as receiving new birth as God's children: "Yet to all who received him, to those who believed in his name, he gave the right to become children of God—children born not of natural descent, nor of human decision or husband's will, but born of God" (Jn 1:12-13). John 3:1-8 clarifies that the Spirit of God is the source of this new birth that constitutes followers of Christ as children of God—"you must be born again . . . born of the Spirit." The restoration of identity as God's children is fundamental to the work of atonement. Why? Because it was fundamentally what was lost in Genesis 2. The Holy Spirit, the Spirit of Pentecost, reconciles people to their identity as God's children and, therefore, is the Spirit of atonement.

Second, the Spirit of Pentecost is the basis of becoming God's children. The indwelling Holy Spirit is the source of "sonship" because the Spirit constituted the Sonship of Jesus Christ—the Holy Spirit was the agent of the Incarnation of the Son of God.[36] The Spirit's work in the Incarnation is the paradigm of the Spirit's work as the Spirit of Pentecost. In other words, symmetry marks the Spirit's work in the Incarnation and grace. What the Spirit achieved in the life of Christ indicates the mission of the Spirit of Pentecost. Jesus Christ was the incarnate Son of God through the activity of the Holy Spirit. The Spirit led and enabled the life and ministry of Jesus Christ (Lk. 4:1 and 14). So also the Spirit constitutes believers children of God and frees their lives from sin and enables them to live in righteousness (Rom. 8:1-11).[37] Reconciliation to identity and life as children of God is pneumatological because the same "Spirit that raised Jesus from the dead is living in you" (Rom. 8:11). Atonement, therefore, entails becoming God's children and sharing in his Spirit-anointed life through the same Spirit that brought about the Incarnation of the Son of God in Jesus Christ. The outpouring of the Holy Spirit on the Day of Pentecost, moreover, "is a public statement

---

between Christ as the Son of God and the identity of Christians as children of the Father. My use of the term is inclusive and, therefore, denotes "children of God."

[36] Volker Rabens also emphasizes the Spirit's role in adoption as God's children. Being children of God consists in the indwelling Spirit enlightening and empowering moral transformation for ethical—Christ-like—living and nurturing relational intimacy with Christ and the Father. I agree with Rabens' case that the Spirit empowers ethical living through relational intimacy with Christ. I also argue, nevertheless, that the work of the Spirit in grace parallels the work of the Spirit in the Incarnation. Without the Spirit-Christ synergy in Incarnation and grace, pneumatological extrinsicism results; the Spirit is instrumental to Christ. Although Rabens' account accentuates the work of the Spirit, it essentially fits within the traditional paradigm of Christ accomplishes and the Spirit applies redemption, the principal work of the Spirit being sanctification. Thus, the Spirit fosters relationship with Christ and empowers sanctified life. My point, however, is that the Spirit, as Spirit of Pentecost, brings the life the Spirit realized in Jesus Christ. The Spirit makes Christians children of God because the Spirit was the foundation of the Incarnation of the Son of God in Jesus Christ. For Rabens, see *The Holy Spirit and Ethics in Paul: Transformation and Empowering for Religious-Ethical Life*, Wissenschaftliche Untersuchungen zum Neuen Testament, 2nd Series, 283 (Tübingen: Mohr Siebeck, 2010), 171–242, esp. 219–35.

[37] Note that becoming the children of God is also inextricably transformative. David Vincent Meconi and Carl E. Olson also make this point in *Called to be the Children of God: The Catholic Theology of Human Deification* (San Francisco: Ignatius, 2016), 11 and 13–14.

from the Father to His children of love and affirmation. They are indeed the sons and daughters of God and are, therefore, the recipients of the promise of the Father."[38] The gift of the Spirit of Pentecost parallels Jesus' baptism with the Holy Spirit. When Jesus came up from the waters of John's baptism, he heard the Father say, "You are my Son, whom I love; with you I am well pleased" (Lk. 3:22). The outpouring of the Spirit on the Day of Pentecost continues to the full consummation of the new creation and offers all people the opportunity to return home to God their Father.

Third, becoming the children of God is eschatological. The new life, the resurrection life of the Spirit, has two eschatological dimensions.[39] First, participating in the new life of the Spirit is to taste the coming new creation (Rom. 8:23 and Heb. 6:4-5). Second, participating in the new life of the Spirit is a work in progress. *Becoming* the children of God will not be fully realized until the final consummation of the new creation.[40] As Andrew K. Gabriel points out, although Christians are children of God, "believers await their full inheritance as God's children."[41] But I also want to emphasize present participation as eschatological. Paul declares that the "law of the Spirit of life set me free from the law of sin and death . . . in order that the righteous requirements of the law might be fully met in us, who do not live according to the sinful nature, but according to the Spirit" (Rom. 8:2-4). Clearly Paul regards living "according to the Spirit" and having "the righteous requirements of the law . . . met in us" as a current reality for Christians. This fulfilling the law by living in the power of the Holy Spirit achieves the promise of Ezek. 36:26-28 that God "will give you a new heart . . . and I will put my Spirit in you and move you to follow my decrees and be careful to keep my laws."[42] Yet, Paul also recognizes that fulfilling the law is an ongoing process that awaits completion in the new creation. For this reason, "the Spirit . . . testifies with our spirit that we are God's children" and "co-heirs with Christ" (Rom. 8:16-17). Living according to the Spirit is the "firstfruits" of the future "glory" and "our adoption" as God's children and the "redemption of our bodies" (Rom. 8:23).

Fourth, recognizing the dynamic, eschatological, nature of becoming God's children is not a source of spiritual anxiety. The Christian need not worry, what if I do not make it? Christians are secure in their identity in Christ. Not because they trust in their relative level of sanctification. But because they trust in the Spirit-

---

[38] Daniela C. Augustine, *Pentecost, Hospitality, and Transfiguration: Toward a Spirit-inspired Vision of Social Transformation* (Cleveland: CPT, 2012), 26.

[39] James M. Scott develops the present and future aspect of becoming children of God in *Adoption as Sons of God: An Exegetical Investigation into the Background of "huiothesia" in the Pauline Corpus*, Wissenschaftliche Untersuchungen zum Neuen Testament, 2 (Tübingen: Mohr Siebeck, 1992), 244–66.

[40] Michael J. Gorman emphasizes that the eschatological character of the Christian life consists in the Holy Spirit's ongoing ethical transformation that eventuates in ontological sharing in the risen Christ's glory. See Gorman, *Becoming the Gospel: Paul, Participation, and Mission* (Grand Rapids: Eerdmans, 2015), 281–2. Douglas A. Campbell also notes that "to bear the image of the Son is to be his brother, although this image is only completed eschatologically." See Campbell, *The Quest for Paul's Gospel: A Suggested Strategy* (New York: T & T Clark, 2005), 76.

[41] Andrew K. Gabriel, "The Holy Spirit and Eschatology—with Implications for Ministry and the Doctrine of Spirit Baptism," *Journal of Pentecostal Theology* 25, no. 2 (2016): 209.

[42] Thanks go to James M. Scott for pointing out this allusion to Ezekiel (*Adoption as Sons of God*, 263–4).

anointed life they have received. The presence and work of the Holy Spirit in their lives is "a deposit, guaranteeing what is to come" (2 Cor. 1:22, 5:5 and Eph. 1:14). Jesus Christ's identity as the Son of God was never in doubt. Christ was the Spirit-anointed messiah from the moment of the Incarnation. And yet, his life developed. He did not proceed directly to make intercession before the Father at the first moment of the Incarnation. His Spirit-anointed life, his fulfillment of the human vocation to image God, emerged throughout his life and culminated in his death, resurrection, and ascension. His identity as the Son of God emerged in the particularities of his historical life and ministry. Considering the ascension and what it meant for the way Jesus experienced his identity as the Son of the God and his relationship with the Father sheds light on the Christian's dynamic identity as God's children. Theologically, Jesus Christ was the Son of God without remainder at the inception of the Incarnation. Experientially, Jesus grew into his identity as the Son of God. A conundrum resides in the Incarnation. The Son of God in Christ remains in indissoluble union with the Father. In other words, even though the Father sent the Son into the world in the Incarnation, the Son did not leave the immanent fellowship of the triune God. And yet, the Son became incarnate in the humanity of Jesus Christ. The critical point is that the Son's incarnate life in Christ became the primary point of reference for his relationship with the Father. For this reason, he describes his relationship with the Father in spatial terms. For example, Jesus says "I have come down from heaven . . . to do the will of him who sent me" and "for I came from God and now am here. I have not come on my own; but he sent me" (Jn 6:38 and 8:42). The incarnate Son in Jesus Christ experienced relational distance from the Father. His father remained in heaven and sent him into the world to carry out his redemptive work. Theologically and ontologically the Son remained in union with the Father in the immanent Trinity. But in respect to his experience as the incarnate Son of God in Jesus Christ, his relational or, perhaps better, emotional connection with the God the Father fluctuated. In other words, his relationship with the Father had a thoroughly human dimension and would have varied depending on circumstances. During his baptism, when he hears the voice of his Father declare "You are my Son, whom I love; with you I am well pleased" (Lk. 3:22), his experience must have been of unmitigated intimacy. Later in the Garden of Gethsemane, God the Father must have seemed remote and unresponsive to his pleas to take the cup of suffering from him (Lk. 22:42–44). Indeed, on the cross, Jesus experiences the totality of absence when he cries out "my God, my God, why have you forsaken me?" (Mk 15:34). Indicating his return to the Father however, Jesus had previously assured his disciples that "I came from the Father and entered the world; now I am leaving the world and going back to the Father" (Jn 16:28). The ascension narratives reinforce Jesus' return to the Father (Mk 16:19; Lk. 24:51; as well as Acts 1:1-11). They narrate his relational return to unmitigated fellowship with the Father. This relational reality of the Incarnation demonstrates that being children of God can be an enduring theological reality and an unfolding experience as well. From an eschatological perspective, the Christian's identity as a child of God is firm. As Paul affirms, nothing can "separate us from the love of God that is in Christ Jesus our Lord" (Rom. 8:38-39). But since redemptive history unfolds, the fullness of that identity emerges along the arc of the eschaton. Thus, all those who have received the Spirit of

Pentecost are and are becoming children of God. The Holy Spirit grounds and secures their identity as God's children (Rom. 8:14-17). Their identity, moreover, as God's Spirit-anointed and -constituted children emerges in the concrete circumstances of their lives until they are resurrected by the Holy Spirit and "share" in the "glory" of the everlasting kingdom of God (Rom. 8:17-24).

What are the implications for pentecostal praxis of the Spirit's eschatological restoration of people to their identity and life as God's children? Recognizing that the Spirit of Pentecost is for "all people" and joins them together in one but diverse family of God subverts any and all prejudices that justify exploiting, degrading, and ultimately dehumanizing people. Tribalism, for example, whether of ethnicity and religion or class and politics, is one of the most potent foundations of discrimination.[43] Yet, from the perspective of the Spirit of Pentecost, there is only one tribe—the Spirit-breathed community of "all people." But does this theology create a tribalism of Pentecost? After all, not all people have opened their hearts to receive the Spirit of Pentecost. No, because all people have their life from the Spirit of God. Murray W. Dempster, in an early foray into a pentecostal theology of social liberation, maintains that the "the doctrine of humankind as God's image bearer provides universal parameters in the application of social justice."[44] All people are Spirit-breathed divine image bearers. They are children of God even if they have not awoken to that reality. The pentecostal community simply marks those who are reconciled to their pneumatic identity. The Spirit of Pentecost does not create a special privilege club of the spiritually gifted but empowers "openness . . . [to embrace] the otherness of the neighbor . . . as an enrichment."[45] The point of the parable of the prodigal son is that the wayward son remains a beloved child of the father. The story rebukes the tribal-minded older brother (Lk. 15:11-32). The Spirit of Pentecost does not create a new and exclusive pentecostal tribe but awakens people to their shared universal fraternity. While not everyone has received the Spirit of Pentecost, everyone is a Spirit-breathed divine image bearer and is one of the "all people" who can receive the Spirit of Pentecost.

Going Home

The Spirit of Pentecost is eschatological because the Holy Spirit takes people home. Atonement is the Spirit taking people to the place the human heart longs to go. The place beyond "tears," "pain," suffering, and "death" (Rev. 21:4). The place beyond the bitter gall of separation and loss. Home for most people is not only a house. It is also the street where you grew up, it is the local store, pizza place, and park. It is

---

[43] E.g., Stevan E. Hobfoll, *Tribalism: The Evolutionary Origins of Fear Politics* (New York: Palgrave Macmillan, 2018). For an example of the vitriolic political and cultural partisanship in contemporary American society, see Emma Green, "Americans Hate One Another. Impeachment Isn't Helping," *The Atlantic* November 2, 2019. https://www.theatlantic.com/politics/archive/2019/11/impeachment-democrats-republicans-polarization/601264/?utm_source=facebook&utm_medium=social&utm_campaign=share

[44] Murray W. Dempster, "Pentecostal Social Concern and the Biblical Mandate of Social Justice," *Pneuma: The Journal of the Society for Pentecostal Studies* 9, no. 2 (1987): 133.

[45] Jean-Jacques Suurmond, *Word and Spirit at Play: Towards a Charismatic Theology*, trans. John Bowden (1994; reprint, Grand Rapids: Eerdmans, 1995), 222.

a friend's house where you had sleepovers and spent your summer days. I always looked forward to going home. For me, coming home is more than a visit to my parents' house. It is seeing N. W. Freeman Street where I grew up and rode bikes and played street football with my sister and other kids. It is seeing the alleyway where we took shortcuts to the park, the "little store"—Northside Grocery—where we went to get pops and candy bars, and McKay Creek where I explored, fished, and trapped crawdads. It is slowing down while driving by W. Verne McKinney Elementary school and its playground. It is seeing the ponds, creeks, and the coast range mountains rising to the west where I learned to fly fish. Going home takes me to a time when my parents were young. It is going back to a childhood place that was good. But my childhood home no longer exists. It was demolished and replaced with infill townhomes. Most of the places that I associate with going home have changed so much that they are no longer familiar. Going home, nevertheless, is nostalgic. Going home takes us to a place where our hearts ache to go. But, as time passes and people and places change, we can't. That place we long to go exists now only in memory. Not everyone, moreover, has warm memories of one or even of any childhood home. Refugees and immigrants are displaced from their homes. For some people, home was and is hell—a place of abuse, addiction, depression, misery, and suffering. My kids have lived in four states and two countries. They have called three apartments and five houses "home." They do not have a "home" to go back to; their childhood was not a unified experience in one place. Of course, houses, streets, and parks are not the most fundamental experience of home. People make houses homes and streets neighborhoods. Christian eschatology is about going home. It is about the Spirit taking us to the place where our hearts ache to go.

The irony is that the Spirit takes us to the place of nostalgia by taking us forward into the horizon of God's kingdom. Reading Genesis 3 makes our hearts ache for the world of Genesis 2, the world before sin, before the thorns and thistles, before death. Even if our home no longer exists or is a place we would never want to go back to, our hearts yearn for the place portrayed in Genesis 2. We long for the world before we needed to hide from God and each other. We long for a world before fear, vulnerability, alienation, futility, and death. Genesis 2, however, is like my childhood home. I can't go back to it. It's gone. Paved over with, what to me are, ersatz houses; things that will never be home to me. Christian eschatology does not take us back to a halcyon time immemorial. The history of redemption is not a return to a pristine primordial place. The Spirit takes us to a world beyond both Genesis 3 and 2. The Spirit redeems us from melancholic nostalgia for the world before Genesis 3 by taking us forward into the coming kingdom God. The Holy Spirit takes us where our hearts ache to go by taking us on the journey with "Abraham ... [who] was looking forward to the city with foundations, whose architect and builder is God. ... All these people ... were looking for a better country—a heavenly one. ... [And] we are looking for the city that is to come" (Heb. 11:8-10, 13-16 and 13:14). The Spirit takes us to the place where "He will wipe every tear from their eyes. [And where] there will be no more death or mourning or crying or pain, for the old order of things has passed away" (Rev. 21:4). When Jesus prepared to leave his disciples, he consoled them with the promise that his Father's house had many rooms and he was "going there to prepare a place for them" (Jn 14:1-

4). Going home is going where you belong. Home includes people and places, and so does the home where the Spirit of Pentecost is taking us.

But what is the nature of the place the Spirit of God is taking us? It is a world beyond Genesis 3. But it is not an off-world place. It is not even a spiritual world. But it is the world the human heart longs for. It is to a restoration of Spirit-breathed life. The Spirit leads people out of the wilderness east of Eden, the land of thorns and thistles, the land of the sweat of the brow and futility, and into "a good and spacious land" (Exod. 3:8). Between Genesis 2 and Revelation 21 and 22 is a macro-narrative of redemption, which consists of exile and exodus. Within that redemptive arc are particular stories that participate in and reflect that larger story—for example, the exodus from Egypt. The Spirit of Pentecost initiates the great exodus from exile that characterizes the history of redemption. Pentecost offers "all people" the opportunity to come home by participating in the Spirit-anointed life of Jesus Christ—the one who personifies exodus from exile through his life, resurrection, and ascension. Receiving the Spirit of Pentecost begins the journey home, not to the proto-Charismatic community of Eden (see Chapter 2), but to the pentecostal community "all people" that finds fulfillment in the "nations" of the new creation (Rev. 21:24).

The eschatological character of the Spirit of atonement suggests that coming home (exodus from exile) is the normative paradigm for the Christian life. Rising in popularity in contemporary North American Christianity, however, is the exile paradigm for the Christian life.[46] The exile metaphor operates on functional and theological levels. Rod Dreher's *Benedict Option* emphasizes functional exilic status. American mainstream culture booted Christianity to the curb. The only realistic response is to accept cultural marginalization and to establish Christian enclaves inspired by monastic practices.[47] Stanley Hauerwas represents the influential movement of theological exilic identity.[48] According to this view, Christians are aliens not only in American culture but in the world itself. This world is a place of pilgrim sojourn. The Christian can never be at home in this world. The eschatological Spirit of Pentecost, however, means that exile cannot serve as a normative paradigm for the Christian life. The outpouring of the Spirit of Pentecost starts the journey home. It signals the end of exile. Exodus from the life of death and dissolution has begun. The journey home includes the renewal of life in all of its Spirit-breathed dimensions. I am not being Pollyannaish. I think Rod Dreher's gloomy forecast on the future of Christian churches in North American society (Western society in general) is more or less correct. Post-Christendom and the marginalization of Christians in contemporary North American and Western societies is real. But the theological question is, what does Pentecost and its eschatological consummation in the new creation say about the Christian's place in and relation to the world? It suggests that life in this world is renewed. The Christian life is the journey out of sin, dysfunction, and death to a world of renewed and abundant life.

---

[46] Lee Beach, *The Church in Exile: Living in Hope after Christendom* (Downers Grove: IVP Academic, 2015).

[47] Rod Dreher, *The Benedict Option: A Strategy for Christians in a Post-Christian Nation* (New York: Sentinel, 2017), 98–9.

[48] Stanley Hauerwas and William H. Willimon, *Resident Aliens: Life in the Christian Colony*, Expanded 25th Anniversary Edition (Nashville: Abingdon, 2014).

The eschatological vision entails all creation and not only the realm of personal spirituality. Consequently, exile cannot be normative for Christian spirituality. The exile paradigm emphasizes estrangement from the life for which God created human beings. Theologically, indeed pneumatologically, "exile" is never a primary identity for Christians. The vision of redemption is return to and renewal in the land. God creates a world of abundance and creates human beings for life in it. The creation of human beings for life in this world and the eschatological hope of the new heaven and the new earth and the New Jerusalem means that restoration and renewal are the fundamental character of the Christian life. Human beings are not aliens in this world. They are not spiritual interlopers in this physical and material world. They do not find their real home in a disembodied and spiritual state that transcends the material. They should be aliens to sin and everything opposed to the new creation. Participating in the Spirit of Pentecost, however, starts the journey home out of exile to the eschatological new creation—the new heaven and the new earth.

An obvious objection is that many people never experience the renewal of life in this world. They live and die oppressed, poor, and discarded. Pentecostals preach healing, but many people succumb to their diseases—indeed, all will at some point. Has God abandoned them? Have they failed to grasp their foretaste of the eschatological kingdom? Were they left behind on the journey out of exile and into the homeland of God's coming kingdom? No. Expecting to experience all the blessings of the consummated kingdom misses the current place in the narrative of redemption just as much as the exile mentality. Suffering and death just as much as renewal, hope, and promise are indicative themes of the present location in the narrative of redemption. The Christian life is a foretaste of the great banquet feast of the consummated kingdom of God (Lk. 14:1-24). A place exists for functional alien status. In cases of extreme persecution and repression, accepting cultural, social, and political marginality may be the only way to survive.[49] But such a status is not aspirational. It is not theologically normative for life renewed by the Holy Spirit any more than is continuing to be bedeviled by self-destructive lifestyle habits. The Spirit of Pentecost leads people into the horizon of the kingdom of God, but the Promised Land still lies beyond the Jordan River. The journey home has begun. Family members are with us. The real joy of fellowship begins to replace nostalgic ruminations. But one more road remains to be traveled and a river to be crossed. Pentecostal eschatology needs to recognize the present place in the history of redemption. This world remains the world of Genesis 3, but it is also the world of the emerging new creation. Pentecostal praxis, from physical healing to reconciled families and economic mobility, are advents of the eschatological home, even though the gates of the New Jerusalem are still in a far-off country.

What is "home" for Pentecostals? Ultimately, it is the resurrection to new life in the new creation. But the Spirit of Pentecost creates communities of faith that glimpse and taste the final homegoing. Describing the pentecostal communities in Latin America, Calvin L. Smith notes that "across a continent where a highly disproportionate

---

[49] See *Bishop of Truro's Independent Review for the Foreign Secretary of FCO Support for Persecuted Christians: Final Report and Recommendations*, 2019. https://christianpersecutionreview.org.uk/storage/2019/07/final-report-and-recommendations.pdf

segment of the population is poor, displaced and marginalized, previously powerless pentecostal believers find a home which stresses their self-worth by virtue of their Spirit-endowed gifts and callings, allowing them to participate and feel they have a worthwhile role to contribute within the local body of Christ."[50] He continues that women find "empowerment . . . in a traditionally *machismo* culture."[51] The pentecostal churches and their fellowship give people a place to belong. Ostracized, vilified, and disregarded people are welcomed as equals and as people dignified with the love and grace of God and the open arms and fellowship of other believers.[52] Pentecostal communities provide "identity, meaning, acceptance, and relationships," especially for young people.[53] Although discussion of Pentecostalism and social liberation often focuses on economic issues, which are important, the pentecostal churches provide a richer social benefit than only economic uplift. They provide nurturing communities that generate social capital. They give people a social enclave in a world that is harsh, unforgiving, and indifferent. They encourage a sense of personal transformation and empowerment in society. They connect people to grassroots networks that stimulate successful civic activity (e.g., economic and political).[54] The experience of coming home for these Latin American Pentecostals stands in continuity with the welcome home and embrace that the poor, the "sinners and tax collectors," and the social flotsam and jetsam received from Jesus (Mt. 9:10). The manifestation of spiritual gifts, moreover, such as speaking in tongues, is the sign of the presence and the grace of this God of love and compassion. Thus, the communities created by the Spirit of Pentecost provide an experience of coming home for people where they share fellowship and love with their brothers and sisters in Christ.

Green Cosmopolitanism

Although hazarding anachronism, describing Eden as a green place is fair. It is vegan. It has not been degraded by human activity. It is an off-the-grid idyll. But human cultural activity is not absent. God intended Adam "to work and take care of" Eden (Gen. 2:15). That cultural activity achieves its most sophisticated expression in the life of the city. So, the history of redemption has two fundamental subject matters. What God has created and what his creation has created. First, God redeems creation and especially the highest expression of that divine creativity—the divine image bearers. Second, God redeems what his creation creates, especially the products of the divine image bearers. Why does God redeem their creation? Because it is the product of their effort, however imperfect, to manifest their Spirit-breathed life and bear the divine image. Daniela C. Augustine adds that the redemption of the city, human cultural activity, is a "radical

---

[50] Smith, "Pneumapraxis and Eschatological Urgency," 186–7.
[51] Smith, "Pneumapraxis and Eschatological Urgency," 187.
[52] Cheryl J. Sanders argues that inner city black pentecostal churches play a similar social role for the poor, functioning as "places of refuge" (*Saints in Exile*, 129).
[53] Douglas Petersen, "A Moral Imagination: Pentecostals and Social Concern in Latin America," in *The Spirit in the World: Emerging Pentecostal Theologies in Global Contexts*, ed. Veli-Matti Kärkkäinen (Grand Rapids: Eerdmans, 2009), 55.
[54] Miller and Yamamori, *Global Pentecostalism*, 23 and Petersen, "A Moral Imagination: Pentecostals and Social Concern in Latin America," 60–2.

gesture of unconditional hospitality in which God subjects the reality of His future to the form of human civilization. Apart from this eschatological openness of divine hospitality, the comprehensive redemption of humanity will be impossible."[55] The resurrection of the children God for life in the New Jerusalem, the new heaven, and the new earth recapitulates God's blessing of creation. The Spirit that God sent to still the primal sea and bring forth life on the earth ever stirs. The Spirit renews the earth, its people, and their creative activity as divine image bearers. Thus, the vision of the new creation includes edenic and cosmopolitan images. But what does the eschatological home look like? In Rev. 7:9, John "looked and there before [him] was a great multitude that no one could count, from every nation, tribe, people, and language, standing before the throne and in front of the Lamb" (Rev. 7:9). How did this multitude arrive before the throne and the Lamb of God? They received the Spirit of Pentecost. The "great multitude" corresponds with the "all people" of Pentecost (Acts 2:17). John also saw "the Holy City, the new Jerusalem, coming down out of heaven from God" (Rev. 21:2). The "nations" will enter the city that has "the river of the water of life . . . flowing . . . down the middle of the great street of the city. On each side of the river stood the tree of life, bearing twelve crops of fruit, yielding its fruit every month. And the leaves of the tree are for the healing of the nations" (Rev. 22:1-2). John's vision of the new heaven and the new earth reflects a multicultural and green cosmopolitanism.[56]

Inclusive multiculturalism is a hallmark of the outpouring of the Holy Spirit on the Day of Pentecost. Although hackneyed platitudes in contemporary political and social discourse, "inclusive" and "multicultural" capture both the nature of Pentecost and the vision of the everlasting kingdom in Revelation. Pentecost is the promise that the Holy Spirit is available to "all people." On the Day of Pentecost, "God fearing Jews from every nation under heaven" received the outpouring of the Holy Spirit (Acts 2:5 and 21). Although these people were Jews and Gentile converts to Judaism, they were ethnically diverse—including people from regions that are today called the Middle East, Iran, North Africa, Turkey, and Italy. Pentecost entails not only ethnic, and thus also cultural, but also class and demographic diversity. Quoting Joel 2, Peter clarifies that "all people" takes in "sons and daughters," "young" and "old," and "even servants, both men and women" (Acts 2:17-18). It includes the single mom working in a Wal-Mart in a forgotten Rust-Belt town and the Wall Street Investment Banker. The stories in the book of Acts narrate the progressive realization of the Holy Spirit being poured out on all people and the difficulty of the early Christians in coming to terms with that promise. From Jews and erstwhile Gentile converts to Judaism, the Spirit radiates out from Jerusalem to include Samaritans and Gentiles in the kingdom of God. Although from chapter 10 onward, Acts focuses on the missionary adventures of the Apostle Paul, it also tells the expanding story of the Spirit of Pentecost being poured out on all people. The story of Acts, the story of the Spirit of Pentecost, concludes with the "great multitude that no one could count, from every nation, tribe, people, and

---

[55] Augustine, *Pentecost, Hospitality, and Transfiguration*, 68.
[56] Pentecostal scholar Daniela Augustine develops a theology of pentecostal cosmopolitanism based on the Holy Spirit empowering Christ-like hospitality that embraces the genuine differences of all people rather than the pseudo-diversity of Western multiculturalism. See Augustine, *Pentecost, Hospitality, and Transfiguration*, 43–72.

language, standing before the throne and in front of the Lamb" (Rev. 7:9). In sum, the eschatological vision of redemption marries edenic and cosmopolitan features. The new creation is a green cosmopolitan world centered on the edenic New Jerusalem.[57] The final vision of redemption in Revelation includes people from all the nations, renewed cities, and the restoration of edenic paradise.[58] But how does a green cosmopolitan vision connect with the telocity of the Spirit of Pentecost?

First, the magnifying nature of biblical eschatology arises from the fecundity of the Holy Spirit. The narrative of the Spirit is not simply a return to a prior pristine state. But neither does it abrogate the world that arose from creation. The eschaton, moreover, is not transport to an off- and otherworldly place. Traditional pentecostal eschatology regards this world in almost entirely negative terms. This world is something to be escaped by going to heaven. But biblical eschatology envisions the renewal, the recreation, of the world. As Eva Maria Räpple notes, "life in the city of God enters a new dimension. It has its origin and roots in the worldly city."[59] In other words, a fundamental continuity pertains between the original and the new creation.[60] Why? Because the Spirit that is the source of creation and that animates life redeems and renews it. At the same time, Douglas Farrow offers an important reminder that the "*ordo Spiritus*" is an "*ordo progressivus*."[61] Spirit's work in eschatological new creation is something new. The Spirit renews creation, but also takes it to a new place. For this reason, although continuity characterizes the new creation, so do discontinuity.

Second, the story of the Spirit begins with creating the heavens and the earth and ends with their renewal in the new heaven and the new earth.[62] The earth brought forth from the darkness over the deep was a place of plenitude, a place where life

---

[57] After selecting the terminology of "green cosmopolitanism," I found my theological instinct corroborated in Mark B. Stephens' reference to "The New Jerusalem as a Garden City." See Stephens, *Annihilation or Renewal? The Meaning and Function of New Creation in the Book of Revelation*, Wissenschaftliche Untersuchungen zum Neuen Testament, ed. Jörg Frey, 2nd series, 307 (Tübingen: Mohr Siebeck, 2011), 250–4. Also, I take the symbol of the New Jerusalem as a place and a people; it describes in some way the embodied and communal nature of resurrected life in the eschaton (cf. Stephens, *Annihilation or Renewal?* 232–3). Some scholars, however, take the New Jerusalem as a symbol of the resurrected saints and not as an eschatological place. For this latter interpretation, see Robert H. Gundry, "The New Jerusalem: People as Place, not Place for People," *Novum Testamentum* 229, no. 3 (1987): 254–64.

[58] On the redemption of the nations in Revelation, see Allan J. McNicol, *The Conversion of the Nations in Revelation*, Library of New Testament Studies, ed. Mark Goodacre, vol. 438 (London: T & T Clark, 2011), 120–1 and 129–30.

[59] Eva Maria Räpple, *The Metaphor of the City in the Apocalypse of John*, Studies in Biblical Literature, vol. 67, gen. ed. Hemchand Gossai (New York: Peter Lang, 2004), 105.

[60] Amos Yong affirms the same in *The Spirit Poured Out on All Flesh: Pentecostalism and the Possibility of Global Theology* (Grand Rapids: Baker Academic, 2005), 96. Allan J. McNicol maintains that Revelation has a "consistent theme of a correlation of first and last things. The perfect rule of God that existed in the creation will return in a perfect way at the end." See McNicol, *The Conversion of the Nations in Revelation*, 80 and 98–9. Grant Osborne raises the question of whether or not the new creation will be physical in nature. I agree with his surmise that "we know little of what form [it] will take." But given the emphasis on the "physicality" of the new creation and the resurrection of the saints, it "is best to affirm some type of continuity within the wholly 'new' order." See Grant R. Osborne, *Revelation* (Grand Rapids: Baker Academic, 2002), 730.

[61] Douglas Farrow, *Ascension Theology* (New York: T & T Clark, 2011), 133.

[62] For renewal rather than destruction and replacement in the new creation, see Stephens, *Annihilation or Renewal?* esp. 238–43.

proliferated.⁶³ Although human life returns to the dust, God's Spirit remains its animating principle along its journey. During that time, the Spirit nurtures life that embodies the divine image. In this sense, the Spirit has always been working as the Spirit of Pentecost. Pentecost, by way of the history of redemption and especially the Spirit's work in Christ, reveals the telos of the Spirit's perennial work in creation. Pentecost renews the life given in creation. The Spirit that brings life from the darkness of the deep and creates the divine image bearer from the dust is the Spirit of Pentecost. That Spirit, moreover, gives rise to the dynamism of human history, which finds its most sophisticated expression in the life of the city. The creative work of human beings arises from and manifests their Spirit-breathed life.

Third, the narrative of redemption concludes with "the New Jerusalem coming down out of heaven from God" (Rev. 21:1-2). Even though urban life is not part of the original Eden story, God redeems it in the "new heaven and the new earth" (Rev. 21:1).⁶⁴ Why? The cultural activities that are subject to the Spirit's renewal are themselves the fruit of people embodying the Spirit-breathed divine image over the course of the narrative of the Spirit of God. Human cultural activity arises from Spirit-breathed life (Gen. 2:15). The expansion of human cultural activity into the life of the city was not a fall from the bucolic idyll of Eden. God's Spirit gave humans embodied life to image God in the world. Engaging in activity that nourishes the flourishing of life is the closest way that humans embody the Spirit-breathed divine image.⁶⁵ The synthesis of urban and edenic imagery in the New Jerusalem fulfills the human vocation to "not only *preserve* Eden as sacred space, but to further *extend* Eden by 'filling the earth' and transforming that which lies outside the garden into the same kind of sacred space."⁶⁶ Thus, the narrative of the Spirit that culminates in the new heaven and the new earth is not a return to a prelapsarian time before culture. On the contrary, it redeems the sophisticated diversity and breadth of human activity.⁶⁷ Thus, the vision of the new creation in Revelation includes the people of many nations. The chief metropolis, the New Jerusalem, is a bustling city that integrates edenic and urban features (Rev. 22:1-2). The cosmopolitan vision of the new creation is the culmination of the Spirit of

---

63 Although I am emphasizing continuity in the history of redemption, discontinuity should not be ignored. The new creation eradicates the deep of Genesis 1, the symbol of cosmic chaos, along with death (Rev. 21:1). See Stephens, *Annihilation or Renewal?* 235–7.
64 As Jon Morales notes, "the final vision presents a *reversal* of the hostility between the nations and the people of God." See Jon Morales, *Christ, Shepherd of the Nations: The Nations as Narrative Character and Audience in John's Apocalypse*, Library of New Testament Studies, ed. Chris Keith, vol. 577 (London: Bloomsbury/T & T Clark, 2018), 131 (emphasis original).
65 For a holistic eschatology that entails the renewal of creation, see Richard J. Middleton, *A New Heaven and a New Earth: Reclaiming Biblical Eschatology* (Grand Rapids: Baker Academic, 2014), 155–75 and my *A Pentecostal Political Theology for American Renewal: Spirit of the Kingdoms, Citizens of the Cities*, Charis: Christianity and Renewal—Interdisciplinary Studies (New York: Palgrave Macmillan, 2016), 157–73. Amos Yong also affirms an embodied ("holistic") eschatological experience of the coming kingdom of God. See Yong, *The Spirit Poured Out on All Flesh*, 190.
66 Stephens, *Annihilation or Renewal?* 247 (emphasis original).
67 For similar views that the New Jerusalem suggests the renewal of human culture and civilization, see Gordon Campbell, "Antithetical Feminine-Urban Imagery and a Tale of Two Women-Cities in the Book of Revelation," *Tyndale Bulletin* 55, no. 1 (2004): 86; Ryan S. Schellenberg, "Seeing the Whole World: Intertextuality and the New Jerusalem (Revelation 21-22)," *Perspectives in Religious Studies* 33, no. 4 (2006): 475; and Stephens, *Annihilation or Renewal?* 252.

Pentecost. The people of many nations received the outpouring of the Spirit on the Day of Pentecost, which continues "to the ends of the earth" to take in "all people" (Acts 1:8 and 2:17). This outpouring of the Spirit finds its consummation in the "healing of the nations" in the new creation (Rev. 22:2). Atonement includes their renewal because they are part of the narrative of the Spirit. Indeed, the cosmopolitan communities of the new creation are already emerging. For example, pentecostal scholar Nimi Wariboko regards the emerging global cities as the Charismatic City. The Charismatic City is the trans-territorial and trans-spatial nexus point for the people and cultures of the world that characterize life emerging in the global cities of the world. They are, moreover, the result of the Spirit's work in the world and, thus, are becoming the Charismatic City. Wariboko refers to the Charismatic City in the singular because it serves as the metaphor, not for any one city, but the emerging form of life in the early twenty-first century.[68] The Spirit does not ultimately abandon life to the dust but renews it in all its manifold dimensions. The Spirit of atonement renews the life that emerges from the Spirit over the course of the history of redemption. Atonement is not restoration to the paradisiacal place before sin—Genesis 2. But the renewal of life that emerges during the history of redemption, including the peoples of the nations, and culminates in the green cosmopolitan vision of Revelation 21 and 22.

Fourth, the new earth and its capital city are cosmopolitan. Cosmopolitanism proposes that all people are members of a common and shared community. This notion squares with the biblical theology that human life emerges from the breath of God's Spirit and that the same Spirit, as the Spirit of Pentecost, is the foundation of the divine-human fellowship of "all people" that are resurrected in the new heaven and the new earth and that come to worship God in the New Jerusalem. In other words, the people of the nations included in the new creation share in their fidelity to and fellowship with the God of the New Jerusalem and the new creation. The cosmopolitan vision, however, is not the uniformity of a Borg collective. It comprises the peoples of distinct nations united in fellowship with each other and their God living in a renewed edenic earth.[69] The new creation consummates the fullness of atonement because it restores people to their unmitigated fellowship with God and with each other. The

---

[68] Wariboko, *The Charismatic City and the Public Resurgence of Religion*, esp. 7–12 and 169–93. Wariboko's Charismatic City bears conceptual similarity with Michael Hardt and Antonio Negri's vision of the advent of global empire, according to which the decentralized and deterritorialized global capitalist system is replacing state imperialism (Michael Hardt and Antonio Negri, *Empire* [Cambridge, MA: Harvard University Press, 2000]). Like Hardt and Negri, the Charismatic City is eschatological for Wariboko. But the Charismatic City does not culminate in the Empire of the globalized economic market system and culture, but inclusion in the body of Christ through the life-giving presence of the Holy Spirit. I also make an argument for the life of the city as the collective responses of Spirit-breathed divine image bearers in *A Pentecostal Political Theology*, 141–73.

[69] Scholars are mixed on the meaning of the "nations" in Revelation 22. One view regards them as Christian converts from before the eschatological judgment. An alternative, more universalist soteriology, regards them as ongoing people redeemed from the lake of fire. I do not want to adjudicate this issue but affirm that the "nations" in Revelation stand for distinct people and their diverse cities and cultures that nonetheless share a cosmopolitan identity in the New Jerusalem and loving fellowship with its God. For background on the interpretation of the nations, see David Mathewson, *A New Heaven and a New Earth: The Meaning and Function of the Old Testament in Revelation 21.1–22.5*, Journal of the Study of the New Testament Supplement Series, 238 (New York: Sheffield Academic Press, 2003), 169–77.

long history of atonement from the animal skins to the tabernacle and temple offerings were partial. They all operated according to the "the old order of things" (Rev. 21:4), the world of Genesis 3. They never opened the door for people to be fully restored to relationship with their God and with each other.[70] But the gates of the New Jerusalem are always open and a temple is no longer necessary because "now the dwelling of God is with men, and he will live with them. They will be his people, and God himself will be with them and be their God" (Rev. 21:3 and 21:22-25). This new heaven and new earth and its New Jerusalem are the telos of the Spirit of Pentecost. Waking to life in the new creation with all the people of Pentecost and entering with them through the doors of the New Jerusalem is the consummation of atonement and the consummate chapter in the narrative of the Spirit of Pentecost.

Conclusion

The chapter concludes a pentecostal theology of the atonement. It argued that the Spirit of atonement is eschatological. Atonement is the dynamic result of the Spirit of Pentecost restoring people to their identity as children of God and the life for which they were created. Entailed in that work is the renewal of God's creation. The Spirit of atonement reaches its zenith in the eschatological new heaven and new earth when all the people of Pentecost will come together to worship the resurrected Christ in green cosmopolitan New Jerusalem.

---

[70] Osborne regards the dwelling of God with the saints in the New Jerusalem as the fulfillment of the various programs for mediating divine presence, one of which was the sacrificial system of atonement. See Osborn, *Revelation*, 726-7.

12

Epilogue

This book develops a pentecostal theology of the atonement. The Spirit of Pentecost is the fundamental gift of atonement. That is the central theological claim that grounds this pentecostal theology of atonement. It is also what makes this book potentially contentious. Making a case for the Holy Spirit's fundamental place in the work of redemption should not be contentious. After all, the Holy Spirit is an equal member of the Trinity. The Day of Pentecost is a major event in the history of redemption that creates the church of Jesus Christ. The Holy Spirit sanctifies Christians. These are claims that most Christians believe. The argument developed throughout this book that the Holy Spirit is central to a pentecostal theology of atonement is, nevertheless, controversial. The question is, why? The following details four reasons that also serve as summative statements on this pentecostal theology of atonement. Ironically, all of these reasons both arise from the biblical narrative of redemption and challenge the common logics of atonement that focus almost exclusively on Christ's crucifixion and that render the work of the Holy Spirit a minor thread in the work of redemption.

First, Christocentric and crucicentric narratives dominate most atonement theologies. The Holy Spirit, consequently, plays little to no role in most traditional atonement theologies. A pentecostal atonement theology upends that imbalance. It does not replace Christocentrism with pneumacentrism. A pentecostal atonement theology integrates pneumatology and Christology. It also means that Pentecost, not the cross, is the telos of redemption. Atonement is the result of the Holy Spirit's redemptive work that emerges in the biblical narrative from creation and the Garden of Eden to promises of exodus from exile, restoration to the land, the renewal of the people, and the coming of the Spirit-anointed messiah. The history of the Holy Spirit and the work of atonement is an eschatological narrative of redemption that carries on into the new creation.

Second, it means that atonement is transformational. It is not primarily a legal drama between the Father and Son performed in the historical past. Participating in the life the Holy Spirit realized in Jesus Christ is the essence of atonement. The Spirit of Pentecost transforms and renews life in the image of the Spirit-breathed life realized in Jesus Christ. Pentecost is the nexus from the particularity of the Spirit-breathed life revealed and realized in Christ to the universal outpouring of that life on and for all people. Pentecost makes the horizon for participation in the Spirit-breathed life realized in Christ universal.

Third, atonement is trinitarian and relational. The Holy Spirit makes people children of God the Father by drawing the "all people" of Pentecost into union with the Son of God in Jesus Christ (Acts 2:17). Pentecostal atonement is, moreover, the ongoing experience of growing into identity as the children of God. The dynamic, indeed eschatological, experience of atonement matches Martin Luther's description of baptism as the daily experience of the new person emerging in grace and righteousness.[1] Atonement reconciles human beings to their identity as the Spirit-breathed children of God. The Spirit of Pentecost transforms and renews their life in the image of the Spirit-breathed life realized in Jesus Christ.

Fourth, this argument for a pentecostal theology of the atonement takes the pentecostal praxis of the Holy Spirit as indicative of an approach to a pentecostal atonement theology. The Spirit of Pentecost is the systematic starting point for a pentecostal theology of the atonement. But wait. Theology should start with the Bible. In principle that is correct. The problem is that the Christocentric and crucicentric theological tradition obfuscates the role of the Holy Spirit in the history of redemption. The global pentecostal movements are a product of the work of the Holy Spirit. They showcase the transformative experience and empowerment of the Holy Spirit. The question is, does the prominence of the Holy Spirit in pentecostal praxis find corroboration in the biblical narrative of redemption? The answer is "yes." The pentecostal experience of the Holy Spirit, therefore, suggests a hermeneutical correction to the traditions of Christocentrism and crucicentrism.

Although interacting with historical pentecostal theology and wider traditions of Christian theology throughout the course of this book, the primary focus has been presenting a constructive pentecostal theology of atonement. At this closing point, therefore, it is appropriate to consider how this project contributes to and challenges both the pentecostal and the wider Christian traditions of atonement theology. For pentecostal traditions, this project contributes to the move away from the compartmentalized understanding of Christ and the Holy Spirit in Classical Pentecostalism. Rather than locating the primary work of the Spirit in a post-conversion experience of spiritual empowerment, it provides pneumatological categories for Pentecostals to understand and expand their holistic and transformative praxis of the Spirit of Pentecost. In this respect, this project contributes to the constructive work of contemporary pentecostal theologians such as Daniela Augustine, Terry Cross, Andrew Gabriel, Frank Macchia, Wolfgang Vondey, Nimi Waiboko, and Amos Yong. The narrative approach of this project that integrates Christology and the Spirit of Pentecost, moreover, provides a more expansive theological vision for articulating the global diversity of pentecostal praxis than do the doctrinal categories of Classical Pentecostalism.

For the ecumenical Christian traditions, a pentecostal theology of the atonement challenges popular Western atonement theologies to rethink their Christocentrism and crucicentrism as well as their atomistic tendency to separate soteriology into objective (Christological) and subjective (pneumatological) categories. Without marginalizing Christ and the cross, a pentecostal atonement theology integrates them in a wider narrative of the Holy Spirit that stretches from creation to eschaton. It expands the

---

[1] *Small Catechism*, "The Sacrament of Holy Baptism." http://bookofconcord.org/smallcatechism.php#baptism

scope of atonement from an intra-trinitarian judicial proceeding between the Father and the Son and a forensic acquittal of sin to the renewal of life in this world as the proleptic participation in the new creation. Although sharing fundamental continuities with the Eastern Orthodox vision of grace, it transcends its residual Christocentric and ecclesiocentric tendencies.

In sum, what is the yield of this book? It carries on a critical conversation with Western atonement theology and especially the way this tradition shaped classical pentecostal theology. It resources the pneumatic and holistic nature of global pentecostal practice and theology. It engages in a critical-dialogical conversation with the wider ecumenical and historical traditions of atonement theology. It develops an innovative pentecostal theology of the atonement based on the pentecostal experience of the Holy Spirit and the place of the Spirit in the biblical narrative of redemption. It does not marginalize Christology and the cross. But contextualizes Christology in light of the outpouring of the Spirit of Pentecost. It achieves a synergy between Christ and the Spirit too often absent from traditional atonement theologies. Doing so yields a theology of atonement that reflects both the character of the biblical narrative of redemption and the pentecostal experience of the Holy Spirit.

Of course, this book does not cover every important topic related to atonement. One area that calls for further consideration is the nature of death both for Christ and the Christian and the Holy Spirit's place in it. In what sense, does Christ die, especially since he overcame death, hell, and the grave (Rev. 1:18 and Acts 2:24)? And how should theology understand death for those in Christ because they share in his victory over death and yet they clearly die? Daniela Augustine's pentecostal discussion of this issue by way of Eastern Orthodox theology is an excellent starting point for exploring this matter.[2] One area likely to be charged with neglect is the relationship between the atonement as receiving the Spirit of Pentecost and the Hebrew Bible's sacrificial system. That is a fair question. Although the logic of penal atonement comes under critical evaluation throughout the book, it avoids diving into the labyrinthine points of biblical exegesis and theological argumentation used to support penal atonement. Why make this decision? Having rejected its fundamental logic and reading atonement in terms of the Holy Spirit's role in the wider narrative of redemption, little reason remains to journey those exegetical and theological corridors. Chapter 4 on the crucifixion, nevertheless, addresses this question on a programmatic level. It argues that sacrifice was God's concession to the cultural expectations of people living in the ancient Near East. What is vital about the death of Christ on the cross is not that it conforms to human expectations of retributive punishment. The atonement is less about God operating within the punitive expectations of human beings and more about subverting those expectations. The crucified Christ yields himself to the forces of violence, hate, and retribution not to ameliorate God the Father's appetite for penal justice. He sacrifices himself so that all the people who receive the Spirit of Pentecost can walk in his Spirit-anointed life and transcend that cycle of cruelty.

---

[2] Daniela C. Augustine, *The Spirit and the Common Good: Shared Fellowship in the Image of God* (Grand Rapids: Eerdmans, 2019), 84–9.

Subject Index

American Enterprise Institute for Public Policy Research 144
ancient Near East 73
Anselm 57, 65 n.40
Apostle Paul 66–7, 81, 82, 86, 97, 166, 168 n.15, 171, 174
Arya Mahila Samaj 111
Assemblies of God Great Britain 5 n.18
Assemblies of God USA 5, 57 n.8, 118 n.43, 119–20, 151
Assemblies of God Zimbabwe 139
Athanasius 70 n.54
Augustine 57 n.6
Azusa Street 110, 115–21, 125

baptism 170–3
Basil the Great 68
Bowler, Kate 93 n.4
Brookings Institution 144

Calvin, John 58–60
Centre for Development and Enterprise 139
Chalcedonian theology 51
Cheong, Weng Kit 121 n.56
Church-Sect Theory 131–2
Christian and Missionary Alliance 141
Christian Century 130
Christocentrism 2, 4, 6, 10, 12, 17, 19, 21, 79, 128–9, 136, 164–5, 174, 201–2, *see also* Christology
Christology 8, 19–20, 27, 37–55, 70–1, 80–1, 94, 136, 155, 200
Christus Victor 79
classical pentecostalism 2, 5, 6, 10, 134–8, 168, 179, 201
creation 8, 12, 19, 20–33, 35, 44–9, 55, 62, 75, 89, 96, 98–9, 114, 129, 168, 170, 176, 185 n.32, 193, 194, 200, *see also* new creation

crucicentrism 2, 4–5, 6, 10, 12, 17, 19, 56 n.1, 57 n.4, 59–60, 62–3, 69, 79, 88, 128–9, 154, 167–8, *see also* crucifixion
crucifixion 56–76, 79, 171–2, 200

Dispensationalism 94, 181

Eastern Orthodox 10, 43, 48 n.28, 50, 53–4, 55, 57 n.5, 70, 73–4, 77 n.4, 78 n.5, 89 n.61, 94 n.7, 98 n.14, 183, 202
ecumenism 3, 67 n.45, 201
Elim Pentecostal Church (UK and Ireland) 5 n.18
eschatology 8–9, 12, 19 n.8, 32, 39, 63, 67, 88, 93–105, 133, 135, 142–3, 152, 170, 173, 179–99, *see also* new creation
Evangelicalism 2, 3–4, 6, 17, 41–2, 43, 93 n.2, 131
exile 63, 94, 96–7, 115, 169–70, 193, 200
exile-exodus 28–33, 96–9, 114, 170 n.23, 200
exodus 94, 96–7, 114–15, 169–70, 172 n.30, 200
Ezekiel 34–6, 52

Fall, the 8, 27–8, 33, 35, 38, 66–7, 83–4, 88–9, 101, 151, 179, 185, 187, 192
feminism 113, 114 n.26
filioque 54
Full Gospel 10, 128, 134–8, 150–1
fundamentalism 93 n.2

global Pentecostalism 10, 13
Gospel of John 27, 52, 67, 151 n.12, 157
Gospel of Luke 49, 64 n.39, 83
Gospel of Matthew 63, 66, 83, 156

healing (gift of) 136, 150–4, *see also* spiritual gifts
holiness 33–4, 117, 150 n.1, 159 n.38, 165

Incarnation   12, 40–55, 63, 67, 70–1, 104, 128–49, 154, 155–7, 189
Isaiah   34, 37–8, 48, 83
Islam   139, 140, 183

Jerusalem Council   81
Joel   34–5
John the Baptist   63
justification   4, 9, 43, 57 n.8, 59–61, 78–80, 153, 154, 164, 170, 172 n.29, 176–7, 180

Keswick Movement   111
kingdom of God   63, 65, 69, 73, 142–3, 155, 162–3, 179, 190, 191, 193

liberalism   51
liberation theology   146–7
Living Faith Church (Eglise de la Foi Vivante; Ngaoundéré, Cameroon)   139–40
Luther, Martin   57 n.7, 58–9, 201

mission   56, 62
Mukti Mission   110–15, 125
multiculturalism   195

new creation   8–9, 17, 19, 27, 33, 37, 39, 83, 88, 97–100, 105, 115, 164–78, 192, 196–9, 202
New York Times   145

penal-substitutionary atonement   2–3, 8, 9, 42, 46–7, 50, 56–62, 65, 69–70, 72–5, 77 n.2, 78, 80, 154, 156, 159, 171, 202
Pentecost   7, 9–10, 17–39, 61–2, 79, 88–91, 94–9, 109, 119–20, 122–3, 147, 155, 180, 192, 195–6, 198, 200
Pentecostal Assemblies of Canada   5 n.17
Pentecostalism in Africa   138–40, 147–9, 182 n.18

Pentecostalism in Brazil   146, 148
Pentecostalism in Cameroon   138–40, 143
Pentecostalism in Chile   147
Pentecostalism in Vietnam   140–4, 149
Pew Research Center   1, 3, 121, 126, 131, 183
Platonism   26 n.37, 64
post-Christendom   96, 125, 192
premillennialism   93, 181
Progressive Pentecostals   182
prophecy (gift of)   136, *see also* spiritual gifts
prosperity Gospel   93, 131, 139–40, 143, 148, 152–3, 159, 162

reformation   26 n.37, 57, 157
resurrection   48, 57, 59, 77–92, 99 n.15, 152, 172–8
Roman Catholic   43, 177

sanctification   5, 9, 43, 59, 137, 150, 165, 172 n.29, 176–7, 188–9
Spirit baptism   3, 5, 11, 17, 19 n.8, 49, 99–105, 121, 135, 136, 180, 186, *see also* tongues (speaking in)
spiritual gifts   7, 25, 136, 174, 184, *see also* tongues (speaking in)
Synoptic Gospels   45, 48
systematic theology   6

tongues (speaking in)   5 n.18, 6–7, 109, 118, 135, 136, *see also* Spirit baptism; spiritual gifts
Trinity, The   10, 18, 40 n.1, 41, 50–5, 85, 157, 168 n.16, 186, 189, 200–201, *see also filioque*

Valley Gate Vineyard (Nova Scotia, Canada)   110, 124–6

Westminster Confession of Faith   176

Modern Name Index

Abrams, Minnie 111
Adkins, LaTrese 146
Ahmed, Abiy 183
Alexander, Estrelda Y. 7 n.21
Alfaro, Sammy 7 n.21, 183, 185 n.30
Allen, David M. 104 n.37
Allen, Gustav 51
Althouse, Peter 130 n.10, 132–3, 185 n.31
Álvarez, Miguel 7 n.21
Anderson, Allan 7 n.21, 136
Anderson, Robert Mapes 130, 132, 180–1
Augustine, Daniela 10, 69, 194–5, 201, 202
Aulén, Gustav 57 n.7, 58 n.19

Badcock, Gary D. 5 n.15
Baker, Mark D. 57 n.4
Bapat, Ram 112 n.10
Barth, Karl 21 n.15, 53 n.39
Beach, Lee 124
Beale, Dorothea 113
Beeke, Joel R. 42 n.6
Belousek, Darrin 56, 65 n.41, 66 n.43
Bird, Michael F. 79 n.15, 87 n.56, 168 n.15
Bishop, Bill 122 n.62
Bhakiaraj, Paul Joseph 113 n.16
Blackwell, Ben C. 168 n.15, 175
Blumhofer, Edith L. 111 n.5
Bodley, Rachel L. 113 n.21
Boersma, Hans 57 n.6, 58 n.19, 61 n.38
Boff, Leonardo 71
Bouteneff, Peter 68, 70, 73–4, 89 n.61
Bowler, Kate 131
Bowles, Tuere A. 146
Brooks, David 144
Bulgakov, Sergius 53 n.41
Burke, Trevor J. 186 n.34
Burton, Antoinette M. 113

Campbell, Constantine R. 170 n.24
Campbell, Douglas A. 88, 91 n.70, 158 n.37, 168 nn.15–16, 173 n.31, 188 n.40
Campbell, Gordon 197 n.67
Cartledge, Mark 128–9, 154
Castelo, Daniel 1
Charette, Blaine 95 n.8
Chism, Jonathan Langston 147
Churchill, Winston 19 n.9
Cimpean, Florin T. 174 n.38
Clark, Joseph 137 n.39
Clark, Matthew S. 5 n.18
Clarke, Clifton 7 n.21
Cook, Stephen L. 31 n.46
Courey, David 159 n.39
Cox, Harvey 7 n.21, 131–2, 160–1, 183–4
Craig, William Lane 59 n.23
Cross, Terry 3, 201
Cucchiari, Salvatore 146
Cushing, Robert G. 122 n.62

Dahles, Heidi 131 n.12, 132 n.22
Davis, Martin M. 43 n.19
Dayton, Donald 2 n.7, 181
Demarest, Bruce 69, 73, 79 n.10
Dempster, Murray W. 190
de Petrella, Lidia Susana Vaccaro 182–3
Dreher, Rod 192
Drønen, Tomas Sundnes 139
Dunn, James D. G. 48 n.30, 82, 84–5, 176 n.43, 177 n.51
Dunning, H. Ray 56 n.3, 69 n.50

Eberhart, Christian A. 90 n.63, 101 n.22, 104 n.39
Embry, Bradley 23 n.25
Eskola, Timo 91 n.69
Espinosa, Gastón 116 n.34

Farrow, Douglas 196
Faupel, D. William 179 n.1

Fee, Gordon D.   84–7, 173 n.33
Fergusson, Niall   75
Fiddes, Paul S.   8 n.22, 9, 51, 57 n.4, 67, 68 n.47, 70 n.53, 74, 75
Freeman, Dena   147–8
Frykenberg, Robert Eric   111 n.9

Gabriel, Andrew K.   188, 201
Gaffin, Richard   87 n.56
Ganiel, Gladys   123
Garrison, William Lloyd   113
Gause, Hollis   164–5
Gerrard, Nathan L.   131 n.16
Gifford, Paul   140 n.48
Gorman, Michael J.   157, 170 n.25, 188 n.40
Green, Joel B.   57 n.4
Grey, Jacqueline   38 n.58
Grudem, Wayne   42
Gundry, Robert H.   196 n.57
Gunton, Colin E.   8 n.22

Habets, Myk   45 n.22
Hahn, Roger L.   175, 177 n.50
Hardt, Michael   198 n.68
Harner, Philip B.   31 n.43
Hart, Larry D.   57 n.8
Hauerwas, Stanley   192
Hays, Richard B.   80
Heath, Gordon L.   162
Hill, Graham   152 n.14
Hodge, Charles   58 n.18, 59 n.20
Hodges, Melvin   119
Hodson, Alan K.   104 n.38
Hollenweger, Walter J.   7 n.21
Holm, Randall   151
Hooker, Morna D.   176 n.44
Horton, Stanley M.   57 n.8
Hultgren, Arland J.   171–2
Hunt, Stephen   132 n.23

Isgrigg, Daniel D.   180 n.4

Jacobsen, Douglas   4, 7 n.21
Jamieson, R. B.   60–1, 90 n.68
Jewett, Robert   48 n.30
Joh, Wonhee Anne   71
Johns, Cheryl Bridges   4, 118, 120
Johnson, Nathan C.   83

Kalu, Ogbu   7 n.21
Kay, William K.   153 n.24
Keener, Craig S.   2 n.6, 82
Kim, Hyn Chul Paul   31–2
King, Larry L.   134 n.30
Köhrsen, Jens   133 n.29, 166–7
Kosambi, Meera   112 n.11

Lamp, Jeffrey S.   37 n.57, 93 n.3
Le, Vince   141
Leach, Monica T.   146
Lee, Edward S.   115–16
Leithart, Peter J.   90 n.68, 158
Letham, Robert   42–3, 58 n.18, 59, 61 n.37
Lincoln, Abraham   113
Lindhardt, Martin   7 n.21, 133 n.27, 147
Longnecker, Richard N.   81, 174
Löning, Karl   20 n.11
Lossky, Vladimir   19 n.10, 40 n.3, 53–4, 69 n.50, 74 n.67, 98 n.14

Ma, Wonsuk   180 n.8, 183
McCall, Thomas H.   40 n.2, 61 n.36
Macchia, Frank   1, 11, 17 n.1, 18, 40 n.1, 49 n.34, 102, 128 n.1, 186 n.33, 201
McClymond, Michael J.   111 n.4, 120
McDowell, Catherine L.   24 n.31
McGee, Gary B.   119
McGlothlin, Thomas D.   99 n.15, 176 n.44
McGrath, Alister E.   58 n.19
Macleod, Donald   41, 42, 44 n.21
McNicol, Allan J.   196 n.58, 196 n.60
McQueen, Larry R.   93 n.1
Mariz, Cecília Loreto   146
Marshall, Christopher D.   71–2
Marshall, I. Howard   57 n.9, 60 n.27, 77 n.2, 87 n.55, 155
Marti, Gerardo   121 n.59, 122, 123
Martin, Craig   26 n.37
Martin, Bernice   146
Martin, David   148 n.85, 182 n.18
Martin, Pamela P.   146
Matera, Frank J.   47, 85 n.44, 171 n.26
Mathewson, David   98 n.13, 198 n.69
Mauser, Ulrich   38 n.59
Maxwell, David   139
Meconi, David Vincent   187 n.37
Medina, Néstor   183
Menzies, Robert P.   152

Menzies, William W.   5, 57 n.8, 152
Meyendorff, John   54 n.45, 98 n.14
Middleton, Richard J.   26 n.36, 197 n.65
Miller, Donald E.   133, 137, 182
Moffitt, David M.   89, 101, 103
Moo, Douglas J.   169, 172 n.29
Morales, Jon   197 n.64
Morales, Rodrigo J.   97
Moussa, Iya   139–40

Negri, Antonio   198 n.68
Niebuhr, H. Richard   132

Oblau, Gotthard   151 n.4
Oliverio, L. William   4
Olsen, Carl E.   187 n.37
Osborne, Grant R.   48 n.30, 103 n.35, 196 n.60, 199 n.70

Park, Andrew Sung   61 n.38
Parker, Stephen   26 n.38
Payton, James R.   43
Perry, David   1
Pinnock, Clark   2, 78
Putnam, Robert D.   144

Rabens, Volker   187 n.36
Rahner, Karl   53 n.39
Ramabai, Pandita   109–15, 119, 125, 127
Räpple, Eva Maria   196
Robeck, Cecil M.   115 n.31, 117 n.38
Rohr, Richard   50 n.35, 51 n.38, 73 n.66
Rusch, William G.   5 n.15
Rutledge, Fleming   2 n.4, 79

Sánchez, Arelene M.   136
Sanders, Cheryl J.   148 n.86, 182, 194 n.52
Sanders, E. P.   168 n.15
Schafroth, Verena   34 n.50
Schmemann, Alexander   78 n.5
Schnelle, Udo   168 n.16
Schreiner, Thomas R.   42, 77 n.3
Schuele, Andreas   24 n.29, 34 n.53, 48 n.29
Schwadel, Philip   131
Scott, James M.   28 n.39, 83–4, 188 n.39, 188 n.42
Seifrid, Mark A.   91 n.69, 177
Seymour, William   109, 115–21, 125, 127, 132–3

Sheppard, Gerald T.   93 n.2
Smilde, David   142 n.58
Smith, Calvin L.   132 n.22, 180 n.6, 183 n.25, 193–4
Smith, Mark S.   20 n.13
Snyder, Meredith P.   116–17
Stackhouse, Ian   153 n.26
Stavropoulos, Christoforos   54 n.46
Stephens, Mark B.   196 n.57, 196 n.62
Stephenson, Lisa P.   6 n.19, 44, 45 n.23, 129
Stroope, Samuel   137 n.39
Stuhlmacher, Peter   48 n.30, 84 n.34, 177 n.47
Stump, Eleonore   2 n.4, 8 n.23
Sugirtharajah, R. S.   112 n.15
Sunday, Billy   134 n.30
Swoboda, A. J.   2
Synan, Vinson   7 n.21

Tankersley, Lee   78–9, 87 n.56
Tarango, Angela   119, 165–6
Thomas, Alma   119
Thomas, John Christopher   103 n.35, 151 n.12, 153 n.29
Thomas, Rebecca   26 n.38
Thomas, V. V.   133
Thompson, Matthew K.   93 n.2, 185 n.31
Torrance, T. F.   42 n.6, 43, 48–9, 94 n.5
Towner, Philip   86
Treier, Daniel J.   43
Tripp, Thomas Alfred   130
Troeltsch, Ernst   132
Tubman, Harriett   113

Vance, J. D.   144
VanWolde, Ellen   23 n.26
Vidu, Adonis   61 n.36, 68 n.48
Villafañe, Eldin   185 n.30
Vondey, Wolfgang   2, 10–11, 17 n.3, 49 n.34, 94 n.6, 135, 151, 201

Wacker, Grant   7 n.21, 130–2
Waltke, Bruce   21 n.15
Ward, Graham   100
Ware, Frederick L.   146 n.77, 181 n.11
Wariboko, Nimi   198, 201
Warrington, Keith   137 n.35
Washburn, Alta   119
Watson, Rebecca S.   21 n.18, 22 n.21

Weaver, J. Denny 77 n.1
Weber, Max 132, 139, 147–8
Wellman, Jack 162
Westfall, Cynthia L. 90 n.63
White, Vernon 49
Whitsett, Christopher G. 81 n.19, 82 n.26
Wilfong, Marsha M. 24 n.33
William, Joseph W. 150 n.3
Wimber, John 151 n.5

Wright, N. T. 28 n.39, 67 n.45, 71 n.56, 81, 85 n.44, 87 n.58, 169, 171 n.26

Yamamori, Tetsunao 133, 137, 182
Yong, Amos 2, 7 n.21, 11, 17 n.1, 18 n.7, 49 n.34, 128, 133 n.24, 146, 160, 196 n.60, 201

Zenger, Erich 20 n.11

www.ingramcontent.com/pod-product-compliance
Lightning Source LLC
Chambersburg PA
CBHW072235290426
44111CB00012B/2099